MELVILLE: THE CRITICAL HERITAGE

THE CRITICAL HERITAGE SERIES

GENERAL EDITOR: B. C. SOUTHAM, M.A., B.LITT. (OXON.)
Formerly Department of English, Westfield College, University of London

---

For a list of books in the series see the back end paper

MELVILLE

THE CRITICAL HERITAGE

Edited by
WATSON G. BRANCH
Assistant Professor of English
University of California, Santa Barbara

ROUTLEDGE & KEGAN PAUL : LONDON AND BOSTON

First published in 1974
by Routledge & Kegan Paul Ltd
Broadway House, 68–74 Carter Lane,
London EC4V 5EL and
9 Park Street,
Boston, Mass. 02108, U.S.A.

ISBN 0 7100 7774 2
Library of Congress Catalog Card No. 73–86570

Printed in Great Britain
by Richard Clay (The Chaucer Press) Ltd
Bungay, Suffolk
Set in Monotype Bembo

For

HERSHEL PARKER
with admiration

and for

EREN
con amore

General Editor's Preface

The reception given to a writer by his contemporaries and near-contemporaries is evidence of considerable value to the student of literature. On one side we learn a great deal about the state of criticism at large and in particular about the development of critical attitudes towards a single writer; at the same time, through private comments in letters, journals or marginalia, we gain an insight upon the tastes and literary thought of individual readers of the period. Evidence of this kind helps us to understand the writer's historical situation, the nature of his immediate reading-public, and his response to these pressures.

The separate volumes in the *Critical Heritage Series* present a record of this early criticism. Clearly, for many of the highly productive and lengthily reviewed nineteenth- and twentieth-century writers, there exists an enormous body of material; and in these cases the volume editors have made a selection of the most important views, significant for their intrinsic critical worth or for their representative quality—perhaps even registering incomprehension!

For earlier writers, notably pre-eighteenth century, the materials are much scarcer and the historical period has been extended, sometimes far beyond the writer's lifetime, in order to show the inception and growth of critical views which were initially slow to appear.

In each volume the documents are headed by an Introduction, discussing the material assembled and relating the early stages of the author's reception to what we have come to identify as the critical tradition. The volumes will make available much material which would otherwise be difficult of access and it is hoped that the modern reader will be thereby helped towards an informed understanding of the ways in which literature has been read and judged.

B.C.S.

Contents

General estimates (1889–92)

Preface and Acknowledgments

The selection of reviews, essays, and other documents in this volume is intended to present a broad and accurate picture of the contemporary critical response to Melville's works and his own reaction to that criticism. The period covered begins with a review of his first book, *Typee*, in 1846 and ends with another review of *Typee* (and three other books) in 1892, the year after Melville died. This collection of criticism is designed to be representative of the total response to Melville's books. Very often the short, superficial notices included here are more typical of the general attitude toward a given book than are the longer, more perceptive ones that make up the main portion of this volume. Reviews were chosen, too, to show the range of judgments by the critics. No attempt has been made to correlate the number of reviews reprinted here to the number of known reviews of each work, nor to balance the proportion of American to British (or French) reviews. The guiding principle of selection was simply the relative contribution of the review or essay to a full understanding by today's reader of Melville's critical reception during his lifetime.

Nearly all references to dates and events in Melville's life are based on transcriptions of documents printed in the following sources: *The Letters of Herman Melville*, eds Merrell R. Davis and William H. Gilman (New Haven: Yale University Press, 1960); Julian Hawthorne, *Nathaniel Hawthorne and His Wife* (Boston: Houghton, Mifflin, 1884); *Journal of a Visit to Europe and the Levant, October 11, 1856–May 6, 1857, by Herman Melville*, ed. Howard C. Horsford (Princeton University Press, 1955); *The Melville Log: A Documentary Life of Herman Melville, 1819–1891*, 2 vols, ed. Jay Leyda (New York: Harcourt, Brace, 1951; reprinted, 'With a New Supplementary Chapter,' New York: Gordian Press, 1969); Eleanor Melville Metcalf, *Herman Melville: Cycle and Epicycle* (Cambridge, Mass.: Harvard University Press, 1953); *Journal of a Visit to London and the Continent by Herman Melville, 1849–1850*, ed. Eleanor Melville Metcalf (Cambridge, Mass.: Harvard University Press, 1948); Merton M. Sealts, Jr, *Melville as Lecturer* (Cambridge, Mass.: Harvard University Press, 1957); Nathaniel Hawthorne, *The English Notebooks*, ed. Randall Stewart

(New York: Modern Language Association of America, 1941; reprinted, New York: Russell & Russell, 1962); and G. Thomas Tanselle, 'The Sales of Melville's Books,' *Harvard Library Bulletin*, 18 (April 1969), 195–215. The Introduction to this volume depends especially upon the Davis-Gilman *Letters* and the Leyda *Log*. Much of the information regarding the reviewers and the periodicals was derived from the following sources: Homer F. Barnes, *Charles Fenno Hoffman* (New York, 1930); George Willis Cooke, *John Sullivan Dwight* (Boston, 1898); Walter Graham, *English Literary Periodicals* (New York: Nelson, 1930); Hugh W. Hetherington, *Melville's Reviewers, British and American 1846–1891* (Chapel Hill: University of North Carolina Press, 1961); Leslie A. Marchand, *The Athenaeum, A Mirror of Victorian Culture* (Chapel Hill: University of North Carolina Press, 1941); Perry Miller, *The Raven and the Whale* (New York, 1956); Frank Luther Mott, *A History of American Magazines*, vol. I, *1741–1850* (New York: Appleton, 1930), and vol. II, *1850–1865* (Cambridge, Mass.: Harvard University Press, 1938); *The Recognition of Herman Melville*, ed. Hershel Parker (Ann Arbor: University of Michigan Press, 1967); Merton M. Sealts, Jr, 'Melville and Richard Henry Stoddard', *American Literature*, 43 (November 1971), 359–70; John Stafford, *The Literary Criticism of 'Young America'* (Berkeley: University of California Press, 1952); and various entries in the *Dictionary of American Biography*, the *Dictionary of National Biography*, the *Dictionnaire de Biographie Française*, and the *National Cyclopedia of American Biography*.

The Melville Collection in The Newberry Library, Chicago, Illinois, contains photostatic, typewritten, or original copies of almost all the known contemporary reviews of Melville's books. The collection was based on the reviews discovered since the 'Melville Revival' of the 1920s by such scholars as Charles R. Anderson, John H. Birss, Leyda, Hetherington, Meade Minnigerode, O. W. Riegel, Willard Thorp, and Mentor L. Williams, and it has grown much larger during the preparation of the Northwestern-Newberry edition of *The Writings of Herman Melville*. I owe special thanks to the edition's editors, Harrison Hayford, Hershel Parker, and G. Thomas Tanselle, and to The Newberry Library for granting me access to the collection. Professor Parker also supplied me with copies of several reviews that he found after I had made my original selections from those in the Melville Collection. Professor Sealts generously provided me with copies of the pieces on Melville by Richard Henry Stoddard.

I am certainly grateful to scholars of this and earlier generations whose efforts and accomplishments form the foundation for this volume. And I would like to thank the University of California, Santa Barbara, for granting me a leave of absence in the fall of 1972 so that I might complete the book.

Introduction

I

MELVILLE'S REPUTATION: CONTEMPORARY AND LATER

American and British literary critics generally applauded the advent of Herman Melville as an author when *Typee* appeared in 1846. The tale of exciting adventure in a little-known area of the world told by a man who claimed to be a common sailor fascinated the reviewers. The applause continued and even grew wider the following year in response to *Omoo*, a sequel that presented much the same kind of material as its highly successful forerunner. But the acclamation became sporadic and mixed with censure when *Mardi* was published in 1849. Melville had attempted to go beyond writing simple tales of nautical adventure, and many critics expressed disappointment at the change or were derogatory of the author's attempts at allegory and political satire. In an apparent effort to regain critical approval and to achieve financial success, Melville hurriedly wrote in the summer of 1849 two rather straightforward stories of nautical life, *Redburn* (1849) and *White-Jacket* (1850), based, respectively, on his first voyage as a sailor and on his experiences as a crewman aboard a United States Navy frigate. The reviews, though fewer in number than for his earlier books, generally approved Melville's return to the kind of writing that first earned him fame. But Melville's next book, *Moby-Dick* (1851), once again disappointed many reviewers, who decried the mixture of modes and of subjects in what they considered an extravagant though often powerful production. The variety of response with which *Moby-Dick* was received changed to almost totally negative comment with *Pierre* (1852). The book was a flat failure, and said to be deservedly so for its stylistic and moral outrages. A silence of general neglect greeted the rest of Melville's writing except *The Confidence-Man* (1857), which elicited a mild revival of interest, especially in England where several major periodicals gave the book long and often perceptive notices. After 1857 Melville published only volumes of poetry: *Battle-Pieces* (1866), *Clarel* (1876), *John Marr* (1888), and *Timoleon* (1891). The first two received but the scantest critical attention, and the last two, being privately printed in editions of twenty-five copies each, were totally ignored save for one known review of the earlier volume.

Melville evidently was quite sensitive to the critical reception of his books during the eleven years—1846–57—when he sought to earn his living as an author. Comments in his personal letters and journals show this, and sometimes the books themselves reflect Melville's response to the published criticisms of his earlier productions—in the prefaces or passages that seek to answer directly specific objections of the critics and in certain aspects of form and content that attempt to conform to the critics' expressed aesthetic and moral preconceptions. The reviewers often berated Melville for failing to control his powerful imagination so that his writings would be in accord with the accepted canons of literary art. Also they thought that his sailor usages, irreverence toward religion, and treatment of indelicate subjects—usually those having to do with sex—were inappropriate, tasteless, and often immoral.

Melville was forgotten by both the critics and the reading public as the years went by, and the news of his death in 1891 surprised many who happened to remember the once famous author from forty years before: they thought him already dead. Even to the members of the literary world at the end of the nineteenth century, the name of Herman Melville meant nothing until they were reminded of his career by the spate of obituary notices that appeared in New York and New England. The state of nearly total oblivion in which Melville's reputation rested was not broken until almost thirty years after his death when a second advent took place: in the 1920s Melville was once again acclaimed, though often for reasons different from those given by earlier critics. The social and literary changes since Melville's books were first published created a new critical context in which his writings, especially *Moby-Dick*, were typically read as the record of a man's rebellion against the oppressive forces in his society. More recently Melville's books have been studied from a number of varied critical perspectives focusing on all aspects of form and content and on relationships of the works to their author. The growth of Melville's reputation since the 'Melville Revival' of the 1920s has more than matched its decline during his lifetime. Melville has been canonized as one of America's greatest authors—considered *the* greatest by some advocates, an honor not even his most sympathetic reviewer would have bestowed on him.

II

FIRST FAME: *Typee* (1846) AND *Omoo* (1847)

The obscurity of his death was not unlike the obscurity of his life before *Typee* appeared. The book, with its avowed autobiographical content, made him famous immediately as an author and, as he was later to say with some regret to Nathaniel Hawthorne, 'as a "man who lived among the cannibals"!' But so unusual were the events recorded —his desertion of a whaler in the South Seas and his captivity and escape from cannibals on the island of Nukuheva in the Marquesas— and so unfamiliar was the setting for these extraordinary adventures that Melville had trouble at first getting his book published. In mid-1845 he sent his completed manuscript to the New York publishing house of Harper & Brothers where the narrative was rejected because 'it was impossible that it could be true and therefore was without real value.' The rejection and undaunted belief in the merits of the book led his brother Gansevoort, recently appointed Secretary of the American Legation in London, to seek a publisher for the manuscript when he went to England in August. Henry Murray agreed to bring the book out as a part of his Home and Colonial Library, an inexpensive series containing narratives of true adventures in unusual settings around the world. But Murray also doubted that the story was absolutely authentic: it seemed like the work of 'a practised writer' who could have created the exciting tale out of his imagination. Gansevoort had to assure him that his brother was 'a mere novice in the art' and that 'the adventurer, and the writer of the adventure are one & the same person.' Apparently Murray's worries about the acceptance of the book as authentic could be calmed only by the addition of some more factual matter regarding life on the island, so Melville wrote three new chapters which Gansevoort delivered to the publisher, noting that they would 'go far to give a more life-like air to the whole, an[d] parry the incredulity of those who may be disposed to regard the work as an ingenious fiction.' But the chapters apparently did not go far enough: the reviewers of *Typee* questioned the authenticity both of the events and of their adventurer-author.

Gansevoort also secured an American publisher for *Typee*, the New York firm of Wiley & Putnam. Probably encouraged by Washington Irving—himself a Wiley & Putnam author—who read part of the manuscript and prophesied its success, Gansevoort contacted George

Palmer Putnam at the firm's London office. Putnam was delighted by the narrative and agreed to publish it. Proof sheets of the English edition were sent to New York for Wiley & Putnam to use in preparing its edition. There John Wiley was worried not about authenticity but about a lack of taste and delicacy, especially in Melville's treatment of the missionaries and in his picture of sailor life. A comparison of the first English and first American edition indicates that Wiley probably ordered a bowdlerization of the text, but the pressure of time—he wanted simultaneous publication with the English edition—and the expense of revision apparently brought that enterprise to an early end. Wiley's efforts, to judge by the responses of many of the reviewers, had as sound a basis as Murray's and were equally unsuccessful.

These matters of authenticity and taste were closely related to the chief subjects of critical discussion: *Typee*'s style, its narrative of Melville's adventures, and its picture of life in Polynesia.

The style was universally praised by the reviewers—even those who complained about the 'moral tone' of the book—with only minor objections to 'certain sea freedoms . . . that might as well have been removed before issuing it for family reading.' The reviewers noted the 'careless elegance' of Melville's language, 'so easy, so graceful, and so graphic,' not only 'plain and unpretending, but racy and pointed' as well.[1]

The style of *Typee* was compared—not always favorably—with that of *Two Years Before the Mast* (1840), Richard Henry Dana's autobiographical account of a gentleman serving as a common sailor. Dana's book, along with the sea fiction of James Fenimore Cooper, provided a literary precedent for the ability of a sailor who shipped 'before the mast' to write with the skills that the reviewers noted in *Typee*. In England the critics discussed at length the possibility that 'Herman Melville' was in fact a man of letters who created the adventures of *Typee* out of his imagination. *John Bull* (No. 4) found it difficult to believe that *Typee* was 'the production of a common sailor,' and *The Times* (No. 11) said Melville's 'style throughout is rather that of an educated literary man than of a poor outcast working seaman.' But the English critics generally—like the American—treated Melville as the real-life hero of actual adventures.

There was some dissent, to be sure, from this opinion regarding the authenticity of the events recorded in *Typee*, and its basis was logical rather than social: the adventures related were declared impossible, or extremely improbable. Even George Duyckinck, the brother of Evert

Duyckinck, an editor at Melville's American publishers, had expressed his doubts in a letter to a friend less than a month after the book appeared:

I am glad you like *Typee* though I cannot join with you in taking it all for sober verity. . . . His exploits in descending the waterfalls beat Sam Patch and can you enlighten me as to how he gets down the last one. If I remember rightly he is on the top of a precipice at the end of one chapter and safe and sound at the bottom at the beginning of the next.

Many reviewers thought the events at least highly-colored and exaggerated for effect, yet they perceived an overall *vraisemblance* in the narrative. Others were more severe, like the *Morning Courier and New York Enquirer* (17 April), which declared of *Typee* 'in all essential respects, it is a *fiction*,—a piece of Munchausenism,—from beginning to end.' Though Melville may have visited the Marquesas, the reviewer still did not have 'the slightest confidence in any of the details, while many of the incidents narrated are utterly incredible.' Since the book was put forth 'as a simple record of actual experiences,' it must be judged as 'a statement of facts,' and as such it has 'no merit whatever.'

This attack on his veracity was too much for Melville, and he took corrective measures. First he had a comment inserted in the Albany, New York, *Argus* account of *Typee*'s continuing success (21 April): 'The author desires to state to the public, that *Typee* is a true narrative of events which actually occurred to him. Although there may be moving incidents and hairbreadth escapes, it is scarcely more strange than such as happen to those who make their home on the deep.' Then Melville wrote on 23 May to A. W. Bradford, co-editor of the *American Review*, sending him an article (now lost) written for anonymous publication as a direct rebuttal to the piece in the *Morning Courier and New York Enquirer*:

Herewith you have the article we spoke of. I have endeavored to make it appear as if written by one who had read the book & beleived it—& morover—had been as much pleased with it as most people who read it profess to be. . . . Bye the by, I received to day among other papers, a number of *Chambers's Edinbrgh Journal* containing an abridged account of the adventure—& I could not but feel heartily vexed, that while the intelligent Editors of a publication like that should thus endorse the genuineness of the narrative—so many numskulls on this side of the water should heroically avow their determination not to be 'gulled' by it. The fact is, those who do not beleive it are the greatest 'gulls'.—full fledged ones too.—

What I have written embodies some thoughts which I think will tell with the public if they are introduced thro' the proper channel.—That channel is the *C*[*ourier*] *& Enquirer,* as it contained the obnoxious review.—I feel confident that unless something of this kind appears the success of the book here as a genuine narrative will be seriously impaired. I am told that, that malicious notice (for it certainly has that sort of edge to it) has been copied into papers in the Western part of the state.—It will do mischief unless answered.

Not only the genuineness of Melville's narrative but also his observations and judgments were subject to attack by the reviewers. Most accepted the descriptions of the Marquesas themselves and the natives there as factual and highly interesting, especially because little-known at the time. But Melville's treatment of the Typee cannibals as members of a utopian society and his obvious preference for the 'savage' over the 'civilized' life were harshly criticized in some quarters. 'What ROUSSEAU, in his famous Dijon thesis, traced out in theory,' said the *Critic* (No. 2), 'Mr. MELVILLE endeavours to exhibit in practice. Both are wrong.'

Even more offensive to some reviewers was Melville's picture of the missionaries. Many secular papers either agreed with Melville's appraisals of the 'good' done by the missionaries or deferred judgment of that aspect of the book for lack of first-hand knowledge, though the *Critic* told Melville that 'a twelve-months' mental discipline under the weakest of the disinterested class whom he reviles would be to him of the greatest service; it would teach him the value of moderation, charity, and truth-seeking,' and the *American Review* (April) thought his statements about the missionaries to be 'prejudiced and unfounded.' The religious papers, as George Duyckinck had said, hauled *Typee* 'over the coals for its treatment of the missionaries and some other points.' He was probably referring to a review in the *Evangelist* (No. 12) that accused Melville of 'the sheerest ignorance, and utter disregard of truth.' The longest and most vituperative attack was to appear in the July issue of the *Christian Parlor Magazine* (No. 16) which sought to rebuke Melville—the 'Traducer of Missions'—for his 'flagrant outrages against civilization, and particularly the missionary work.'

Melville's veracity got some unexpected support on 1 July when the Buffalo, New York, *Commercial Advertiser* carried a letter to its editor written by 'Toby,' one Richard Tobias Greene, the real-life original of the character in *Typee*:

In the *New York Evangelist* I chanced to see a notice of a new publication in two parts, called *Typee, a residence in the Marquesas,* by HERMAN MELVILLE. . . .

The *Evangelist* speaks rather disparagingly of the book as being too romantic to be true, and as being too severe on the missionaries. But to my object: I am the true and veritable 'Toby,' yet living, and I am happy to testify to the entire accuracy of the work so long as I was with MELVILLE, who makes me figure so largely in it. . . .

The *Commercial Advertiser*'s editor prefaced Toby's letter with the comment, 'His turning up here is a strange verification of a very strange and, as has hitherto been deemed, an almost incredible book.'

Melville was elated at the discovery of Toby, and wrote to Evert Duyckinck two days after the letter appeared:

There was a spice of civil scepticism in your manner, My Dear Sir, when we were conversing together the other day about *Typee*—What will the politely incredulous Mr Duycknck now say to the true Toby's having turned up in Buffalo, and written a letter to the *Commercial Advertiser* of that place, vouching for the truth of all that part (what has been considered the most extraordinary part) of the narrative, where he is made to figure.—Give ear then, oh ye of little faith—especially thou man of the *Evangelist*—and hear what Toby has to say for himself.—

Seriously, My Dear Sir, this resurection of Toby from the dead . . . can not but settle the question of the book's genuineness. . . .

Later in the month Melville wrote to Murray, informing him that Toby had 'come to life':

the impression which Toby's letter has produced is this—i e—that every thing about it bears the impress of truth.—Indeed, the whole *Typee* adventure is now regarded as a sort of Romance of Real Life.—You would be greatly diverted to read some of the comments of our Western Editors and log-cabin critics.

And he told Murray of his plans for 'a short Sequel to *Typee* containing a simple account of Toby's escape from the valley as related to me by himself.'

The letter also contained the news that a revised edition of *Typee* was soon to be published in America, one evidently occasioned at Wiley's insistence because of the adverse reaction to the picture of the missionaries. (In a letter written to Evert Duyckinck on 15 July, Melville said, '*Typee* has come out measurably unschathed from the fiery ordeal of Mr Wiley's criticisms.') And Melville felt it necessary to defend the revisions to Murray:

The revision will only extend to the exclusion of those parts not naturally connected with the narrative, and some slight purifications of style. I am persuaded that the interest of the book almost wholly consists in the *intrinsick merit of the narrative alone*—& that other portions, however interesting they may be in themselves, only serve to impede the story. The book is certainly calculated for popular reading, or for none at all.—If the first, why then, all passages which are calculated to offend the tastes, or offer violance to the feelings of any large class of readers are certainly objectionable.

—Proceeding on this principle then, I have rejected every thing, in revising the book, which refers to the missionaries. Such passages are altogether foreign to the adventure, & altho' they may possess a temporary interest *now*, to some, yet so far as the wide & permanent popularity of the work is conserned, their exclusion will certainly be beneficial, for to that end, the less the book has to carry along with it the better.—Certain 'sea-freedoms' also have been modifyed in the expression—but nothing has been done to effect the general character & style of the book—the narrative parts are untouched—In short—in revising the work, I have merely removed passages which leave no gap, & the removal of which imparts a unity to the book which it wanted before.

Still Melville was aware of what he had done, for he wrote to Duyckinck on 28 July, 'The *Revised* (Expurgated?—Odious word!) Edition of *Typee* ought to be duly announced.' When it did appear the next month, it was in fact more 'expurgated' than 'revised,' leaving it in a condition that pleased even the *Christian Parlor Magazine* (September 1846), which admitted that the 'most objectionable parts' had been removed, 'an evidence that, for some reason, the counsels of truth and decency have been regarded.'

Murray, who was not bothered by Melville's treatment of the missionaries because the English reviewers in general were not bothered, did not use the revised edition. But he still wanted some 'documentary evidences' that Melville had in fact been in the Marquesas, a request the author saw not as a mark of disbelief on Murray's part, but as a search for something substantial to 'stop the mouths of the senseless sceptics—men who go straight from their cradles to their graves & never dream of the queer things going on at the antipodes.' (It was almost two years before Melville could supply Murray with such 'evidences.') Curious to see what the sceptics and other critics were saying, Melville asked Murray to send him 'any further notices' of *Typee*, and he was obviously disappointed when the 'sagatious Critic' of the London *Literary Gazette* (12 December 1846) refused to believe in Melville's existence or in the veracity of his story, berating his 'contemporary periodical brethren' for doing so:

as we happened to fancy the name of Melville to be equivalent to that of Sinbad the Sailor, we certainly abstained from noticing that clever and entertaining production; as an apology for which, we beg Mr. Melville to accept this explanation, and do us the honour to dine with us on the 1st of April next: we intend to ask only a small party,—Messrs. Crusoe, Sinbad, Gulliver, Munchausen, and perhaps Pillet, Thiers, Kohl, and a few others.

Melville's displeasure at the reception of *Typee*'s authenticity was, perhaps, greater than was merited, considering how much the product of imagination the story really was. As Leon Howard has said, '*Typee* was, in fact, neither literal autobiography nor pure fiction. Melville drew his material from his experiences, from his imagination, and from a variety of travel books when the memory of his experiences failed him or when his personal observations were inadequate.'[2]

The reviewers' doubts about *Typee*'s authenticity and their censure of its treatment of the missionaries preoccupied Melville during the composition of his next book, *Omoo*. In December of 1846, shortly before signing an agreement with the Harpers for the publication of the new work, Melville asked Evert Duyckinck to look over several chapters of the manuscript that referred 'more or less to the missions & the condition of the natives.' After seeing these chapters, Duyckinck wrote his brother, George, that Melville 'owes a sailor's grudge to the Missionaries & pays it off at Tahiti.' Melville made a serious attempt to forestall the kind of criticism that beset *Typee* by writing a preface in which he explained his intentions and proclaimed his veracity. The work was intended, Melville wrote, 'to convey some idea' of sailor life in the South Seas, 'by means of a circumstantial history of adventures befalling the author,' and to give 'a *familiar* account of the present condition of the converted Polynesians, as affected by their promiscuous intercourse with foreigners, and the teachings of the missionaries, combined.' Foreseeing the reviewers' reaction to the latter subject, Melville announced that in 'every statement connected with missionary operations, a strict adherence to facts has, of course, been scrupulously observed. . . . Nothing but an earnest desire for truth and good has led him [the author] to touch upon this subject at all.' However he did protect himself by issuing a disclaimer of 'precision with respect to dates' because he depended on 'simple recollection' rather than a written record of his experiences. And he made no 'pretensions to philosophic research,' indulging only in occasional 'spontaneous' reflections upon what he witnessed.

Still, when *Omoo* appeared in England, published by Murray on 30 March 1847, and in America just over a month later, the reviewers once again raised the same questions. They did so in great part because *Omoo* contained much the same subject matter as its predecessor: the adventures and observations of a young American sailor on shipboard and among the natives and foreigners in the South Seas. In the preface Melville stated that *Omoo* necessarily began where *Typee* concluded but that it had 'no further connection with the latter work.' The reviewers could not separate *Typee* and *Omoo* so easily, and often the two were considered in the same article, especially by critics who had missed *Typee* and were noticing Melville for the first time. Melville, as one reviewer said, shared the good fortune of Lord Byron, 'that of going to bed at night an unknown personage and finding himself famous when he got up the next morning.'[3] As a result of this sudden fame, more reviewers took notice of *Omoo* than of *Typee*. The author was most anxious to see how his *Omoo* would be 'received by the sagatious Critics of the English press,' and he asked his agent in London, John Broadhead, 'to have an eye, occasionaly, upon the Reviews, & to cause to be collected & sent me, in their original form, whatever notices may appear of the book.' If *Omoo* was a critical success, he promised Murray he would 'follow it up by something else, immediately.'

The reviewers generally were surprised and pleased to find that *Omoo*, unlike most sequels, equalled its predecessor, though to the disparagers of *Typee* this meant that the new book was 'replete alike with the merits and the faults of its forerunner.' Once again Melville's style was extolled on both sides of the Atlantic by critics who described it as 'vivacious,' 'simple and unpretending,' 'richly good natured,' and 'brilliant and captivating.' Melville's ability to draw interesting characters in *Omoo* received special attention, particularly his picture of the 'capital' Doctor Long Ghost, a 'jewel of a boy, a complete original, hit off with uncommon felicity.' Another reviewer thought the character sketches 'exquisite' and just as amusing as those in the *Pickwick Papers*.[4]

Omoo proved Melville, according to the New York *Tribune* (No. 30), 'a born genius, with few superiors either as a narrator, a describer, or a humorist.' But some critics found Melville's artistic ability a dangerously seductive disguise for the book's diseased moral tone and for the 'lies' about the missionaries. A brief notice in the *Evangelist* (27 May) typified this response:

These lively sketches steal one's favor and approbation in spite of himself. They are so graphic and spirited, and narrate scenes of such strange and surpassing interest, that the reader is borne along through the checkered history, without stopping to inquire how much is true or false, or what reliance is to be placed on the author's most deliberate statements. But on arriving at the end and looking back, the conviction speedily arises that it is but little else than romance. Its only merit is what a well-told tale, founded on some Polynesian facts, would have. The author's mendacity is sometimes flagrantly visible, as well as his spite against religion and its missionaries.

The battle lines were drawn on the question of Melville's veracity as a reporter on the condition of the missions and the natives in the South Seas. On the attack were the reviewers for the religious periodicals and their supporters in the secular press, and on the defense were Melville's friends among the literati in New York City and other reviewers who believed his picture to be accurate. Before the *Evangelist*'s notice appeared, several periodicals had accepted Melville's accounts as factual: 'a plain and honest statement,' said one, by a 'candid and impartial witness,' said another. It was near the end of June that Horace Greeley in the New York *Tribune* expressed disappointment that the book's 'diseased' moral tone, caused by the 'racy lightness' with which Melville treated 'objectionable' incidents, would undermine his otherwise 'lucid and apparently candid testimony' on the missions. But the attacks started in earnest with George Washington Peck's assault in the *American Review* (No. 31) on Melville's veracity and personal behavior and on his artistic ability as well. Melville's 'licentiousness' among the natives led to a hatred and fear of the missionaries, and while his book is entertaining, there is no truth in it; one must read it with 'a perpetual recoil.' Peck's article got support on 14 July from the *Morning Courier and New York Enquirer*, of which Peck was an assistant editor. On the other side of the public controversy (privately, in his diary, Duyckinck had called Peck's review 'grossly abusive') was Jedediah B. Auld, who, a week later in the New York *Evening Mirror* (No. 32), first took issue with the *American Review* and then with the *Courier and Enquirer* for sanctioning Peck's 'disgusting loathsomeness and personal blackguardism.' And the satirical *Yankee Doodle* (24 July) ran a paragraph, probably written by Duyckinck, cutting Peck's 'high parsonical style.'

Another frontal assault against Melville was launched by William Oland Bourne, who had earlier pilloried the 'Traducer of Missions' in his review of *Typee*. In a letter to his friend Greeley, published in the *Tribune* on 2 October, Bourne pronounced Melville's book, 'so far as its pretended facts are concerned, a tissue of uninformed misrepresentations, of prejudiced ignorance, and of hostility,' obviously the work of a 'pertinacious traducer of loftier and better men.' Once more the *Evening Mirror* came to Melville's defense, berating Bourne for his 'ill-natured and bigoted notice' of *Omoo*. These attacks on his personal conduct and on his reportorial accuracy, when compared to the more sympathetic treatment on the other side of the Atlantic, led Melville to write to Duyckinck on 23 October.[5] He thanked his friend for sending along an English review—probably that in *The Times* (No. 33)—and remarked, 'Upon my soul, Duyckinck, these English are a sensible people. Indeed to confess the truth, when I compare their reception of *Omoo* in particular, with its treatment here, it begets ideas not very favorable to one's patriotism.' And Melville must have felt even less patriotic if he read Bourne's last word on *Omoo* in a long review titled 'Missionary Operations in Polynesia' in the *New Englander* (January 1848), a religious quarterly published in New Haven, Connecticut. As in his attack on *Typee*, Bourne cited many other authorities on the South Seas in his attempt to refute Melville's 'cavils' about the missions.

The controversy over the veracity of Melville's picture of the missions went on for years. The London *English Review* in March 1848 censured Melville for 'a laxity of moral feeling, an absence of religious principle throughout both works.' According to the Boston, Massachusetts, *Christian Examiner* (May 1848), *Typee* and *Omoo* had been 'taken up by the Catholics as authority, and made the groundwork of a new attack upon Protestant missions'—this referring to the *Catholic Magazine*'s treatment of the two books in articles in November 1847 and January 1848. And in October 1850 the London *Eclectic Review* accused Melville of being one of the 'partisans of popery,' who 'is guilty of deliberate and elaborate misrepresentation' and 'is a prejudiced, incompetent, and truthless witness' regarding the Protestant Missions in Tahiti. This attack, occasioned by the publication of a pirated edition of *Omoo* in England, was reprinted by two American periodicals. The *Literary World* answered the charges for Melville, rebuking the 'stupidity' of the English reviewer who 'evidently considers the author a *Jesuit in disguise*, bent on the destruction of Protestantism in the Islands.'

But the furor and fervor of the religious writers finally faded away, and *Typee* and *Omoo* served through the rest of the nineteenth century as a touchstone for judging later books on the Polynesian islands. As the London *Athenaeum* wrote (11 November 1854), 'Every place, sooner or later, finds its voice,—finds somebody to paint it to the eyes of cultivated, speculative Europe—to furnish a picture of it which, according to the skill of the artist, remains its "ideal" for generations more or less numerous.' *Typee* and *Omoo* did this for America as well as for Europe.

III

GREATER EFFORT; LESS SUCCESS: *Mardi* (1849)

The more immediate critical response to *Omoo* in 1847 apparently encouraged Melville to think in terms of the new book he had mentioned to Murray on 31 March. At least on 19 June he asked another English publisher, Richard Bentley, who had made overtures to Melville in May, what value he would place on 'the English copy right of a new work of South Sea adventure, by me, occupying entirely fresh ground.' Perhaps the prospect of his marriage to Elizabeth Shaw, which was to take place on 4 August, prodded him to write something more lucrative than his series of anonymous satirical pieces on General Zachary Taylor—'Authentic Anecdotes of "Old Zack" '—to be carried by *Yankee Doodle* in the late summer. By 22 September Evert Duyckinck could write to his brother that Melville, now living and writing in New York City, was 'preparing a third book which [will] exhaust the South Sea marvels.' A month later Melville expressed to Murray his 'gratification' at *Omoo*'s English reception and reported that he had 'engaged upon another book of South Sea Adventure (continued from, tho' wholly independent of, *Omoo*).' Melville believed the 'signal success' of his two earlier books, '& other considerations peculiar to the case, leave little doubt as to the success of a third.' He projected delivery of the new manuscript no later than the fall of 1848 but wanted to arrange 'the sale of the book *now*' and at a better price than he had received for *Omoo*:

> Surely, if the probable sale of *Omoo* in England is to be estimated by the notices of it which have appeared there, & also by its known sale *here*, you can not be surprised, that to say the least, the book in my estimation brought less than it has proved to be worth, in a merely business point of view.

Murray disabused Melville in his answering letter: taken together the two books represented as of 3 December a loss of more than £6 to his firm. So the quibbling over the value of the new book continued by mail into 1848 while Melville worked hard on the uncompleted manuscript.

During these months Melville spent a lot of time reading the works of other authors as well as writing his own book. He bought copies of Robert Burton, Coleridge, Defoe, Shakespeare, Montaigne, and Froissart and borrowed other works, some, such as travel books, from the New York Library Society, and others, including Sir Thomas Browne and Rabelais, from Duyckinck, whose literary circle he had entered as the newly-discovered sailor-author of *Typee* and *Omoo*. The enlightening contacts with books and literary men changed the course of his book so much that on 25 March Melville had to confess to Murray that a great deal had happened to his manuscript since he had last written:

> the work I then had in view was a bona-vide narrative of my adventures in the Pacific, continued from *Omoo*—My object in now writing you—I should have done so ere this—is to inform you of a change in my determinations. To be blunt: the work I shall next publish will [be] in downright earnest a 'Romance of Polynisian Adventure'—But why this? The truth is, Sir, that the reiterated imputation of being a romancer in disguise has at last pricked me into a resolution to show those who may take any interest in the matter, that a *real* romance of mine is no *Typee* or *Omoo*, & is made of different stuff altogether. . . . —As for the policy of putting forth an acknowledged *romance* upon the heel of two books of travel which in some quarters have been recvd with no small incredulity—That, Sir, is a question for which I care little, really.—My *instinct* is to out with the Romance, & let me say that instincts are prophetic, & better than acquired wisdom—which alludes remotely to your experience in literature as an eminent publisher.

Murray's reply seemed 'Antarctic' to Melville—'I fear you abhor romances,' he told the publisher—but he would not be moved from his desire to write the kind of book he wanted to. *Mardi* turned out to be, as Elizabeth S. Foster has said, 'a continuum of adventure in an open boat and a derelict ship, wild allegorical romance, and fantastic travelogue-satire,'[6] having developed through those stages from the spring of 1847 to near the end of 1848. Melville signed an agreement with the Harpers for the publication of *Mardi* on 15 November on terms that included a $500 advance and half-profits after expenses. Murray refused the 'romance' but Bentley quickly took it, and on 3 March 1849 agreed to advance Melville £210 against the half-profits from sales of the book. For reasons of copyright the English edition once again preceded the American: Bentley published *Mardi* in three volumes on 16 March and the Harpers in two volumes on 14 April.

Melville saw *Mardi* as a step forward for him as an artist, one that had needed over a year and a half to complete, and he took some time off after it was finished to rest and to think about the next step. He went to Boston to stay at the home of his father-in-law, Judge Lemuel Shaw, while his wife, Elizabeth, awaited the birth of their first child, born on 16 February 1849. The next week he wrote to Duyckinck that he had been passing his time 'very pleasurably' there, reading Shakespeare and attending cultural events, among them a lecture by Emerson. Even in his letter of 5 April to Duyckinck—just nine days before *Mardi* was published—there is no suggestion that he thought the new book would fail:

I am glad you liked that affair of mine. But it seems so long now since I wrote it, & my mood has so changed, that I dread to look into it, & have purposely abstained from so doing since I thanked God it was off my hands.—Would that a man could do something & then say—It is finished.—not that one thing only, but all others—that he has reached his uttermost, & can never exceed it. But live & push—tho' we put one leg forward ten miles—its no reason the other must lag behind—no, *that* must again distance the other—& so we go till we get the cramp & die.

In Melville's mind *Mardi* had been a ten-mile step forward and his next book should surpass that. But with the appearance of the reviews Melville knew that *Mardi* was generally considered, as *Blackwood's Edinburgh Magazine* was to say, a 'backsliding performance' and that it would probably be a financial as well as a critical failure.

As in *Omoo*, Melville used his preface as an apologia for his book:

Not long ago, having published two narratives of voyages in the Pacific, which, in many quarters, were received with incredulity, the thought occurred to me, of indeed writing a romance of Polynesian adventure, and publishing it as such; to see whether, the fiction might not, possibly, be received for a verity: in some degree the reverse of my previous experience.

This thought was the germ of others, which have resulted in *Mardi*.

Despite Melville's claim that he was writing a new kind of book, the descriptions of nature and life at sea in the opening chapters of *Mardi* seemed to the reviewers a happy continuation of the best aspects of *Typee* and *Omoo*. Up to the point where the sea adventures gave way to the travels through the islands of Mardi, the critics, even those hostile to the book as a whole, were bothered only by some extravagances of style. But the varied aspects of the later portions of the book led to confusion among the critics about the book's genre and, as a result, they despaired of ever finding out what *Mardi* was all about.

The *Athenaeum* (No. 34) said, 'If this book was meant as a pleasantry, the mirth has been oddly left out—if as an allegory, the key of the casket is "buried in ocean deep"—if as a romance, it fails from tediousness—if as a prose-poem, it is chargeable with puerility.' The reviewer for the London *Critic* (1 April) was disappointed in Melville for destroying even the illusion that the book might be fact rather than fiction by calling it a romance in his preface. But, the reviewer continued, *Mardi* is not purely a romance:

> It is an extraordinary mixture of all kinds of composition, and of the strangest variety of themes. There are philosophical discourse, political disquisition, the essay, scientific and humourous, touches of poetry, and episodical adventure, with descriptions of countries and people, strung together by the slight thread of a story which is not very intelligible.

In America much the same opinion was expressed in the Boston *Post* (No. 39), which, after extolling the genius exhibited in *Typee* and *Omoo*, said the 'unreadable' *Mardi* became 'mere *hodge-podge*' after the opening sea scenes and contained 'a mass of downright nonsense.' In response to Melville's preface, the reviewer gave some practical advice to the young author: 'He had better stick to his "fact" which is received as "fiction," but which puts money in his purse and wreathes laurels round his head, than fly to "fiction" which is not received at all . . . .' The New York *Tribune* (No. 43) said Melville had 'failed by leaving his sphere, which is that of graphic, poetical narration, and launching out into the dim, shadowy, spectral, Mardian region of mystic speculation and wizard fancies.'

The reviewers recognized the allegorical and satirical elements of *Mardi*, but most, disturbed by the book's disorganization, refused to take the time to search out the meanings and the targets. Those few who did look deep into *Mardi* generally found it a great step forward in Melville's development as an artist. The circle of New York literati that Melville had recently joined particularly praised the book, perhaps because they felt they had had a hand in its author's progress from 'common sailor' to man of letters. In the *Literary World* (No. 38), Duyckinck declared *Mardi* a 'purely original invention' and, in his role as supporter of things American in literature, asked, 'Is not this sign of a true manhood, when an American author lifts his voice boldly to tell the truth to his country people?' Even more exuberant was Duyckinck's friend, William Alfred Jones, who in the New York *United States Magazine and Democratic Review* (No. 45), said *Typee* and

Omoo were to *Mardi* 'as a seven-by-nine sketch of a sylvan lake . . . compared with the cartoons of Raphael.' The reader who wants to be entertained by an ordinary romance need not open *Mardi*, but 'whoso wishes to see the spirit of philosophy and humanity, love and wisdom, showing man to himself as he is, that he may know his evil and folly, and be saved from them, will be reverently thankful for this book.' Not only Melville's New York friends but some of the English reviewers, too, saw growth of talent over the earlier books. The *Critic* wrote that *Mardi*

> will better please the refined and thoughtful reader, but it will prove less interesting to the mere seeker after amusement. Much will be learned from it by those who look to be instructed by what they read, for a lesson and a moral are conveyed in every incident. Beyond question, it is a production of extraordinary talent.

But other reviewers considered Melville's development to have a rather parasitic dependence on earlier writers that led to obscurity and verbosity in *Mardi*. Among the authors most cited as Melville's apparent models were Carlyle, Emerson (and transcendental writers in general), Defoe, Swift, Sir Thomas Browne, Robert Burton, Sterne, Rabelais, and 'Ossian.' The London *Spectator* (21 April), in a very harsh review, noted similarities to the *Arabian Nights* and to *Gulliver's Travels* and then declared, 'It is not plagarism that is the ground of censure; it is the manner in which the "conveyed" goods are disfigured and deprived of value without gaining any character in place of what is lost.' As to Melville's efforts to move into the field of romance, the *Spectator* judged that he 'has neither the mind nor the mental training requisite for fiction; and in aiming to become what he is not, he spoils what he is.'

The reviews evidently upset Melville. On 23 April, shortly after he and his family returned to New York City from Boston, he wrote to Judge Shaw:

> I see that *Mardi* has been cut into by the London *Atheneum*, and also burnt by the common hangman in the Boston *Post*. However the London *Examiner* & *Literary Gazette*; & other papers this side of the water have done differently. These attacks are matters of course, and are essential to the building up of any permanent reputation—if such should ever prove to be mine.—'There's nothing in it!' cried the dunce, when he threw down the 47th problem of the 1st Book of Euclid—'There's nothing in it—'—Thus with the posed critic. But Time, which is the solver of all riddles, will solve *Mardi*.

He also defended *Mardi* against the attacks of the critics in a letter on 5 June to Bentley:

> The critics on your side of the water seem to have fired quite a broadside into *Mardi*; but it was not altogether unexpected. In fact the book is of a nature to attract compliments of that sort from some quarters; and as you may be aware yourself, it is judged only as a work meant to entertain. And I can not but think that its having been brought out in England in the ordinary novel form must have led to the disappointment of many readers, who would have been better pleased with it, perhaps, had they taken it up in the first place for what it really is.—Besides, the peculiar thoughts & fancies of a Yankee upon politics & other matters could hardly be presumed to delight that class of gentlemen who conduct your leading journals; while the metaphysical ingredients (for want of a better term) of the book, must of course repel some of those who read simply for amusement.—However, it will reach those for whom it is intended; and I have already received assurances that *Mardi*, in its higher purposes, has not been written in vain.
>
> You may think, in your own mind that a man is unwise,—indiscreet, to write a work of that kind, when he might have written one perhaps, calculated merely to please the general reader, & not provoke attack, however masqued in an affectation of indifference or contempt. But some of us scribblers, My Dear Sir, always have a certain something unmanageable in us, that bids us do this or that, and be done it must—hit or miss.

But with a wife and child to support and with the hostile reviews indicating little in the way of financial success to be expected from *Mardi*, Melville apparently decided to manage the 'something unmanageable.' Perhaps, too, he consciously accepted the counsel of the Boston *Post* to stick to fact which put 'money in his purse,' for in the spring of 1849 he began writing a new book which he described to Bentley in the same letter:

> I have now in preparation a thing of a widely different cast from *Mardi*:—a plain, straightforward, amusing narrative of personal experience—the son of a gentleman on his first voyage to sea as a sailor—no metaphysics, no conic-sections, nothing but cakes & ale. I have shifted my ground from the South Seas to a different quarter of the globe—nearer home—and what I write I have almost wholly picked up by my own observations under comical circumstances. In size the book will be perhaps a fraction smaller than *Typee*; will be printed here by the Harpers, & ready for them two or three months hence, or before. I value the English Copyright at one hundred & fifty pounds, and think it would be wise to put it forth in a manner, admitting of a popular circulation.

IV

TWO JOBS: *Redburn* (1849) AND *White-Jacket* (1850)

Melville worked hard, at an almost frantic pace in fact, during the summer of 1849, writing in a way designed to avoid offending the critics and to gain financial success. The result was two nautical narratives, *Redburn* and *White-Jacket*, based on his experience in the first instance as a 'green hand' aboard a merchant ship in 1839 and in the second as an 'ordinary seaman' on a United States Navy man-of-war in 1843–4. By July he had arranged for the publication of *Redburn* by the Harpers and by Bentley. He corrected the proof sheets supplied by the Harpers while he was working on the manuscript of *White-Jacket* in late July and in August, and he sent a set of those proofs to Bentley for his use in preparing the English edition of *Redburn*. On 13 September the Harpers agreed to publish *White-Jacket*, two months before their edition of *Redburn* appeared. Bentley brought out *Redburn* on 29 September, two weeks before the Harpers edition, in order to avoid giving any other English firm the chance to publish an unauthorized edition using the American text as its source. Though at this time no legal protection was afforded to an American author in England (or English in America) or to his authorized publisher there, yet by gentlemen's agreement the English publishers respected priority of publication of foreign authors in England as establishing the rights to the book.

Melville planned to sail to England to arrange for the publication of *White-Jacket* since he had not had time to carry out any such transaction by mail during the hectic period of the book's composition. No reviews of the English edition of *Redburn* had reached the United States before he left on 11 October, taking a set of *White-Jacket* proof sheets with him, and the American edition did not appear for another month. In expectation of these reviews, Melville told his father-in-law in a letter written a few days before his departure:

> For *Redburn* I anticipate no particular reception of any kind. It may be deemed a book of tolerable entertainment;—& may be accounted dull.—As for the other book, it will be sure to be attacked in some quarters. But no reputation that is gratifying to me, can possibly be achieved by either of these books. They are two *jobs*, which I have done for money—being forced to it, as other men are to sawing wood. And while I have felt obliged to refrain from writing the kind of book I would wish to; yet, in writing these two books, I have not

repressed myself very much—so far as *they* are concerned; but have spoken pretty much as I feel.—Being books, then, written in this way, my only desire for their 'success' (as it is called) springs from my pocket, & not from my heart. So far as I am individually concerned, & independent of my pocket, it is my earnest desire to write those sort of books which are said to 'fail.'—Pardon this egotism.

Melville had not been in England since the journey that formed the basis for *Redburn*, and the change in his station led him to remark in his journal on 4 November, 'This time tomorrow I shall be on land, & press English earth after the lapse of ten years—*then* a sailor, *now* H.M. author of "Peedee" "Hullabaloo" & "Pog-Dog." ' The first reviews the 'author' saw were in *Bentley's Miscellany* (his publisher's own periodical) and *Blackwood's* (No. 53). The latter review he characterized in his journal as a

long story about a short book. It's very comical—seemed so, at least, as I had to hurry over it—in treating the thing as real. But the wonder is that the old Tory should waste so many pages upon a thing, which I, the author, know to be trash, & wrote it to buy some tobacco with.

Two days later, on 8 November, he visited Bentley's offices to try to arrange for the publication of *White-Jacket*. There he was shown notices from the English press concerning *Redburn*; he found them 'laughable.' This judgment probably grew out of Melville's own opinion regarding the book and out of his evolving disregard and perhaps contempt for the opinions of the critics except as those opinions affected the financial success of his books. In general the English notices that appeared before he went to Bentley's that day spoke highly and in some cases enthusiastically about *Redburn*, as did the ones that appeared later in England and in America after its delayed publication there.

Reviewers on both sides of the Atlantic praised the fidelity with which Melville rendered 'common and real life' in *Redburn*, so that it seemed, as the Boston *Post* (No. 55) said, 'to be *fact* word for word.' They were speaking mainly of the sea sections of *Redburn*, for the episodes in Liverpool and London in the second half of the book were usually treated as contrived, unrealistic melodrama, especially by the British critics. The sea scenes encouraged comparison with other writers of nautical fiction: Dana, Smollett, Cooper, and Marryat. The voyage to Liverpool, said the *Literary Gazette* (No. 48), 'is as perfect a specimen of the naval yarn as we ever read.' Another frequently made comparison was with Defoe—the *Literary World* (No. 54) called Melville 'the De Foe of the Ocean'—the clear and simple style, life-like characters, and fidelity to the details of nature of the English author seemed taken over by Melville in *Redburn*.

A major compliment paid Melville was for his artistic skill in making interesting the commonplace events and often-written-about material of the sea voyage. The incidents, *Holden's Dollar Magazine* (No. 61) said, are 'clothed in the fresh and poetic style' that makes them more charming 'than novelties . . . in a less beautiful dress.' The London *Athenaeum* (10 November 1849) concluded that *Redburn* 'wants the novelty of interest and of subject' of *Typee* and *Omoo*, 'but that on the whole it is better written than either,' and the New York *Literary American* (24 November) could not but wonder 'at the interest with which [Melville] leads the reader through the ordinary details of a sailor's life.'

The characters, with the major exception of Harry Bolton, were generally considered well-drawn and life-like. Jackson was often cited as an original portrait, and the description of his fall to his death was excerpted by several periodicals. The hero himself, Wellingborough Redburn, drew the attention of many reviewers. They found the 'green hand's' perspective on his first voyage entertaining and perhaps even instructive for young men who might read the book in anticipation of going to sea. But the critics questioned the inconsistency in the characterization: *Blackwood's* noted that 'Redburn, a sharp enough lad on shore, . . . seems converted, by the first sniff of salt water, into as arrant a simpleton as ever made mirth in a cockpit,' and the reviewer in the London *Daily News* (No. 52) felt a 'discrepancy' between 'the author and the biographer' because the hero enveloped his many silly actions 'with rich thought and keen observation. How can we admit the fool in action with "the wit in mind?" '

Despite these various reservations, the reviewers in general welcomed *Redburn* as a return by Melville to his best area—the simple, straightforward tale of nautical adventure—perhaps not as interesting or novel as *Typee* and *Omoo* but certainly an improvement over *Mardi*. Dissent from this opinion came from those few critics who considered *Mardi* a substantial artistic advancement from the earlier works. But Melville was probably satisfied as he read the reviews that *Redburn* would gain the kind of financial 'success' he had intended for it.

He had still to sell the rights to the English edition of *White-Jacket*, and in November he visited a number of London publishing houses in an attempt to get a good price for the book. Several publishers used the ambiguous state of the copyright law as an excuse for rejecting *White-Jacket*. In his journal and in letters home Melville complained about this, telling Duyckinck on 2 December that 'the confounded state of the Copyright question in England . . . has prevented me from receiving an immediate supply of cash,' so he must return to the United States sooner than he wanted. In a continuation of this letter dated 14 December Melville expressed his surprise about *Redburn*'s favorable reception:

I am glad of it—for it puts money into an empty purse. But I hope I shall never write such a book again—Tho' when a poor devil writes with duns all round him, & looking over the back of his chair—& perching on his pen & diving in his inkstand—like the devils about St: Anthony—what can you expect of that poor devil?—What but a beggarly *Redburn*! And when he attempts anything higher—God help him & save him! for it is not with a hollow purse as with a hollow balloon—for a hollow purse makes the poet *sink*—witness *Mardi* But we that write & print have all our books predestinated—& for me, I shall write such things as the Great Publisher of Mankind ordained ages before he published 'The World'—this planet, I mean—not the Literary Globe.—What a madness & anguish it is, that an author can never—under no conceivable circumstances—be at all frank with his readers.—Could I, for one, be frank with them—how would they cease their railing—those at least who have railed.—In a little notice[7] of *The Oregon Trail* I once said something 'critical' about another man's book—I shall never do it again. Hereafter I shall no more stab at a book (in print, I mean) than I would stab at a man.—I am but a poor mortal, & I admit that I learn by experience & not by divine intuitions. Had I not written & published *Mardi*, in all likelihood, I would not be as wise as I am now, or may be. For that thing was stabbed *at* (I do not say *through*)—& therefore, I am the wiser for it.

A few days later he signed an agreement with Bentley, selling him the copyright for *White-Jacket* for £200; and on Christmas Day, his business finished, Melville sailed for home.

The day after his arrival in New York on 1 February 1850 Melville presented a copy of the English edition of the much abused *Mardi* to Duyckinck, with the expressed hope that 'if *Mardi* be admitted to your shelves, your bibliographical Republic of Letters may find some contentment in the thought, that it has afforded refuge to a work, which almost everywhere else has been driven forth like a wild, mystic Mormon into shelterless exile.'

The reception of *White-Jacket* was to be much more hospitable than that of *Mardi*, and even somewhat warmer than that of *Redburn*.

Bentley got the new book out near the end of January 1850, and the Harpers' edition appeared on 21 March. *White-Jacket* proved to many reviewers that Melville was the leading writer of nautical fiction, a type of literature, according to an article in the London *Weekly Chronicle* (3 February), that seemed 'of late to have gone out of fashion.' The reviewers compared Melville favorably with other writers of sea tales—such as Cooper and Marryat—and, as in their reviews of *Redburn*, praised Melville's artistic skill in making interesting the material of the sea and ships that many thought already exhausted by those other writers. 'We cannot recall,' said the *Athenaeum* (No. 63), 'another novelist or sketcher who has given the poetry of the Ship—her voyages and her crew—in a manner at all resembling his.' Melville's powers of observation and description were credited with enabling him to paint more truthfully than had ever been done the life at sea on board a man-of-war.

The reviewers noted much more than just a factual narrative in *White-Jacket*, and they reacted variously to the inclusion of 'fiction,' 'disquisitions,' 'essays,' 'discussions,' 'anecdotes,' 'sketches,' and other matter in the book. *Britannia* (No. 64) used a putative want of continuity and of motive as an excuse to lecture on a general fault among American writers: 'In this respect Mr. Melville resembles the great majority of his countrymen who aspire to literary eminence. They imagine everything depends on mental vigour, and nothing on mental discipline.' As for Melville in particular, he 'has strength, but he is not skillful in the use of it; he has fancy, but he knows not how to restrain and guide it.' The equally chauvinistic London *Morning Post* (12 February), while recommending *White-Jacket* 'in the strongest manner,' declared,

> The mind of young America, keen, sensitive, but unmatured, lies before us. With all the ardour of a youth first opening upon the stories of nature and literature, the author pours forth in unchastened eloquence the thoughts that rise profusely to his mind. He has not learnt, or has not cared to practise, the art of giving to each subject its due weight, to each motive its proper influence in the matters of which he treats.

But British national feeling was pleased by Melville's flattering picture of the English Navy, particularly in his contrasts to American naval practices. These contrasts, however, led the critic for the *United States Magazine and Democratic Review* (No. 70) to say that *White-Jacket* was 'evidently manufactured for the English market.'

Melville's picture of abuses in the United States Navy gained wide attention in the American periodicals, especially his chapters on flogging, an unpopular practice much in the news at that time and soon to be abolished by Congress. Some of Melville's expressed thoughts on other abuses raised countering arguments by reviewers on both sides of the Atlantic, including the one for the Boston *Post* (No. 72), who declared Melville incompetent to discuss the 'great practical subjects' of naval life: they were best left to 'men of character, wisdom and experience—not men of theories, fancies and enthusiasm.'

While a few reviewers objected once again to Melville's 'too great freedom in touching on sacred subjects,' the objections were minor in comparison with the general praise of the book. And most would have agreed with the *Knickerbocker* (No. 73) that Melville was 'on the right ground at last.' After the sad mistake of *Mardi*, '*Redburn* reässured us; and now comes *White-Jacket*, to reïnstate the author in the best good-graces of the reading public.'

V

LEVIATHAN AND KRAKEN: *Moby-Dick* (1851) AND *Pierre* (1852)

With an eye to maintaining himself in these collective 'good-graces,' Melville began composing, in the spring of 1850, another book of nautical adventure. Evidently his experiences on a whale ship formed the basis for the new book, because on 1 May he answered a letter from Richard Henry Dana, Jr, on that subject:

> About the 'whaling voyage'—I am half way in the work, & am very glad that your suggestion so jumps with mine. It will be a strange sort of book, tho', I fear; blubber is blubber you know; tho' you may get oil out of it, the poetry runs as hard as sap from a frozen maple tree;—& to cook the thing up, one must needs throw in a little fancy, which from the nature of the thing, must be ungainly as the gambols of the whales themselves. Yet I mean to give the truth of the thing, spite of this.

Two months later he offered Bentley the copyright of the 'new work,' to be delivered in the late fall, for the sum of £200. Melville extolled the 'great novelty' of the book which would make it sell well: 'I do not know that the subject treated of has ever been worked up by a romancer; or, indeed, by any writer, in any adequate manner.' Melville should have been an expert on that subject because for months he had been buying and borrowing books on whales and whaling and on Pacific voyages. His usual writing practice—one he had certainly followed in the five earlier books—was to supplement his personal knowledge and to refresh his memory on his subject by referring to books by other authors.

In early August Evert Duyckinck wrote his brother, George, that Melville's new book was 'mostly done—a romantic, fanciful & literal & most enjoyable presentment of the Whale Fishery—something quite new.' The letter was sent from Pittsfield, in the Berkshire mountains of western Massachusetts, where Duyckinck was visiting and where Melville was spending the summer with relatives prior to buying a house there that would be his home for the next several years. One highly important event took place during this holiday visit that changed the course both of the 'mostly done' work and of Melville's future: he met Nathaniel Hawthorne, who was living in nearby Lenox. The immediate consequence of this new friendship was that Melville read a collection of Hawthorne's tales, 'Mosses from an Old Manse,' and wrote a long appreciative essay, 'Hawthorne and His Mosses' (No. 74), that Duyckinck printed in two parts in the *Literary World* on 17 and 24 August. A second and ultimately more important consequence was that Melville, when he revised his new book, operated under the influence of what he had described in the essay as being the essential nature of Hawthorne's genius.

Hawthorne's more privately expressed opinion on Melville's abilities as a writer can be seen in a letter to Duyckinck late in August at a time when Hawthorne did not know who had written the 'Mosses' essay:

> I have read Melville's works with a progressive appreciation of the author. No writer ever put the reality before his reader more unflinchingly than he does in *Redburn*, and *White Jacket*. *Mardi* is a rich book, with depths here and there that compel a man to swim for his life. It is so good that one scarcely pardons the writer for not having brooded long over it, so as to make it a great deal better.

The two authors met and corresponded from time to time over the next year as Melville was working on his manuscript. In December 1850, Melville described to Duyckinck how he spent his time in Pittsfield, writing on the new book from after breakfast to 2.30 p.m. each day. In the face of this effort he wondered if it were not true that 'a book in a man's brain is better off than a book bound in calf—at any rate it is safer from criticism.' Melville felt that by making public his thoughts he was making himself vulnerable to the reviewers' objections, and yet to write as those reviewers dictated resulted in unsatisfying 'jobs' like *Redburn* and *White-Jacket*. His growing disdain for public opinion probably accounts for his refusal in February to send Duyckinck a daguerreotype portrait he had requested of Melville:

> The fact is, almost everybody is having his 'mug' engraved nowadays; so that this test of distinction is getting to be reversed; and therefore, to see one's 'mug' in a magazine, is presumptive evidence that he's a nobody. So being as vain a man as ever lived; & beleiving that my illustrious name is famous throughout the world—I respectfully decline being oblivionated by a Daguerretype . . . .

Melville's acquired attitude toward the hazards and rewards of authorship can be seen in his letter early in June to Hawthorne (No. 75), sent while he was finishing his new book. To write as he wanted to would not pay, yet, despite his financial needs, he could not bring himself to write completely the '*other* way.' The books that resulted from a compromise between the need for self-expression and the need for money were all 'botches.' And regarding this new book, Melville told Hawthorne that he would bring it to a conclusion soon: 'What's the use of elaborating what, in its very essence, is so short-lived as a modern book? Though I wrote the Gospels in this century, I should die in the gutter.' He had written five books, but his 'horrible' reputation still seemed to be based solely on the first of them: 'Think of it! To go down to posterity is bad enough, any way; but to go down as a "man who lived among the cannibals"! . . . I have come to regard this matter of Fame as the most transparent of all vanities.'

In 1851 he was almost $700 in debt to the Harpers because the combination of advances on his earlier books and his purchases of other authors' works through the firm was not covered by his share of the profits from the sales of his own books. For this reason the Harpers refused his request for an advance on the work being composed. Bentley accepted the new book in July but could advance him only £150 against his share of the profits, citing the condition of the international copyright question as his reason for offering such a small sum. Melville found it necessary, therefore, to borrow money in order to support his wife and children. When the new book was finally published—as *The Whale* in England on 18 October and as *Moby-Dick* in America on 13 November—the reviews gave little hope that it would be the kind of critical and financial success Melville needed.

Once again Melville had violated the literary canons of the reviewers by creating a book that left them 'at a loss to determine in what category of works of amusement to place it.' The reviewer for the *Dublin University Magazine* (February 1852) complained, 'All the rules which have been hitherto understood to regulate the composition of works of fiction are despised and set at naught' by the book. It put, said the New York *Tribune* (No. 89), 'all regular criticism at defiance' by its 'lawless flights.' Almost every reviewer who examined *Moby-Dick* at any length noted the mixture not only of fact and fiction—a usual complaint against his earlier works—but of modes and of subjects as well. 'This sea novel is a singular medley of naval observation, magazine article writing, satiric reflection upon the conventionalisms of civilized life, and rhapsody run mad,' reported the *Spectator* (No. 79). Other reviewers characterized it as 'a salmagundi of fact, fiction and philosophy;' 'a romance, a tragedy, and a natural history, not without numerous gratuitous suggestions on psychology, ethics, and theology;' 'an intellectual chowder of romance, philosophy, natural history, fine writing, good feeling, bad sayings.'[8] The resulting judgments of the book and its author were sometimes quite harsh. Melville, said the *Athenaeum* (No. 77),

> must be henceforth numbered in the company of the incorrigibles who occasionally tantalize us with indications of genius, while they constantly summon us to endure monstrosities, carelessnesses, and other such harassing manifestations of bad taste as daring or disordered ingenuity can devise.

But most critics simply regretted the 'extravagant' or 'exaggerated' or 'rhapsodical' parts because they detracted from what otherwise was an interesting and often exciting book. Even reviewers who did not like *Moby-Dick* as a whole discovered manifestations of Melville's original genius and great—though, unfortunately, ill-controlled—powers of imagination and expression. Some even thought *Moby-Dick* more indicative of these powers than any of his books.

The British critics were further confused by the omission from *The Whale* of the Epilogue explaining how Ishmael alone survived to tell the tale. They objected to the lack of verisimilitude caused when all the characters in a story die leaving no one alive who could have witnessed the events; how, asked the *Literary Gazette* (No. 91), did 'the imaginary writer, who appears to have been drowned with the rest,' communicate his notes for publication to Mr. Bentley?

The characterizations in *Moby-Dick* also suffered the charge of extravagance. Ahab, especially, was labeled exaggerated, though many reviewers accepted his monomania as reason enough for his wild actions, and they admitted the need for an extraordinary human being to do battle with the white whale. The other characterizations represented 'truthful portraitures' and 'a unique picture gallery' to some critics—even 'Shakspearean' in delineation—but others considered them 'amongst the poorest things' Melville had done: 'phantom-like, un-human, and vaguely uninteresting.'[9]

Melville's style, usually praised by the reviewers no matter what their judgments on the books as wholes, also was believed cursed with the same fault of over-doing. The tale was 'disfigured by mad (rather than bad) English,' said the *Athenaeum*. American critics dismissed sections of the dialogue as 'ravings' by the characters or as unbelieveable representations of 'seaman's lingo.' What one American critic called a 'quaint though interesting style, . . . with an easy, rollicking freedom of language and structure' was considered too American by many on the other side of the Atlantic.[10] Somewhat more charitably, *John Bull* (No. 78) was ready to forgive all 'that is idiomatically American' in the slang—though it might grate 'upon civilized ears'—but it could not forgive the 'occasional thrusts against revealed religion.' This objection was made, too, in a number of American reviews, including the *Literary World* (No. 84) and the New York *Methodist Quarterly Review* (January 1852), which regretted Melville 'should allow himself to sink so low.'

Melville's dissatisfaction with the critics and with Evert Duyckinck in particular would be manifested in *Pierre*, the book he was writing as the reviews of *Moby-Dick* appeared in late 1851 and early 1852. But he was more than satisfied with Hawthorne's perceptive and flattering comments in a letter sent soon after the book appeared. What exactly Hawthorne said to Melville is not known, for the letter is lost, but on 1 December Hawthorne wrote Duyckinck, saying, 'What a book Melville has written! It gives me an idea of much greater power than his preceding ones. It hardly seemed to me that the review of it, in the *Literary World*, did justice to its best points.' Hawthorne must already have praised those 'points' in his letter to Melville, and on 17 November Melville answered his neighbor's 'joy-giving and exultation-breeding letter,' finding it an unexpected reward for his 'ditcher's work' in writing *Moby-Dick*:

not one man in five cycles, who is wise, will expect appreciative recognition from his fellows, or any one of them. Appreciation! Recognition! Is love appreciated? Why, ever since Adam, who has got to the meaning of this great allegory—the world? Then we pygmies must be content to have our paper allegories but ill comprehended. I say your appreciation is my glorious gratuity.

Then, looking ahead to yet another book to be written, Melville asked Hawthorne, 'when shall we be done growing? As long as we have anything more to do, we have done nothing. So, now, let us add *Moby Dick* to our blessing, and step from that. Leviathan is not the biggest fish;—I have heard of Krakens.' Apparently Melville was well under way on his new book by Christmas. Another neighbor of his, Sarah Morewood, at whose home the Melville family ate Christmas dinner in 1851, wrote a few days after the event to George Duyckinck:

I hear that he is now engaged in a new work as frequently not to leave his room till quite dark in the evening—when he for the first time during the whole day partakes of solid food—he must therefore write under a state of morbid excitement which will soon injure his health—I laughed at him somewhat and told him that the recluse life he was leading made his city friends think that he was slightly insane—he replied that long ago he came to the same conclusion himself—but if he left home to look after Hungary the cause in hunger would suffer . . . .

So Melville refrained from involvement with the problems of the 'Hungarys' of the world and stayed at home to earn his bread by completing the new book, which, he promised Sophia Hawthorne soon after the first of the year, would be 'a rural bowl of milk' rather than 'a bowl of salt water' like *Moby-Dick*. Evidently he was trying to write a book that would appeal to the feminine audience that made up the majority of the novel-reading public—at least the early sections of *Pierre* indicate such an intention. On 20 February he received a $500 advance from the Harpers against the royalties that were expected from the new book. An attempt to have it published in England stalled in disagreements with Bentley over terms. He told Melville early in March that he foresaw an eventual loss of more than £350 from the four books he had already published and therefore could offer Melville no advance payment for *Pierre*. Bentley would, however, agree to publish it if Melville would accept half-profits as they accrued after the expenses of publication had been paid and if the author would allow certain 'alterations' by Bentley's editors in order to make the book more acceptable in England than *Mardi* and *The Whale* had been. Melville would not accept these terms, and when *Pierre* did appear in

England, it was in the form of pages printed in the United States by the Harpers and shipped to England where they were bound and distributed by Sampson, Low, Son, and Company. The failure to have an English publisher limited severely the British notices of *Pierre*: only the review in the *Athenaeum* (No. 109) has been located. But in America Melville's latest work was received with a hostility beyond that of any other of his books.

Melville may have foresworn the hope for critical approval of *Pierre* while he was in the process of writing the book. His experiences with the reviewers certainly had disappointed him, as is evident in earlier comments in his personal letters and journals. But Melville chose to air the problems of authorship publicly in the latter sections of *Pierre*, especially books XVII (No. 97), XVIII, XXI, XXII, and XXV, where he presented his young hero's attempts to become a successful writer. With sardonic irony Melville drew a parodic picture of the course of his own artistic career over the last five or six years: the strain, both physical and mental, of writing; the difficulty in dealing with short-sighted publishers; the ill-treatment at the hands of ignorant or prejudiced critics. Though only one reviewer took note in print of these satiric sections of *Pierre*, the rest certainly saw them. Their displeasure at such abuse from an author may account for that virulence of the tone of personal attack on Melville evident in several of the reviews. As Hershel Parker has observed, the few attempts 'to comprehend *Pierre* were submerged in the foul wash of publishing gossip, old literary feuds, new personal attacks, and morally and aesthetically outraged diatribes.'[11]

The hostile critics stabbed at every aspect of *Pierre*, the 'craziest fiction extant,' according to the Boston *Post* (No. 98), filled with 'trash of conception, execution, dialogue and sentiment.' They found the incidents impossible in real life, the characters unnatural, and the style absurd—on the whole 'a dead failure.' The moral tone of *Pierre* upset the critics still further. Its 'most immoral *moral*' seemed to be 'the impracticability of virtue.' And for the author to hint at 'that fearfullest of all human crimes,' incest, was unforgivable to many reviewers.[12] The New York satirical weekly *Lantern* (16 October) even abandoned its indirect mode to counsel Melville 'either to resign his pen altogether or to choose different subjects. He must not dance on the tight rope between morality and indecency longer—dullness is better than meretriciousness.'

One explanation for this 'crazy' book might be, the Charleston,

North Carolina, *Southern Quarterly Review* (October) and others suggested, that its author had lost his mind:

> That Herman Melville has gone 'clean daft,' is very much to be feared; certainly, he has given us a very mad book . . . . The sooner this author is put in ward the better. If trusted with himself, at all events give him no further trust in pen and ink, till the present fit has worn off. He will grievously hurt himself else—or his very amiable publishers.

Even so, many reviewers remarked that Melville's 'unmistakable power' occasionally peeped through the nonsense and ambiguities of *Pierre*. 'There are passages in this book that absolutely glitter with genius,' said the *Morning Courier and New York Enquirer* (21 August). 'There are scenes and portraitures that nothing but the most extraordinary skill could execute.' The 'force and subtlety' of thought behind the book impressed others, and to the reviewer for the New York *Home Journal* (4 September) the story was 'psychologically suggestive. It is subtle, metaphysical, often profound, and has passages of bewildering intensity.' On the whole, however, *Pierre* was thought 'utterly unworthy of Mr. Melville's genius,' which would be much better and more profitably directed to writing sea stories like *Typee* and *Omoo*.[13]

VI

MAGAZINE WRITING: THE TALES (1853–6) AND *Israel Potter* (1855)

Evidently the response to *Pierre* discouraged Melville from writing anything more, for a while at least. During a trip to Nantucket with his father-in-law in July 1852, he heard an interesting tale of some natives of that island, but instead of working it up into 'a regular story' himself, he offered it in August to Hawthorne, who, in Melville's opinion, 'would make a better hand' at dealing with that particular material. Two months later Melville made some further suggestions to Hawthorne on how 'the story of Agatha'—as he referred to the tale—might be developed. But by the end of November he had decided, apparently at Hawthorne's urging, to write the story himself. If Melville did complete the story, he never published it though he may have tried to. Perhaps the 'Agatha' story was the 'work' that he told the Harpers he was 'prevented from printing' in the spring of 1853. And Melville's mother wrote to her brother on 20 April of that year that Melville's absorption in a 'new work, now nearly ready for the press,' had kept her son from taking 'proper, & necessary measures to procure' a post as consul in some foreign city. His mother and the rest of his family had decided, in her words, that a 'change of occupation' was necessary because the 'constant working of the brain, & excitement of the imagination' had worn him out and evidently was ruining his health. Influential family friends were enlisted to support Melville's candidacy for a consulship under the new administration of President Franklin Pierce, but to no avail.

So, as his health improved in the summer, Melville began to write pieces of short fiction for the magazines. At least he could expect some money on publication, and Melville certainly needed income at this time. Besides personal debts to his father-in-law and others, he still owed the Harpers nearly $300 in March 1853, and he foresaw no success for *Pierre* to help relieve this burden. The Harpers had been publishing a monthly magazine for several years, and in October 1852 the firm of G. P. Putnam & Company had solicited Melville's 'assistance as a contributor' to an 'Original periodical' they were starting. In the second issue (February 1853) *Putnam's Monthly Magazine* carried a long and not very sympathetic article on Melville by Fitz-James O'Brien (No. 110). In its eleventh issue (November 1853) it carried Melville's first contribution, part one of 'Bartleby.' From that time through the first half of 1856 *Putnam's* published seven of Melville's tales and his serialized *Israel Potter* while *Harper's New Monthly Magazine* printed six other tales and one sketch, paying Melville at the average rate of about five dollars a page.

After the scathing reaction to *Pierre*, Melville took particular care not to offend the moral, philosophical, or aesthetic sensibilities and preconceptions of the reviewers. When he offered the story of Israel Potter to George Palmer Putnam in June 1854, Melville wrote, 'I engage that the story shall contain nothing of any sort to shock the fastidious. There will be very little reflective writing in it; nothing weighty. It is adventure.' He had made the same sort of disclaimer to Bentley when offering the English publisher *Redburn* in the wake of the disastrous critical reception of *Mardi*. But Melville apparently needed to express certain ideas even if he had to disguise them so that they would not be noticed by the public. The tales he wrote during the 1850s may be, as Jay Leyda has said, 'an artist's resolution of that constant contradiction—between the desperate need to communicate and the fear of revealing too much.'[14] One of those tales, 'The Two

Temples, must have been too obvious a statement on religious subjects because *Putnam's* editor, Charles F. Briggs, rejected it in 1854 to avoid 'offending the religious sensibilities of the public.'

The critical response to the tales was minimized by the reviewers' normal practice of surveying only briefly the contents of the monthly magazines with the very shortest of comments on the individual pieces. Also, the kind of personal attack that marked the reviews of *Pierre* was forestalled to some degree by anonymous publication of works of original fiction, though Melville's name was often attached to his tales by reviewers who had sources of information at his two magazines. The critics evidently did not notice or were not disturbed by whatever uncommon or controversial thoughts Melville expressed beneath the 'thoroughly magazinish'[15] surfaces of his tales. The *Literary World*'s (3 December 1853) one-sentence comment on 'Bartleby' said that it was 'a Poeish tale, with an infusion of more natural sentiment.' Almost as brief was the comment in the New York *Citizen* (30 December 1854) on the seventh part of *Israel Potter*: 'This is a stirring narrative, and admirably written; so that if you begin you must finish it.'

Israel Potter was republished in book form by G. P. Putnam & Company in March 1855 just before that firm was purchased by J. H. Dix, head of Dix & Edwards. The reviews of *Israel Potter*, though few, were generally favorable: it was considered an improvement, in style and subject matter, over *Pierre*, though it did not reach the high level of *Typee* and *Omoo*. The *Morning Courier and New York Enquirer* (17 March 1855) reaffirmed its judgment of the serialized version that the story's 'manly' and 'direct' style was in pleasant contrast to Melville's last book. The reviewers' disagreements regarding the important characterizations of Benjamin Franklin and John Paul Jones ranged from complaints about the lack of reality in Melville's portraits to encomia for the genuine dramatic feeling in their conception and development. The critics disputed, too, the proportions of historical fact and imaginative fiction contained in a book that claimed in its dedication to preserve, 'almost as in a reprint, Israel Potter's autobiographical story.' Perhaps it was Melville himself who responded to this question—the same one many reviewers had plagued him with in regard to earlier works—in the Editorial Notes section of *Putnam's* (May 1855): a comparison of *Israel Potter* with the old book the author cites as his source shows that 'Mr. Melville departs considerably from his orginal. . . . How far he is justified in the historical liberties he has taken, would be a curious case of literary casuistry.' The kind of ironic perspective possibly present in this commentary seemed vividly apparent, to one reviewer at least, in the book itself. In a brief review the New York *National Magazine* (May 1855) noted a 'tinge of obscure sarcasm,' especially in the dedication, which Melville must have composed 'in a half-comic, half-patriotic vein.' The patriotic side attracted Ém. Montégut's attention in a long article in the Paris *Revue des deux mondes* (1 July 1855). Israel Potter represents the democratic American hero, the man of the crowd whose disinterested self-sacrifice brought success to the United States.

Even while he was writing short or serialized fiction for *Putnam's* and *Harper's,* Melville was also working on longer, book-length pieces. He had received in December 1853 a $300 advance from the Harpers for a book 'of Tortoise Hunting Adventure' that was supposed to be 'ready for the press' the following January but was never delivered to them. Melville may have used up some of the material planned for the proposed book when he wrote 'The Encantadas,' a series of sketches carried in *Putnam's* in 1854. Probably in May 1855 he began another long piece. The new book centered on the escapades of a confidence man, an idea perhaps inspired by newspaper articles announcing that the 'Original Confidence Man,' famous for his unique swindles in New York City in 1849, had reappeared in Albany, New York. The book may have been far enough along in a few weeks time to allow Melville to propose it to J. H. Dix as a novel in early summer. But work on it was slowed during the following months by Melville's ill-health (rheumatism, sciatica, and failing eyesight), by his composition of shorter pieces for the magazines, and by his preparation for Dix & Edwards of a one-volume collection of the stories that had appeared in *Putnam's* from November 1854 to December 1855. Concerning the latter project, Dix's editorial advisor, the novelist George William Curtis, told the publisher on 2 January 1856, 'I don't think Melville's book will sell a great deal, but he is a good name upon your list. He has lost his prestige,—& I don't believe the *Putman* stories will bring it up.'

Melville's 'name' was sufficiently well known to have his works surveyed in two long articles printed at this point in his career. The *Cyclopaedia of American Literature* (No. 118), edited by Evert and George Duyckinck and published in New York in late 1855, discussed Melville's life as well as his works, and a piece in the *Dublin University Magazine* (No. 119) in January made Melville, with Cooper and Dana, one of 'A Trio of American Sailor-Authors' who had 'written either nautical novels or narratives of the highest degree of excellence.'

Only some short reviews greeted the publication of the collected stories, called *The Piazza Tales*, perhaps because merely one of them, 'The Piazza,' was new to the reading public. The New York *American Publishers' Circular* (31 May 1856) gave the tales credit for helping to raise *Putnam's* 'to its present proud position—the best of the American *Monthlies*.' In general the reviewers treated the book in a cursory manner, usually noting the wide range of subjects and styles and picking one or two tales for special mention. 'The Encantadas' gained the most attention, probably because its South Seas setting reminded the reviewers of Melville's first two books, which were listed on the title page of this, his latest one. But the scant critical examination of *The Piazza Tales* can better be understood as a result of the general attitude, expressed by the reviewer for the New York *Times* (No. 125) that the 'author of *Typee* should do something higher and better than Magazine articles.'

VII

VALEDICTION: *The Confidence-Man* (1857)

As the reviews of *The Piazza Tales* were appearing in the summer of 1856, Melville completed 'something higher and better': *The Confidence-Man*. The writing of this book, the last long work of prose fiction Melville ever published, evidently wore him out. His father-in-law, Judge Shaw, told his son Samuel on 1 September 1856 that Melville 'overworks himself & brings on severe nervous affections. He has been advised strongly to break off this labor for some time, & take a voyage or a journey, & endeavor to recruit.' Suffering as he was from pains in his back, hip, and head, Melville apparently saw the wisdom of such a vacation, and leaving the final negotiations for publication of *The Confidence-Man* in the hands of his brother Allan, he sailed for Glasgow on 11 October. In Liverpool he visited Hawthorne, appointed consul there by President Pierce, and the description of their meeting in Hawthorne's Notebooks gives the best picture available of Melville's state of mind just after completing his tenth book in as many years of active though increasingly disappointing authorship:[16]

A week ago last Monday, Herman Melville came to see me at the Consulate, looking much as he used to do (a little paler, and perhaps a little sadder), in a rough outside coat, and with his characteristic gravity and reserve of manner. . . . we soon found ourselves on pretty much our former terms of sociability and confidence. Melville has not been well, of late; . . . and no doubt has suffered from too constant literary occupation, pursued without much success, latterly; and his writings, for a long while past, have indicated a morbid state of mind. . . . Melville, as he always does, began to reason of Providence and futurity, and of everything that lies beyond human ken, and informed me that he had 'pretty much made up his mind to be annihilated'; but still he does not seem to rest in that anticipation; and, I think, will never rest until he gets hold of a definite belief. It is strange how he persists—and has persisted ever since I knew him, and probably long before—in wandering to-and-fro over these deserts, as dismal and monotonous as the sand hills amid which we were sitting. He can neither believe, nor be comfortable in his unbelief; and he is too honest and courageous not to try to do one or the other. If he were a religious man, he would be one of the most truly religious and reverential; he has a very high and noble nature, and better worth immortality than most of us.

Melville left Liverpool on 18 November to continue his voyage to the Near East and the Continent. Comments in his journal suggest he may have had plans for a sequel to the manuscript he left behind, a manuscript that ended with the sentence, 'Something further may follow of this Masquerade.' But the reception of *The Confidence-Man* when it appeared the following spring probably discouraged any such project. While Melville travelled, his new book was published in New York by Dix, Edwards & Company on 1 April and a week later in London by Longman, Brown, Green, Longmans, and Roberts under an agreement signed on Melville's behalf by Hawthorne. A few days prior to publication, the April issue of *Putnam's* appeared containing the longest contemporary American critical commentary on the book, part of an article surveying Melville's works (No. 130). There are just over a dozen known American reviews, all but three of them quite brief. The British reviews, though somewhat fewer, were much longer and in general much more thoughtful. Melville's reputation was experiencing a mild revival, especially in England, but no book he could now write would ever restore his name to the position it occupied in the wake of *Typee* and *Omoo*. Because he was in Italy when the book was published, Melville could not have seen the critical commentary immediately. He arrived in London two weeks after the first British reviews appeared and returned to the United States on 20 May, in both cases after most of the reviews had already been circulated. However, his own and his wife's families saw some articles when they first came out: his sister, Augusta, wrote in a letter on 15 April, 'To-day's mail brought us several highly complimentary notices of Herman's new book.' But a letter from Lemuel Shaw, Jr, to his brother Samuel is probably a better indicator of his family's thoughts on the book, and it agrees in general with the known American critical response:

A new book by Herman called *The Confidence Man* has recently been published. I have not yet read it; but have looked at it & dipped into it, & fear it belongs that horribly uninteresting class of nonsensical books he is given to writing—where there are pages of crude theory & speculation to every line of narrative—& interspersed with strained & ineffectual attempts to be humorous. I wish he could or would do better, when he went away he was dispirited & ill—& this book was left completed in the publisher's hands.

The reviewers found too much metaphysical and theoretical writing for their tastes and not enough of what the Albany, New York, *Evening Journal* (2 April 1857) called the 'vivid, graphic delineation based on real life' that characterized *Typee* and *Omoo*. The satirical elements were thought overgeneralized and therefore not as effective as they might have been had the targets been more narrowly defined. Even the British reviewers who enjoyed so much the satire on American 'smartnesses' thought the picture of life in the United States somewhat exaggerated.

The combination of different modes in *The Confidence-Man* once again, as with some of Melville's earlier works, made it difficult for the critics to categorize the book. The 'novel, comedy, collection of dialogues, repertory of anecdotes, or whatever it is,' said the London *Illustrated Times* (No. 139), can at least be called 'a fiction,' though 'its *génre* is the *génre ennuyeux*.' The nature of the title character and the purpose of his masquerade were equally hard for the critics to discover. The London *Critic* (15 April) wondered if the philosophic 'apostle of geniality' were not 'an arch-impostor of the deepest dye,' but the American reviewers seemed more willing to accept him as simply a confidence man, and one critic, in the Burlington, Vermont, *Free Press* (25 April), even identified the real-life original for Melville's character:

The story of the chap who managed to diddle many out of their property lamenting their want of confidence in him till they were willing to prove its reality by trusting him with a watch, a gold pencil case or a five dollar bill, never to be seen again by their owners, has furnished the hint on which the volume is made up.

Despite all the complaints about other aspects of the book, most reviewers praised the style, which, though 'difficult to manage,' said the *Athenaeum* (No. 133), was now under Melville's 'mastery.'

The mixed reception of *The Confidence-Man* did not help its sales in England or the United States, but even more disturbing as far as the future of Melville's literary career was concerned was the scarcity of reviews by major American periodicals. The commercial failure of Dix, Edwards & Company less than a month after *The Confidence-Man* was published certainly contributed to the book's poor sales, but even in England, where a large number of pre-publication advertisements announced Melville's new work, Longman's managed to sell only 343 copies in the first three months and just thirty-four more in the year that followed, leaving the author's account still £24 8*s*. short of expenses.

VIII

TOWARD OBLIVION: THE POETRY

Discouraged by his lack of success with the critics and the public, Melville, on his return to the United States in May 1857, decided to give up trying to make a living as an author. Lemuel Shaw, Jr, told his brother Samuel in a letter on 2 June, 'Herman says he is not going to write any more at present & wishes to get a place in the N.Y. Custom House.' Melville did not get that 'place' until after the American Civil War. In the meantime, in order to support his wife and four children, Melville chose to become a lecturer, a profitable occupation for many literary men in mid-nineteenth-century America, though often denigrated by them as a prostitution of their talents and their art.

For the next three lecture seasons, 1857–60, Melville travelled the circuit through the eastern and northern United States with 'Statuary in Rome,' 'The South Seas,' and 'Travel' as his successive annual topics. A review of his lecture in Cincinnati, Ohio, in the *Enquirer* (2 February 1858) contains the gratuitous evaluation of his writings: 'Mr. M.'s authorship is toward the nadir rather than the zenith, and he has been progressing in the form of an inverted climax.' After the second lecture season ended, Melville was visited in April 1859 by two Williams College students who described 'the renowned author of *Typee*, &c.' as 'evidently a disappointed man, soured by criticism and disgusted with the civilized world' and as having the air of one 'who has suffered from opposition, both literary and social.' The third season was a failure, probably because Melville simply was not an exciting or accomplished speaker and the novelty of hearing in person the author of *Typee* and *Omoo*—for it was in this capacity that he was best remembered—wore off after the first season or two. His chronic ill-health might also have contributed to his decision to give up lecturing.[17]

Later in 1860 he did try to have a volume of verse published, showing a willingness to have his writings before the public once more, though with little in the way of expectation of income. In a letter to his brother Allan regarding the poems, Melville wrote, 'Don't stand on terms much with the publisher—half-profits after expenses are paid will content me—not that I expect much "profits"—but that will be a fair nominal arrangement.' The effort failed because the publisher approached, Charles Scribner, could not afford another volume of poetry that year; he had already issued two and did not expect to meet expenses with either one.

In 1861 family and friends were once again busy trying to prevent Melville from writing by securing for him the consular post at Florence, Italy, from the newly-elected president, Abraham Lincoln. They were convinced, as his father-in-law said, 'of the necessity of Herman's getting away' from Pittsfield where his 'solitary' life, 'without exercise or occupation' except the strains of authorship, was adversely affecting his mind and body.

The effort to get the post was unsuccessful, and Melville had no job during the next few years. This left him with time to write a number of new poems inspired by the events of the Civil War. They were collected and then published by the Harpers in August 1866 as *Battle-Pieces and Aspects of the War*. Melville had made one visit to the front, in April 1864, but most of the poems had their sources in news reports reaching New York City—where he had moved his family in 1863—and originated, as he said in a prefatory note to the volume, 'in an impulse imparted by the fall of Richmond' on 3 April 1865. The critics in general took little note of the volume even though about 300 copies of the 1,260 printed had been sent out to the periodicals. The few who reviewed it at any length were not very impressed by Melville 'in his new character as a poet.' In particular they objected to the irregularities of the verse. His pages contained 'at best little more than the rough ore of poetry,' in spite of the 'gleams of imaginative power' and occasional good lines.[18] The critic for the New York *World* (No. 147) expressed the feeling of several of the reviewers when he cited *Battle-*

Pieces as an example of the fact that 'the poetic nature and the technical faculty of poetry writing are not identical.' Melville's prose may very well have been 'poetic,' but his poetry failed as formal verse.

Late in 1866 Melville finally got a position as inspector at the New York Custom House where he served for the next twenty years. It paid only four dollars a day (and in 1875 it was reduced to $3.60), but that was something at least, and it did take Melville out of his house, away from writing, and put him in contact with other people—much to the satisfaction of his family. During the next decade Melville was nearly forgotten by the critics. When *Putnam's Magazine* was revived in January 1868 after ten years of silence, Charles F. Briggs asked in an article that Melville must have found quite ironic, 'where . . . is Herman Melville? Has that copious and imaginative author . . . let fall his pen just where its use might have been so remunerative to himself, and so satisfactory to the public?' Melville never contributed to the new magazine, though he did express his intention to do so. Perhaps his thoughts on literary fame at this period in his life are best seen in his marginal comment on a passage he marked in Matthew Arnold's *Essays in Criticism*, which he had acquired in July 1869. Arnold quoted Maurice de Guérin, 'The literary career seems to me unreal, both in its essence and in the rewards which one seeks from it, and therefore fatally marred by a secret absurdity,' to which Melville responded, 'This is the finest verbal statement of a truth which every one who thinks in these days must have felt.'

During the 1870s and 1880s excerpts from Melville's works were occasionally included in anthologies, and short sketches of his career appeared in books on American literature, but in neither case was he given a position of any eminence. He continued to produce poetry, however, writing many short pieces and the long narrative poem *Clarel*, based on his travels in the Holy Land in the winter of 1856–7. Its publication in June 1876 by G. P. Putnam & Company was paid for by Melville's uncle, Peter Gansevoort, who, shortly before he died in January 1876, sent his nephew a check for $1,200 to cover the costs. Facing the first page of the text, Melville had printed the following statement:

> If during the period in which this work has remained unpublished, though not undivulged, any of its properties have by a natural process exhaled; it yet retains, I trust, enough of original life to redeem it at least from vapidity. Be that as it may, I here dismiss the book—content beforehand with whatever future awaits it.

Melville's expressed attitude was fortunate because *Clarel*'s future did not prove very bright as far as its reception and its sales were concerned. The few reviewers who did notice the book generally found it a plotless and puzzling affair but with many powerful passages of description. Some good lines were noted, but on the whole its verse was considered highly imperfect. Perhaps, the reviewers felt, it should have been written as prose because Melville certainly disregarded 'the first principles of poetic art.'[19] Only the London *Academy* (No. 154) had the perceptiveness to see this disregard as intentional, and in its review it compared Melville with Arthur Hugh Clough. Melville apparently had expected something like this general disapproval, for he referred to *Clarel* eight years later in a letter to the English classicist James Billson as 'a metrical affair, a pilgrimage or what not, of several thousand lines, eminently adapted for unpopularity.'

It seems that British literary men gave Melville more attention during the last decade of his life than did their American counterparts even though his books after *The Confidence-Man* had not been published in England. Melville developed several friendships by correspondence with British writers, among them W. Clark Russell, a sea novelist who wrote several articles praising Melville's books (see Nos 155 and 163), and Henry S. Salt, a critic, biographer, and classicist, who also wrote on Melville for the periodicals (see Nos 157 and 164). Melville dedicated his next book of poetry, *John Marr and Other Sailors* (1888), to Russell. This volume and Melville's next and last book of poems, *Timoleon* (1891), were privately printed in editions of twenty-five copies each, allowing for little in the way of critical reception, and only one review is known, that of *John Marr* in the New York *Mail and Express* (No. 156). When the English poet Robert Buchanan came to America in the mid-1880s and inquired about the American author whose books he so admired, he had trouble finding out from his New York literary acquaintances if Melville were even alive, let alone what had become of him. In his poem 'Socrates in Camden,' which was in praise of Walt Whitman, Buchanan included some lines on Melville and then, apparently fearing that Melville might not be remembered, added a footnote in which he declared him 'the one great imaginative writer fit to stand shoulder to shoulder with Whitman on that continent.'

Melville resigned his post as Inspector of Customs at the end of 1885, thus removing himself even further from public view. In one of the few mentions of him to appear in the press in these last years, the New

York *Commercial Advertiser* (14 January 1886) reported that Melville, who, 'after all his wanderings, loves to stay at home,' exemplified 'the transiency of literary reputation. . . . To-day, his name would not be recognized by the rising generation.' Many people, said Edward Bok in November 1890 (No. 158), believed Melville to be dead.

During the last three years of his life, Melville may not have been highly visible in person or in print, but he was busy writing poems, some collected in *Timoleon* and others unpublished in his lifetime. He also worked from 16 November 1888 to 19 April 1891 on the manuscript of a book he would never offer to the public: *Billy Budd*.

The obituary notices and editorials that appeared immediately after Melville died on 28 September 1891 often exhibited the general state of ignorance regarding the man and his works, but somewhat later and more reflective articles showed sensitivity and appreciation as well as greater knowledge of the facts. Melville simply had outlived his reputation. Had he died forty years earlier, his passing would have attracted a great deal of attention on both sides of the Atlantic. But in 1857 he had quit his role as prose writer and had resigned from active literary life except to publish his poems. A phrase he wrote in *The Confidence-Man* to describe the withdrawal of the mute from the attention of his fellow passengers might be applied to Melville's own exit from the scene after publishing that valedictory book: 'by stealing into retirement, . . . he seemed to have courted oblivion, a boon not often withheld from so humble an applicant as he.'

Ironically the news of his death awoke a small revival of interest in his books. During his lifetime something over 50,000 copies had been sold by his authorized publishers in America and England, bringing him the really insignificant income of a little more than $10,000 in forty-five years. None of the books made any money for him after *Pierre*, which itself brought only $157.75 in royalties to its author. *Typee* was the biggest success with more than 16,000 copies sold while Melville was alive, and *Moby-Dick* was sixth in rank, trailing *Omoo*, *White-Jacket*, *Redburn*, and *Mardi* as well as *Typee*. In 1892 the United States Book Company brought out editions of *Typee*, *Omoo*, *White-Jacket*, and *Moby-Dick*, edited by Arthur Stedman. This company and its successor, the American Publishing Corporation, managed to sell almost 8,000 copies of the four books—again *Typee* sold best—before the latter firm went bankrupt in 1898. Some of the books—270 copies of each—were sold to G. P. Putnam & Company for distribution in England. There in 1893 Melville's first English publisher, Henry

Murray, brought out new, illustrated impressions of his editions of *Typee* and *Omoo*, but it took many years to exhaust the 1,012 copies of each.[20] John St Loe Strachey reviewed the four books of the Stedman edition in the London *Spectator* (24 June 1893), praising them generally as sea tales but also offering some criticism that sounded a note much heard in the reviews of forty years earlier:

> Mr. Melville is no mean master of prose, and had his judgment been equal to his feeling for form, he might have ranked high in English literature on the ground of style alone. Unfortunately, he was apt to let the last great master of style he had been reading run away with him.

This review was the last serious critical appraisal of Melville to be published for almost a quarter of a century except for Archibald MacMechan's essay on *Moby-Dick*, 'The Best Sea Story Ever Told,' in the *Queen's Quarterly* (October 1899). In the histories of American literature and in the textbooks, Melville was treated as a very minor writer of sea and adventure stories.

IX

REVIVAL

This was all changed by one man: in 1917 Carl Van Doren published a four-page essay in the *Cambridge History of American Literature*, of which he was an editor, showing for the first time in the twentieth century adequate appreciation for and understanding of Melville's writings. Van Doren, noting the upcoming centennial of Melville's birth, also moved Raymond Weaver to the investigations that led not only to an article for the New York *Nation* in the centenary year of 1919 but also to the first full-length biography, *Herman Melville, Mariner and Mystic* (New York: George H. Doran Company, 1921). Frank Jewett Mather, Jr, long an admirer of Melville, also wrote a sympathetic and perceptive centennial essay which appeared in the New York *Review* (9 August 1919). In England those who proclaimed their esteem for Melville in print were fewer in number but perhaps even more appreciative, H. L. Tomlinson of the London *Nation and Athenaeum* foremost among them.

Thus began the 'Melville Revival' of the 1920s and early 1930s, and the Melville that the American critics revived was a rebel out of step with the values of his age, a philosopher who later turned cynic, the author of one truly great book, *Moby-Dick*, which expressed his innermost thoughts and feelings. In England, where the need to relate a national author to the social conditions of the critics' own age was not as great as in America, Melville received more temperate treatment. Because the three decades of disregard for Melville had resulted in the loss of much valuable biographical material, the critics mined his works for autobiographical 'facts' and revelations of his personal character; then they used these 'facts' and discoveries in their appraisals of the author and his books.

One great benefit of the 'Revival' was the extrication of the manuscript of *Billy Budd* from among the surviving Melville papers which had been carefully preserved of late by his granddaughter, Eleanor Melville Metcalf. Weaver edited the novel and published it for the first time in 1924 in volume XIII of the Standard Edition of Melville's *Complete Works* (London: Constable & Company) and again in 1928 in a slightly different version in the *Shorter Novels of Herman Melville* (New York: Horace Liveright).[21] Thus the critical reception of *Billy Budd* began three decades after the story was left as a semi-final draft by its author at the time of his death. Weaver himself in his 1921 biography commented on the story even before it had been published:

> The novel, *Billy Budd*, is built around the character of Jack Chase, the 'Handsome Sailor.' In the character of Billy Budd, Melville attempts to portray the native purity and nobility of the uncorrupted man. Melville spends elaborate pains in analysing 'the mystery of iniquity,' and in celebrating by contrast the god-like beauty of body and spirit of his hero. Billy Budd, by his heroic guilelessness is, like an angel of vengeance, precipitated into manslaughter; and for his very righteousness he is hanged. *Billy Budd*, finished within a few months before the end of Melville's life, would seem to teach that though the wages of sin is death, that sinners and saints alike toil for a common hire. In *Billy Budd* the orphic sententiousness is gone, it is true. But gone also is the brisk lucidity, the sparkle, the verve. Only the disillusion abided with him to the last.

When the Constable edition came out, John Middleton Murry, writing in *The Times Literary Supplement* (10 July 1924), commented on the last years of Melville's life:

> With the mere fact of the long silence in our minds we could not help regarding *Billy Budd* as the last will and spiritual testament of a man of genius. We could not help expecting this, if we have any imaginative understanding. Of course, if we are content to dismiss in our minds, if not in our words, the man of

genius as mad, there is no need to trouble. Some one is sure to have told us that *Billy Budd*, like *Pierre*, is a tissue of naivety and extravagance: that will be enough. And, truly, *Billy Budd is* like *Pierre*—startlingly like. Once more Melville is telling the story of the inevitable and utter disaster of the good and trying to convey to us that this must be so and ought to be so—chronometrically and horologically. He is trying, as it were with his final breath, to reveal the knowledge that has been haunting him—that these things must be so and not otherwise.

Murry read the tale as a conflict of good and evil—'the clash of absolutes'—and said *Billy Budd* was 'Melville's final word, worthy of him, indisputably a passing beyond the nihilism of *Moby Dick* to what may seem to some simple and childish, but will be to others wonderful and divine.'

Another British critic, John Freeman, in the first English biography, titled *Herman Melville* (London: Macmillan, 1926), compared *Billy Budd* with *Paradise Regained* after comparing *Moby-Dick* to *Paradise Lost*:

Like *Moby-Dick* this late and pure survival of Melville's genius has a double interest, the interest of story and the interest of psychology. *Billy Budd* is the narrative of one who, like Pierre, is unpractised in the ways of life and the hearts of other men; guilelessness is a kind of genius and the better part of innocence in this handsome young sailor. His offence is his innocence, and it is Claggart, a subtle, dark, demon-haunted petty-officer, that his innocence offends. Claggart's was the mania of an evil nature—the 'natural depravity' of Plato's definition.

Freeman summarized the action, quoting at length, and then focused on the 'final scene, to which with unlabouring imagination Melville imparts a strange serenity and solemn ease. . . . Exaltation of spirit redeems such a scene from burdens which otherwise might appear too painful to be borne.' The death scene was for Freeman the 'public vindication of the law, and the superior assertion at the very moment of death of the nobility of a pure human spirit.' He closed his discussion by saying:

Finished but a few months before the author's death and only lately published, *Billy Budd* shows the imaginative faculty still secure and powerful, after nearly forty years' supineness, and the not less striking security of Melville's inward peace. After what storms and secret spiritual turbulence we do not know, except by hints which it is easy to exaggerate, in his last days he re-enters an Eden-like sweetness and serenity, 'with calm of mind, all passion spent,' and sets his brief, appealing tragedy for witness that evil is defeat and natural goodness invincible in the affections of man. In this, the simplest of stories, told with but little of the old digressive vexatiousness, and based upon recorded incidents, Herman Melville uttered his everlasting yea, and died before a soul had been allowed to hear him.

At the end of the first decade of the 'Melville Revival,' Lewis Mumford in his biography *Herman Melville* (New York: Harcourt, Brace & Company, 1929) found 'graceful but diminished energies' in Melville's late prose. *Billy Budd* 'is not a full-bodied story': it has 'just statement, wise commentary, apt illustration' but it lacks 'an independent and living creation' that would include the 'body and colour' of epithet of *Moby-Dick* and the 'fecundity and energy' of *White-Jacket.* There is a structural concentration that strips the story for action and leaves the characters with 'a Platonic clarity of form.' Mumford concluded his psychological study with this reading of the novel:

> *Billy Budd* is the story of three men in the British Navy: it is also the story of the world, the spirit, and the devil. . . . Good and evil exist in the nature of things, each forever itself, each doomed to war with the other. In the working out of human institutions, evil has a place as well as the good: Vere is contemptuous of Claggart, but cannot do without him: he loves Budd as a son and must condemn him to the noose: justice dictates an act abhorrent to his nature, and only his inner magnanimity keeps it from being revolting. These are the fundamental ambiguities of life: so long as evil exists, the agents that intercept it will also be evil, whilst we accept the world's conditions: those universal articles of war on which our civilizations rest. Rascality may be punished; but beauty and innocence will suffer in that process far more. There is no comfort, in this perpetual Calvary, to find a thief nailed on either side of the Cross. Melville had been harried by these paradoxes in *Pierre.* At last he was reconciled. He accepted the situation as a tragic necessity; and to meet that tragedy bravely was to find peace, the ultimate peace of resignation, even in an incongruous world. As Melville's own end approached, he cried out with Billy Budd: God bless Captain Vere! In this final affirmation Herman Melville died.

In the 1930s there was something of a backlash against the sudden growth of Melville's reputation. Representative of this was Ludwig Lewisohn's statement in *Expression in America* (1932) that the 'recent reëstimate' by enthusiastic readers of Melville had 'overshot the mark.' It was not until 1938 that Melville was generally considered an important and serious enough writer to merit study by university scholars. Willard Thorp was responsible for making Melville academically 'respectable,' and it was he who first approached Melville at length in a scholarly way. In his introduction to *Herman Melville: Representative Selections* (1938) Thorp separated fact from fiction in regard to Melville's life and put the man and his works into their political and social contexts. From that time to the present day, almost every imaginable aspect of Melville's writings—from his sources to his metaphysics, from his diction to his aesthetics—has received published attention from members of the academic community. The range of approaches and of topics considered has been as varied as the quality of execution. Though a large number of intelligent, perceptive, and sympathetic studies have appeared since 1938, many a critic has tried to cut and stretch Melville's works to fit the Procrustean bed of his own preconceptions. A plethora of articles and books on Melville has developed in recent years, reflecting the breadth and greatness of the vision of reality that can inspire such general interest. It reflects, too, the problematical nature of the expression of that vision, for Melville's art has allowed widely divergent interpretations of his works. The critical heritage of Herman Melville grows and changes with each generation of readers; his works abide.

NOTES

1 Unidentified quotations in this paragraph are from, respectively, the London *Spectator* (No. 1), the New Bedford, Massachusetts *Daily Mercury* (No. 5), the London *John Bull* (No. 4), and the New York *American Review* (April 1846).

2 Historical Note for *Typee*, vol. I of the Northwestern-Newberry Edition of *The Writings of Herman Melville*, eds Harrison Hayford, Hershel Parker, and G. Thomas Tanselle (Evanston and Chicago: Northwestern University Press, 1968), p. 291.

3 New York *Columbian Magazine* (June 1847).

4 Unidentified quotations in this paragraph are from, respectively, the New York *Tribune* (No. 30), the London *Spectator* (No. 18), the New York *Knickerbocker* (No. 29), the Brooklyn, New York *Daily Eagle* (No. 21), the New York *Evening Mirror* (No. 25), *Blackwood's Edinburgh Magazine* (No. 28), and Philadelphia *Godey's Magazine and Lady's Book* (July 1847).

5 This letter is dated '10? or 31? July 1847' in the *Letters* and 'Early July' in the *Log*, but the internal evidence seems to point to 23 October 1847 as a more likely 'Saturday Morning' for Melville to have written it to Duyckinck.

6 Historical Note for *Mardi*, vol. III of the Northwestern-Newberry Edition, p. 657.

7 This was Melville's anonymous and rather unsympathetic review of Francis Parkman's *The California and Oregon Trail* that Duyckinck printed in the *Literary World* (31 March 1849).

8 Unidentified quotations in this paragraph are from, respectively, the London *Britannia* (No. 81), the New York *Commercial Advertiser* (28 November 1851), the New York *Harper's New Monthly Magazine* (No. 90), and the New York *Literary World* (No. 84).

9 Unidentified quotations in this paragraph are from, respectively, the London *Spectator* (No. 79), the New York *Harper's New Monthly Magazine* (No. 90), the Washington, D.C., *National Intelligencer* (No. 93), the London *Atlas* (1 November 1851), and the London *Morning Chronicle* (No. 94).

10 Unidentified quotations in this paragraph are from, respectively, the Charleston, South Carolina *Southern Quarterly Review* (No. 95), the New York *Albion* (No. 88), and the Springfield, Massachusetts *Republican* (No. 85).

11 Historical Note for *Pierre*, vol. VII of the Northwestern-Newberry Edition, p. 383.

12 Unidentified quotations in this paragraph are from respectively, the New York *Albion* (No. 101), the New York *Literary World* (No. 102), and again the *Albion*.

13 Unidentified quotations in this paragraph are from, respectively, the Boston *Post* (No. 98), the Philadelphia *Graham's Magazine* (No. 107), and the Washington, D.C., *National Era* (No. 100).

14 Introduction to *The Complete Stories of Herman Melville*, ed. Jay Leyda (New York: Random House, 1949), p. xviii.

15 This phrase is used by George William Curtis in his letter of 7 September 1855 to J. H. Dix, publisher of *Putnam's*, to characterize a tale Melville submitted to the magazine. He also called the piece 'a capital, genial, humorous sketch.' Twentieth-century critics, however, have found beneath the surface of this tale, 'I and My Chimney,' an allegorical description of a supposed examination of Melville to see if he were insane.

16 *The English Notebooks of Nathaniel Hawthorne*, ed. Randall Stewart (New York: Modern Language Association of America, 1941), pp. 432–3.

17. See Merton M. Sealts, Jr, *Melville as Lecturer* (Cambridge: Harvard University Press, 1957) for a complete examination of Melville's career as a lecturer.

18 Unidentified quotations in this paragraph are from, respectively, the New York *Herald* (No. 144) and the New York *Nation* (No. 145).

19 New York *Tribune* (No. 150).

20 See G. Thomas Tanselle, 'The Sales of Melville's Books,' *Harvard Library Bulletin*, xviii (April 1969), 195–215 for an informative study of Melville's publishers' records.

21 The situation surrounding the first edition of *Billy Budd* is similar to that of

The Whale, in which the British reviewers had problems dealing with the story because the Epilogue was omitted from the English edition. The first edition of *Billy Budd* available to the critics likewise did not represent Melville's final intention regarding the story, as nearly as that intention can be determined from the state in which the manuscript was left at his death. Among the most egregious errors was the printing of a putative Preface, using what was in fact a discarded fragment of the manuscript. Critics have often read this 'Preface' as Melville's purposeful setting of tone and as a base of reference to which he expected his readers to return in reading the rest of the story. The results of such assumptions can be, of course, disastrous for any interpretation of *Billy Budd.* A second text, edited by H. Barron Freeman, was published in 1948 by the Harvard University Press. While Freeman corrected some of Weaver's errors, he followed him in others—such as printing the 'Preface'—and introduced still other mistakes concerning the manuscript. This unsatisfactory situation has been corrected by Harrison Hayford and Merton M. Sealts, Jr, whose completely new and comprehensive scholarly edition of *Billy Budd, Sailor* (University of Chicago Press, 1962) presents a reliable text that finally opens the way for definitive criticism of the book.

Note on the Text

The materials in this volume follow the original texts in all important aspects. However, typographical errors in the reviews and essays have been silently emended, though indicative errors, such as misspellings of Melville's name, his characters' names, or his books' titles, have been allowed to stand. The italicization of titles of books and periodicals have also been regularized. Lengthy extracts, plot summaries, and repetitious or digressive passages in the reviews have been omitted, and the omissions are indicated in the text. The present editor's footnotes are numbered; the critics' footnotes are asterisked, daggered, etc. The texts of documents pertaining to Melville's life are taken from the sources listed in the Preface and Acknowledgments, and any variation between a document as transcribed in those sources and as quoted in this volume—beyond the correction of typographical errors—is based on an examination of the original. However, the idiosyncrasies of Melville's spelling have been preserved in the quotations from his letters and journals.

TYPEE

1846

1. From an unsigned review, London *Spectator*

28 February 1846, 209–10

. . . It will be seen that the *Residence in the Marquesas* consists of adventure and observation. The adventure embraces a portion of the voyage in the Dolly, the narrative of the wanderings among the mountains, and Melville's escape from the Happy Valley, as well as several incidents during his detention,—such as his surprising the worthy household in which he lived examining three smoked human heads, one of which his hasty glance saw to be a White man's, with a first idea that it *might* be Toby's; the cannibal feast, which he is sure took place after a fight with the inhabitants of a neighbouring valley, when bundles consisting of human bodies wrapped in leaves were, as he infers, brought in. And, notwithstanding a tendency to make too much of things by writing about them, wherever there is a story, however slight, the book is very interesting. The descriptive parts are not of so striking a character. The American fluency, which even in the narrative verges upon prolixity, becomes rather uninteresting where there is no action to relieve it: especially as Mr. Melville's mind, though vigorous enough, has not been trained in those studies which enable men to observe with profit; nor did he master the language sufficiently to have comprehended any communication made to him beyond the commonest subject. The book, however, is of great curiosity in one point of view: it is the first account that has been published of a residence among the natives of the Polynesian Islands, by a person who has lived with them in their own fashion, and as near as may be upon terms of social equality: for although hundreds of mariners have lived and died upon these islands, and some of them—as Christian the mutineer—were perhaps capable of writing a book, none of them that we remember have ever done so.

The picture of this life which Mr. Melville draws is very attractive, upon the text,

> Let me enjoy the cheerful day,
>   Till many a year has o'er me roll'd;
> Pleased let me trifle life away,
>   And sing of love ere I grow old.'

The warmth of the Tropics, tempered by the vast Pacific, makes the climate a delightful 'June melting into July'; the fertile soil, with its cocoas and bread fruit and other nutritious vegetation, supports life without labour, (assisted, we cannot help imagining, by some preventive check, notwithstanding our author's vehement disclaimer of infanticide,) whilst a community of goods, and an absence of anything like jealousy or female restraint, realize the Pantisocracy which Southey, Coleridge, and others, fancied the perfection of society during the phrensy of the French Revolution. It is not, therefore, surprising that a sailor, just escaped from the confinement and disagreeables of a South Sea whaler and the low tyranny of its captain, should be enraptured with the mode of life, or should draw comparisons with civilized society or the missionary converts very much in favour of the Typees. At the same time, his theory and practice were different; for he seized the first opportunity of escaping, and his pleasurable existence was constantly damped by the fear that he never should be able to escape.

Had this work been put forward as the production of an English common sailor, we should have had some doubts of its authenticity, in the absence of distinct proof. But in the United States it is different. There social opinion does not invest any employment with caste discredit; and it seems customary with young men of respectability to serve as common seamen, either as a probationership to the navy or as a mode of seeing life. Cooper and Dana are examples of this practice. The wide-spread system of popular education also bestows upon the American a greater familiarity with popular literature and a readier use of the pen than is usual with classes of the same apparent grade in England. Striking as the style of composition may sometimes seem in a *Residence in the Marquesas,* there is nothing in it beyond the effects of a vivacious mind, acquainted with popular books, and writing with the national fluency; or a reading sailor spinning a yarn; nothing to indicate the student or the scholar. Yet we should like to have had the story of the book; to have known the motives of the publication, and whether it is an American reprint or a conjoint appearance, or whether Mr. Murray has the sole right of publishing. There are certain sea freedoms, too, that might as well have been removed before issuing it for family reading.

Much of the book is not beyond the range of invention, especially by a person acquainted with the Islands, and with the fictions of De Foe; and we think that several things have been heightened for effect, if indeed this artistical principle does not pervade the work. Many of the incidents, however, seem too natural to be invented by the author. Such is the following picture, which but requires us to call the savages celestials, to suppose Mr. Melville to have dropped from the clouds instead of 'bolting' from the skipper Vangs, and to fancy some Ovidian graces added to the narrative, in order to become a scene of classical mythology.

[quotes from chapter 18, 'Returning health and peace' to 'endeavors to reach them.']

The 'service' has had the effect of enlarging Mr. Melville's mind, and making him less provincial in feeling than many of his countrymen. It has also given him some knowledge of the South Seas generally, which appears in the comparisons he incidentally introduces; and has impressed him with an indifferent opinion of (to say the least) the self-seeking and worldly spirit of the missionaries. Here is an example of them at the Sandwich Islands.

[quotes from chapter 26, 'Not until I visited' to 'draw their superiors home.']

2. From an unsigned review, London *Critic*

7, 14, 28 March 1846, 219–22, 251–4, 315–20

This is a most entertaining and refreshing book. It details the experiences of an American sailor, who, disgusted with the tedium of a long whaling voyage, and the arbitrary conduct of his captain, availed himself of the vessel's visit to Nukuheva for provisions, to run away and take his chance among the savages of that island.

The picture he has drawn of Polynesian life and scenery is incomparably the most vivid and forcible that has ever been laid before the public. The incidents, no doubt, are sometimes exaggerated, and the colouring is often overcharged, yet in the narrative generally there is a *vraisemblance*[1] that cannot be feigned; for the minuteness, and novelty of the details, could only have been given by one who had before him nature for his model.

The writer of this narrative, though filling the post of a common sailor, is certainly no common man. His clear, lively, and pointed style, the skilful management of his descriptive, the philosophical reflections and sentimental apostrophes scattered plentifully through the work, at first induced us to suppose it the joint production of an American sailor and man of letters, of whom the one furnished the raw materials and the other gave them shape, order, and consistency, so as to tell with more effect upon the public. We have since learned, on good authority, that this was not the case; that, in fact, the narrative is the *bonâ fide* production of a brother to one of the gentlemen officially attached to the American Legation in this country, and his alone.

In America, as in Germany, there prevails among young men a more ardent wish to see and prove the world than actuates those who are first entering upon the business of life among ourselves. In this particular we are less enlightened than those nations; and since nothing is so effective for dissipating prejudices, enlarging ideas, and accumulating a useful stock of imagery for the mind, as travel, it were greatly to be wished the custom of looking more abroad before settling down in the world were generally adopted by the rising generation of Englishmen. The beneficial effect of such a practice is abundantly visible in the

[1] *Vraisemblance*: verisimilitude.

national character, and especially in the literature, of the Germans and Americans. To confine ourselves to the country of our author, the names of COOPER, DANA, and BRYANT, at once present themselves, to which this work adds that of a *confrere* of whom they may justly be proud.

Of adventure this narrative, limited as is the period which it embraces, necessarily affords but little, nor does it abound in stirring incident or action; we propose, however, to give the substance of these, with such extracts as may shew the chief peculiarities of the wild people among whom our author sojourned, and at the same time convey to the reader a tolerably accurate idea of the work he has produced....

[summarizes the first part of the story, quoting six long passages]

The predominant and most objectionable characteristic of this book is the obtrusive earnestness with which its author supports a favourite notion that savage is preferable to civilised life. From the page on which he relates his first interview with the cannibals to that where he gives wild utterance to joy at escaping from them, there are perpetually contrasted the superior happiness and enjoyments the Polynesian in his wild state enjoys, to those which would result to him under the influence of Civilisation. Seldom have savages found so zealous a vindicator of their morals; rarely, too, has Christianity owned so ungrateful a son. What ROUSSEAU, in his famous Dijon thesis, traced out in theory, Mr. MELVILLE endeavours to exhibit in practice. Both are wrong. The first adopted his views solely from a love of paradox, backed by a remark of DIDEROT'S; and though he supported them in a strain of fervid and bewildering eloquence, it afterwards became known that they were as contrary to the deliberate convictions of his judgment as they are specious, imaginary, and unsubstantial. The last, and lesser of the two, fails in his attempt from a want of comprehensiveness in argument. It is true he gives us charming descriptions of savage life—of a people blessed with a divine climate and inhabiting a luxuriant country, where the necessaries of life spring spontaneously to the hand; but the points on which he expatiates are those only favourable to his purpose—the social condition is neither sufficiently scrutinised nor described; while the isolated facts he offers are so tinged with the colouring through which he perversely beholds them as to be little better than worthless, so far as the question he supports is concerned. If we glance but for a moment at his argument, we find it audaciously assumptive, and throughout questionable.

'In a primitive state of society' says he, 'the enjoyments of life, though few and simple, are spread over a great extent, and are unalloyed: but civilisation for every advantage she imparts holds a hundred evils in reserve;—the heart-burnings, the jealousies, the social rivalries, the family dissensions, and the thousand self-inflicted discomforts of refined life, which make up in units the swelling aggregates of human misery, are unknown among these unsophisticated people.' Can anything be falser and shallower than this? We claim not, indeed, for civilised life that its pleasures are 'unalloyed,' but that they are more general, more lasting, more satisfactory, and more pure than those of the savage state, a moment's dispassionate reflection must conclusively shew. Furthermore, does not the author again transgress the truth when he denies the existence of 'heart-burnings, jealousies, social rivalries, and family dissensions,' among the happy islanders from whom he was but too happy to escape? If he does not, then we can only say that the Polynesian differs from every other human family, civilised or savage, that has ever existed. 'The heart of man,' exclaims the Psalmist, 'is prone to deceit, and desperately wicked.' In the natural state the *body* rules predominant; in the civilised it is controlled by the mind: the passions of the one are 'of the earth earthy;' the self-springing emotions and delights of the other are holy and pure, because the soul is itself from God.

That the Polynesians are cannibals our author admits; but he tells us 'they are so only when they seek to gratify the passion of revenge upon their enemies.' That they are treacherous and bloodthirsty we have the strongest inferential evidence in the perpetual apprehension of death or disaster which oppressed him when among them, and the desperate attempt they made to destroy the boat in which he was escaping. That they have few and light ideas of religion, and are idol-worshippers, Mr. MELVILLE admits in a light tone, as if these were circumstances not much to be deprecated; and that their ideas of chastity, of family relations, and social government, are of the loosest possible nature, the unintentional revelations of this book abundantly prove. Such are the people who, it is affirmed, are happier, more comfortable, and better in their primitive state than if the blessings of civilisation had been their birthright.

One more censure we have to pronounce before we rejoin our author in the narrative of his experiences among the Marquesans. In the course of his remarks he has frequent occasion to advert to the labours of the missionaries among these and other islanders of the

South Seas; and it is remarkable that he never speaks of them but in terms either of downright disrespect, of ridicule as often as he can, or to charge them with gross and wilful exaggeration in their statements, or with credulity and blindness in their dealings with the natives. To such an extent does he carry this, that, having a misgiving it will be offensive to his readers, he purposely excuses it as best he can in the preface to his book. The tone of mock respect in which he does this is the more despicable and mischievous because it may betray the unthinking into confidence in his statements, believing that he has the real interests of Christianity very seriously at heart. We caution all such against delusions of this nature, and tell Mr. MELVILLE that a twelve-months' mental discipline under the weakest of the disinterested class whom he reviles would be to him of the greatest service; it would teach him the value of moderation, charity, and truth-seeking, —to draw conclusions warily and after mature consideration, and thus better qualify him for a censor of morals and commentator on a people than he has proved himself in this book.

Having now recounted the blemishes which deform this work, we take up the narrative where, in our last, we left off, and avail ourself of the author's descriptions of life, manners, and scenery, which are always interesting. . . .

[continues the summary of the story, with quotations]

In our last number, it will be remembered, we found occasion to censure Mr. MELVILLE for the unjustifiable and uncalled-for remarks he has made on the missionaries and their labours in the South Seas. Since then, in order to test the accuracy of this author in other particulars, and at the same time take the opinion of another writer who had equally favourable opportunities of forming a correct judgment of the utility and working of missions among the heathens of the Pacific, we have referred to a plainly written and evidently trustworthy book, published last year, and entitled *Adventures in the Pacific*, which has already been noticed in this Journal. Its author, Dr. JOHN COULTHER, surgeon to the ship *Stratford*, like Mr. MELVILLE, passed some time among the Marquesans, who, after tattooing him, compelled him to assume the costume and functions of a chief, and in that capacity to assist in their wars. It adds greatly, in our opinion, to the authenticity of Mr. MELVILLE's book, that its descriptions of the physical aspect of the country, and of the customs and amusements of the natives, are remarkably corroborated by Dr. COULTHER. It is in the respective estimates they draw of the morals and condition of the people that the most obvious difference between them arises. Here they are altogether at issue; the first affirming the natives are happier and more to be envied in the primitive state, and that civilisation is a curse to them; the last pitying and deploring their abject condition, who, with capacities for intellectual culture of a superior kind, are grovelling, sensual, indolent, and brutish. Most accordant with the common-sense view of the case is the view of Dr. COULTHER; and he has a further advantage in this, that, while our author, partly for effect and partly from prejudice, colours his pictures very strongly, he gives nakedly, and without exaggeration, the facts and features as he found them. . . .

[concludes the summary, with quotations]

Here we close our notice of a book which, though deformed with some blemishes, is, as we think the reader must have seen, by the extracts offered, one of the most brilliantly coloured and entertaining that has for a long while past issued from the press.

3. Unsigned review, London *Examiner*

7 March 1846, 147–8

'The Devil is not so black as he is painted,' says the proverb. Cannibals are not so unpleasant as we think them, says Mr Herman Melville. His 'Peep at Polynesian Life' was taken in a Cannibal Valley; and, premising that an intolerable weariness seems as incident to Polynesia as to Abyssinia, the Happy Valley of our dear old *Rasselas* was not a more romantic or enchanting scene.

This is really a very curious book. Its authenticity (it is an importation from America) did not seem very clear to us at first, but on closer examination we are not disposed to question it. A little colouring there may be, here and there; but the result is a thorough impression of reality. In the 'inducement' of the narrative, we are reminded of Mr Dana's *Two Years before the Mast*; though there is not such unaffected vigour and straightforward simplicity in the style of its descriptions. Mr Melville, like Mr Dana, is a young and educated American, who had signed articles as a common seaman on board an American South-Sea whaler. The precise meaning or drift of this custom, we confess we cannot arrive at; unless it be to qualify for the writing of interesting books. The Navy service would hardly exact such a harassing pupilage; and a less desperate mode of initiation into 'life' might surely be hit upon. But so it is. The custom exists, and we owe to it this peep at Polynesia.

Mr Dana's captain was not more unpopular than the captain of the 'Dolly' whaler. Mr Melville's narrative opens with a description of the general weariness and disgust on board at the obstinate tyranny of Captain Vangs, in having kept the ship for six mortal months out of all sight of harbour or headland. He steered at last for the Marquesas group, which, though earliest discovered, have been least described of all the South-Sea Islands. It was in 1842, and the famous Dupetit Thouars had hoisted the French flag but a few days before; wherefore, as they sailed into the lovely bay of Nukuheva, they passed six black-hulled, bristling Frenchmen, surmounted by the tricolour; but this was nothing to a sudden and singular commotion visible in the water a-head of their own vessel, and which proved to be a shoal of 'whinhenies,' or young Polynesian nymphs, who boarded the 'Dolly' with a welcome. It is a curious description, and may be quoted; for its mixture of grace, licence, and oddity, is no bad expression of the general character of the book.

[quotes from chapter 2, 'As they drew nearer' to 'unlimited gratification.']

Mr Melville has some decisive opinions in this part of his narrative on French habits and policy in Polynesia; but we content ourselves with referring to them. He had not been many days in Nukuheva harbour when he resolved to escape from the ship into the bush; stung by the intolerable tyranny of Captain Vangs, and tempted, there is no doubt, by bewitching glimpses of land scenery visible from the decks of his unbewitching 'Dolly.' Yet his bane and antidote were both before him. For whereas, adjacent to Nukuheva, lay the charming valley of Happar, inhabited by a most friendly race,—on the other side of Happar, and closely joining it, lurked the not less magnificent valley of Typee, peopled by cannibals and ferocious tribes. Mr Melville, notwithstanding, resolved to take his chance; and another seaman risked it with him. Their hope was to get so far inland as to be safe from search till the 'Dolly' sailed off; and to be able to live on fruits till they could 'show' without danger in the friendly valley. So with a few biscuits and a quantity of tobacco, the author and his fellow-seaman, Toby, made their desperate venture.

The subsequent details of the escape are extraordinary. To comprehend them the reader must imagine the shore of Nukuheva indented by other extensive inlets, into which descend broad and verdant valleys, intersected by mountains of two or three thousand feet above the level of the sea, which serve thus to define the territories of the several occupants of the valleys, and are never crossed but for purposes of war or plunder. Into these terrible altitudes the two seamen toilsomely ascended; but they found no fruit, they could get no shelter; and starved with hunger, drenched with rain, and overwhelmed by sickness and disease, they had to descend and re-ascend the most frightful ravines; till, grown bewildered and reckless, they resolved to make for some human habitation, no matter whether Happar or Typee. The die went against them, and they found themselves in Typee. We remember few narratives of escape with a more sustained interest, of a more dramatic close.

Typee, however, turned out far from the Golgotha they looked for. Skulls they detected now and then, in suspicious ways, it is true; even 'smoked human heads' were discovered; nay, after a straggling encounter or a fight with a neighbouring valley, it seems pretty certain that the victors had regaled themselves with a feast upon their foes; but in all this there was a singular decency. The skulls had to be hunted out from remote parts of a household; the smoked heads had been carefully put away; and the joints conveyed to the cannibal repast were wrapped up in leaves. On the other hand, Mr Melville and his friend were treated with high hospitality. So high indeed, that poor Toby (quite a character in his way, and most cleverly sketched) conceived a sudden terror that he was fattening for an ulterior purpose; and, too eager to make his escape, disappeared one day altogether. Mr Melville never could make out what became of him—whether a chief, or a cutlet, in Polynesia. He remained himself, meanwhile, in a kind of honourable and hospitable durance; studying the manners and life of this most mysterious, generous, primitive race of cannibals; drawing conclusions by no means favourable to civilization (culinary tastes excepted); and preparing his materials for this curious book.

We must refer to it for details. We could not, without too great minuteness, sketch his observation of the chief people of the valley; the mildly dignified sovereign, Mehevi; the graceful, winning, irresistible, beauty, Fayaway; the household that lodged him; Marheyo, and his wife, the only industrious old body in the valley; the young men of the house, roystering, drinking, laughing and unthinking 'blades of savages;' the young ladies, though in the summer costume of Paradise, coquettish and fantastical, delicate and ladylike, as Parisian belles; and his faithful but hideous body-servant, Kory-Kory. He passed four months with them, living in their own fashion; and is the only man who has described them, we believe, from this very social and familiar point of view.

The impression is odd and startling, as we have said. Savage life, with so little savagery, we could hardly have conceived. All that part of it, at any rate, is dextrously veiled. You have a kind of pantisocracy, or social millennium in little. No need of restraints or laws. No evil passions, malice, or hatred; therefore no mischievous legislation. Plenty to eat, nothing to do, and a delicious climate. Wives with Heaven knows how many husbands; husbands content with ever so small a share of a wife; and no jealousy, and no surplus population. Inducements to South-Sea colonization which we think it almost dangerous to set forth. For, alas! Mr Melville discourses sadly of the effects of European intercourse with these innocent cannibals; and contrasts the scenes of his happy valley with later experiences of that part of the Polynesian group on which the missionaries have bestowed their greatest attention.

[quotes from chapter 26, 'Among a multitude' to 'their superiors home.']

Wives or widows make a very different business of attendances at religious worship in Typee. As we have the volumes open for extract, let us observe some old Typee ladies in mourning for their lords:

[quotes from chapter 23, 'I was amused' to 'of their calamities.']

Our last extract shall be descriptive of an artist in tattooing; from whom, it will be seen, Mr Melville had a close escape. Tattooing, we need not remark, is the universal fashion of these savages; and the more hideous the extent of it, the greater the dandyism; but the lovely

Fayaway had not in even this lost her winning ways, presenting in the tattoo department but three minute dots no bigger than pin heads on either laughing lip, and on either shoulder a graceful undress epaulette.

[quotes from chapter 30, 'I beheld a man' to 'merrily as a woodpecker.']

Such alarms as these had doubtless no small effect on our adventurous seaman's nerves. For with all his sentimental zeal for the cannibal condition of innocence and non-civilization, he seems to have wearied quite as much to get back to wickedness and broadcloth as ever poor Rasselas did to escape from the tiresome valley of Amhara.

The truth is, he felt himself a prisoner, and doubtless was one. He was kept in the upper part of the valley; was very closely watched whenever he approached the sea; and, though greatly feasted and honoured, never could think himself secure. Thus Fayaway herself seems at last to have lost some of her charms. The disappearance of his companion, too, naturally haunted him; since he never saw a dinner cooked with any appearance of mystery, that he did not dread some possible connection with the fate of Toby. At last he found an opportunity of escape by means of the boat of an English ship, and so returned to America to write this clever book, which we thank Mr Murray for having included in his cheap and well-conducted *Colonial Library.*

4. Unsigned notice, London *John Bull*

7 March 1846, 156

Since the joyous moment when we first read *Robinson Crusoe*, and believed it all, and wondered all the more because we believed, we have not met with so bewitching a work as this narrative of Herman Melville's, which forms the thirtieth and thirty-first parts of Mr. Murray's *Home and Colonial Library.* Like Robinson Crusoe, however, we cannot help suspecting that if there be really such a person as Herman Melville, he has either employed a Daniel Defoe to describe his adventures, or is himself both a Defoe and an Alexander Selkirk.

The work professes to be written by an American common sailor, who, with one of his comrades, escaped from the *Dolly*, a South Sea whaler (in consequence of the cruelty of the captain), when she touched at Nukuheva, the principal of that group of islands in the Pacific known by the name of the Marquesas—so called in honour of the Marquess de Mendoza, Viceroy of Peru, under whose auspices, in the year 1595, the navigator sailed who first visited them.

Nothing is said as to whether this work is a reprint from an American edition, or whether it has been transmitted to this country in manuscript for publication; while the tone of the article which appears in the appendix, warmly vindicating the conduct of Lord George Paulet in the affair of the Sandwich Islands, would almost justify the suspicion that the work is not written by an American at all. When too, we consider the style of composition, so easy, so graceful, and so graphic, we own the difficulty we feel in believing that it is the production of a common sailor. It is 'affectionately inscribed' to 'Lemuel Shaw, Chief Justice of the Commonwealth of Massachusetts.' Be the author, however, whom and what he may, he has produced a narrative of singular interest, not merely as regards his own personal adventures, which are in the highest degree exciting and romantic, but as regards the remarkable people (the Typees) among whom he sojourned for some time, and whose manners and customs he delineates with so much power. More than three years, he informs us, have elapsed since the occurrence of the events he has described, and as the account of them, he says, when 'spun as a yarn,' not only relieved the weariness of many a night watch at sea, but excited the warmest sympathies of the author's 'shipmates,' he was 'led to think that his story could scarcely fail to interest those who are less familiar than the sailor with a life of adventure.' There are a few passages, here and there, obnoxious to the same censure which was bestowed upon Dr. Hawkesworth for his account of Otaheite, in Cook's *Voyages*.

5. Unsigned notice, New Bedford, Massachusetts, *Daily Mercury*

23 March 1846

This is a singularly attractive and delightful work. Impelled by the love of novelty and a roving disposition, the author appears to have taken 'French leave' of the whaling ship 'Dolly' at the Bay of Nukuheva, Marquesas Islands, and after a series of wandering and almost incredible adventures and hair-breadth escapes, at length becomes fairly domesticated at the Court of the 'King of the Cannibal Islands' with abundant opportunity and keen perceptions of observation of the habits and manners of the Islanders. His descriptions of Polynesian Life are characterised with a careless elegance of style which suits admirably with the luxurious and tropical tone of the narrative, bespeaking the practised and accomplished writer rather than the inmate of the forecastle. Such instances of rare talent and superior literary acquirements are however by no means of rare occurrence among the motley groups who man the numerous whale ships from our ports. The work is dedicated by the author to Lemuel Shaw, Chief Justice of the Commonwealth of Massachusetts, and is published simultaneously by Messrs Wiley & Putnam, New York, as No. XIII. of their 'Library of American Books,' and in London. . . .

6. Nathaniel Hawthorne, unsigned notice, Salem, Massachusetts, *Advertiser*

25 March 1846

Hawthorne (1804–64) and Melville evidently did not meet until 5 August 1850 when both were living in the Berkshire region of western Massachusetts. Melville's appreciation of Hawthorne can be seen in his essay, 'Hawthorne and His Mosses,' which appeared pseudonymously in the New York *Literary World* (see No. 75), in his letters to Hawthorne (see No. 76), and in the dedication of *Moby-Dick*: 'In token of my admiration for his genius, This Book is Inscribed to Nathaniel Hawthorne.'

Wiley & Putnam's Library of American Books, Nos. XIII and XIV. The present numbers of this excellent and popular series, contain a very remarkable work, entitled *Typee, or a Peep at Polynesian Life.* It records the adventures of a young American who ran away from a whale ship at the Marquesas, and spent some months as the guest, or captive, of a native tribe, of which scarcely anything had been hitherto known to the civilized world.—The book is lightly but vigorously written; and we are acquainted with no work that gives a freer and more effective picture of barbarian life, in that unadulterated state of which there are now so few specimens remaining. The gentleness of disposition that seems akin to the delicious climate, is shown in contrast with traits of savage fierceness;—on one page, we read of manners and modes of life that indicate a whole system of innocence and peace; and on the next, we catch a glimpse of a smoked human head, and the half-picked skeleton of what had been (in a culinary sense) a *well-dressed* man. The author's descriptions of the native girls are voluptuously colored, yet not more so than the exigencies of the subject appear to require. He has that freedom of view—it would be too harsh to call it laxity of principle—which renders him tolerant of codes of morals that may be little in accordance with our own; a spirit proper enough to a young and adventurous sailor, and which makes his book the more wholesome to our staid landsmen. The narrative is skilfully managed, and in a literary point of view, the execution of the work is worthy of the novelty and interest of its subject.

7. Charles Fenno Hoffman, unsigned review, New York *Gazette and Times*

30 March 1846

Hoffman (1806–84), a novelist, poet, and editor as well as a critic, was an important figure in the circle of New York literary men whom Melville met in the wake of *Typee*'s success. He edited several New York periodicals, among them the *Literary World* in 1847 and 1848. The following year he entered a mental hospital where he spent the rest of his life. On 5 April 1849 Melville wrote to Evert Duyckinck:

Poor Hoffman—I remember the shock I had when I first saw the mention of his madness.—But he was just the man to go mad—imaginative, voluptuously inclined, poor, unemployed, in the race of life distanc[d] by his inferiors, unmarried,—without a port or haven in the universe to make. His present misfortune—rather blessing—is but the sequel to a long experience of unwhole habits of thought.—This going mad of a friend or acquaintance comes straight home to every man who feels his soul in him,—which but few men do. For in all of us lodges the same fuel to light the same fire. And he who has never felt, momentarily, what madness is has but a mouthful of brains. What sort of sensation permanent madness is may be very well imagined—just as we imagine how we felt when we were infants, tho' we can not recall it. In both conditions we are irresponsible & riot like gods without fear of fate.—It is the climax of a mad night of revelry when the blood has been transmuted into brandy.—But if we prate much of this thing we shall be illustrating our own propositions.—

This is one of the most delightful and well written narratives that ever came from an American pen; nor could a fresh, graceful and animated style be more fortunately furnished with a suitable theme to set it forth to the best advantage. Mr Melville has made the subject of Typee henceforth wholly his own by his felicitous mode of showing off its wild and novel charms. The account he gives of the manner in which he lighted upon his paradise of the Pacific is very simple. The love of adventure drove him to sea and induced him to go before the mast in a whaler; and the same love of adventure impelled him to run away from his ship when she reached the Marquesas Islands. There, not being safe from arrest as a deserter, among the friendly natives, he was driven to find a refuge among the cannibal Typees: the formidable race of which Commodore Porter gave so striking an account thirty years ago, and which Mr Melville found still in an uncontaminated state of paradisaical barbarism. That is, the men eat their enemies, and entertain their friends with the freest hospitality; and the women in their ball dresses of flowers and feathers 'look like a band of olive-colored Sylphides on the point of taking wing.'

> Would that the desert were my dwelling place,
> With one fair spirit for my minister,

quoth Lord Byron,—and Mr Melville realized the wish by having one of these olive-colored sylphs to 'minister' to him in his wandering through the Island. With this wood Nymph *Fayaway* by name, and a Man Friday called *Kory-kory*, our American Crusoe revelled in all sorts of out-of-doors felicities.

[quotes from chapter 18, 'The first day' to 'everything appear' and 'One day, after' to 'this feat repeated.']

According to Mr Melville's description, nothing can be more uniform and undiversified than the life of the Typees. 'One tranquil day of ease and happiness follows another in quiet succession, and with these unsophisticated savages the history of a day is the history of a life.' The only hard labor known among them is that of striking a light, which is done in the primitive style of rubbing two pieces of wood together. As the introduction of lucifer matches is out of the question, Mr Melville hints that an improvement might be borrowed from old Rome by organizing a community of vestals to keep fire always burning; a plan to which he confesses however that there are some objections among the Typees.

The number of this primitive people is estimated at about two thousand.

[quotes from chapter 26, 'The valley is some' to 'temporal destruction!']

In the remaining portion of this chapter, as well as in others, written in a more serious and earnest vein, Mr Melville is very severe upon some of the missionary establishments of the Pacific. We commend this portion of his book, for verification or reply to those more familiar with this interesting and important matter than we secular journalists can claim to be. Mr Melville, a grandson of Gen. Gansevoort, of New York, is a son of the late Major Melville, of Massachusetts, and a brother of Gansevoort Melville, Esq., United States Secretary of Legation at the Court of St. James. His book shows him to be a man of education, sense and spirit, and his representations therefore upon this subject as on others, will awaken no little attention. We close our extracts from these amazingly clever volumes, with the following history of a day as usually spent in the Typee Valley.

[quotes from chapter 20, 'We were not very' to 'luxurious nap.']

8. Unsigned review, London *Douglas Jerrold's Shilling Magazine*

April 1846, iii, 380–3

Is there any one whose eye may fall on this page, weary of the conventionalities of civilised life—some toil-worn Sisyphus bowed to the earth with his never-ending task of rolling up the hill of life the stone that ever threatens to fall back on himself—dispirited with the energies he has wasted on unrewarded or uncongenial pursuits—cheated with Hope until he regard her as a baffled impostor who shall cheat him no more; whose heart beats no longer high for the future; but whose best affections are chilled, and loftiest aspirations thrown back on themselves. Is there any one sick of the petty animosities, the paltry heart-burnings and jealousies, and low-thoughted cares of what is called, in bitter mockery, society?—Oh! 'if such man there be,' let him take the 'wings of a dove,' or what perhaps will bear safer the weight of himself and his woes—a berth in a South-sea whaler, and try the effects of a 'Residence in the Marquesas,' and take a 'Peep at Polynesian life,' and if he likes the peep make that life his own.

Here, and we call Mr. Herman Melville into court, he need not fear the single rap at the door which dissipates his day-dreams as surely as the kite in the air scares away the feathered minstrelsy of the grove; nor the postman's knock that peradventure brings the letter of the impatient dun or threatening attorney; nor butchers' nor bakers' bills; nor quarter-days with griping landlord and brutal brokers; nor tax-gatherer; nor income-tax collectors gauging with greedy exactness the drops that have fallen from his brow. Here, strange to say, he will find no money, no bargaining, no bankers with overdrawn accounts or dishonoured acceptances; no coin, and therefore no care; no misery, and therefore no crime. No corn-laws, no tariff, no union-workhouse, no bone-crushing, no spirit-crushing, no sponging-houses, no prisons. But he may live as the songster *wish'd*, but dar'd not even to hope he could live——

in an isle of his own
In a blue summer ocean far off;

but *not* 'alone.' For here are Houris even more graceful and lovely than the flowers they are perpetually weaving to adorn themselves with chaplets and necklaces, their only ornaments, but worthy of the court of Flora herself; inviting him to repose his weary limbs beneath the shadows of groves, on couches strewn with buds and fragrant blossoms.

Here the bosom of Nature unscarified by the plough, offers up spontaneously her goodliest gifts; food the most nutritious, and fruits the most refreshing. The original curse on man's destiny, appears here not to have fallen, 'the ground is *not* cursed for his sake;' nor 'in sorrow does he eat of it all the days of his life.'

In this garden of Eden, from which man is not yet an exile, there are no laws, and what is more agreeable still, no want of them; unless it be an Agrarian law, which works to every one's satisfaction. In this paradise of islands, you have only to fix the site of your house, and you will not be called upon to produce your title deeds; and you may call upon your neighbours to help you to build it, without any surveyor being called in to tax their bills. Here you may, instead of going to your office or warehouse, loiter away your morning beneath the loveliest and bluest of skies, on the margin of some fair lake, reflecting their hues yet more tenderly; or join the young men in their fishing-parties or more athletic sports; or if more quietly disposed, join the old men seated on their mats in the shade, in their 'talk' deprived of only one topic, your everlasting one, the weather; for where the climate is one tropical June day, 'melting into July,' it leaves you nothing to wish for, positively nothing to grumble at.

Such is life in the valley of the Typees; and surely Rasselas, if he had had the good luck to stumble on it, would not have gone further in his search after happiness.

There is, however, one trifling drawback—some shadows to temper the light of this glowing picture—the Typees are cannibals! The author makes an elaborate, but to our notion, a very unnecessary apology for this propensity of theirs. The Polynesians have the advantage of the cannibals of civilised life, for we have long since made the pleasant discovery, that man-eating is not confined to the Anthropophagi of the South Seas. The latter have undoubtedly one redeeming distinction—they only devour their enemies slain in battle: there is nothing which man in a civilised state has a keener appetite for than his particular friend. Go to any race-course, and you will find some scented Damon picking his teeth with a silver tooth-pick after devouring his Pythias, as if he had relished the repast. Go to Tattersal's or Cockford's, and you will find that in a single night a man has devoured his own wife and children—having been disappointed in supping off his intimate friends. We know instances of highly respected country gentlemen swallowing at a single election the whole of their posterity; and could quote one huge Ogre who can gorge in his mighty man a few millions of 'the finest peasantry'—nothing, indeed, civilised men are more expert in than picking their neighbours' bones!

Possibly, we may have pushed the parallel to the furthest; but it is impossible to read this pleasant volume without being startled at the oft-recurring doubt, has civilization made man better, and therefore happier? If she has brought much to him, she has taken much away; and wherever she has trod, disease, misery and crime have tracked her footsteps. She finds man a rude but happy savage, and leaves him a repulsive outcast, whose only relation to humanity consists in the vices which stain it!

We have dwelt more on the subject of Mr. Melville's 'Narrative,' and the reflections it excites, than on the book itself, which is one of the most captivating we have ever read. What will our juvenile readers say to a *real* Robinson Crusoe, with a *real* man Friday?—one Kory-Kory, with whom we will venture to say they will be delighted in five minutes from his introduction. The early part of the volume, narrating the author's escape from the prison ship—with his strange comrade Toby, whose mysterious fate, after baffling our curiosity and speculation, is yet to be developed—for the best of all possible reasons, that the author himself has not found it out!—is full of vivid excitement. The hair-breadth escapes of the adventurous seamen, their climbing up precipices and perpendicular rocks, their perilous leaps into cavernous retreats and gloomy ravines, are painted in vivid contrast to the voluptuous ease and tranquil enjoyments of the happy valley which they eventually reach. Although with little pretension to author-craft, there is a life and truth in the descriptions, and a freshness in the style of the narrative, which is in perfect keeping with the scenes and adventures it delineates. The volume forms a part of 'Murray's Home and Colonial Library,' and is worthy to follow Borrow's *Bible in Spain*, and Heber's *Indian Journals*. What traveller would wish for a higher distinction?

9. John Sullivan Dwight, from an unsigned review, Brook Farm *Harbinger*

4 April 1846, 263–6

Dwight (1813–93) graduated from Harvard Divinity School in 1836, the same year he became a member—with Ralph Waldo Emerson, George Ripley, and others—of the Transcendental Club. He took part in the Brook Farm experiment, teaching music and Latin there. The *Harbinger* (1845–9), which succeeded the *Dial* (1840–4) and the *Phalanx* (1843–5) as the vehicle for American Transcendentalist and Fourierist ideas, was first edited by Ripley and then, at the end of 1846, by Ripley and Dwight, who was already literary and music editor.

In the middle of the Pacific Ocean, some nine or ten degrees south of the Equator, lie the Marquesas. Here where the heats of the tropical sun are mitigated by the influence of the vast surrounding expanse of waters, and the climate is perfect and free from excesses of every kind, Nature blooms in a genial and healthy luxuriance such as she can no where else display. No Hesperides ever wore the gorgeous beauty of this southern paradise. Its green valleys stretch away in a loveliness which cannot be described. Hidden in the recesses of rough volcanic hills, their varied features teem with a glory that the dweller in other regions never conceived of. Their precipitous sides, covered with vegetation and with flowers, gleam with silvery cascades; in their evergreen and lofty groves, the golden fruits which supply the wants of their inhabitants, ripen without the labor of man; and little lakes nestling amidst the exuberant foliage, reflect the sky and tempt the beholder into their cool, clear depths. Such are these gems of the ocean, in which Nature, prodigal and unhindered, has hinted the extent of her possibilities, and by a kind of material diffraction has prophecied her own future perfections;—perfections which she shall possess in infinite and universal variety when, through the combined industry and wealth and power of a United Race, she shall have become but the image and expression of the Kingdom of God abiding in the souls and societies of Man!

Of the inhabitants of these islands we have accounts quite as striking as of the islands themselves. All writers unite in declaring them to be most perfect specimens of physical beauty, symmetry and health. . . .

Thus far there is no doubt of the facts; the assertions of the author are sustained by all the evidence relating to the subject. But in the course of his narrative, he makes some statements respecting the social condition and character of the tribe with which he was domesticated, of so remarkable a character that we cannot escape a slight suspicion that he has embellished the facts from his own imagination, in other words, that there is an indefinite amount of romance mingled with the reality of his narrative.

We say this without knowing the author or how far he may be relied on. The name on the title page gives, we take it, no indication either of his what, or his whereabouts; there is, to be sure, a straight forward air in his preface which is worth something, and the fact that the book is dedicated to Chief Justice Shaw, is greatly in favor of the assumption that it is a true history, but yet we cannot avoid the possibility that it may be in the most important particulars, only an amusing fiction. Still there is a verisimilitude about it, which inclines us to the contrary opinion; it relates nothing which is in itself impossible, and, having made the foregoing deductions, we shall consider it as though its facts were not susceptible of doubt.

. . . Their wanderings over mountains and defiles are described with great skill, and indeed we will here say that the whole book is the work of an artist. Since Dana's *Two Years Before the Mast*, we have had nothing to compare with it in point of fresh and natural interest. . . .

What has most interested us in *Typee*, is the social state which is described in the following extracts.

[quotes seven passages on the Typees]

This is certainly a noteworthy condition of social relations. Among these ignorant savages we behold order existing with liberty, and virtues of which, in civilized communities we find only the intellectual ideal, matters of everyday life. How is it that without our learning or our religion these cannibals can thus put to shame the most refined and Christian societies? How is it that in a mere state of nature they can live together in a degree of social harmony and freedom from vice, which all our jails, and scaffolds, and courts of justice, and police officers, and soldiers, and schoolmasters, and great philosophers, and immense politicians, and moral codes, and steam engines, material and spiritual, cannot procure for us? These are questions of some significance, but yet not difficult to answer. The great secret of the whole matter is that in Typee there is *abundance for every person*, and thus the most fruitful cause of the selfishness and crime of our enlightened and philosophic civilization does not exist there. Here is the lesson which the leaders of this nineteenth century may learn from the Typees; here is the doctrine which our legislators and philosophers, aye! and our clergy and churches who *preach* the love of man, and ought to know what are its conditions, need a better understanding of. Said that Coryphaeus of our beneficent modern metaphysics, Victor Cousin, when the oppression and degradation of the laboring classes were urged upon his unwilling attention, 'Eh! Give them good precepts! Give them good precepts! At least they can't abuse them, but if they get money they will only spend it in vice!'

To the winds with such shallow and selfish hypocrisy! Shame upon such intellectual inertia, such scepticism, as will not see that our Father who is in Heaven, has made it our duty to protect our brethren against the evils in which they are involved, and to discover and establish a social state of Justice and generous competence for all! Give them good precepts, but give them something else beside, if you wish to have your precepts effectual. Give them such an abundance of material things as bountiful nature in Typee bestows upon her children, and then when you bid them love each other, your words will not fall dead and unmeaning upon their ears. The peace and good will of that South Sea valley are as possible here as they are there; they are possible here in a far higher degree, on account of our greater refinement and intelligence, and our higher religious development. Here, indeed, in order to produce those blessings, we must in society create the material conditions which there are created by nature; we must have a social system which will produce and distribute to every member of society a complete abundance as the result of a healthy amount of labor, and not a niggardly, starving pittance to nineteen-twentieths of the population as the return for slavish and debasing toil, and enormous wealth to the other one-twentieth, as the fruit of grasping cunning or the wages of stupid and pitiable idleness. It is no deceitful phantasm when in some unknown and distant region we find a tribe of rude savages living in true social brotherhood; if we are wise we shall not hurry to the conclusion that such a state of things is impossible for us, but shall inquire what is the cause which produces it there, and how shall that cause be made to operate here. The cause is plain, and the means of putting it into effect with us not less so. The cause as we have said, is *universal abundance*, and the means of producing such abundance in civilized societies is the organization of industry and the distribution of its products according to principles of exact justice. . . .

10. Margaret Fuller, unsigned review, New York *Tribune*

4 April 1846

Fuller (1810–50), another member of the Transcendentalist group and an editor of the *Dial*, served as literary critic for Horace Greeley's *Tribune* from late 1844 through most of 1846. Her famous 'conversations,' which she created to provide 'a point of union to well-educated and thinking women,' led to her writing *Woman in the Nineteenth Century* (1845). Her review of *Typee* is preceded by comments on *Notes on a Journey from Cornhill to Cairo*.

Typee would seem, also, to be the record of imaginary adventures by someone who had visited those regions. But it is a very entertaining and pleasing narrative, and the Happy Valley of the gentle cannibals compares very well with the best contrivances of the learned Dr. Johnson to produce similar impressions. Of the power of this writer to make pretty and spirited pictures as well [as] of his quick and arch manner generally, a happy specimen may be seen in the account of the savage climbing the cocoa-tree, p. 273, vol. 2d. Many of the observations and narratives we suppose to be strictly correct. Is the account given of the result of the missionary enterprises in the Sandwich Islands of this number? We suppose so from what we have heard in other ways. With a view to ascertaining the truth, it would be well if the sewing societies, now engaged in providing funds for such enterprises would read the particulars, they will find in this book beginning p. 249, vol. 2d, and make inquiries in consequence, before going on with their efforts. Generally, the sewing societies of the country villages will find this the very book they wish to have read while assembled at their work. Othello's hairbreadth 'scapes were nothing to those by this hero in the descent of the cataracts, and many a Desdemona might seriously incline her ear to the descriptions of the lovely Fay-a-way.

11. From an unsigned review, London *Times*

6 April 1846

Mr. Murray's *Home and Colonial Library* does not furnish us with a more interesting book than this; hardly with a cleverer. It is full of the captivating matter upon which the general reader battens; and is endowed with freshness and originality to an extent that cannot fail to exhilarate the most enervated and *blasé* of circulating-library loungers.

[summarizes the story]

We have been somewhat prolix in the narration of this history; first, because the book of Mr. Melville is really a very clever production; and, secondly, because it is introduced to the English public as authentic, which we by no means think it to be. We have called Mr. Melville a common sailor; but he is a very uncommon common sailor, even for America, whose mariners are better educated than our own. His reading has been extensive. In his own province, the voyages of Cook, Carteret, Byron, Kotzebue, and Vancouver are familiar to him; he can talk glibly of Count Bouffon and Baron Cuvier, and critically, when he likes, of Teniers. His descriptions of scenery are lifelike and vigorous, sometimes masterly, and his style throughout is rather that of an educated literary man than of a poor outcast working seaman on board of a South Sea whaler.

The book betrays itself. In the early part of the narrative, and during the frightful incidents of the flight, Mr. Melville has but a spoonful of sodden biscuit daily; his leg is fearfully swollen, his pains are most acute; he is suffering from a raging fever; yet on he goes, day after day, for a week, undergoing exertion and fatigue that would kill a giant in health, yet arriving at last in the happy valley in tolerably good plight notwithstanding.

It must have been impossible, under the circumstances, for the fugitives to have carried 'luggage' with them, yet after two months' spent in the valley a large bundle turns up, which, it appears, Mr. Melville brought with him. After a week or two's sojourn the guest, ignorant of the Typee language when he first set foot in the valley, with most unaccountable facility understands all that is said to him, although the discourse of the chiefs comprehends abstruse points and very complex reasoning; and yet at the end of two or three months, forgetting what happened before, he informs us that gesticulation is required to enlighten him on the most ordinary subjects. At page 112 we find that 'our Typee friends availed themselves of a disaster of Toby to exhort us to a due appreciation of the blessings we enjoyed amongst them, contrasting their own generous reception of us with the animosity of their neighbours. They likewise dwelt upon the cannibal propensities of the Happars, a subject which they were perfectly aware could not fail to alarm us, while, at the same time, they earnestly disclaimed all participation in so horrid a custom. *Nor did they omit to call upon us to admire the natural loveliness of their own abode, and the lavish abundance with which it produced all manner of luxuriant fruits, exalting it in this particular above any of the surrounding valleys.*' Again, immediately afterwards, at page 119, when Herman inquires for the lost Toby, his earnest questions 'appeared to embarrass the natives greatly. *All their accounts were contradictory*; one giving me to understand that Toby would be with me in a very short time; another, that he did not know where he was; while a third, violently inveighing against him, assured me that he had stolen away, and would never come back.' Two months afterwards, when Mr. Melville's knowledge of Typee must have materially increased, we find—for so it is written at pp. 152 and 154—that he was so utterly ignorant of it as to be able to judge of the speaker's meaning only by signs, and very imperfectly by those. The getting rid of poor Toby, the only credible witness of these transactions, is of itself a most suspicious circumstance; so is the exquisite description of Fayaway; how different to what we elsewhere read of South Sea nymphs! So are the scenes that here and there end a chapter, like scenes of a play concluding an act with a *tableau vivant*,[1] and bringing the curtain down in the midst of it—we refer especially to chapter 12, which gives us young girls, darting from surrounding groves, 'hanging upon our skirts, and accompanying us with shouts of merriment and delight, which almost drowned the deep notes of the recitative.'

The evidence against the authenticity of the book is more than sufficient to satisfy a court of justice. Our limits forbid us to prosecute it further. Of evidence against the smartness and talent of the production there is none. The author, be he American or Englishman, has written a charming little book, and, as it appears to us, with a laudable and Christian purpose. Let it be regarded as an apology for the Pagan; a plea for the South Sea Islanders, governments, and missionaries, who understand so little the sacred charge which God commits to them, when He places in their hands the children of His favoured sunny regions; may they learn from fiction a lesson which experience has hitherto failed to teach them—viz., that if it be needful for Christianity to approach the Heathen, it is equally necessary that it should approach him *reverently and tenderly*.

[1] *Tableau vivant:* a scene of grouped persons.

12. 'H.C.,' review, New York *Evangelist*

9 April 1846, 60

The *Evangelist* was founded in the early 1830s 'expressly to promote revivals and missions, temperance, and other reforms,' including abolition.

If this be not sheer romance, (which there is reason to suspect,) it is the extremely exaggerated, but racily-written narrative of a forecastle-runaway from an American whale ship, who met the fortune those fish did in the fable, that he jumped out of the frying-pan into the fire. He had life among Marquesan cannibals to his liking; a plenty of what pleases the vicious appetite of a sailor, or of sensual human nature generally. He seems to have been pleased enough with his captors, but glad to get away uneaten. 'Horrible and fearful (he says) as the custom of cannibalism is, still I assert that those who indulge in it are in *other respects humane and virtuous!*'

The book abounds in praises of the life of nature, *alias* savageism, and in slurs and flings against missionaries and civilization. When the author alludes to, or touches matters of fact at the Sandwich Islands, he shows the sheerest ignorance and utter disregard of truth.

The work was made, not for America, but for a circle, and that not the highest, in London, where theatres, opera-dancers, and voluptuous prints have made such unblushing walks along the edge of modesty as are here delineated to be rather more admired than we hope they are yet among us. We are sorry that such a volume should have been allowed a place in the 'Library of American Books.' It can only have been without reading it beforehand, and from deference to the publisher on the other side.

We have long noted it as true in criticism, that what makes a large class of books bad, immoral, and consequently injurious, is not so much what is plainly expressed, as what is left to be imagined by the reader. Apply this rule to the work in hand, and while everybody will admit it is written with an attractive vivacity, and (except where it palpably lies) with great good humor, it cannot escape severe condemnation.

13. Unsigned notice, *Graham's Magazine*

May 1846, xxviii, 240

This entertaining work belongs to the 'Library of American Books.' Those who love to roam and revel in a life purely unconventional, though only in imagination, may be gratified by following the guidance of Mr. Melville. He writes of what he has seen *con amore*,[1] and at times almost loses his loyalty to civilization and the Anglo-Saxon race. His pen riots in describing the felicity of the Typees; and their occasional indulgence in a little cannibalism, he is inclined to regard somewhat as an amiable weakness, or, at least, as not being worse than many practices sanctioned by polite nations. 'The white civilized man,' he considers to be entitled, in point of 'remorseless cruelty,' to the dubious honor of being 'the most ferocious animal on the face of the earth.' So far he seems to think sailors and missionaries have carried little to the barbarous nations which have come under his notice, but disease, starvation and death. It is the old story of civilization, who, whenever she goes to heathen nations, carries her eternally conflicting implements—rum and religion. Mr. Melville's book is full of things strange and queer to the ears of Broadway and Chestnut street. If the truth about savage nations were not always a little stranger than civilized fiction can be, we should sometimes be inclined to compliment him for his strength in drawing the long bow of travelers; but his descriptions are doubtless transcripts of facts, not imagination, sounding as they do, 'as bad as truth.' Those who desire a 'Peep at Polynesian Life,' had better by all means obtain his work.

[1] *Con amore:* with affection.

14. Unsigned notice, *United States Magazine and Democratic Review*

May 1846, n.s. xviii, 399

These volumes are perhaps of the most interesting of Wiley & Putnam's deservedly popular 'Library of American Books.' The adventures are of a youth in the romantic islands of the Pacific Ocean, among a strange race of beings, whose manners and modes of life are by no means familiar to us. The scenes, described with peculiar animation and vivacity, are of a description that must task the credulity of most plain matter of fact people; yet they are without doubt faithfully sketched, and afford evidence of 'how little half the world knows how the other half lives.' The fairy vales of the Marquesas are represented as presenting all that nature and a most favored clime can contribute to the happiness and enjoyment of man, and inhabited by a primitive race with whom the intercourse of the author appears to have been on the best possible terms. The volumes are of a most amusing and interesting description.

15. Gilbert Abbott à Becket, unsigned lampoon, *Almanack of the Month*

June 1846, i, 368–9

À Becket (1811–56), English playwright and humorist long associated with *Punch*, was editor of the *Almanack*. This piece appeared in the 'Literary Sessions' section.

Alleged Forgery.—An individual who gave the name of Herman Melville was brought up on a charge of having forged several valuable documents relative to the Marquesas, in which he described himself to have been formerly resident. A good deal of conflicting evidence was brought forward on both sides, and it was obvious that whether the papers were forgeries or not, the talent and ingenuity of Herman Melville were of themselves sufficient to recommend him very favourably to a literary tribunal. In the course of the trial, it was suggested that as it would occupy too much of his honour's time to set out the whole of the disputed matter in the pleadings, the jury should take it home to read at their leisure. It was ultimately agreed that the matter should be referred to the superior court of Public Opinion, with a strong recommendation that every one being a member of that tribunal should read the whole of the alleged forgeries without missing a word. The impression was decidedly favourable to Mr. Herman Melville, and though no verdict has been come to upon the question of forgery, he has excited the greatest interest, and is received every where with the most cordial welcome.

16. William Oland Bourne, from an unsigned article, 'Typee: the Traducers of Missions,' *Christian Parlor Magazine*

July 1846, iii, 74–83

Bourne (1819–1901), a New York educator, was a close friend of Horace Greeley. A member of the Reformed Church, he defended the missionaries against what he saw as attacks by Melville in *Typee* and *Omoo*. The review of *Typee* was carried in a magazine designed by its editor, the Reverend Darius Mead, to combat the irreligious and immoral literature of the day. In sections deleted here Bourne quotes from various authorities on the South Seas to prove Melville wrong in his facts and to rebuke his 'flagrant outrages against civilization, and particularly the missionary work.' Bourne also denigrated Melville's character and veracity in a letter to Greeley that the editor published in his New York *Tribune* on 2 October 1847 and in a review of *Omoo* in the New Haven, Conn., *New Englander*, another religious periodical.

An apotheosis of barbarism! A panegyric on cannibal delights! An apostrophe to the spirit of savage felicity! Such are the exclamations instinctively springing from our lips as we close a book entitled *Typee: a Residence in the Marquesas*, lately published in Wiley & Putnam's interesting 'Library of American Books.' It is even so, reader! A work coming from the press of one of the first houses in this country, and published simultaneously by the same house in London, gemmed with enthusiastic descriptions of the innocent felicity of a savage tribe—tinselled with ornate pencillings of cannibal enjoyments—drawing frequent contrasts between the disadvantages and miseries of civilization, and the uninterrupted paradisaical bliss of a tribe which has traced in ominous characters of blood on the outer battlements of its natural fortresses of rock and mountain that omnipotent and talismanic 'TABU.'

We do not purpose in our examination of this book to enter into an analysis of its contents, its literary execution, or its claims to fidelity in the general description it gives of the people among whom our author resided during a period of some four months. Such a 'review' belongs properly to the acknowledged critical journals of the day, and would occupy far more space than we can appropriate to such a task. Nevertheless, we shall attempt to canvass some of its statements, wherein the cause of MISSIONS is assailed, with a pertinacity of misrepresentation and degree of *hatred*, which can only entitle the perpetrator to the just claim of traducer. We know what we are saying when we use these terms; we have read this book word by word; we have studied it carefully with reference to these very points, for to all that appertains to the missionary work we are sensitively alive; and were gladdened when we first saw it, with the prospect of learning something more from an impartial source concerning the practical operations of the missionary enterprise in that interesting region of the earth known as POLYNESIA. But we were soon disappointed; instead of a calm and unbiassed view, we have on every occasion a tissue of misrepresentation, and detraction of the labors of the devoted men and women who have exiled themselves for the purpose of carrying the blessings of the gospel to some of the most degraded and benighted children of Adam—who have been debased from the spiritual 'image and likeness' of their God to naked and roving savages; and who, in the wildness of their character and the helplessness of their social condition, are but little exalted above the 'brutes that perish.' . . .

The book whose title we have given may be called a respectable publication. The author seems to possess a cultivated taste and a fair education, but a deficient reading, and to this latter cause we assign many of his errors of general fact, as well as gross misstatements concerning the missionaries. With a lively imagination and a good and often graceful description, together with a somewhat happy strain of narrative, he has written an attractive history of personal adventure and unwilling *abandon* among the happy and sequestered Typees.

Come, oh celestial Spirit of Primitive Bliss! and waft me on thy golden pinions to the lovely abodes of the Typeeans! Bear me, oh genial spirit of unrefined progression, to the eternal landmarks of thy tabued groves! Waft me, benignant genius of undisturbed repose, to the overhanging peaks of thy untainted solitudes, where the dulcet strains of an uncaring minstrel shall thrill the sighing spirit with the newer life of a 'healthful physical enjoyment!' Come, oh yearning soul of the angelic FAYAWAY! let me henceforth be the chosen partner of thy tabued pleasures! let me bask beneath the mild ray of thine azure eye, and repose on the swelling oval of thy graceful form! No lingering love for the griefs of a civilized home shall tempt *me* to leave thy presence! no profane desires for the pains and miseries of these pent-up cities, and sin-cursed streets, and fashion-worshipping crowds, shall distract my sighing heart, and cause me to leave thee weeping amid the dashing waters of thine entrancing abode. With thee let me sport on the mirror-surface of thy sacred waters, and ramble beneath the refreshing shades of the cocoa and the palm! No recreant will I be to thy matchless love—no reckless fugitive from thy twining arms! So let me rest, and no palaces of earth, or lands of other names and customs more refined, shall tempt me to flee thy loved abodes!

We have remarked that this is a respectable book, but yet we have doubted whether it were worth a notice. To give circulation to such statements as our author makes may seem unwise, but as extracts from it of the nature we condemn are obtaining a channel through the public journals, we have determined to do our part in the work of making him known to the public. Although ordinarily we should not have regarded it as being worth an extended notice, we think the mode of its publication and the rank it holds, deserve a passing remark. In the first place it is dedicated to Hon. LEMUEL SHAW, *Chief Justice of Massachusetts*; it is published by WILEY & PUTNAM, in *New York* and *London*; and it is permanently lettered XIII. and XIV. in their *Library of American Books.* These considerations serve, then, to give the book a respectability and an influence which it could not have without them, and without which we should probably have passed it by.

Before proceeding to our investigation of his statements concerning the missionaries, we remark of the book generally: 1. It is filled with the most palpable and absurd contradictions; 2. These contradictions are so carelessly put together as to occur in consecutive paragraphs; 3. It is throughout laudatory of the innocence and freedom from care of the barbarians of the South Seas, particularly the Marquesans; 4. It compares their condition with civilized society as being the more desirable of the two; 5. It either excuses and wilfully palliates the cannibalism and savage vices of the Polynesians, or is guilty of as great a crime in such a writer, that of ignorance of his subject; and, 6. It is redundant with bitter charges against the missionaries, piles obloquy upon their labor and its results, and broadly accuses them of being the cause of the vice, misery, destitution, and unhappiness of the Polynesians wherever they have penetrated.

Brevity requires us to keep close to the point indicated in the title of our article, or we could furnish numerous extracts to justify the charges. . . .

We are inclined to doubt seriously whether our author ever saw the Marquesas; or if he did, whether he ever resided among the Typees; or, if he did, whether this book is not a sort of romantic satire at the expense of the poor savages . . . .

The worst feature of the book is the undisguised attempt to decry the missionary work in its every feature. . . .

Some of our readers will perhaps be surprised at our review of *Typee: or Residence in the Marquesas*. It is matter of surprise to us that such a work could have obtained the name of LEMUEL SHAW, and such a press as that of WILEY & PUTNAM. The author manifests a palpable ignorance in regard to every question of interest, and redeems that feature by laying his tribute upon the altar of cannibal felicity and barbaric society. He looks at the savage life with a captivated eye, and seals his approbation with a constant phrenzy to be freed from this happy vale—being in almost daily fear of finding himself hashed in the most approved style of Typee epicurean rites, or tenderly roasted and served up in calabashes for 'the regal and noble Mehevi' and his chiefs!

We have borne with the pretensions of this book as though it were a narrative of real events. It may be, and likely is, though somewhat highly colored. But whether true or false, the real or pseudonymic author deserves a pointed and severe rebuke for his flagrant outrages against civilization, and particularly the missionary work. The abuse he heaps upon the latter belongs to the vagabonds, fugitives, convicts, and deserters of every grade—and there let it rest. We have meditated nothing in a spirit of harshness or 'bigotry.' We have sought only to present the other side of the case to the public, with the hope of rendering at least a little service to the cause of truth; while we regret that a book possessed of such high merit in other respects, should have been made the vehicle of so many prejudiced misstatements concerning missions.

We purpose on some future occasion to take a view of the present state of the missionary work, and what is needed to make it more efficient and exceptionless than it is, and shall endeavor to give every side a fair hearing. We shall probably give Typee a glance among the authorities, as a specimen of that genus of writers whose poetry and poetic feelings lead them to admire only what is savage, and condemn, under assumed pretexts, the ripening fruit of the gospel of Christ. The author having anticipated and challenged investigation, will doubtless duly appreciate our pains-taking in comparing his statements with the contemporaneous reports of Capt. Wilkes and other authorities.

OMOO

1847

17. Unsigned notice, London *Britannia*

10 April 1847, 229–30

The reviewer discusses *Omoo* and two other recent books in Murray's Home and Colonial Library under 'Literary Notices.'

. . .—*Omoo, or, Adventures in the South Seas,* relates the experience of an American seaman in the isles of the Pacific, Omoo in the dialect of the Marquesas signifying a wanderer from one island to another. The writer, without being a copyist, has caught the spirit of Cooper's nautical style; and by a free bold style of description, and perhaps some romantic licence in dealing with facts, gives great animation to his pages. His notices of Tahiti are among the latest published. They are melancholy enough; the natives, it appears, will soon become extinct; they are in the most deplorable state, and fast perishing from disease. In 1777 Cook estimated the population of the island at two hundred thousand; four or five years ago the number was reduced to nine thousand. They are in that state, it is said, 'where all that is corrupt in barbarism and civilization unite, to the exclusion of the virtues of either state.'

18. From an unsigned review, *Spectator*

10 April 1847, 351–2

Unlike most sequels, *Omoo*, or 'a narrative of Adventures in the South Seas,' is equal to its predecessor. There are not so many unusual hardships, and dangerous but necessary gymnastics, as in the hungry wanderings of Melville and his companion Toby among the mountains of Nukuheva; nor such elaborate pictures of the daily life and manners of the unsophisticated Polynesians as were furnished by the residence of the adventurers in the valley of the Typees. Neither is there the same novelty of subject in *Omoo* as there was in *Typee*. Mr. Dana and some imitators have painted nautical life and character as seen from the foremastman's point of view, and many writers have described the inhabitants of the different Polynesian Islands *au naturel*, and in their various aspects of civilization, or as our author would say, their simple and corrupted nature. Still, from circumstances, and the position in which its writer was placed, *Omoo* has sufficient freshness; as it derives interest from his fluent vivacious style, and a natural aptitude for describing a scene or telling a story. It is probable, however, that neither scene nor story suffers at his hands from want of embellishment.

The leading subjects of *Omoo* are threefold,—first, life and character on board an old ill-found colonial vessel, scantily and badly manned, where needy or unprincipled speculators risk their own property, and the lives of such people as they can pick up, in a game with the odds, it would seem, greatly against them. Secondly, adventures at Tahiti (the Otaheite of Cook); where the crew carried the vessel into the harbour, distinctly refused to do duty, were taken on board a French frigate, and ironed, under the requisition of Mr. Consul Wilson, the *locum tenens*[1] of the notorious Pritchard, and, though subsequently released from this custody, were put into a prison on shore. Thirdly, the adventures of Melville and a companion, when they went away by night from a sort of free custody, to take service with a couple of runaway sailors, who had established a 'plantation' on the neighbouring island of Imeeo; with their excursions about this latter place, till Melville finally shipped on board an American whaler.

[1] *Locum tenens:* holding place.

There is some adventure in the volume, with a good many sketches of life and nature at the Society Islands, as well as a comparison between the past and present state of the Polynesians, and an estimate of the results of missionary exertion. The true characteristic of the book, however, is its nautical pictures, and the glimpses it gives of the strange characters that are to be found scattered over the South Seas. The outcasts of all nations would seem to congregate there. The little law anywhere, its total absence in some of the islands, the readiness with which a subsistence may be procured, and the *dolce far niente*[2] indulged in a climate where fuel and clothes may both be dispensed with, are all attractions to the runaway convict or the broken-down adventurer. The long voyage, hard living, and laborious service of the sperm whale-fishery, naturally induce seamen to desert from a harsh captain in an ill-provisioned ship, especially as the number of these whalers gives a man an opportunity, or at least a good chance, of quitting any place after a few months' residence, by engaging for a limited voyage in a vessel short of hands. In such a congregation the straitlacedness of a conventicle or a Quaker's meeting is not to be looked for; and deeds of ruffianism and brutality must be perpetrated, when such men are excited by liquor, passion, or opposition. Yet it seems wonderful what a sense of right and wrong obtains among them towards Europeans; and if they do not extend the same feeling to the natives, it seems owing to ignorance, and the example of their superiors: nor indeed has this catholic morality long prevailed even in England, as it does not yet in many nations of Europe. Little ill-treatment of the natives by the sailor or the outcast, however, appears either in Dana or Melville; and perhaps little takes place, unless in a brawl. Polynesian hospitality satisfies their wants; the general licentiousness gratifies their passions; and they lead an easy and uncontrolled life, removed from all temptation which requires violence or crime to indulge in. . . .

. . . the character of the composition . . . is clear, vivacious, and full of matter. Melville's descriptions not only convey distinctly what he wishes to present, but they abound in subordinate or incidental pictures respecting the whole of the life described. As in *Typee*, there are a few free passages, that might as well have been omitted.

[2] *Dolce far niente:* sweet leisure.

19. Unsigned notice, *John Bull*

17 April 1847, 248

They who have read the *Residence in the Marquesas Islands* will take up the present work with expectations not easily to be satisfied; but we can promise all such that whatever their expectations may be, they will experience no disappointment. It is, in fact, a continuation of the former volume, commencing with the escape of the author from Typee, and narrating his subsequent adventures in the South Seas until his return to the United States. Nothing can exceed the interest which Mr. Melville throws into his narrative; an interest which arises mainly from two causes, the clearness and simplicity of his style, and the utter absence of all approach to prolixity. He dwells upon no subject long enough to exhaust it; and yet his rapidity is never at the expense of sufficient fulness to place every subject distinctly before the reader. When there is occasion, too, he is as sly, humorous, and pungent as need be. He seems somewhat apprehensive, indeed, that his comic descriptions may be misinterpreted, for in the Preface he says, 'should a little jocoseness be shown upon some curious traits of the Tahitians, it proceeds from no intention to ridicule; things are merely described as, from their entire novelty, they first struck an unbiassed observer.' At Tahiti the author resided for a considerable period, and his account of the island, of the natives, of the proceedings of the French, and of the conduct of the missionaries (whom he is not inclined to spare), form by far the most valuable and interesting portions of the work. Upon the last mentioned subject he asserts that an 'earnest desire for truth and good' has been his great inducement for mentioning the evils which he has unveiled; while another object has been to give a '*familiar* account of the present condition of the converted Polynesians.' The title of the work (*Omoo*) is borrowed from the dialect of the Marquesas Islands, where, among other uses, the word signifies a rover, or rather, a person wandering from one island to another. . . .

20. From an unsigned review, London *People's Journal*

17 April 1847, 223–4

There seems to be springing up in the literary world a new and very interesting class of authors; consisting of men, who, led on by a romantic love of adventure, and an inquisitive spirit, plunge themselves into the roughest of life's paths, taking cheerfully their share in the hardest, and most unromantic work; submitting to the most painful privations; and harder still, to the most bitter personal humiliations; making danger their daily companion and helpmate; and who, after experiencing themselves what life is in the track they have followed, possess the skill to describe it in the freshest and most vivid colours to others. And such, indeed, should be the principle through all literature. Experience—whether the experience be of the outer or the inner world—whether it be what a man has seen, or done, or thought, is the only thing worth listening to—the only valid plea for a man's asking the world of readers to listen to him.

Hermann Melville, if that indeed be his true name, is an American, who, in 1842, visited the Marquesas Islands, as a sailor before the mast, in an American ship, brought thither by the attractions of the sperm whale fishery. He left his ship on reaching the island of Nukuheva, and wandered about until he came into the valley of Typee. Here, among a tribe of primitive savages, he was detained in a kind of pleasant captivity for about four months. He was relieved by the captain of a vessel that had anchored in the neighbourhood; and the present volume describes his reception in the ship, his comrades, their adventures, ending in a kind of mutiny, and in a party of the crew quitting the vessel (at first as prisoners) at Tahiti, which gave Hermann Melville a fresh opportunity of wandering about from island to island, and making himself acquainted with the people who have of late engaged so much attention in England, on account of the intrigues of the French and English residents to obtain for their respective nations the greater amount of influence over the Queen Pomare, and through her, over her subjects and the country generally.

It would be difficult to imagine a man better fitted to describe the impressions such a life and such scenes are calculated to call forth, than the author of *Omoo*. Every variety of character, and scene, and incident, he studies and describes with equal gusto. Among his characters, perhaps the medical man, 'Doctor Long Ghost,' is the most truly characteristic both of the individual, and of a class common in all those remote parts of the world, where men either seek to recruit the fortunes and the reputation that have been sacrificed at home, or to plunge still deeper into the reckless, desperate, licentious courses, that first seduced them from the ordinary and honourable path. . . .

21. Walt Whitman, unsigned notice, Brooklyn, New York, *Daily Eagle*

5 May 1847

Whitman (1819–92) and Melville, so far as is known, never met, nor is there any known commentary on each other's work besides this notice and possibly a brief notice of *Typee* that has been attributed to Whitman (see *Log*, p. 211). The notice of *Omoo* appeared while Whitman was editor of the *Daily Eagle*.

Omoo, the new work (Harpers, pub.) by Mr. Melville, author of *Typee*, affords two well printed volumes of the most readable sort of reading. The question whether these stories be authentic or not has, of course, not so much to do with their interest. One can revel in such richly good natured style, if nothing else. We therefore recommend this 'narrative of adventures in the south seas,' as thorough entertainment—not so light as to be tossed aside for its flippancy, nor so profound as to be tiresome. All books have their office—and this a very side one.

22. Charles Gordon Greene, unsigned notice, Boston *Post*

5 May 1847

Greene (1804–86), editor of the *Post* from 1831 to 1875, was active in Democratic party politics from as early as 1827 when the Philadelphia *National Palladium*, which he edited, was the first daily newspaper in Pennsylvania to support the presidential candidacy of Andrew Jackson. Greene knew Melville's older brother, Gansevoort, who was an advocate of President Polk.

The readers of *Typee* will need no invitation to read *Omoo*, in spite of its heathenish and *cattle-ish* appellation, which we are told signifies a 'rover' in the Tahitian language. Whether or not Mr Melville has ever visited the places which he describes, it is unnecessary to discuss, but if he have not, his books are worthy a place with Robinson Crusoe and Gulliver. If he have, it must be owned that he has the descriptive power in greater abundance than any traveller of the age. That *all* in his book is actually true we can hardly believe, but he imparts a great deal of information tallying with the reports of former voyagers, and in addition, gives an array of characters as interesting as those of romance with acuteness and power. *Omoo* pictures the life of a rover in a whale ship and on the Society Islands for the space of several months. Columns on columns of pleasant extracts might be given, but we are forced to refer our readers to the volumes themselves. They will find them filled with stirring incident and beautiful description, with here and there a touch of the genuine comic. The long doctor is an actual creation, while the Tahitian girls are sprites of fun, softness and beauty. One wishes that Mr Melville had not been quite so chary of relating his own adventures with the fair Tahitians. We hope his next book may have a Christian title.

23. Unsigned notice, New York *Albion*

8 May 1847, 228

A new work by the author of *Typee* will find its way into the hands of every reader. Mr. Melville has more than sustained his widely spread reputation in these volumes. Treating as they do on familiar topics connected with Otaheite, that we had thought had been exhausted by other authors, we are agreeably delighted to find so much of what is positively new in *Omoo*. There is a freshness and novelty in the graphic sketches of society as it now exists in these islands, that we look for in vain in the writings of other travellers. Mr. Melville contrives to throw around his personal adventures all the interest and charm of fictitious narrative. *Omoo* and *Typee* are actually delightful romances of real life, embellished with powers of description, and a graphic skill of hitting off characters little inferior to the highest order of novelist and romance writers.

24. Charles Fenno Hoffman, from an unsigned review, New York *Literary World*

8 May 1847, 319–21

Hoffman took over as editor of the *Literary World* with this issue, replacing Evert Duyckinck until October of the following year.

Few American books have awakened the lively interest excited by Mr Melville's unique and delightful volumes on Typee. To many, the theme was entirely new; to others, Commodore Porter's once famed, and now nearly forgotten journal, had long since commended it, and they seized upon Mr. Melville's book with the avidity that children take up any new volume which purports to be a continuation of *Robinson Crusoe*. In the city of New York, especially, from which the three or four of Porter's surviving officers hailed originally, Typee was remembered in years far back as the theme of many a dinner-table yarn, when men used to tell longer and *stronger* stories over their Madeira than is now the fashion among modern sherry drinkers. And while the world abroad were showing their acuteness in detecting Mr. Melville as a veteran bookmaker, who, being master of a brilliant style, had ingeniously fashioned a most readable piece of Munchausenism while sitting in his library, his work was at once recognised as a genuine narrative in the city where it was published.

The close of his volumes on Typee, it may be remembered, left Mr. Melville just gaining the deck of a vessel which 'hove to' at the mouth of the harbor to aid his escape. The present narrative opens with his reception on board the barque Julia, and reveals to the reader a fresh series of adventures in the South Seas; which are related with all the animation, the picturesqueness, and felicity of style which commend his first writings to a second reading, even after curiosity is satisfied by tracing out the singularity of his story.

In the Julia, though placed at once among other seamen in the forecastle, the state of his health exempted him from duty for a season; and here a capital character turns up as his messmate, who is thus described.

[quotes from chapter 2, 'All English whalemen' to 'an absolute godsend.']

With this worthy we have other characters associated, who are drawn with a pencil of equal vigor; and perhaps the portion of these volumes which sets off the author's literary talents in the strongest light is that relating to the open ocean, when, with no external objects to vary the monotony of a portion of the cruise, his ship scenes are made full of interest and attraction, by the graphic humor with which he paints an interior . . . .

When painting the scenery of the shore, Catherwood's 'Bay of Islands' will doubtless recur to all who enjoyed a sight of that magnificent panorama, so vivid are the author's descriptions of nature. . . .

Not less refreshing are the descriptions of tropical vegetation; the regal 'Ati' with its massive trunk, and broad laurel-shaped leaves; and the beautiful, flowering 'Hotoo,' with its pyramid of shining leaves, diversified with numberless small white blossoms; and the fruits profuse and delicious; red ripe avees; guavas, with the shadows of their crimson pulp flushing through a transparent skin; oranges of scarlet freshness, tinged on the sunny side to a berry brown; fat bananas, in their buff jackets of mellowness; and 'great jolly melons, which rolled about in very portliness. All ruddy, and ripe, and round—bursting with the good cheer of the tropical soil whence they sprang.' Then, too, the hazel-eyed nymphs, so beautiful-limbed, in their wavy motions, and fresh and bright as the blossoms of their own luxuriant clime; but Mr. Melville's limning needs no encouragement on this score—and we turn from this rural carnival of wild nature to the more sober scenes where Christianity begins to give a different interest to the ever-changing masque.

[quotes chapter 44, complete]

Scenes not unsimilar to these Mr. Melville might have witnessed in many a country church within the realms of civilization, which seems to have effected little more among these islanders than giving them our absurdities, as well as our vices and maladies. . . .

25. Unsigned review, New York *Evening Mirror*

21 May 1847

Under the heading 'Polynesian Life' the reviewer discusses both *Typee* and *Omoo*.

Many doubts have been expressed as to the truth of Mr. Melville's revelations of Polynesian life. Such as have assumed a tangible form in the literary journals, are based upon the assumption that the adventures narrated are of too marvellous and extraordinary a character to be of actual occurence. They are incredible only because novel to the reading public.— The absurdity of such objections is sufficiently proved by incidents in the career of almost every sailor who has spent a few years in the Pacific. What is there incredible in Melville's adventures? The facts as stated by the author are simply these: He visits the Marquesas in a whaler. At the port of Nukuheva he deserts with a shipmate on account of the ill treatment, and makes his way over the mountains to the valley of Typee. In this wild ramble, occupying five or six days, he endures much suffering from hunger and thirst, and after a reasonable amount of jumping and climbing, falls into the hands of a very hospitable set of barbarians—a tribe of savage gentlemen, who, knowing nothing of the vices of civilized life, live in a state of primitive simplicity, very much at their ease, and give our adventurer many hints by which more polished nations might profit. So far, not only are the incidents probable, but we have good reason to know that perhaps a third of the crew of every Pacific whaler, can testify from practical experience, to twenty similar desertions and escapes. Comparatively few cases of the kind reach the public ear, because every sailor who deserts from a whale-ship, preferring land-savages to sea-savages, is not a genius or the son of a genius. But what are we to think of the little paradise in savagedom—the happy valley, with its Fayaways, and Mehevis, and Kory-Korys! Is it possible such a race of beings inhabit our sublunary sphere? Why, for that matter, we see either nothing impossible or improbable in it. Very far, indeed, from being purely etherial are these curious people; they are carnal enough, in all conscience. The old King and his retainers are strongly suspected of devouring their neighbors, and the author's lady-love (a delicious young creature) eats raw fish. If they are mere imaginary personages, 'woven from beams of light,' it must be admitted that they have a most extraordinary relish for substantial diet. More than half the beauties of a thousand similar valleys and scenes not less enchanting, and many striking peculiarities of a native character, are lost to the ordinary adventurer, and we are not disposed to doubt Mr. Melville's word because he describes what fell under his observation in a style so picturesque and fascinating.

Robert Drury's narrative of a shipwreck in the Mozambique Channel, and subsequent captivity and wonderful adventures in the interior of Madagascar, is not doubted. He was an uneducated sailor and related his adventures in the homely language of an unlettered man, and obtained credit for veracity—though Heaven knows, compared with our Polynesian adventurer, he was a downright Munchausen. Captain Little, who spent twenty years at sea, relates in his *Sketches of Ocean*

Life, instances of captivity among the savage islanders of the Pacific, far more extraordinary than anything in these volumes—yet, being an uneducated man and a member of the Church, he is believed. The survivors of the crew of a New Bedford whaler, wrecked on Lord North's island, have given, in a little work published a few years since, a thrilling account of captivity and adventures on that island, which may in fact be considered miraculous—but it is not doubted by those who have read it, because it is very roughly written. We might multiply examples, but we are not so Quixotic as to undertake a serious crusade against windmills. The truth of the matter is, *Typee* is an extraordinary book, only because it is written in a most brilliant and captivating style. Gentlemen who have visited the Marquesas and Society Islands have assured us personally that Melville's description of the natives, their manners and customs, and the progress of civilization in that interesting region, are strictly and vividly accurate.—An officer attached to the frigate Brandywine in 1845, when she touched at Tahiti, declared within our hearing that in reading *Omoo* he actually imagined himself on the spot—so graphic are the sketches of life and scenery interspersed throughout that work.

It is not altogether the truthfulness of these sketches, however, that constitutes their great charm—a daguerreotype could be merely accurate; it is the warmth, the tropical luxuriance, the genial flow of humor and good-nature—the happy enthusiasm, gushing like a stream of mellow sunshine from the author's heart—all these, and a thousand nameless beauties of tone and sentiment, are the captivating ingredients of *Omoo*. Who can follow our young adventurer in his wanderings through those quiet valleys and leafy glens, and listen to his pleasant discourse, without feeling completely regenerated? Ushered gradually into a world of primitive beauties, enveloped in a spell of delicious enchantment, humanized and spiritualized at the same time—the reader unconsciously yields to the charm and finds himself a dreamy inhabitant of the sunny South Sea Isles. Cold, indeed, must be his heart, if it does not inspire him to grasp the hand of his roving cicerone in the very intensity of right-down cordial good-fellowship. And as for Dr. Long Ghost—if you don't see him, and hear him and *feel* him through every fibre of your mortal body—why, all we can say is, you ought to be condemned to read Wilkes' *Narrative*.

Not even the grand dignitary of the quarter-deck, though he looks so sublime in his sultanic mightiness of power,—not even he, who makes you quake as you read of him, can compare with you in point of independence. *You* have no intricate problems in Bowditch to work out; no impossible observations to take in hazy weather; no crazy instruments with distracting angles to adjust; no brain-distracting questions in nautical jurisprudence to decide; no visions of grumbling owners to haunt you for every generous impulse; no shadowy goblins of drowsy mates, false chronometers, coral-reefs, typhoons, and flying Dutchmen to startle you from your midnight slumbers. All is easy sailing and fine weather to you. The wide world is open to you with a polite invitation to live at your ease. Make yourself comfortable, therefore, and if you are violently moved by the spirit of adventure, rob your neighbor's hen-roost and request the nearest magistrate to place you in solitary confinement.

Mr. Melville's remarks on the manner in which the Missionary system is conducted in Tahiti and other islands of the South Seas are deserving of serious consideration. Here we have the testimony of a candid and impartial witness—one who while friendly to the cause, is not impelled by a blind fanaticism to magnify the beneficial results which have sprung from it.—Indeed, he has given us in a familiar style a greater amount of reliable information on this subject than is contained in all the Missionary works ever palmed off upon the credulity of the public. The moderation and forbearance with which he treats of clerical despotism and evangelical tyranny, cannot fail to produce a deep impression on the minds of all reasonable men. Such testimony, bearing intrinsic evidence of candor and impartiality, will for that very reason be unpalatable to the mass of our church-bigots, who regard these things as too sacred to be placed in the category of worldly matters. It is not a question to be classed with human imperfections and ordinary realities. Of course Mr. Melville can no longer claim to be a Christian—he has taken the part of the poor savage, and questioned the propriety of scourging him into the traces of fat Missionary ladies and Christianity—and is therefore an Atheist. Thus, having proved him, out of his own mouth, to be an enemy of religion, because he is opposed to evangelizing the natives into draught horses and beasts of burden, the corollary is irresistible—is he entitled to credit? Assuredly not! This summary mode of putting down a well authenticated fact, will not, however, satisfy those who are so wicked as to exercise the gift of reason. To say the least of it, the established system of Christianizing the heathen, places him in a very embarrassing situation. The French, for instance, send three Catholic priests to Tahiti. These sleek and oily gentlemen (who while worshipping God, contrive to devote a little private worship to their creature comforts)—these devout soldiers of Zion, tell the benighted natives they must bow down and worship the true cross or a graven image of the Virgin as the case may be, or their soul will be lost. Ministers of other denominations warn the dusky sinners, in tones of thunder, to abandon their pagan idols and heathenish rites or they cannot be saved. Thus, they are assured of perdition whichever way they go; they must be lost under any circumstances. What difference can the poor natives see between idol-worship of one kind and idol-worship of another—man-worship of one kind and man-worship of another. It too often happens that the prostitution of the natives is indirectly made as source of revenue to the clerical establishment; and although this charge has been denied, it is none the less true on that account. Nearly every intelligent traveller who has visited the islands of the Pacific bears verbal testimony to the fact, though few have the hardihood to commit their views to print. It is always a thankless task to expose abuses of this kind. The American public have become so accustomed to one side of the question, that the bare intimation of another is an outrage not to be tolerated. In sober truth, these deluded philanthropists have, by deluding others, built up an immense institution, requiring annually several hundred thousand dollars to support it; and now they are deluding the natives with the idea that it is all for *their* good. This talk about glorious revivals among the heathens, is the veriest nonsense that ever emanated from the muddled brains of madmen. A few ignorant islanders are harangued into a state of mere animal phrenzy, frightened into the grossest absurdities, and finally reduced to a state of slavery—and all this is heralded as a grand triumph of religion! Really it is quite humiliating enough that such a state of things should prevail in our own civilized country; we are sorry to see the unoffending natives imposed upon.—Let them be taught something that they can understand, and civilized before they are beset with mysteries which an educated man can but very imperfectly comprehend. Let the sailors who visit their ports be civilized, and it will be ample time, when all this is effected, to enlighten the natives on spiritual matters.

This subject reminds us of an anecdote related by Dubois, a French priest, who spent many years in the India Mission—quite as good authority as any of the same profession. When the American Missionaries first commenced their labors in a certain part of India Proper, they encountered great difficulty in making converts; and so slow was their progress that they seldom had a triumph to boast of in the Home organ. An old sea-captain who understood the native character, learning the disheartening state of affairs went to the Missionaries and gave them a plan by which they converted the natives at an extraordinary rate. A barrel of Sirack was placed in a convenient place, and the inhabitants were informed that every man who listened to a sermon would receive a dram at the conclusion. They soon flocked in by dozens, and many of them joined the church on condition that they should receive a dram every day. The design of the Missionaries was to dispense with the intoxicating potations, as soon as the sermons should produce an effect, but the natives when they lost their beloved Sirack, lost the moving spirit and became incorrigible backsliders.

In conclusion; to sum up our judgment of *Typee* and *Omoo*. We consider them, in a word, the best works on Polynesian life yet published, either in this country or England; and no work within the range of our nautical reading can compare with them in the spirit and vividness of their forecastle revelations.—There is a rolicking felicity, a hearty abandonment pervading throughout rather than in any particular instance, which is peculiarly characteristic of sailor-life in the midst of its privations; and this is most happily developed in *Omoo*. If you wish to read the details of forecastle life they are to be found in other works; but if you desire a vivid and masterly picture of a whale ship, inside and outside, fore and aft, with living, moving, wide-awake characters, full of fun and desperately mutinous, read *Omoo*. A perusal of *Typee* will sharpen your appetite for the repast in store for you. Both are published in the best style of type and paper.

26. Unsigned review, Washington, D.C., *National Intelligencer*

26 May 1847

On 28 May the *National Intelligencer* concluded its review by printing extracts from *Omoo*.

Although the age be a very impressible age, and civilization, worn out and *blazé* with its old dissipations, seems to seek, like a battered *roué*, counterfeit sensations, any pleasures but the genuine, and almost any thing so it be unexhausted and novel; and although, for no more critical reason than this, it runs after any literary anomaly, much as the crowds of all Paris rush to see and be delighted with the last monster or abortion of the Boulevards—the wild woman caught in a Hungarian forest; a live Feejee cannibal; a North American savage, from the remotest prairie, in his skins and paint, with the scalps about him and howling his war-song within hearing of Pasta and Lablache; or Tom Thumb, or the last grand juggler; and though, therefore, the learned transports of now-a-days be very frequent and very rapturous, few books, except the *Old Curiosity Shop*, or the *Course of Time*, or Alison's *History of Europe*, have, for a long time, more excited the easy enthusiasm of our times than that of which the present is the sequel—namely, Mr. MELVILLE's *Typee*. Certainly, Borrows's *Bible in Spain* and Warburton's (but is it his?) *Eothen* had much the same success and a charm quite akin: but *Typee* united, in no small degree, the imaginative cast of the first with the adventurous air of the second, and bore off the advantage over both in presenting us scenes still remoter from the life of coats, breeches, and fur hats. In a word, *Typee* was, we take it, an almost unmingled *Sea Romance* of lands, waters, and people, skilfully chosen to affect the fancy of a generation highly sensuous and wonder-loving, much-rejoicing in its refinement and its morality, but exceedingly content to be helped to an imaginary sojourn with barbarism and an ideal plunge into such a state of Nature as the loosest voluptuary may sigh for.

Of *Typee*, because appearing at that season (the close of the fall) when literature must, in our columns, yield to politics, we were not able to speak while it was fresh. It is, however, so strictly connected with the new volume before us, that we have no choice as to reverting to it, although no longer within our reach—so that we must confine ourselves to general terms in speaking of it.

Not possessing, and indeed hardly preferring, any claim to the character of a historic-descriptive performance, a regular survey of the physical or moral face of a region, we can hardly exact in it the proper merits of a Book of Travels: sober and full information, exactness, and even scrupulous attention to matter-of-fact in *all* that is told, are hardly to be required. It is, in a word, a thing written to please, not instruct: to please by a general conformity to fact; but to please chiefly, and with the license of some suppression and some embellishment—a license which, it strikes us, Mr. Melville has abundantly used, and without which he would, no doubt, have failed, just as much as St. Pierre would have done, if, instead of those two airy pastoralities over which everybody melts back into innocence and tenderness—his *Paul and Virginia*—he had applied himself to tracing, with the most perfect authenticity, the lazy and graceless childhood of two little French creoles in the Isle of Bourbon. Or, to take another instance, *Typee* is, we imagine, quite as true, in its particulars, as Sterne's *Sentimental Journey*; of the want of verity in which nobody ever thought of complaining, inasmuch as the fictions were such as Horace enjoins, 'agreeable to Nature,' and obviously more pleasing than unadorned truth could possibly have been rendered.

Among the critics of England (the earliest to applaud the production —which, indeed, first appeared there as part of Murray's 'Colonial Library') much debate seems to have been held upon this question, purely speculative as we take it to be, of the reality of the facts related in *Typee*. They all agree that the tale is a singularly agreeable one. Now, inasmuch as, to make it so, *fact* was always to be sacrificed to *effect*, and *probability* only to be observed as instrumental to the same main purpose, they should surely have seen that it was one of those works in which to create and sustain the illusion of truth, but by no means to tell it, is the business of an able writer—a business in which Mr. Melville has, in our opinion, shown himself a great adept, in *Typee*, if (whether from carelessness or a subject less capable of admitting invention *ad libitum*) only a considerable proficient in *Omoo*.

The French—that very skilful people in all the art of communicating with others—have it for a sort of axiom that 'there is nothing which you may not say to a man, provided you say it *politely*.' A like principle is so true of mere fact that it is difficult to say *what* people may not be made, by a certain charm in the telling, to credit as perfectly veracious. The trick is one not hard to explain, and, with *Typee* for an example, not difficult to understand. You begin with an air of the greatest simplicity and ingenuousness—just as Count Cagliostro and Mesmer (those masterly impostors) led you, by an obscure street and a very plain vestibule, into their palaces of wonder. Then, of a sudden, by a harmonious style and seducing images, you seize and captivate the senses—much as the Rosicrucians set at work the imagination of their initiates, by perfumes breathed around them, low sweet music from unseen instruments, and the fantastic strangeness of a great saloon, richly decorated and dimly lighted. Men's minds once agitated in this way, through unusual and bewitching sensations, you may proceed to play off upon them almost any jugglery you like. They are entranced and see no longer with the eyes of their common sense, but those of the fancy which you have opened—eyes which they the more easily believe, because they are not conscious of possessing them. This dreamy state, this temporary hallucination and ecstacy into which men may be thrown by certain mesmeric manipulations and passes of the style, followed up by a poetic playing-off of a whole crowd of intoxicating and dazzling ideas, is readily produced in children, whose fresher susceptibilities are easily made to act with force enough to get the better of their little judgments; and, next to them, it is facile in the ignorant (who are but tall children) and women, whose more nervous organization renders them prompt dupes of their own imaginations. We need scarcely add that which every body must have remarked, that as poetry, acting on the ears through its melodious cadences and on the other senses through its figurative and sensuous diction, excites the fancy much more than prose, with its limited resorts of sound and of picturesque language can do, so we can away with things in verse which would be incredible even in the best prose.

As to *Typee*, we certainly read it with just the same delight and much the same faith as we yielded, when some thirty years younger, to the most charming of fairy tales—in our own language, the 'Legends of the South of Ireland'—the 'Red Cup' and other German stories of Grimm; the delicious lies of Perrault and of Count Anthony Hamilton, (quite as witty perhaps as true, and certainly altogether as moral as his 'Memoirs of Grammont,' his brother-in-law.) The author (Mr. Melville, we mean) of course maintains the authenticity of all he has told: that is his business; and his friends stand by his invariable veracity: that is their duty; for, as we have already explained, the illusion of truth is necessary to the literary effect of such a work. Avow it a hoax, or even a sophistication of facts, a masquerade of reality, and the charm would be gone, except for folks like us, who, being fond of *Gulliver* and the *Arabian Nights*, and familiar with the court chroniclers of three or four successive Administrations near us, have learnt to read with very little necessity of believing. We perceive, certainly, that, with a very laudable ingenuity, (a continuation of the book being in view,) the proprietors or friends or author of *Typee* have fished up somewhere a live witness—no less than Toby himself, whilom supposed, in the narrative, to have been devoured by the Typees. But who will believe a thing any the more for Toby's swearing? What sailor will not stand up to the *yarns* of a messmate ashore? And, for that matter, who can say that this is the veritable (let alone the veracious) Toby? Where is the proof of his personal identity? For our part we cling to the story as written: we love to be persuaded that Toby *was* made a *rôti suffoqué* of, was *boucanisé à la Polynésienne.*[1] In a word, we stand out upon the want of identification, and urge what Hamlet, as quoted by Mrs. Malaprop, says of the matter in his soliloquy:

Toby, or not Toby? that is the question.

Seriously, however, we look upon the *Typee* as in sooth nothing but a very agreeable and fanciful sea-romance. Whether it was meant to be such, or written with the aid of certain raptures of the fancy which always seize some people when they relate what they have seen or heard, we do not pretend to say: but, in either case, the same poetic temperament, only voluntary in one case and involuntary in the other, is betokened. Clearly Mr. Melville has a great warmth and beauty of the imagination: to describe and relate as he does one must have that faculty which makes pictures in the mind—which recalls and re-embodies at pleasure all that has passed before the mind or the eyes, and at will 'raises a world of gayer tint and grace' out of every thing. To come more minutely, however, to the grounds of our incredulity, they are these:

There is a great poetic exaggeration in the height of cliffs and waterfalls and the depths of chasms, across which our fugitives make their way to the vale of Typee. Commodore Porter (see his cruise of the

[1] *Rôti suffoqué:* smothered roast; *boucanisé:* smoked.

Essex) took a considerable body of marines into the interior of the same island, and gives one not the smallest idea of his having encountered any very serious natural impediments to the march of armed bands of men. Then that tumbling over the sides of precipices, so judiciously practiced by Herman and Toby, as to light in the tops of palm trees, and thus merely break their fall instead of their necks, is a thing which has no possibility out of romance. A more enormous sailor's *yarn* has seldom been heard. Nor can one conceive it within the range of human folly that two unarmed mariners should voluntarily seek refuge from aboard ship, and for little else but a shore-frolick among a wild tribe, whom they supposed to be man-eaters. One is forced to conclude that such a residence could only be selected for an imaginary visit: that upon the frequented part of Nukahivah some vague account of such a quarter of the island had been collected, and that upon these reports and what the adventurer had seen of the rest of the land and its inhabitants the story was feigned. This supposition is to us greatly strengthened by the extreme thinness, scantiness, and indistinctness of the particulars which the narrative furnishes concerning the manners and customs of this secluded nook: they consist of nothing but a few traits, such as might be gathered or inferred from a slight acquaintance with any of the savages of inter-tropical Polynesia. It is like that case so skilfully made out by Mr. Laing in his *History of Scotland* against the authenticity of MacPherson's *Ossian*. The narrative poet (he argues) who writes in the midst of the acts and manners which he describes, necessarily animates his verse with their forms of life, their religious rites, their social usages, their political institutions, and all that. In Homer, for instance, every thing is the moving and speaking image of an actual people; and so of all other works of fiction, prose, or poetry, that belong to the times which they delineate. But *Ossian* offers no such identity and individuality: it exhibits nothing but the distant shadow of times imagined, not seen: scarcely a religious idea, and not a single religious observance, can be traced in it: as little, except that some of the hereos are styled kings, can you collect any notion of their mode of government: the women appear to possess but one single article of clothing—a veil; and the male costume nowhere consists of any thing but a helmet and a shield. Their eating and drinking are equally obscure: it is always 'the feast of shells;' and of their bill of fare you arrive at nothing further. Now, all these objections to the authenticity of *Ossian* are decisive; and it strikes us that they apply with almost equal force to *Typee*. Except the playing of the girls and children in their morning bath—a scene charmingly painted, but which might be beheld in any other Polynesian isle just as well as in Nukahivah—all has to us a most shadowy indistinctness: neither the domestic, nor the civil, nor the religious life presents any living or certain form. The little that one learns of the last of these in no manner agrees with Commodore Porter's account of the matter, if we at all remember that account. Finally: all the conduct of the natives towards him, both in his stay and at his escape, is involved in such mere mystery as appears to us the voluntary resort of the story-teller only, who chooses, by the vague horror of cannibalism, to keep to the last what young ladies and the magazines written for them entitle the 'thrilling interest' of the tale.

It will easily be seen that all we have thus urged implies to us nothing that does not leave *Typee* a literary performance of great merit and beauty. This repeated, by way of caution, it is time that we should proceed to the examination of the sequel of *Typee*—that is, the voyage and sea-haps which befall our wanderer, after his evasion of being cooked in Nukahivah and during his residence in Otaheite and other islands of the Elysian cluster.

In general, it bears the unexhausted characteristics of the same talent; but applied to incidents less congenial, because much less rarely offering scope for the grace and sweetness of fancy, the glow of wild nature and romance, which is almost every where flung over the previous adventures. These are, in great part, scenes of mess, either on deck or ashore, amidst a lawless and drunken crew, three-fourths of whom are plainly as mere scoundrels as

Ever scuttled ship or cut a throat;

so that their wild doings, bordering generally upon mutiny, sometimes on murder, and, in their mildest shape, licentious and reckless in the extreme, make up all the first half of the narrative. The second consists of the joint wanderings, in Otaheite and its neighbor islets, of Typee and his chum of the cruize, a sort of degraded sea-surgeon, whom his shipmates distinguish by the descriptive name of Doctor Long Ghost. Of his messmates, the author himself gives, near the outset, a general character which all that he tells of their subsequent conduct certainly justifies to the full:

The crews manning vessels like these are, for the most part, villains of all nations and dyes; picked up in the lawless ports of the Spanish Main and among the savages of the islands. Like galley-slaves, they are only to be governed by scourges and chains. Their officers go among them with dirk and pistol—concealed, but ready at a grasp. *Not a few of our own crew were men of this stamp.* (P. 30.)

It is a little singular, however, that, after such an account of the morals of this gang, Mr. Melville should go on to indicate, by all that he tells us of his *acts*, his co-operation with them—though sometimes but of a passive sort; his sympathy with their lawless deeds aboard and on shore, though sometimes related as if he condemned them. He really makes himself out to be very little better than they, except in point of education and intelligence. Why it has pleased Mr. Melville to paint himself in a semblance so bad and (as it must be) so untrue, we are totally unable to imagine. The elegance of his mind, the grace, beauty, sweetness of his fancy, bespeak refinement of the sentiments, cultivated affections, and every thing of morals and feeling that would harmonize the least with such brutal society; and yet, for some inconceivable reason, he chooses to represent himself as participating in a mutiny, as almost one of its ringleaders: they are on the verge of committing *one* murder, and every where show themselves to be such desperadoes as no man in his senses would league with in any thing that implied force; for any resort to that renders probable, upon resistance, bloodshed, and, in case of submission, every sort of excess and outrage. As for his friend, Doctor Long Ghost, who seems meant as little less than the hero of the tale, he appears to us, in all his conduct, a most unprincipled vagabond, hardly less witless than he is worthless. As an eccentric comrade in strolling about the Society Islands, in hunting wild cattle and hogs, or hiring themselves to labor with a view to get wages, but do no work, and all that, he may do very well for a strange figure in a fiction; but, as for presenting him to us either for admiration or amusement, it is out of the question; and, as a principal character, we must regard him as a complete failure.

These are some of the faults of the book as to the management of the subject. We reserve for another day what our readers will more enjoy—some of its beauties.

27. 'B.,' review, *National Anti-Slavery Standard*

27 May 1847, 207

The *Standard*, published in New York from 1840 to 1864, was the organ of the American Anti-Slavery Society.

Typee proved the most successful hit in book-making, since the publication of Stephens's first book of Travels. An English critic said it was 'Yankee all over.' By which he meant that it was entirely new, fresh, and devil-may-care; free from the dry, stale, and wearisome conventionalities of trained literature. It was a book of itself, not made up of pickings from other books, but from the personal observations and individualities of the author. This was enough to insure it popularity; but, in addition to this, it opened to the reading world views of a new existence, more novel and startling than any of the revelations of Swedenborg, in his *Heaven and Hell.* In truth, *Typee* resolved 'the great problem of the age,' and proved that happiness was not only possible without the aid of pastry cooks, lawyers, tailors, and clergymen, but that men could be happier without these excresences of civilization than with them. It proved another important fact, the most important of all facts for Americans, that Slavery is not, as Charles J. Ingersoll told Mrs. Maury, indigenous to the tropics, and, like mosquitoes, always most troublesome when the weather is hottest. It is true that the Typees eat their enemies, but then they do not eat them alive; they have the humanity to wait until their victims are dead before they begin to feast upon them. Here, we reverse the rule, and feed on each other while living. One dead enemy was sufficient to feast a whole tribe of Typees; but with us, a hundred slaves hardly suffice to furnish food for one Southern family. The Typee craunches the tendons and muscles of his dead enemy between his molars, but inflicts no pain upon him; but with us, the Calhouns, Clays, and Polks, feed daily upon the sweat, the tears, the groans, the anguished hearts and despairing sighs, of living men and women; they do not eat the insensible flesh of their dead slaves, but they lacerate it when alive with whips, and cauterize it with hot branding-irons. We would advise our readers who are sick at heart, from reading the daily reports of the murders committed by our army in Mexico; or of the inhuman cruelties of our slaveholders at the South; or of the daily outrages upon the rights of humanity practised by Christian judges and lawyers in our Halls of Justice, to turn for relief to the amiable savages of Typee, whose greatest cruelty consists in devouring the body of an enemy who has been killed in a hand-to-hand scuffle.

Omoo is a continuation of the author's adventures in the Pacific after he escaped from the valley of the Typees. It is written in the same free and jocular style as *Typee*, but it contains nothing so purely novel as some of the scenes recorded in that pleasant and bewitching volume. The sketches of sea-life and character, are very lively and accurate, and the insight which it gives of the state of society in the half-Christianized islands of the Pacific, entertaining and instructive. Mr. Melville has had the misfortune to encounter the same kind of doubters, who attempted to discredit the narratives of Bruce, but we have found nothing in his volumes that contradicts or transcends the many oral and written accounts we have received from travellers in that part of the world which he visited.

28. John Wilson, from an unsigned review, *Blackwood's Edinburgh Magazine*

June 1847, lxi, 754–67

Wilson (1785–1854), who wrote under the pseudonym of 'Christopher North,' was a Scottish author and professor of Moral Philosophy at the University of Edinburgh. He began contributing to *Blackwood's* in 1817, and his articles were numerous and influential, often quoted or reprinted in American periodicals. At his death, *Putnam's Monthly Magazine* characterized him as 'the slashing reviewer, the genial essayist, the sturdy moralist, the boon companion, the hearty lover of Nature, the stubborn Tory, the gentle poet, the rollicking satirist, the learned critic, the wise teacher.'

We were much puzzled, a few weeks since, by a tantalising and unintelligible paragraph, pertinaciously reiterated in the London newspapers. Its brevity equalled its mystery; it consisted but of five words, the first and last in imposing majuscules. Thus it ran:—

OMOO, by the author of TYPEE.

With Trinculo we exclaimed, 'What have we here? a man or a fish? dead or alive?' Who or what were Typee and Omoo? Were things or creatures thus designated? Did they exist on the earth, or in the air, or in the waters under the earth; were they spiritual or material, vegetable or mineral, brute or human? Were they newly-discovered planets, nick-named whilst awaiting baptism, or strange fossils, contemporaries of the Megatherium, or Magyar dissyllables from Dr Bowring's vocabulary? Perchance they were a pair of new singers for the Garden, or a fresh brace of beasts for the legitimate drama at Drury. Omoo might be the heavy elephant; Typee the light-comedy camel. Did danger lurk in the enigmatical words? Were they obscure intimations of treasonable designs, Swing advertisements, or masonic signs? Was the palace at Westminster in peril? Had an agent of Barbarossa Joinville undermined the Trafalgar column? Were they conspirators' watch-words, lovers' letters, signals concerted between the robbers of Rogers's bank? We tried them anagramatically, but in vain: there was naught to be made of Omoo; shake it as we would, the O's came uppermost; and by reversing Typee we obtained but a pitiful result. At last a bright gleam broke through the mist of conjecture. Omoo was a book. The outlandish title that had perplexed us was intended to perplex; it was a bait thrown out to that wide-mouthed fish, the public; a specimen of what is theatrically styled *gag*. Having but an indifferent opinion of books ushered into existence by such charlatanical manœuvres, we thought no more of Omoo, until, musing the other day over our matutinal hyson, the volume itself was laid before us, and we suddenly found ourselves in the entertaining society of Marquesan Melville, the phœnix of modern voyagers, sprung, it would seem, from the mingled ashes of Captain Cook and Robinson Crusoe.

Those who have read Mr Herman Melville's former work will remember, those who have not are informed by the introduction to the present one, that the author, an educated American, whom circumstances had shipped as a common sailor on board a South-Seaman, was left by his vessel on the island of Nukuheva, one of the Marquesan group. Here he remained some months, until taken off by a Sydney whaler, shorthanded, and glad to catch him. At this point of his adventures he commences *Omoo*. The title is borrowed from the dialect of the Marquesas, and signifies a rover: the book is excellent, quite first-rate, the 'clear grit,' as Mr Melville's countrymen would say. Its chief fault, almost its only one, interferes little with the pleasure of reading it, will escape many, and is hardly worth insisting upon. *Omoo* is of the order composite, a skilfully concocted Robinsonade, where fictitious incident is ingeniously blended with genuine information. Doubtless its author has visited the countries he describes, but not in the capacity he states. He is no Munchausen; there is nothing improbable in his adventures, save their occurrence to himself, and that he should have been a man before the mast on board South-Sea traders, or whalers, or on any ship or ships whatever. His speech betrayeth him. His voyages and wanderings commenced, according to his own account, at least as far back as the year 1838; for aught we know they are not yet at an end. On leaving Tahiti in 1843, he made sail for Japan, and the very book before us may have been scribbled on the greasy deck of a whaler, whilst floating amidst the coral reefs of the wide Pacific. True that in his preface, and in the month of January of the present year, Mr Melville hails from New York; but in such matters we really place little dependence upon him. From his narrative we gather that this literary and gentlemanly common sailor is quite a young man. His life, therefore, since he emerged from boyhood, has been spent in a ship's forecastle, amongst the wildest and most ignorant class of mariners. Yet his tone is refined and well-bred; he writes like one accustomed to good European society, who has read books and collected stores of information, other than could be perused or gathered in the places and amongst the rude associates he describes. These inconsistencies are glaring, and can hardly be explained. A wild freak or unfortunate act of folly, or a boyish thirst for adventure, sometimes drives lads of education to try life before the mast, but when suited for better things they seldom persevere; and Mr Melville does not seem to us the manner of man to rest long contented with the coarse company and humble lot of merchant seamen. Other discrepancies strike us in his book and character. The train of suspicion once lighted, the flame runs rapidly along. Our misgivings begin with the title-page. 'Lovel or Belville,' says the Laird of Monkbarns, 'are just the names which youngsters are apt to assume on such occasions.' And Herman Melville sounds to us vastly like the harmonious and carefully selected appellation of an imaginary hero of romance. Separately the names are not uncommon; we can urge no valid reason against their junction, and yet in this instance they fall suspiciously on our ear. We are similarly impressed by the dedication. Of the existence of Uncle Gansevoort, of Gansevoort, Saratoga County, we are wholly incredulous. We shall commission our New York correspondents to inquire as to the reality of Mr Melville's avuncular relative, and, until certified of his corporality, shall set down the gentleman with the Dutch patronymic as a member of an imaginary clan. . . .

. . . There is a world of wild romance and thrilling adventure in the occasional glimpses of the whale fishery afforded us in *Omoo*; a strange picturesqueness and piratical mystery about the lawless class of seamen engaged in it. Such a portrait gallery as *Typee* makes out of the Julia's crew, beginning with Chips and Bungs, the carpenter and cooper, the 'Cods,' or leaders of the forecastle, and descending until he arrives at poor Rope Yarn, or Ropey, as he was called, a stunted journeyman baker from Holborn, the most helpless and forlorn of all land-lubbers, the butt and drudge of the ship's company! A Dane, a Portuguese, a Finlander, a savage from Hivarhoo, sundry English, Irish, and Americans, a daring Yankee *beach-comber*, called Salem, and Sydney Ben, a runaway ticket-of-leave-man, made up a crew much too weak to do any good in the whaling way. But the best fellow on board, and by far the most remarkable, was a disciple of Esculapius, known as Doctor Long-Ghost. Jermin is a good portrait; so is Captain Guy; but Long-Ghost is a jewel of a boy, a complete original, hit off with uncommon felicity. . . . Long-Ghost was a sort of medical Tom Coffin, a raw-boned giant, upwards of two yards high, one of those men to whom the between-decks of a small craft is a residence little less afflicting than one of Cardinal Balue's iron cages. And to one who 'had certainly, at some time or other, spent money, drunk Burgundy, and associated with gentlemen,' the Julia's forecastle must have contained a host of disagreeables, irrespective of rats and cockroaches, of its low roof, evil odours, damp timbers, and dungeon-like aspect. The captain's table, if less luxurious than that of a royal yacht or New York liner, surely offered something better than the biscuits, hard as gun-flints and thoroughly honeycombed, and the shot-soup, 'great round peas polishing themselves like pebbles by rolling about in tepid water,' on which the restive man of medicine was fain to exercise his grinders during his abode forward. As regarded society, he lost little by relinquishing that of Guy the Cockney, since he obtained in exchange the intimacy of Melville the Yankee, who, to judge from his book, must be exceeding good company, and to whom he was a great resource. The doctor was a man of learning and accomplishments, who had made the most of his time whilst the sun shone on his side the hedge, and had rolled his ungainly carcass over half the world. 'He quoted Virgil and talked of Hobbes of Malmsbury, besides repeating poetry by the canto, especially Hudibras. In the easiest way imaginable, he could refer to an amour he had in Palermo, his lion-hunting before breakfast among the Caffres, and the quality of the coffee to be drunk in Muscat.' Strangely must such reminiscences have sounded in a whaler's forecastle, with Dunks the Dane, Finland Van, and Wymontoo the Savage, for auditors. . . .

Touching the proceedings on board the French man-of-war, its imperfect discipline, and the strange, un-nautical way of carrying on the duty, Typee is jocular and satirical. American though he be—and, but for occasional slight yankeeisms in his style, we might have doubted even that fact—he has evidently much more sympathy with his cousin John Bull than with his country's old allies, the French, whom he freely admits to be a clever and gallant nation, whilst he broadly hints that their valour is not likely to be displayed to advantage on the water. He finds too much of the military style about their marine institutions. Sailors should be fighting men, but not soldiers or musket-carriers, as they all are in turn in the French navy. He laughs at or objects to every thing; the mustaches of the officers, the system of punishment, the sour wine that replaces rum and water, the soup instead of junk, the pitiful little rolls baked on board, and distributed in lieu of hard biscuit. And whilst praising the build of their ships—the only thing about them he does praise—he ejaculates a hope, which sounds like a doubt, that they will not some day fall into the hands of the people across the Channel. 'In case of war,' he says, 'what a fluttering of French ensigns there would be! for the Frenchman makes but an indifferent seaman, and though for the most part he fights well enough, somehow or other, he seldom fights well enough to beat:'—at sea, be it understood. We are rather at a loss to comprehend the familiarity shown by Typee with the internal arrangements and architecture of the Reine Blanche. His time on board was passed in fetters; at nightfall on the fifth day he left the ship. How, we are curious to know, did he become acquainted with the minute details of 'the crack craft in the French navy,' with the disposition of her guns and decks, the complicated machinery by which certain exceedingly simple things were done, and even with the rich hangings, mirrors, and mahogany of the commodore's cabin? Surely the ragged and disreputable mutineer of the Julia, whose foot had scarcely touched the gangway, when he was hurried into confinement below, could have had scanty opportunity for such observations: unless, indeed, Herman Melville, or Typee, or the Rover, or by whatever other *alias* he be known, instead of creeping in at the hawse-holes, was welcomed on the quarter-deck and admitted to the gun-room, or to the commodore's cabin, an honoured guest in broad-cloth, not a despised merchant seaman in canvass frock and hat of tarpaulin. We shall not dwell on these small inconsistencies and oversights in an amusing book. We prefer accompanying the Julia's crew to Tahiti . . . .

Throughout the book, however, fun and incident abound, and we are consoled for our separation from poor little Jule, by the curious insight we obtain into the manners, morals, and condition of the gentle savages, on whom an attempted civilisation has brought far more curses than blessings. . . .

. . . They had been so long on the rove, that change of scene had become essential to their happiness. The doctor, especially, was anxious to be off to Tamai, an inland village on the borders of a lake, where the fruits were the finest, and the women the most beautiful and unsophisticated in all the Society Islands. Epicurean Long-

Ghost had set his mind upon visiting this terrestrial paradise, and thither his steady chum willingly accompanied him. It was a day's journey on foot, allowing time for dinner and siesta; and the path lay through wood and ravine, unpeopled save by wild cattle. About noon they reached the heart of the island, thus pleasantly described. 'It was a green, cool hollow among the mountains, into which we at last descended with a bound. The place was gushing with a hundred springs, and shaded over with great solemn trees, on whose mossy boles the moisture stood in beads.' There is something delightfully hydropathic in these lines; they cool one like a shower-bath. He is a prime fellow, this common sailor Melville, at such scraps of description, terse and true, placing the scene before us in ten words. In long yarns he indulges not, but of such happy touches as the above, we could quote a score. . . .

29. Unsigned notice, *Knickerbocker*

June 1847, xxix, 562

Without being equal in spirit and interest to its popular predecessor, this is yet a very clever and entertaining work. Aside from the fact that the volumes are full of incident, which if not always striking is nevertheless generally attractive, the *style* of the writer—simple and unpretending, with no apparent aim of forcing the attention and admiration of the reader, and by that very circumstance securing both—is one of its very highest recommendations. Mr. MELVILLE gives us at times, in his narrative, admirable limnings of life on board whaling vessels, filled as they too generally are with the most motley crews, reckless sailors from every nation in the known world, who, when not on ship-board, harbor among the barbarous or semi-civilized islands of Polynesia, or along the western coast of South America. A familiar (and but for the solemn assurance of the author to the contrary, we should add, high-colored) account is given of the present condition of the 'converted' Polynesians, as affected by their promiscuous intercourse with foreigners, and the teachings of the missionaries, combined. In a modest preface, Mr. MELVILLE tells us that the present narrative has no other connection with *Typee*, save that it necessarily begins where that work left off. Its title is derived from the dialect of the Marquesas Islands, where the word, '*Omoo*,' among other uses, signifies a rover, or a person wandering from one island to another, like some of the natives. The author professes to describe merely what he has seen; and so evidently natural are his pages, that we are bound to take him at his word, and to believe farther, that the reflections in which he occasionally indulges are spontaneous, and such as would suggest themselves to the most casual observer. *Omoo* has already passed to a third edition.

30. Horace Greeley, initialled review, New York *Weekly Tribune*

23 June 1847, 5

Greeley (1811–72) was a newspaper writer and editor whose work for the Whig party papers led to friendships with Thurlow Weed and William H. Seward. With their encouragement he founded the New York *Tribune* in April 1841, and he edited it over thirty years. His editorials made the paper an often-quoted and influential voice in American politics.

The review of *Omoo* was included in an Editorial Correspondence date-lined 'Up the Lakes, June 8, 1847,' and prefaced by this sentence: 'Blest, since leaving New York, with a long-coveted opportunity to devote some hours to the deliberate perusal of a few lately-issued works of remarkable character, I wish to speak of them in revisal or confirmation of what may have already been uttered.'

Omoo, by HERMAN MELVILLE, is replete alike with the merits and the faults of its forerunner, *Typee*. All of us were mistaken who thought the fascination of *Typee* owing mainly to its subject, or rather to the novel and primitive state of human existence it described. *Omoo* dispels all such illusions and proves the author a born genius, with few superiors either as a narrator, a describer, or a humorist. Few living men could have invested such scenes, incidents and persons as figure in *Omoo* with anything like the charm they wear in Melville's graphic pages; the adventures narrated might have occurred to any one, as others equally exciting have done to thousands of voyagers in the South Seas; but who has ever before described any so well? *Typee* and *Omoo*, doubtless in the main true narratives, are worthy to rank in interest with *Robinson Crusoe* and in vivacity with the best of Stephens's *Travels*.—Yet they are unmistakably defective if not positively diseased in moral tone, and will very fairly be condemned as dangerous reading for those of immature intellects and unsettled principles. Not that you can often put your finger on a passage positively offensive; but the *tone* is bad, and incidents of the most objectionable character are depicted with a racy lightness which would once have been admired but will now be justly condemned. A *penchant* for bad liquors is everywhere boldly proclaimed, while a hankering after loose company not always of the masculine order, is but thinly disguised and perpetually protruding itself throughout the work. This is to be deplored not alone for the author's sake, nor even for that of the large class which it will deter from perusing his adventures. We regret it still more because it will prevent his lucid and apparently candid testimony with regard to the value, the effect and the defects of the Missionary labors among the South Sea Islanders from having its due weight with those most deeply interested. It is needless here to restate the hackneyed question as to the proper mode of effecting the desired renovation of savage, heathen tribes.—'Preach the Gospel to them,' say the devout: 'convert them to Christianity, and their Civilization follows of course.' —'Nay,' interposes another class: 'you must civilize them, to some extent, before they can even comprehend Christianity, much less truly embrace and adhere to it.'—The Truth obviously lies between these assertions, or rather, embraces them both. A Christianity which does not include Civilization, a Civilizing which does not involve Christianizing, will not answer. Above all, alike to their conversion and their civilization a change in their Social condition and habits—a change from idleness and inefficiency to regular and well directed industry—is absolutely essential.—Without this, the convert of to-day is constantly in danger of relapsing into avowed and inveterate heathenism. This is the moral of Mr. Melville's facts, as indeed of all other impartial testimonies on the subject. Reiterating my regret that he has chosen so to write that his statements will not have that weight with the friends of Missions which the interest of Truth requires, I bid adieu to *Omoo*.

31. George Washington Peck, from an initialled article, *American Review*

July 1847, vi, 36–46

Peck (1817–59) came from Boston to New York and joined the staff of the *Morning Courier and New York Enquirer* in 1847. He was known, too, as a music critic and had founded the short-lived *Boston Musical Review* in 1845. Peck may have been the author of the rather negative review of *Typee* in the April 1846 issue of the *American Review*, an avowed Whig journal.

It was in an unguarded moment that the writer of these lines was drawn into promising an article for the issue of sultry midsummer. A lovely afternoon in the middle of June, he was walking alone in a grove, meditating and breathing the sweet air, when the Editorial Power met him, and from that hour to this his soul has not known peace. Had we reflected that all the days of the interim were to be equally inviting—that the fields were to be as green and fragrant as the valleys of Tahiti, and more refreshing in their fragrance, since the odors of our own country summers are wafted from the Sabean shore of childhood—had we bethought ourselves that we must take from our afternoons so many hours out of the prime of the year—we could hardly have been so rash, to oblige any Editorial or other Power, ever so pen-compelling—not even stern Necessity. But *Omoo* seemed so easy—the fancy so naturally loves to wander away to those fair islands whither the romance of nature has been gradually banished—that it appeared the lightest task that could be, to run off a few pages giving a common-place estimates of its merits, and selecting some of the most striking passages, after the approved custom of reviewers.

Here, again, we deceived ourselves; for upon re-reading the book, we find that what we wasted a couple of hours over very agreeably, is not strong enough to bear up a somewhat careful review, which it most certainly deserved, if it deserves anything, at our hands; to that we must look for a reason for taking so much notice of it as to write an article, rather in the interest with which it has been, and will continue for a while to be, received, by the readers of cheap literature, than by what we feel in it ourselves. Hence, we come to our task unwillingly; and were it not that something *ought* to be said respecting *Omoo*, more than has yet been, we should prefer almost any other subject.

Perhaps it is from this feeling that we have a difficulty in arranging our thoughts into order, and so beginning what we would say in the regular manner. In general, and at first, we can barely observe that we have read *Omoo* with interest, and yet with a perpetual recoil. We were ready to acknowledge that it was written with much power; that the style, though loose in sentences and paragraphs, was not without character, and the pictures it presented vividly drawn; yet we were ready to say, in the words of the old epigram—

'I do not like thee, Doctor Fell,' &c.

The reckless spirit which betrays itself on every page of the book—the cool, sneering wit, and the perfect want of *heart* everywhere manifested in it, make it repel, almost as much as its voluptuous scenery-painting and its sketchy outlines of stories attract. It is curious to observe how much difficulty the newspapers have had in getting at these causes of dislike. They are evidently not pleased with the book; but—as most writers would, sitting down to write a hasty notice of it immediately after running it through—the daily critics find nothing worse to say respecting it than that they do not believe it. Generally, all over the country, in most of the newspapers which we have seen, (and our opportunities are quite as extensive as any one could desire,) this has been the burden of the short notices of the press, where intended to be critical at all. And, generally, too, the reason for not believing in the truth of *Typee*'s and *Omoo*'s stories is not given; but the writers content themselves with manifesting their incredulity in some *naif* or querulous manner that is often amusing. They disbelieve, not so much on the account of improbability of the statements, as from the manner in which the statements are made. Even in the East, where every one fond of adventure has heard, time out of mind, whaling captains and retired boat-steerers tell just such adventures—and there is nothing after them so particularly marvellous in these books—we doubt if there are many readers of good perceptions who have more than a general belief in their truth. They lack *vraisemblance*, and though they are such adventures as might have been true, so much is out of keeping in the minor points of the narratives, and they are 'reeled off' in such an abandoned spirit, that we cannot believe them. The writer does not seem to care to be true; he constantly defies the reader's faith by his cool superciliousness; and though his preface and the first part of the first volume are somewhat better toned, the reader does not reach the second without ceasing to care how soon he parts company with him. . . .

. . . If we turn back to the 27th page of the first volume, where this 'Doctor Long-Ghost' is introduced, it is said 'he quoted Virgil, and talked of Hobbes of Malmesbury, beside repeating poetry by the canto, especially Hudibras. He was moreover a man who had seen the world.' 'He had more anecdotes than I can tell of—then such mellow old songs as he sung—upon the whole Long-Ghost was as entertaining a companion as one could wish; and to me in the Julia, an absolute god-send.' We fear the Doctor himself could scarcely return the compliment paid him in the last sentence. His cool young friend whom he entertained so much, afterwards gets home and writes a book in which he contrives to represent him as playing Pantalon to his own Harlequin, whenever he mentions him. Is it likely that the Doctor, as he is here described, could have been so simple as he is sometimes shown, and so shrewd as he is seen at others? A man of the world, a good storyteller, full of jest, a jolly companion, is one half the time depicted as a sort of Dominie Sampson, or mere foil to set off the author's smartness, while the other half he appears in his original shape. Take him for all in all, he is an impossible monster, a battered wooden Soldan, whom our Sir Oliver Proudfute has set up in the garden of his fancy to breathe himself upon. He has no keeping, and is no more a character than those singular creations of the melodrama, who are formed by the necessities of the story, who have nothing to do but to conform to the exigencies which gave them birth—to be tragic or comic, natural or extravagant, as occasion requires.

This same want of keeping appears not more in our author's character drawing, and in the course of his book taken at large, than in the minute particulars of his narratives. He makes always a striking picture, and, as we skim rapidly over one after another, it does not always occur to us at first to question the truth of the details. But when we come to look at them through a second reading, these details are seen to be thrown in with such a bold disregard of naturalness and congruity as one could never put on who was painting from the actual. . . .

. . . we wish not to have this sort of writing forced upon us under any other than its own proper name. It is mere frothy, sketchy outlining, that will bear the test of comparison with nature as little as would scene painting or the pictures on French paper hangings. If Typee were to tell his stories as he does, in the witness box, he would be a poor lawyer who could not make it evident to a jury that they would not stand sifting; his readiness and flippancy might make a brief impression while he was giving his evidence in chief, but it would take no very rigid cross-examination to bring him into discredit.

The truest pictures of nature will bear examination by a magnifying glass; but a painter is not expected to give daguerreotype likenesses. Neither is a writer of narrative expected to put in all the incidents of a matter; for the history of the most tedious day of our common life would fill a folio; but he is to follow nature so far as he can and so to suggest the rest that we shall seem to see the actual as he saw it. This there are many ways of accomplishing. Some writers go far into detail and yet are full of the truth-seeing eye—the imaginative power; others have this power with less of detail. Shakspeare could paint a whole landscape, yea, and make it more vividly real than even if it were depicted on canvas, in a few lines. 'The heaven's breath smells wooingly here!' one can scarcely read that description of Macbeth's castle without inhaling the breath, as in walking over the brow of a hill in summer, when the wind blows upward from new-mown meadows. De Foe is the commonly cited instance of excellence in the other or detailed style of descriptive writing. We have all taken the walk with him where the brook flowed 'due East' and the whole country seemed like 'a planted garden,' yet the spell that was over us while we wandered into that delicious region, was not one that operated by startling flashes, but by a steady, constant influence—the low murmuring music that as we read on in him is ever falling with a gentle lull upon the mind's ear.

Now in either of these kinds of description, a writer who affects us as true, must have the *truth in him*; that is, he must have the ideal in his mind which he would paint to us, and must draw and color from that, without being led astray either by his chalk or his colors. He must mean to describe faithfully what is before his mind's eye at the outset, and must so control his fancy and so use his language that neither shall mislead either himself or his readers, aside from his purpose. In this tedious process of writing and compelling the fancy to dwell upon far-off scenes, despite the temptations of the present, despite the glory of nature that is around us, despite of mortal heaviness, care, passion, personal grief, what infinite trouble is it to keep the impatient spirit under due obedience! Even as we write these sentences, our thoughts are oftener away than they are upon this writing; somewhat has come over us with years, it matters not what, so heavily that we can no more lose ourself, as the phrase goes, 'in our subject.' Other minds may be more happily constituted, but one may observe that those who trust their fancy most and yield to it farthest, are most liable to be led astray by it. It is only the great poets who seem to acquire control in and by the very tempest and whirlwind of their passion. With what perfect recklessness, yet what perfect self-possession, wrote our Shakspeare and Milton! Flight after flight, bolder than was that of him who was borne of Dedalian pinions, is dared and accomplished till it seems as if their will were almost godlike, and gave birth to power. Many times in running through a play of Shakspeare hastily, we have felt the same feeling that we experienced in hearing one of HANDEL's mighty chorusses —a kind of mysterious awe at the near presence of such terrible, burning strength; to read the glorious comedy of 'As you like it' rapidly, for example, affects us like going into the engine room of one of our great Atlantic steamers, when she is just starting (a homely comparison and one the reader is welcome to smile at if he cannot understand)—or standing by a railroad track when a heavy train is passing—any such exhibition of irresistible force and motion. This feeling we have when we let the play rush through the mind—thought crowding upon thought and all glowing and sparkling; but in the midst of this fiery tumult, if we read more carefully, the great genius as smiling and placid as the expression of the bust we have of him would tell us he was; full of playfulness, delicacy, gentleness. O for such mental discipline. But all the mathematics in all the colleges in New England could never teach it.

Nor shall we be likely to learn it of the author of *Omoo*. For this control and discipline of the fancy seems to us just wherein he fails. He has all the confidence of genius, all its reckless abandonment, but little of its power. He has written a very attractive and readable book, but there are few among those who have an eye for nature and a lively fancy, but who could write as good a one if they had the hardihood—if they could as easily throw off all fear of making the judicious grieve. Were he put to his confession, there is no doubt but he would own that, in drawing pictures, he does not rigidly adhere to a fixed image, something that he has seen or remembers; that he does not endeavor to present his first landscape in a clear, strong, rich light, but often, as his narrative grows road weary, lets it throw the bridle rein of strict veracity on the neck of his fancy, and relieve itself by an occasional canter.

At any rate the passage we have quoted, and hundreds of others, are quite as satisfactory evidence that he does so as would be such an admission.

But let us thank the author for the good he has given us before further considering the bad. We have more sympathy with recklessness than with obedient diligence, since it is the rarer and more difficultly combining element of a great soul. A man who seems to write without the least misgiving—who dares the high with a constant conceit—will carry his point where a modest one, with ten times the inert strength, shall fail. There are men that can live years and ruffle it with the gayest, eat, drink and wear of the best, and owe whomsoever they please, by mere force of countenance, while a nervous one, whom a lady's eye abashes, may be either starving in a garret, or slaving for the ambitious, who catch him with the chaff of friendship. We confess we have more respect for your Brummells, than for your Burritts, that eat their way up in the world by devouring lexicons. The latter are good creatures in their way, to be sure; they do all the hard work for us and deserve to gain all they strive after; nay, we do not object to a modest man, for a small party, but at all times and places, we most especially admire impudence—admire—the word is not strong enough—we 'cotton' to it; we envy it!

And if the reader sees the spirit of envy coloring this article, let him attribute it to this feeling. We do most heartily envy the man who could write such a book as *Omoo*, for nothing disturbs his serenity in the least; he is always in a good humor with himself, well pleased with what he writes, satisfied with his powers, and hence never dull. It must be owned he has some ground for complacency. He exhibits, on almost every page, the original ability to be an imaginative writer of the highest order. Some of his bits of description are very fine, and that in the highest and most poetic way. . . .

. . . It is an ably written book; so good, in fact, (in point of ability, we mean—of its moral tendency we shall speak presently)—that we are not pleased with it because it is not better. The author has shown himself so very capable of using a great style, and comes, at times, so near excellence, that we feel disposed to quarrel with him for never exactly reaching it. He is bold and self-contained; no cold timidity chills the glow of his fancy. Why does he not, before abandoning himself to the current of Thought, push out till he comes over the great channel of Truth? Or, not to speak in a parable, why does he not imitate the great describers, and give us pictures that will bear dissection, characters true to themselves, and a style that moves everywhere with the same peculiar measure?

Alas, Omoo finds it easier to address himself to the pit of the world than to the boxes. His heart is hard, and he prefers painting himself to the public of his native land as a jolly, rollicking blade—a charming, rattling, graceless ne'er-do-well. He meets no man, in all his wanderings, whom he seems to care for—no woman whom he does not consider as merely an enchanting animal, fashioned for his pleasure. Taken upon his own showing, in two volumes, and what is he but what a plain New Englander would call a '*smart scamp?*'

The phrase is a hard one, but it is certainly well deserved. Here is a writer who spices his books with most incredible accounts and dark hints of innumerable amours with the half-naked and half-civilized or savage damsels of Nukuheva and Tahiti—who gets up voluptuous pictures, and with cool, deliberate art breaks off always at the right point, so as without offending decency, he may stimulate curiosity and excite unchaste desire. Most incredible, we style these portions of his stories, for several reasons.

First: He makes it appear always, that he was unusually successful with these poor wild maidens, and that his love-making was particularly acceptable to them. Now, if this had been so, we fancy we should have heard less of it. A true manly mind cannot sit down and coin dramas, such as these he gives us, for either others' delectation or its own. . . .

. . . Native manhood is as modest as maidenhood, and when a man glories in his licentiousness, it raises a strong presumption that he is effete either by nature or through decay.

And this remark leads to our *second* reason for doubting the credibility of these amours. Taking the evidence of imbecility afforded by the reason just given, in conjunction with all that Omoo would have us believe he did (for he does not speak out in plain words like old Capt. Robert Boyle), and it cannot be possible, without Sir Epicure Mammon's wished-for elixir, that he could have the *physical ability* to play the gay deceiver at such a rate among those brawny islanders. This body of ours is very yielding it is true, and if a man resolutely sets his mind to imbrute himself he may go a great way; but a half year of such riotous life would have sufficed for one so proud of his exploits (if, indeed, this very display is not rather the result than one of the causes of a *blasé* condition—perhaps it is both).

Thirdly. We do not believe these stories, for the reason that those poor savage maids could not possibly have been such as Omoo describes them; they are not half so attractive. We have seen the drawings of Catlin, the elaborate French engravings of the South American Indians, Humboldt, Deprez, also some of New Zealand and those of our Exploring Expedition, and never yet saw we a portrait of a female half so attractive as the dumpiest Dutch butter-woman that walks our markets. . . .

It seems necessary nowadays, for a book to be vendible, that it be venomous, and, indeed, venereous. Either so, or else it must be effeminate—pure, because passionless. The manliness of our light literature is curdling into licentiousness on the one hand and imbecility on the other; witness such books as *Omoo*, and the namby-pamby Tennysonian poetry we have of late so much of. Hence, authors who write for immediate sale are obliged to choose their department and walk in it. In some cases it is possible some have assumed vices which they had not, and in others affected an ignorance of temptation which was by no means their condition. We are willing to believe that Omoo is not so bad as he would have us think. He is merely writing in character, and it seemed necessary to pepper high. He may have more heart than he exhibits; and in a few months, when the last edition of his books has been sold, and all the money made from them that ever can be, he may repent him that he did not aim nobler. At the worst, he is no such chief of sinners that we need single him out for special condemnation. Have we not Don Juan? Is not the exhaustless invention of Gaul coining millions out of 'nature's frailty?' When we consider the crimes of some of the modern novel-writers, Omoo seems but a 'juvenile offender.'

But we must not deal too leniently with him neither. That he is a Papalangi whose heart is set in him to do evil, appears no less by his glorying in his misdeeds, than by the spirit he manifests towards the Christian teachers of those ignorant pagans, whose vices he did all in his power to foster. The *blue shark* is on his forehead, and he is as palpable a barbarian as any tattooed New Zealander we ever saw stumbling, with jacket wrong side before and feet that till then never knew shoe, through the streets of New Bedford. He hates the missionaries. This is evident whenever he has occasion to mention them, and whereever there is room for a covert sneer at the little good they have accomplished. He was evidently afraid of them. It does not appear that he sought their acquaintance; but, from his whole way of speaking of them, the reader will not fail to gather the impression that he kept out of their way as much as possible. The spirit which he manifests towards them is what we should expect him to exhibit after his displaying his success with the damsels, 'his particular friends.' But the two spirits neutralize each other. A native of a Christian land, well-educated, and with a fair reputation for truth and veracity—that is to say, any man in his senses, with the common feelings of humanity, and worthy of belief, would have endeavored to make himself known to the missionaries, or indeed to any one in that remote and isolated spot who could speak English; on the other hand, a man who, under those circumstances, should not endeavor to make himself so known, but should prefer to associate with the savages, ought not to be entitled to credit when he speaks slightingly of the results of missionary labor. That the missionaries have not done all things as wisely as they might, had they known more; that they have been, and are, in many respects wrong and in error, may be very true; but Omoo is not the man to tell us so. He, who, by his own confession, never did anything to the islanders while he was among them but amuse himself with their peculiarities and use them for his appetites, is not the one to come home here and tell us the missionaries are doing little or nothing to improve them. All he did tended to make them worse, and it would be out of character if he should have now a benevolent purpose in so coloring his narratives as to make it appear that the missionaries are making them no better.

We are ourselves forced to believe the accounts of the good the missionaries have effected in far countries exaggerated. We cannot help thinking that in general, the men who most frequently abandon home and country and volunteer to spend their lives in teaching Christianity and civilization in those benighted lands, are not the best who might be selected out of enlightened society at large. . . .

Still, unsuitable as many of the teachers are who go out among the heathen, narrow, unreasonable, and unphilosophical, as may be their modes of conversion, and notions of goodness, they are at least sincere in their purpose of doing all the good they can. . . .

. . . Seen through the pages of *Omoo*, the missionaries affect us like some mysterious baleful *presence*, some invisible power that delights in exercising arbitrary sway over the poor natives, without any adequate motive—it cannot be so. Men do not change their natures by sailing a few thousand miles over the rotundity of this orb. . . .

. . . We have felt obliged, as a conservative in literature, (and what true lover of literature is not one,) to say many severe things—the more severe, because they are against the tone and spirit of the book, and therefore apply more directly to its author. But if the reader will observe how cautious we have been to praise all that is good in the book, to the extent of making our article wear two faces, he will not suspect us of any malicious design. And if he will read the book itself, we have confidence that, notwithstanding all the extravagant encomiums it has received from the press, he will be ready to admit that we have not been studying to say the worst things of it that might be said, but only to estimate it fairly. The result of all we have said only brings us back to the remark with which we commenced, viz: that *Omoo* is a book one may read once with interest and pleasure, but with *a perpetual recoil*. It is poetically written, but yet carelessly, and in a bad spirit. Of the truth of this general estimate of its merit the reader will judge for himself. . . .

We had intended, when we began this article, to have expatiated, somewhere in the course of it, upon the glorious landscapes of those fair islands we all love to read of so well, and to have examined why it comes that the fancy so loves to roam among them. We meant to have enlarged upon the various respects that make calamity of life to poetically-disposed people in this wretched world of enterprise, and then to have observed how naturally we turn to a region of better promise. But this would have been forgetting that the actual world is much the same everywhere, and that here, although we may be unblest with hope and happiness, in mind, body, or estate, we are, on the whole, better off than we should be there; and we leave all such reflections to the reader, who, perchance, may never have been so wrought upon as to discuss with himself whether it were not better to turn renegade to civilization, and to whom, therefore, our speculations would seem but mere sentimental melancholy. We had rather he should rejoice with us at parting; there is cause to be merry; the sun is yet high, and the green fields and woody hills of West Hoboken are waiting for us.

32. Jedediah B. Auld, initialled reply to *American Review*, New York *Evening Mirror*

21 July 1847

Auld was another of the 'Young America' group that gathered in New York. With Evert Duyckinck, William A. Jones, and Russell Trevett he founded the Tetractys Club in 1836 for the discussion of literature and literary projects. Apparently Melville sometimes attended the meetings in the late 1840s when the group had expanded. Auld, like Melville's brother Gansevoort, was a staunch Locofoco Democrat. His reference to 'an austere morning paper' is to the *Morning Courier and New York Enquirer*, which a week earlier had reported that *Typee* and *Omoo* 'are reviewed in a just and highly interesting paper by G. W. Peck. . . . This article evinces uncommon critical acumen and a clear-sighted discriminating sympathy with what is sound and healthy in literature and morals.'

The *American Review*, July, 1847.—In all nature there is not a single animated object to be found without at least one parasitical annoyance; in the literary kingdom the same rule holds, and critics and snarlers are the crawling and creeping things of the world of letters. How was it possible for Mr. Colton, who has the credit of literary discrimination, to admit so execrable an article into his magazine as the disgusting and spiteful review of *Omoo*? We should have supposed that the voice of the public would have outweighed the captious snarlings of any small clique even if accompanied by what Mr. Colton might consider a gratuitous advertisement.

We happened, like the vast majority of readers here and abroad, to read *Omoo* with feelings of unmixed delight; we shared in the exuberant jollity of the venturous and careless sailors, and wandered a life of boyish holiday over the sunny groves of the coral islands. In our mind, the illusion was perfect, and the incidents and scenes were as vivid and natural as ever words painted. But the critic comes, and in a pet demolishes poor Omoo, calls him reckless liar and shameless pander, and brands every delighted reader as a fool or sensualist. Unblushing assurance! We never dreamed of sensuality in the perusal, and no one has made the accusation but this one over sensitive or querulous mortal.

But if Omoo is free from the guilt of pandering to a depraved taste, so is not the reviewer. Finding a fair chance to disgorge on the public a little of his own filth, in the pleasant disguise of a moralist and conservative, he launches forth as much disgusting loathsomeness and personal blackguardism as could be crammed in the compass of his few pages.

The grossness and spite of the reviewer, indeed, is the protection of the author, but if indecent flippancy deserves reproof, it justifies our defence. And yet, strange as it may seem, this affected jumble of smuttey morality and personal abuse finds favor in an austere morning paper famous for stern conservativeism. Or is it possible to account for the high praise bestowed on this atrocious specimen of falsehood, silliness and nastiness, on the supposition that there exists among the numerous writers for that journal a *société d'admiration mutuel,*[1] and that one of their fellows is the savage Juvenal of the *Whig Review.*

33. From an unsigned review, London *Times*

24 September 1847

A long session of Parliament and a general election are sad enemies to light literature, as authors and publishers have no doubt discovered before us. But for the prior and sterner claims of both, the following notice of a most deserving little volume would have appeared long ere this. We take an early opportunity to do justice to a work which, on many accounts, merits the attention of the critic and the reader.

Herman Melville is as clever and learned as ever. Sailor before the mast as he is, he discourses as pleasantly and humorously of Nature in her hundred aspects as the gentle Washington Irving himself, the Prince

[1] *Société d'admiration mutuel:* mutual-admiration society.

of story-tellers, the most delicate and touching of painters. Melville professes to be born in the same region as Irving, and we are bound to believe him. But the man puzzles us. Common sailor he is not. If he be an American, he is quite as familiar with English literature and London streets as he is with Bryant and Longfellow, Broadway and Long Island. If he needs an illustration, Regent-street occurs to him as it would to Mr. Dickens; the cockney not the Kentuckian is the subject of his satire, and King John and George IV, supply matter for discussion which Washington and Jackson fail to furnish. To say the least, these are suspicious facts.

Last year we pronounced *Typee* the most charming and ingenious *fiction* of the season. The soft impeachment was denied. The internal evidence, conclusive to our own minds, was set aside by the positive assurances of the author and his friends given somewhere and generally accepted. *Omoo* is not a whit less charming than *Typee;* neither does it appear to us one shade more authentic. Quite as fascinating a production as *Robinson Crusoe*, it is twenty times less probable. Had Mr. Melville lived 50 years ago, and had he been a merchant or a man of education, wrecked upon the happy coasts which he describes, there would have been an air of truthfulness and consistency in his narrative which it certainly now lacks. We never stop in our progress with *Crusoe* to exclaim, 'Impossible!' or to inquire, 'Can this be true?' Adventurous, wonderful, and striking as the incidents may be, they are precisely what might, could, would, or should have happened under the given circumstances. It is the air of wild reality which wins our sympathy, more than the incidents themselves. Everybody knows that *Robinson Crusoe* is a tale of the imagination, yet nobody publicly acknowledges the fact. If it be not sound and simple truth, it ought to be; it is a shame that it is not. Now something very like the contrary to all this holds good of *Omoo* and *Typee*. They profess to be genuine histories, and yet the hitches occur so often that children will be disposed to question their authenticity. The illusion is not perfect. The artificial is mixed with the natural; the *vraisemblable*[1] with the utterly improbable; the craftsman peeps out where the untutored traveller should alone be visible; the man of letters writing for Mr. Murray clashes alternately with the sailor frisking at his ease with the natives of the Southern seas.

We are not disposed to quarrel with Mr. Melville because we believe his delightful books, though unquestionably founded on fact, to be on

[1] *Vraisemblable:* probable.

the whole untrue. Let him write as much as he will, provided always that he writes as well as now, and he shall find us greedy devourers of his productions. He has a rare pen for the delineation of character; an eye for the humorous and grotesque which is worth a Jew's; for the description of natural scenery he is not to be beaten, either on this side of the Atlantic or the other. His pencil is most distinct, the colouring beautiful and rich. As for invention, he will bear comparison with the most cunning of the modern French school, who are famous for the faculty. Put him alongside the French at Tahiti, or cheek by jowl with the missionaries in Papeetee, and no satirist more quiet and stinging. That Mr. Melville has visited the spots which he describes, we think there can be no doubt; that he is acquainted with the South Sea Islanders, their habits and manners, is equally clear. The general features of the picture are evidently drawn from the life; the filling up, the grouping, the composition, are the afterwork of the artist. A better material has not for years fallen into the way of the creator and the poet; a more skilful workman it has been seldom our lot to welcome. But the raw article is far from being exhausted. At the last page of his second work Mr. Melville is as fresh and vigorous as at the first line of the book which preceded it. Like his reader, he leaves off with an appetite. We are much mistaken if the acquaintance formed between the two does not ripen into friendship; and if for years to come we shall not find the sailor before the mast, profitably handling the sheets before the public in Albemarle-street. A more dignified retirement for a poor son of the ocean we can hardly conceive. Greenwich Hospital and a groat a day look poor at the side of 16 guineas a sheet, and what Mr. Webster of the Haymarket calls in the playbills, 'contingent advantages.' America does much for her navy when she enables her sailors thus to retire into the bosom of private life. Let us see if we cannot imitate our sister, and do something for the army. The new regulations offer a wide field for speculation and hope. With a ten years' enlistment, and barrack schools, who knows but that we may have a new edition of the *Subaltern* by Private Johnson, and a philosophical history of the second Lahore campaign by Corporal Bigglesmith, of the 96th. Literary gentlemen by profession, we bid you look to it!

. . . In his first work, our author had but one object in view, that of describing the manners and customs of the Marquesese people, and he accomplished it with credit. In this volume he confesses his object to be twofold. Ist. To convey some idea of life on board of a whaler; and, secondly, to give a familiar account of the present condition of the converted Polynesians as affected by their promiscuous intercourse with foreigners and the teachings of the missionaries combined. Nothing can be more perfect than the success of the writer. The account of the ship, the characters of its crew, the records of its doings, are admirable. . . .

. . . We strongly recommend the reader to take a cruise with Omoo, the Doctor, and Jermin, and to invigorate his soul with the healthy breezes of the South Pacific. Rough though his companions be, sorry the craft, he shall be all the better for a short existence away from the wearisome, insipid, and monotonous doings of our sadly enervated and too political generation. One sight of Tahiti shall give him a seven years' lease of life. How surpassingly beautiful must that island be! How enviable the rude sailor's hand which can trace its form so sweetly clear upon the canvas!

Lovely land, happy people!—land doomed to be defaced and polluted by the foot of civilization; people left to be brutalized, corrupted, and destroyed by the professors of Christianity. Strange that the boasted triumphs of five centuries' ardent prosecution of science, art, and noble deeds, and the mildest, holiest faith the world has ever seen, can be transplanted to the antipodes only to bring havoc to innocence and misery to unoffending virtue! Shall we sum up the good that France has effected in Oceanis, or that English missionaries have produced in the benighted islands which, under their half-spiritual, half-civil government, have become far more gloomy? Alas! the most painful of all contemplations is the contemplation of the work, hideous, shameful, and cruel, which the hand of the white man has produced in the distant regions which, by what Horace Walpole calls a sort of 'piratic jurisprudence,' he has lawfully though impudently made his own. It is a singular fact, that, clever and rational as Europeans generally are, they continue most stupidly ignorant of an obstacle to all success in the way of improving the condition of their fellow creatures, which would seem obvious to the merest observer. In all kinds of instruction two conditions are absolutely necessary—a teacher able to instruct, a pupil competent to learn. In the vegetable world, the soil must be favourable to the sustenance of the plant, or the plant sickens and dies. If this simple law were always kept in mind, we should have spared much bloodshed ere this by not seeking to force a political constitution upon nations unable to comprehend and unwilling to receive it, and unquestionably have preserved much morality and virtue amidst pagans who have lost both in yielding customs which they understood and revered, and in attempting to naturalize others for which neither Heaven nor earth had prepared or designed them. Mr. Melville's account of missionary doings agrees with all that has reached us from trustworthy travellers; corroborates all that we know of such proceedings, whether they take place in Bagdad in Persia, or in the city of London. They are without the elements of success. . . .

We have said that the hand of Omoo is at home in description. Nothing can be finer, more vigorous and graphic than 'the hunt in the mountains,' and the pursuit of Taurus, his wife and child, to wit, his cow and calf in the woods. We recommend the picture to Edwin Landseer; it is worthy his genius, and no painter but himself can do it justice. The account is short like all the descriptions of our author, but it is terse, life-like, and masterly. . . .

That Mr. Melville will favour us with his further adventures on board the Leviathan, and upon new shores, we have no doubt whatever. We shall expect them with impatience and receive them with pleasure. He is a companion after our own hearts: his voice is pleasant, and if we could see his face we are sure we should find it a cheerful one.

MARDI

1849

34. Henry Fothergill Chorley, unsigned review, *Athenæum*

24 March 1849, 296–8

Chorley (1808–72), a critic for the *Athenaeum* from 1833 to 1871, gained his principal fame for his articles and books on music. His literary criticism was said to be sound in judgment and sincere in intention though not particularly imaginative nor appreciative of innovation.

On opening this strange book, the reader will be at once struck by the affectation of its style, in which are mingled many madnesses. Some pages emulate the Ercles' vein of the *Wondrous Tale of Alroy*:—not a few paragraphs indicate that the author has been drinking at the well of 'English bewitched' of which Mr. Carlyle and Mr. Emerson are the priests. Here and there, in the midst of a most frantic romance, occur dry little digressions showing the Magician anxious half to medicine half to *bamboozle* his readers after the manner of *The Doctor*. In other passages of his voyage, where something very shrewd has been intended, we find nothing more poignant than the vapid philosophy of Mr. Fenimore Cooper's *Monikins*. If this book be meant as a pleasantry, the mirth has been oddly left out—if as an allegory, the key of the casket is 'buried in ocean deep'—if as a romance, it fails from tediousness—if as a prose-poem, it is chargeable with puerility. Among the hundred people who will take it up, lured by their remembrances of *Typee*, ninety readers will drop off at the end of the first volume; and the remaining nine will become so weary of the hero when for the seventh time he is assaulted by the three pursuing *Duessas* who pelt him with symbolical flowers, that they will throw down his chronicle ere the end of its second third is reached—with Mr. Burchell's monosyllable by way of comment.

The Critic, of course, is the one intrepid mariner who holds out to the end. With ourselves such persistence was at once a duty, and in some measure a service of hope; because, in spite of all its tawdry faults of style, the commencement of the story impressed us strongly in a strange witch-like way. The narrator begins by telling us how he was on board a sperm-whaler in the Pacific; the captain of which protracted the ship's voyage till our rover and a mate of his, becoming totally ocean-weary when a thousand miles from land(!), resolved to give the *Arcturion* the slip,—and executed their resolution in a manner not very probable but abundantly breathless. Then follow the good pages of this provoking book. The story of their boat voyage, albeit overwrought and extravagant, is full of pictures 'from the under-world.'—

[quotes from chapter 13, 'Though America' to 'at a gulp.']

After going on in this way for many days—the interest of their marvellous voyage being portentously heightened by a calm—the two 'make' a lonely ship.—

[quotes from chapter 19, 'As we came nearer' to 'ever heard before.']

Few who read the above will contest the power of the picture: or not long to see what vision next was revealed to the adventurers. But very shortly after this point the romance ends, and the harlequinade begins. How the narrator and his *Achates* fall among the savages—how they rescue a maiden about to be offered as a human sacrifice, who is well nigh as beautiful as Maturin's *Immalee*—how subsequently, the narrator being received by the Mardi islanders as a Divinity, is fain for security's sake to accept the greatness thrust upon him—these events are told with considerable spirit. But as we proceed the improbability deepens: the author trifles with his tale for some purpose too deep for our plummet to fathom—becomes more and more outrageous in the fashion of his incidents and in the forms of his language.—Losing the maiden he had rescued, he sets out in chase of her with sundry islanders; and they pass many islands such as *Gulliver* might have visited,—haunts peopled by folks who are not human creatures, but merely Follies or Wisdoms tattooed or feathered,—'drinking wild wine' or telling stupid stories as may be. Throughout this voyage of discovery the white man is dogged by three herald*esses* in a boat who bring him enigmatical messages and botanical solicitations from their queen—a sort of *Circe* of the Pacific. Matters become crazier and crazier—more and more foggy—page by page—until the end—which is no more an end than the last line of Coleridge's 'Kubla Khan'—is felt to be a happy release. Few besides ourselves will take the pains of reaching it.

35. From an unsigned review, London *Atlas*

24 March 1849, 185–6

The immense variety of subjects and of information in the present day offers peculiar temptations to the romancing philosopher. The stock ideas of centuries on religious, political, and social questions receive ever and anon a new garb from their association with new facts, or the habits and peculiarities of a new people. We are often glad to meet our old friends in their new dress; and frequently discover in this way features that we had never recognized before, or in such a way that we had not perceived their comeliness. Many a philosophic notion may receive an illustration which enables us at once to perceive its value, by an analogy drawn from the habits of a South Sea Islander.

Again, the multitude of pursuits enables modern ingenuity to see the same thing in every possible aspect. Of several voyagers who should notice the shoals of strange monsters in the ocean, each views them with different eyes. The merchant ruminates on the oil and bone, and calculates the probable gain or loss of a vessel sent to catch them. The naturalist looks at their snouts and fins—examines the difference between the broad tails and the narrow tails—imagines long Latin names in his brain—and conjures up a meeting of the Linnean Society, before which he (the naturalist aforesaid) brings six new species of his own finding, with six new names of his own invention. The gourmand wonders how they would taste. The man of imagination invests them with the fancies of his own wild mind—peoples with them a strange and fantastic creation, in which he revels in heterogeneous notions and ideas of every shade and hue.

To the latter class belongs the author of this book. Before we criticize his notions, let us briefly analyze the frame-work of the tale on which he hangs them. . . .

The work is a compound of *Robinson Crusoe* and *Gulliver's Travels*, seasoned throughout with German metaphysics of the most transcendental school. The great questions of natural religion, necessity, free-will, and so on, which Milton's devils discussed in Pandemonium, are here discussed on a rock in the Pacific Ocean by tattooed and feathered sceptics. They are treated with much ingenuity, and frequently with a richness of imagination which disguises the triteness of the leading ideas. Politics takes their share of the work—not often well, sometimes most absurdly illustrated. The habits of modern society come in for an occasional fling. But the great merit of the work is its fanciful descriptions of nature amid all her variations. Some of the cleverest, even the most brilliant, passages occur when the author fairly gives himself up to his own singular and quaint contemplations of nature. Witness the following description of a calm. Describing a landsman's sensation when becalmed, he says:—

[quotes from chapter 2, 'At first he is' to 'in the bass drum.']

A whole chapter, narrating the passage of the boat through the sea monsters of the Pacific, is about the cleverest and tersest description of animated nature we ever encountered. We regret that we have not space to extract it. We give, however, from another chapter his description, with illustrations, of the sword fish of the South Seas:—

[quotes from chapter 32, 'And here let me' to 'of his foe.']

. . . We cannot follow the author through all his discussions of things real and unreal, nor would we if we could. The style is that of the true German metaphysician—full of tender thoughts and false images—generally entertaining—often ridiculous—attaining sometimes the brightest colourings of fancy, and at others talking the most inaffable bombast. . . .

Altogether we regard this as a remarkable book. When a man essays a continual series of lofty flights, some of his tumbles will be sufficiently absurd; but we must not be thus hindered from admiring his success when he achieves it.

36. Unsigned review, *Examiner*

31 March 1849, 195–6

Manifold were the doubts of the veracity of *Typee* and *Omoo*, but Mr Melville is resolved to have no such questions raised as to *Mardi*. From first to last it is an outrageous fiction; a transcendental *Gulliver*, or *Robinson Crusoe* run mad. A heap of fanciful speculations, vivid descriptions, satirical insinuations, and allegorical typifications, are flung together with little order or connexion; and the result is a book of which the interest is curiously disproportioned to the amount of cleverness and ability employed in it.

Mr Melville still continues in the region where his former scenes were laid, and shows his chief power, as in those striking books, on the waters of the Pacific. Indeed the opening incident of *Mardi* is the same as in *Typee*—the escape, with a companion, from a sea voyage that had become inexpressibly wearisome. They are on a cruise for the huge sea-swimmer 'whose brain enlightens the world;' are a thousand miles from land (so says Mr Melville, and it is not for quiet landsmen to dispute the possibility); and have become so ocean-weary that their hammocks seem to tell centuries, as, pendulum-like, they swing to the ship's dull roll, and tick the hours and ages. This description throws out into capital contrast the excitement of their escape in the whaling boat, and the perils through which they pass from dwellers in the deep. No one paints a shark better than Mr Melville. He makes us see the difference at a glance between the Brown individual, or sea attorney, and the Blue specimen, or dandy of the deep. It would not be easy to say which is the most infernally heartless; but there is nevertheless the widest possible distinction between the hard and inveterate horny snout of the one, and the slender waist, careless fin, indolent tail, and gentlemanly cold-bloodedness of the other. The Tiger shark, again, being of the ruder sort, has a savage swagger peculiar to himself; while the shark with the Shovel nose, attended by his pilot-fishes who scout for him and are quite in anguish when he is killed, seems to have winning as well as sharking ways that make him worthy of the honour he receives from Mr Melville.

We are not going to tell how the deserters from the Arcturus whaler fall in with a wrecked and desolate couple of South Sea Islanders, nor how the hero, or the author, for the story is told in the first person, becomes possessed of a certain wonderful, mystical, mythological maiden, who had been a vine-blossom soon after she was born, and through other changes since has fallen into the hands of a priest, whose murder narrowly saves her from immolation. Suffice it to observe that, with this prize, the hero and his friend Jarl and other companions land on Mardi, where the king is a demigod, and where the author himself receives demi-divinity. Here he dwells with his allegorical maiden, Yillah, till the reader, not always seeing clearly the intention, gets tired of the allegory; and even the all-wise critic, somewhat sharing the reader's dulness in that respect, thinks it safest to say as little as may be about the profundities of allegorical meaning which appear to be involved. However, the natural descriptions are always good and pleasing—and such nice little touches as where Yillah is seen rising out of slumber, are better than all the philosophy she suggests or figures in. You see the first dawn of consciousness breaking along the waking face, then peeping from out the languid lids, then shining forth in longer glances, 'till, like the sun, up comes the soul, and sheds its rays abroad.'

On the sudden disappearance of Yillah the main adventures of the book begin. The author, attended by his friend the King of Mardi, and a great many other companions, pursues her in fruitless search from island to island, each representing some fresh and novel aspect of island eccentricity, and the island creatures introduced comprising pigmies and philosophers, singers and sages and saints, fat men and fools, elfs and antiquaries, speaking oracles and pagodas, monarchists and republicans. We have sundry varieties of questions discussed by the way, with sly hits at many mortal absurdities. Mardi's sovereign, who is a sensible fellow, discusses trial by jury, and other valued institutions of that pitiable part of the world which he thinks uncivilised, with good effect. We also like the jolly old Lord Borabolla, whose name is as round and fat as himself, and whose thoughts waddle as much as his legs. There is something to be learned, too, from the old woman who partakes of twenty unripe bananas, and then makes a company of respectable elfs responsible for all her sufferings.

For examples of thoughtful writing, and very extensive reading, much in the manner of Sir Thomas Browne, and with a dash of old Burton and Sterne, we think the best chapters in the book are those on subjects apart from its ostensible purpose; such as the essays interposed on Time and Temples, on Faith and Knowledge, on Dreams, and on Suppers. Pipes are discussed, too, and noses, with the learning of a Slaukenbergius; and we are taken into catacombs of ancient and curious MSS, which throw light upon history and the many methods of writing it. Thus there lie by the side of the life of old Philo the philanthropist complete in one chapter, no less an instalment than one hundred books of the yet unfinished biography of the great and glorious king Grandissimo. In the matter of dreams Mr Melville's taste is unexceptionable. All men more or less may be masters of their dreams, occupy worlds of their own, and inhabit as many nations as Mungo Park rested in African cots; but Mr Melville shows the best taste when he desires to be served like Bajazet, and to have Bacchus for his butler, Virgil for his minstrel, and Philip Sydney for his page. Better than all his fancies in this sort, however, is the supper he imagines at Pluto's table, and the tip-top company he places there. We have Emperors and Czars, Great Moguls and Great Khans, Grand Lamas and Grand Dukes, Prince Regents and Queen Dowagers. Tamerlane hob-a-nobs with Bonaparte, and Antiochus with Solyman the Magnificent. Pisistratus pledges Pilate; and Semiramis eats bons bons with Bloody Mary, and her namesake of Medicis. The thirty tyrants quaff three to one with the Council of Ten; and Sultans, Satraps, Viziers, Hetmans, Soldiers, Landgraves, Bashaws, Doges, Dauphins, Infantas, Incas and Caciques, form the ordinary lookers on at the banquet. Charles Lamb might have conceived such a party.

There are several political allusions in *Mardi*. Of course Socialism, Republicanism, and Monarchy, are themes for exposition and satirical discussion. Mr Melville talks sensibly on all these subjects. Though an avowed republican, and the subject of a republican state, he has no dogmatic bigotry of opinion. He is too well aware of what he calls the 'inbred servility of mortal to mortal' to think that republics any more than monarchies can be universally suited to all men. He may think them in the abstract best, but he also knows that for many nations monarchies are better, and will always remain so. To be politically free is after all not the prime end, but only the means to it. 'Better be the subject of a king, upright and just, than a freeman in Franco, with the executioner's axe at every corner.' He has also the courage to tell his American fellow-countrymen that if they are proud of their government, they should be still more proud of their origin and geographical position, to which they are more exclusively indebted for it than to any exertions of their own; and in another part of his book he warns them of qualities and dispositions whose indulgence threatens to endanger all they have heretofore obtained. 'It is not freedom to filch,' he pithily observes. He also, with unconcealed reference to the defects of his countrymen, delivers himself thus wisely and manfully. 'It is not gildings, and gold laces, and crown jewels alone, that make a people servile. There is much bowing and cringing among you yourselves, sovereign kings! Poverty is abased before riches, all Mardi over; anywhere, it is hard to be a debtor; anywhere, the wise will lord it over fools; everywhere, suffering is found. Freedom is more social than political. And its real felicity is not to be shared. *That* is of a man's own individual getting and holding. It is not, Who rules the state, but Who rules me.'

Nothing could be better said. And that we may part from Mr Melville in as good humour as his former books have always left us in, we will here close *Mardi*.

37. From an unsigned review, *Bentley's Miscellany*

April 1849, xxv, 439–42

This periodical was the house organ of Melville's English publisher for *Mardi*, *Redburn*, *White-Jacket*, and *Moby-Dick*, Richard Bentley.

Novelty in literature is always delightful, like novelty in love. When we have penetrated completely into the mystery of any form of composition it ceases to have attractions for us, and are consequently easily persuaded to quit it in search of something which promises more, whether it be able to keep the promise or not. In acting thus we obey one of the most powerful impulses of our nature, which impels us everlastingly forward, and gives birth to what is denominated progress, used as a synonyme for improvement.

Under this impression, the author of '*Mardi*,' a man intoxicated with imagination, has evidently written. For feeling in its ordinary shapes he has no toleration, and he thinks, not altogether perhaps without reason, that the world also is growing weary of it. He endeavours, therefore, to imitate one of the most striking processes of civilisation, and to build up for fancy a distant home in the ocean. In the development of this design he is guilty of great extravagance; but while floating between heaven and earth, creating archipelagos in the clouds, and peopling them with races stranger and more fantastical than

> —The cannibals that each other eat;
> The Anthropophagi, and men whose heads
> Do grow beneath their shoulders,

he contrives to inspire us with an interest in his creations, to excite our passions, to astonish us with the wild grandeur of his landscapes, and to excite in us a strong desire to dream on with him indefinitely.

. . . the story is the least part of the work, which consists of an infinite number of episodes and digressions, descriptions and speculations, theories and commentaries sometimes immeasurably fantastical. Occasionally the author determines to display his learning, when vanity gets the upper hand of him, bewilders his judgment, and makes us laugh heartily at the weakness of human nature. Rabelais himself, however, is scarcely more discursive. He has something to say on every imaginable topic, from the Berkeleyan theory to the immortality of whales, which he has not the conscience to dismiss into the night of annihilation, because they are eighty feet long and so many yards about the waist.

We have no objection to a writer's setting down his opinion on all possible subjects, and therefore we would rather encourage this intellectual gambolling, especially when it is done in jest, and no offence in the world is meant; but we have some dislike to meeting with ideas in so thick a haze that we are unable to perceive distinctly which is which, except where, as in the ultimate dalliance with Hautia, something so exceedingly delicate is to be shadowed forth, that the more opaque the veil the better. In such passages an author's skill is put to the test. He would not be misunderstood, and yet to lift the Eleusinian veil and expose the mysteries hinted at to the vulgar gaze, would be to forfeit all claims to the praise of an adept.

Of course, there is nothing in such cases to be said of mere style, which is a contexture of language and ideas framed after certain principles and accommodated more or less correctly to the rules of art. Mr. Melville abjures all connection with such rules and principles. His cardinal notion is, that provided you effect your purpose, awaken interest, and excite admiration, it signifies very little by what means your design is accomplished. He occasionally, therefore, soars into verse, occasionally sinks to the ordinary level of prose, but habitually operates through a medium which is neither the one nor the other, but a singular compound of both, which tolerates the bold licences of the former and the minuteness and voluminousness of the latter.

It must be allowed, however, that the subject being given, it would not be easy to find a style better fitted for recommending it to the reader. The thing to be achieved is no less than the reconciling of the mind to the creation of an Utopia in the unknown latitudes of the Pacific, to call into existence imaginary tribes and nations, to describe fabulous manners; and to glass them so distinctly in the fancy that they will appear to have been implanted there by memory. This was obviously to be effected either by the exaggeration of ideas, or by exaggeration of language, or by both. Had ordinary language been employed, as in Swift's *Gulliver*, to mask the portentous extravagance of the ideas and inventions, our memory would have been thrown back upon numerous achievements of the past—there would have been no novelty. On the other hand, had the incidents and scenes been probable, but made known to us through the instrumentality of a highly exaggerated style, we should have felt the disparity between the things and their representatives, and disgust would have taken the place of pleasure. Nothing was left, therefore, but to give to strange thoughts and ideas a strange utterance, and by churning up language, as the gods in the Indian fable churned the ocean, to create in the reader a sense of bewilderment and dizziness, which must put to flight all wish to revert to a simple phraseology.

To follow the fugitives from the deck of the Arcturion, from the time they drop their boat into the ocean till the last of them is swept from our view in a cloud of spray, is to move through a gorgeous dream, where the scenes change so rapidly, where danger and strife and plunder alternate with tranquillity and ease and serenity, and where the most stupendous of the known phenomena of nature are exaggerated infinitely by the insatiable appetite of human fancy.

And yet it is scarcely possible to set bounds to the magnificence witnessed by those who move among the wonders of the great deep. Sober travellers have sometimes been overtaken by visions of beauty which their pens refuse to chronicle, because they would not be suspected of dealing in the fabulous. It is not so much, however, what we see, as with what eyes we see it, that constitutes the difference between man and man. Our imagination may almost be said to make the world it looks upon, so completely does it mould and colour the aspect of nature. Language, besides, experiencing its inability to paint with precision the world without us, flings itself almost in despair into exaggeration, and substitutes towering images for a faithful report of reality.

Everywhere there is freshness, originality, or a new way of treating old things. The sea is not the cold sea of the north, veiled by chilly vapours, or reflecting from its surface the shivering shores, but a warm fluid, rolling over coral reefs, clear to the depth of many fathoms, and embracing, as it flows, innumerable verdant isles laden with fruit and flowers to the water's edge. It is, consequently, not greatly to be wondered at if Mr. Melville should run riot in luxuriant descriptions, that he should confound visions with realities, and take transcendental views of nature which render it preternatural. He deals with materials very different from those of the ordinary novelist and romance writer; wild and fabulous he is, and full of Utopian fantasies. But in his company we at least escape from those vapid pictures of society which, differently brushed up and varnished, have been presented to us a thousand times before. *Mardi* is a book by itself, which the reader will probably like very much or detest altogether, according to the measure of his own imagination. In us it has excited, on the whole, very pleasurable sensations. There is a good deal, perhaps, to which—in a lengthened critique—we might object; but in a summing-up like the present, it is unnecessary to be hypercritical when confessedly the agreeable greatly predominates over the contrary. We recommend the reader to try his luck with *Mardi*, and to see whether a trip into the Pacific may not prove quite as agreeable as a lounge through Belgravia. The chances, we think, are in favour of the ocean.

38. Evert A. Duyckinck, from an unsigned review, *Literary World*

14, 21 April 1849, 333–6, 351–3

Duyckinck (1816–78) first met Melville when he was an editor at Wiley & Putnam, Melville's first American publisher. In October 1848 the Duyckinck brothers, Evert and George (1823–63), bought the *Literary World* and served as editors and publishers until it failed in 1854. Leyda says that Evert Duyckinck tended to regard Melville 'with that mixture of admiration & condescension usually directed to a protégé, and enjoyed M[elville] as talker & companion perhaps as much as artist' (*Log*, xxv). Melville often borrowed from Duyckinck's large library, especially during the time *Mardi* was being composed.

By Melville's request the Harpers, his second American publisher, sent Duyckinck a pre-publication copy of *Mardi* so that the *Literary World* could be the only periodical to publish in advance extracts from his new book. The extracts first appeared in the 7 April 1849 number, pp. 309–10.

It is a critical period in the life of an author, when, having received ample honors for his early productions, having on a first appearance achieved a distinguished reputation, he comes before the public again, after an interval, with a new book. The question of his intellectual stamina is to be decided. It is to be determined by a full and accurate survey, a calculation of bearings and distances, and the relations of the whole heavenly system; whether 'the comet of a season' is to assume a steady rank in the great planetary world; whether there is heat as well as light in the brilliant body which has attracted the public gaze. To drop metaphor, Mr. Herman Melville, American sailor, fresh from the Pacific, one summer morning, appears before his countrymen and another great audience in England, in the wondrous tale of *Typee*. The narrative is immediately caught up from its freshness, vivacity, the grace of the story, the humor and ease of the style. 'A very uncommon

common sailor, even for America!' quoth the London *Times*. Hard working Jerrold laps himself in the Typee Elysium. The venerable old *Gentleman's* Sylvanus Urban, older than old Parr, nearing his second centennial, feels youthful blood revive in his veins, even as when he read *Rasselas* (fresh from the press), and sighs 'Ah! thou gentle and too enchanting Fayaway!' Blackwood shrugged his broad Scot shoulders and cried, 'There is no Melville! Can such things come out of a forecastle?' At home the wonder was not less and the sale was as great. Poets took up Fayaway and turned capital prose into indifferent verse; the daily newspapers ran out their vocabulary on the spot. The book was 'racy'—'exceedingly racy,' said the *Courier*; 'readable,' said the *Morning News*; 'a charming book,' the hundred-eyed *Argus*. There was no mistaking the matter. *Typee* was a hit, a palpable hit—and the arrows from that quiver are not exhausted yet. *Typee* is constantly getting printed and going off in new editions, which it is quite too much trouble to put upon the title page. *Omoo* followed, less unique, but full of entertainment, humor, and character. It was and is successful—as it deserved. The good humor of the *Times* was again poured out in a column or two of that broad sheet, and

Blackwood murmured soft applause.

But these were books of Travels; and books of Travels, though written in a highly artistic style, will not sustain a great literary reputation. American travellers have frequently written successful Travels. The national quickness of observation coming in contact with new scenes, the freshness of view which belongs to an American in the old world, and the national curiosity at home, have been prolific of popular Tours and Travels. Was there anything more in the author of *Typee*?

That question MARDI is to decide.

It is exactly two years since Mr. Melville's last book. The interval has undoubtedly been devoted conscientiously and laboriously to *Mardi*, which is not only a very happy, genial production, in the best mood of luxurious invention, but a book of thought, curious thought and reflection. There is 'something in it' everywhere. We read on and on for simple amusement; but we find these pictures leave traces on the memory, and are reproduced with our thoughts, pointing many a significant moral.

If we were seeking for comparisons, to give the reader an idea of *Mardi*, we should suggest something of Rabelais—but the reader will be better prepared to understand that when he has read the book through.

What is the book? A purely original invention. Says Mr. Melville, in his brief preface:—'Not long ago, having published two narratives of voyages in the Pacific, which, in many quarters, were received with incredulity, the thought occurred to me, of indeed writing a romance of Polynesian adventure, and publishing it as such; to see whether the fiction might not, possibly, be received for a verity: in some degree the reverse of my previous experience. This thought was the germ of others, which have resulted in *Mardi.*' The romance of Polynesian adventure is the romance of real life, human nature in a new setting, the romance of Rasselas, Gaudentio di Lucca, the Voyage of Panurge.

To begin at the beginning. We think the first chapter of *Mardi* one of the happiest passages of description to be found anywhere. . . .

. . . The preparations for the escape, the escape itself, are told with the author's accustomed ability, in cultivated, picturesque narration, brief and pregnant, not getting you over rapidly (a trait of the lowest kind of successful description), once and for all, but inviting you to linger and repeat the journey, by numerous felicities of expression and tricks of good feeling. The escape is accomplished, and the great Pacific is before the voyagers. Whither turn? Before the trades to the luxurious islands of the line, virgin, coral-bound, lagune-watered, sheltered, verdant, 'unattempted yet' by prow or sailor. Such islands yet linger, reluctant of discovery, in the broad genial Pacific. No romance can outdo their beauties, or heighten to the privations of a northern imagination their exquisite tropical luxuries. . . .

We soon embark upon a tour of the Islands coming early upon a highly poetical legend related by the old chronicler, Braid-Beard, of a young sovereign, who, in accordance with an ancient prophecy, was confined to the royal groves of his island, which he could not pass. The life of man bound even by the most luxurious restraints, is still slavery. In the condition of this prince we have a picture of elegant satiety, of a man immersed in every tropical delight of this sensuous world, but unable to escape the shadow of himself. The descriptions of the natural scenery of his retreat of Willamilla, of its hanging groves and sequestered gardens, of its regal device of the twin palaces of the Morning and Afternoon, following the course of the sun, of the feastings and banquetings, not unmingled with more solemn tints; all these are in the highest style of invention, oriental richness, and moral truthfulness to the whole race of man. Many a reader will turn back again and again after he has concluded this book, accomplishing the many wanderings through the isles of Mardi, to the sensuous, melancholy Donjalolo, imprisoned monarch of Willamilla. . . .

In fact it is beginning to be pretty evident now to the reader that this Mardi into which he has been led, in spite of the glorious feasting, and drinking, and lounging, the eloquent dissertations on Meerschaums and the like, is quite a serious region after all. Indeed is it, for Mardi expands before us from the coral-cinctured isle of summer seas, the reef-girt lagune-watered atoll of Polynesia, with its chieftain palms and Eden gardens, into a wider circuit, broad as that enveloped by old ocean on the wonderous shield of Achilles. The sea has many isles, and the continents are but isles in Mardi—Mardi is the world. Be not surprised then, reader, at finding thyself flitting about, here and there, among its characters, or at seeing thy birthplace and country figured on its ample map. What is this isle of Dominora and its king Bello, of Vivenza, this Porpheero, with its volcanic eruption—marvellously like John Bull, America, and Republican France! . . .

Is not this sign of a true manhood, when an American author lifts his voice boldly to tell the truth to his country people? There has been a time when the land could not bear this strong meat, but forsooth must be fed on windy adulation. As she grows stronger, and girts herself for stouter enterprises, she appears less afraid to look at her own faults. This is a good sign! *Mardi* probes yet deeper.

States and kingdoms, however, do not touch the whole matter yet. The individual world of man, the microcosm, is to be explored and navigated. To this must all true literature come at last. The Poets but begin

> in gladness
> Whereof in the end comes despondency and sadness.

There is no such thing as trifling in a genuine book. Set even a Thomas Hood, lightest of word-wreathers, down to spin rhymes, and we find ourselves soon caught in a mesh in which the soul is struggling. Most mirthful, most serious of men was Hood. Set a Rabelais upon invention, with the widest range of the earthy, and there will be solemnity enough under his grotesque hood. The irony of Swift, and his persecution of humanity, but prove his love for the race. Is it not significant that our American mariner, beginning with pleasant pictures of his Pacific Ocean, should soon sweep beyond the current of his isles into this world of high discourse: revolving the condition, the duties, the destiny of men? No vagrant lounger, truly, into the booths of literature, where frivolous wit is sold in the fashion of the hour, but a laborious worker, of a rare discipline, on our American book shelves.

Mardi is a species of Utopia—or rather a satiric voyage in which we discover—human nature. There is a world of poetical, thoughtful, ingenious moral writing in it which Emerson would not disclaim—gleams of high-raised fancy, quaint assemblages of facts in the learned spirit of Burton and the Doctor. *Mardi* exhibits the most various reflection and reading. It is an extraordinary book.

We have indicated but a part of its contents, not the whole. The party embraced on the voyage with King Media include a speculative, moralizing philosopher, Babbalanja, very fond of quoting from the ancient writings of one Bardianna (a species of Herr Teufelsdroch authority, an eloquent author, and quite to the point), and occasionally getting into the regions of the incomprehensible; a youthful poet Yoomy, a fair type of the class, all sensibility and expression; the antiquarian Mohi. As for our unphilosophic friend Jarl, of the first volume, he seems to have not been wanted in this learned company; so he was left behind at one of the islands to be killed off by the natives. The discourse of these parties is generally very poetical, at times quite edifying, excepting when they get into the clouds, attempting to handle the problem of the universe.

Mardi will undoubtedly add to Mr. Melville's reputation. The public will discover in him, at least, a capital essayist, in addition to the fascinating novelist and painter of sea life. In these there can be no question of his powers. We might multiply instances of ingenious thought, raised by a subtle fancy, or point to the slender resources of savage life, upon which he has built up the most varied and probable superstructure of manners and character. But enough. It will be felt that America has gained an author of innate force and steady wing, a man with material and work in him—who has respect for his calling, in company with original powers of a high order; with whom the public, we trust, may walk hand in hand, heart in heart, through many good years of goodly productiveness.

39. Charles Gordon Greene, unsigned review, Boston *Post*

18 April 1849

Five days after this review appeared Melville wrote to his father-in-law, Judge Lemuel Shaw, 'I see that *Mardi* has been . . . burnt by the common hangman in the Boston *Post*' (*Letters*, 84).

Many a *nine shillings*, we imagine, will be wasted on these two externally handsome volumes. Mr Melville's reputation as a writer of commingled fact and fiction is deservedly high, but we have always thought it not so high as it ought to be. His *Typee* and *Omoo* are much more than graceful, fascinating and vivacious books—they are filled with powerful descriptions, and strongly drawn, well filled and natural characters. His personages purport to be real people, but it is almost needless to say that they must be, in the main, and as much as most fictitious characters are, the mental creations of the author. And it is for this unpretending, homely, real delineation, found in the midst of so much that is wild, light, fanciful and gorgeous, that Mr Melville has not received sufficient praise; and while his productions have been commended quite as much as they deserve to be for the last named attributes, the portions displaying the most genius, tact and knowledge of human nature have usually escaped the general eye, as far at least as the remarks of reviewers are concerned. In his two former books the author under notice is quite worthy of being called a modernised Defoe—much of the strength, homeliness and naturalness of the great original being overlaid with a coating of modern grace and spiritualness. It was with these feelings that we began to read *Mardi*, and we have written the preceding sentences, not to raise up that we might the more effectually knock down, but to show that we have a cordial appreciation of Mr Melville's previous writings, and that in commencing the present one, we had no sort of prejudice against it or him.

With these premises, it is almost needless to say that we were disappointed with *Mardi*. It is not only inferior to *Typee* and *Omoo*, but it is a really poor production. It ought not to make any reputation for its author, or to sell sufficiently well to encourage him to attempt any thing else. 'The Voyage Thither' is interesting enough, though even this is almost spoiled by the everlasting assumption of the brilliant, jocose and witty in its style. After the arrival at 'Mardi,' the book becomes mere *hodge-podge*, reminding us of the *talk* in Rabelais, divested of all its coarseness, and, it may be added, of all its wit and humor. In his preface, Mr Melville intimates, that having previously written truth which was believed to be fiction, he has now attempted a romance 'to see whether it might not possibly be received as a verity.' We think he need be under no apprehension that the present volumes will be received as gospel—they certainly lack all show of truth or naturalness. He had better stick to his 'fact' which is received as 'fiction,' but which puts money in his purse and wreathes laurels round his head, than fly to 'fiction' which is not received at all, as we opine will be the case with *Mardi*, in a very short time, and in spite of the all extending and pervading influence of his publisher. We doubt not, however, that the book will sell and be read, for a time, but if the 'man who read the *Monikins*' was one of the greatest curiosities in the land, we think the 'man who read *Mardi* and *liked it*' will be an *unexampled* product of the age—he may be the 'coming man,' perhaps, spoken of by Punch and the Transcendentalists. We have said that *Mardi* is *hodge-podge*. It describes adventures in the Polynesian Islands, but lacks incident and meaning. The conversations are like nothing one ever read or heard, and, if they have any significance, are too recondite, at least, for our intelligence to fathom. Sometimes it seems as if the book were a satire upon matters and things in general, but this idea is soon dispersed by the appearance of a mass of downright nonsense. The characters are 'legion' and uninteresting—the whole book is not only tedious but unreadable. In a word, *Mardi* greatly resembles Rabelais emasculated of every thing but prosiness and puerility.

40. William Young, unsigned review, *Albion*

21 April 1849, 189

Young (1809–88), an Englishman who came to live in New York, edited the *Albion* from 1848 to 1867. The journal, which reprinted many articles from the British periodicals, also published six extracts from *Mardi* on the same day as this review (pp. 182–3).

These two duodecimo volumes contain an infinite fund of wit, humour, pathos, and philosophy. In them may be found the same charming powers of description already evinced by the author in his *Typee* and *Omoo*; whilst the range of the subject is far more comprehensive, and the abilities of the writer are in consequence still farther developed. His plan, and the license he allows himself, are hinted in the following pithy little preface.

> Not long ago, having published two narratives of voyages in the Pacific, which, in many quarters, were received with incredulity, the thought occurred to me, of indeed writing a romance of Polynesian adventure, and publishing it as such; to see whether the fiction might not possibly be received for a verity; in some degree the reverse of my previous experience. This thought was the germ of others, which resulted in *Mardi*.

Availing himself of this happy conceit, Mr. Melville records a fabulous desertion in a whale-boat from a South Seaman, with all the *vraisemblance*[1] of a log-book, interweaves, at pleasure, classical allusion and scholarly lore with such portions as suit his purpose of the mythology of the South Sea Islanders, treats his readers to some delicate satire, and some sound political hints on men and things in our own and other countries—and in short, with the Pacific Archipelago for his ground-work, has put forth a lively, pungent, instructive, and exceedingly clever bundle of his thoughts and imaginings. Parts may be read by the most careless reader, and be enjoyed in the dozes of a summer's afternoon—other parts require a wide-awake application, or, as in

[1] *Vraisemblance:* verisimilitude.

Gulliver's Travels, one half the aroma will be lost. Though the United States be plainly enough portrayed in *Vivenza*, the British Isles in *Dominora*, *Kaleedoni*, and *Verdanna*, France in *Franko*, and Canada in *Kanneeda*, the book invites study, and deserves that close investigation which appertains to reviewers, for whom indeed it will be a *bonne bouche*.[1] We give copious extracts elsewhere, and what we do not give is as good as what we select. In Mr. Melville's style we notice a too habitual inversion, an overstraining after antithesis and Carlyle-isms, with the not unfrequent sacrifice of the natural to the quaint. These defects, however, are spots in the sun; and we welcome *Mardi* to a place on all book-shelves and a cupboard in the chambers of the memory.

41. From an unsigned review, *John Bull*

21 April 1849, 247

In these volumes the talented author of two narratives of adventures in the South Seas has made use of the materials with which his former residence among the islanders supplied him, for the purpose of weaving the web of a fictitious story which, in more than one sense, is entitled to the appellation 'novel.' . . .

Such is the main outline of the story, evidently intended for an allegory. Yillah,—the dreamy damsel who, unacquainted with her origin, is a stranger to all life's realities, and mysteriously disappears under the baneful spell of Hautia,—representing the poetry of the soul's high romance, and its ideal happiness, before it has become effaced by contact with a base world, while Hautia is the personification of selfishness, of gross desires, and of material enjoyment. A very large, not to say the largest, portion of the book, however, consists of allegoric representations of the real world, and especially of Europe and of this country. Under this mask, which is often of the very thinnest

[1] *Bonne bouche:* tidbit.

texture, the author indulges in much keen satire, and in great license of discussion on topics of every description, chiefly political and religious. While it is impossible not to admire the brilliancy of colouring with which the whole tale is invested, and the striking truth of many of the allegorical remarks and frequent home-thrusts, we cannot but express our profound regret that a pen so talented, and an apparatus so fascinating, as those which the author of *Mardi* commands, should have been made use of for the dissemination of sceptical notions. To introduce the Saviour of mankind under a fabulous name, and to talk down the verities of the Christian faith by sophistry, the more than irreverence of which is but flimsily veiled, is a grave offence, not against good taste alone; and we could heartily wish that Mr. Melville had confined himself to the lively and picturesque scenery of which his pencil is master, and, if he pleased, to such subjects as offer a fair scope for the indulgence of his satirical vein, without introducing crude metaphysics and unsound notions of divinity into a craft of a build far too light for carrying so ponderous a freight.

42. 'A Page by the Author of *Mardi*,' unsigned lampoon, *The Man in the Moon*

May 1849, v, 284–5

Angus B. Reach edited this London monthly humor magazine, which failed the same year the lampoon of *Mardi* was published.

And so the grey-eyed dawn, pale daughter of Night, broke upon the coral island, and the sea, and the temple of the god Jumbo. Indeed the rustle of his godship's wings came pealing down the breeze of the morn, and the light of his eye sparkled in the surf which gemmed the green shores of Mardi.

So that the fishes rejoiced swimmingly, and swam rejoicingly on their way amid the green waters, wagging tails and pointing fins, and diving into the extreme depths, where anchors float, and beneath which ingots of virgin gold descend not—held hovering there by the spirits whose unseen hands form the power which Sir Isaac Newton (prompted by me) called Gravitation.

Let us be merry then, and rejoice and sing under the banyan and over the plantain, and cleave the lightsome air with glad voices, chaunting the hymns of the Sagas and the Scalds, in that old Runic rhyme which Lapland witches sung when they sold shipmen a wind, and invoked the hammer of Thor, near to the roar of the whirling Lofoden!

Jarl is near me—sea green his locks, and streaming. Yillah basks beside me—her great black eyes, lustrous and full orbed, the doors through which Angels and Spirits float into her being from that heaven which is higher than the seventh seen by the camel-driver in his vision; and Samao, also, is nigh, with a fish's bone stuck through the cartilage of his nose.

Ruler of aspirations and despot over the unimaginable vortices of the soul—great Jumbo, god of Mardi—whose father sprang from the tortoise on whose back rests the world, aid me while I strike an airy harp, and upon strings of summer wind fling melody abroad upon entranced creation! The pulsations of Yillah's heart grew musical and dim, and bending over her goddess-like form I heard this song, in the depths of her being—

SONG OF YILLAH'S HEART.

I am a heart, and I pump the blood
　　Through body and limb.
I beat for love, and I cause the blush,
Scarlet and crimson and mellow, to rush
　　(For a whim)
Over the face and over the breast
Of the maid who obeys the high behest
　　　Of Cupid—so slim!
　　　　Slim! slim!!
　　　　　Slim!!!

Then calling upon my Vyking Jarl, we unmoored the whale-boat from the beach. No canoes gemmed the sea—the waves rose and sunk unloaded—so we pushed the whale-boat off the land. Then the legion of the fish came with us, and we sailed away, away, away, for months and months, and years and years, and centuries and centuries—over the sea!

43. George Ripley, initialled review, New York *Tribune*

10 May 1849

Ripley (1802–80) succeeded Margaret Fuller as literary critic for the *Tribune*, a position he held from 1849 to 1880. He was a graduate of the Harvard Divinity School (1826) and was one of the original members of the Transcendental Club. Ripley founded Brook Farm in 1842. Among his duties there was the editorship of the *Harbinger*.

We have seldom found our reading faculty so near exhaustion, or our good nature as critics so severly exercised, as in an attempt to get through this new work by the author of the fascinating *Typee* and *Omoo*. If we had never heard of Mr. Melville before, we should soon have laid aside his book, as a monstrous compound of Carlyle, Jean-Paul, and Sterne, with now and then a touch of Ossian thrown in; but remembering our admiration of his former charming productions, we were unable to believe that the two volumes could contain so little of the peculiar excellence of an old favorite, and only mock us with a constant sense of disappointment.

Typee and *Omoo* were written under the immediate inspiration of personal experience.—The vivid impressions which the author had received from his residence among those fairy Edens of the Sea had not faded from his mind. He describes what he saw and felt, with the careless hilarity of a sailor, relating a long yarn to his shipmates in the forecastle—he has no airs, but airs from the perfumed islands where he revelled so jubilantly in the wild freedom of nature—he has no reputation to keep from damage, except that of a good fellow who has seen strange things in his day—and he talks on in his riotous, rollicking manner, always saucy, often swaggering, but ever revealing the soul of a poet and the eye of a painter; and accordingly, his books have had a popular run, that might gratify the proudest author in modern literature. They have been read with equal delight by the rough sailor, who had to spell out the words by his dim lantern, and the refined scholar who gladly turned from graver toils to these enchanting scenes—by the lawyer amid waiting clients, the seamstress at her needle, and the mechanic at his bench.

The present work aims at a much higher mark but fails to reach it. It professes to be a work of imagination, founded on Polynesian adventures, and for a portion of the first volume maintains that character with tolerable success. In the description of the escape of the 'Ancient Mariner' and himself from the whale ship—their strange voyage in an open boat over a thousand miles of ocean—of their gaining unexpected possession of a new craft, MELVILLE is himself—and this is saying a great deal. There are passages in this part of the work, which, taken as separate pictures, display unrivaled beauty and power—the same simple, unaffected grace—the same deep joy in all the rare and precious things of nature—and the same easy command of forcible, picturesque language, which in his former productions called forth such a gush of admiration, even from the most hide-bound reviewer.

But the scene changes after we arrive at 'Mardi' and the main plot of the book (such as it is) begins to open.

We are then presented with a tissue of conceits, fancifully strung about the personages of the tale, expressed in language that is equally intolerable for its affectation and its obscurity. The story has no movement, no proportions, no ultimate end; and unless it is a huge allegory —bits of which peep out here and there—winding its unwieldy length along, like some monster of the deep, no significance or point. We become weary with the shapeless rhapsody, and wonder at the audacity of the writer which could attempt such an experiment with the long suffering of his readers.

We should not think it worth while to express ourselves so unambiguously on the character of this work, if we did not recognize in Mr. MELVILLE a writer not only of rare promise, but of excellent performance. He has failed by leaving his sphere, which is that of graphic, poetical narration, and launching out into the dim, shadowy, spectral, Mardian region of mystic speculation and wizard fancies.

Even the language of this work is a hybrid between poetry and prose.—Every page abounds in lines which might be dovetailed into a regular poem without any change in the rhythm. It can easily be read aloud so that the nicest ear could not distinguish it from heroic verse. Let the author return to the transparent narration of his own adventures, in the pure, imaginative prose, which he handles with such graceful facility, and he will be everywhere welcomed as one of the most delightful of American writers.

44. Philarète Chasles, from '*Voyages réels et fantastiques d'Hermann Melville*,' Paris *Revue des deux mondes*

15 May 1849, ii, 541–70

Chasles (1798–1873), a widely-known French critic, was especially interested in national literatures and their influences on other nations. He introduced several foreign writers to France, among them Gozzi, Richter, and Melville. This long article surveys his three works, giving special attention to *Mardi*.

The translation presented here is that published by the New York *Literary World* (4, 11 August 1849, 89–90, 101–3). The *Literary World* article is important in itself for the currency it gave Chasles' views—showing the widening European reputation of a young American author—and for the concluding commentary on Chasles and on Melville. One aspect of Chasles' review that cannot be exhibited in any translation is the true nature of *his* translations of passages from *Mardi*. Elizabeth S. Foster discusses this important question in her Historical Note to the Northwestern-Newberry edition of *Mardi* (vol. 3, *The Writings of Herman Melville* [Evanston and Chicago, 1970], 670):

He bestowed the highest praise of his review upon what purported to be a three-paragraph excerpt from *Mardi* in French translation, beginning:

'Salut, mon Amérique libre, terre du printemps!' 'There are few lyric chants more beautiful than this,' he exclaimed. But alas for the author of *Mardi*. The author of the beautiful lyric chant is M. Philarète Chasles, though he does incorporate a few images from Yoomy's song about Yillah in Chapter 154 and a phrase from Babbalanja in Chapter 159. If the translation in the *Literary World* had not omitted all Chasles's excerpts from *Mardi*, or rather pseudo-excerpts, someone would have noticed, and would probably have pointed out long ago, that it was his own amendments of and substitutions for Melville that Chasles found most worthy of wonder and praise. He concluded his essay with his own fervent advice to revolution-prone France, but again he pretended that the passage came from *Mardi*. 'The words which he [Melville] addresses to France,' he gravely said, 'deserve to be pondered.'

PARISIAN CRITICAL SKETCHES

THE ACTUAL AND FANTASTIC VOYAGES OF HERMAN MELVILLE

By M. Philarète Chasles

We have here a curious novelty, an American Rabelais. Fancy what the prodigious Pantagruel would have been, if our Meudon *curé* had added elegiac, transparent, and pearl-like tints to the canvas of his vigorous irony, and enhanced the originality of his arabesques with Pantheistic philosophy. Fancy Daphnis and Chloe, or Paul and Virginia in the bosom of a cloud, dancing I know not what strange gavotte, with Aristotle and Spinoza, escorted by Gargantua and Gargamelle. A work such as was never before heard of, worthy of a Rabelais without gaiety, a Cervantes without grace, a Voltaire without taste. *Mardi and a Voyage Thither* is none the less one of the most singular books which has appeared anywhere upon the face of the globe for a long time. You might accumulate upon it all the epithets that Madame de Sevigné affectionated; an extraordinary and vulgar book, original and incoherent, full of sense and nonsense, stuffed full of interesting facts and repetition, profound instruction, and indifferent epigrams. You might call it the dream of an ill-educated cabin boy, who has intoxicated himself with hashish, and is swayed to and fro by the wind on the fore-top during a midsummer night in the tropics.

This bizarre work, commencing as a novel, turning into a fairy tale, and availing itself of allegory to reach the satirical after passing through the elegy, the drama, and the burlesque novel, piqued greatly my curiosity as a critic; I did not understand it after I had read it, I understood it still less after I had re-read it; a key was necessary not only for the comprehension of the facts, the proper names, and the doctrines which the author introduced, but above all to the composition of such a book, which appeared to have no reason in the world to be in the world. With that love of the truth and that necessity of going to the bottom of things which I neither can nor would extinguish, I set to work to solve a problem which had all the more interest as relating to an entirely new literature, which is still, so to speak, in the egg-shell. I consulted the English criticisms; they told me what I already knew—in the first place that the work was an extravagant one, and in the second, that they saw their way no more clearly than I did. They also informed me that Mr. Herman Melville was a pseudonym for the author of the apocryphal romance-voyages, *Typee* and *Omoo*, which exhibit vigorous power of imagination and great hardihood in lying.

In consequence I read *Typee*, or as we should pronounce the word, *Taïpie*, and also *Omoo* (*Omoū*), and I did not agree with the English critics. They treat without doubt of a thousand strange adventures, of nymphs, lovelorn and savage, of idyllic and philosophical cannibals, of temples buried in the woods and perched on tops of the rocks of Nukuheva, of beautiful *Morais* in the villages, of innocent scenes of anthropophagism varied with sentimental dances, but pretty much these identical things are found in the pages of Bougainville, Onga, Ellis, and Earle. There was an impression of truth, a savor of an unknown and primitive nature, a vivacity of impression which struck me. The colors appeared to me to be real, although a little too warm and somewhat heightened for effect, while the romantic adventures of the author were turned off with sufficient probability. Our hero, after having been, as he tells us, devoured with caresses by his Polynesian hosts, came near being devoured by them in flesh and bones; they had prodigally bestowed upon him those attentions of gastronomic hospitality, of which the animals of our farmyards are the subject. Fed, lodged, and entertained at the expense of the state, he had for amusement the opera, native poetry, balls, and the conversation of the most distinguished bayadères. They took care of his life, his happiness, his good humor, his physical and moral health, with a love and watchfulness which make one shudder. He hastened to escape from a people who were so careful of their guests. A long odyssey, full of redoubtable wanderings, terminated in his escape from the barbaric banquet. He, however, left *en route* his valet de chambre, a sort of sailor Sancho Panza, named Toby, a diverting personage. His master, who doubted not that the Typeeans had served up Toby à la broche, or fried in sheets of paper, shed a few tears to his memory and returned to Boston, where he published this history.

It was taken for a *hoax* of the first calibre. The style, without being pure or elegant, had vivacity, and carried the reader along with it. The public were astonished to find an American so imaginative and so much of a Gascon, but admired him none the less. The Americans understand pleasantry, except when it touches the national honor; they are fond enough of it, and like it none the worse with a high seasoning. They say strange things in their legislative chambers. Certain grave and highly esteemed journals always prefix to their announcements of marriages a small vignette representing a mouse trap, with these words beneath in enormous letters,—Matrimonial Mousetrap. It is also an ancient English and Puritan custom, cultivated with remarkable dexterity by Daniel Defoe, to entrap the public in this way by fictions adorned with all the details of verisimilitude. 'The Revelation of Mrs. Veal, made on her Death-bed,'—a sheet which was cried in the streets of London about 1688,—deceived many good Calvinistic souls for the benefit of their salvation. So the pleasantry displeased no one, and Mr. Herman Melville passed for a very original and amusing *story-teller.*

Meantime, an austere journal, the New York *Evangelist*, handled these romantic inventions of Mr. Melville very severely, treated him as an ill-timed jester, and reproached him for having spoken lightly and calumniously of the missionaries at Typee and the Marquesas. It did not concern the author to find himself thus refuted. He made no answer, but all of a sudden, in January, 1846, a letter of the sailor valet de chambre Toby appeared in one of the journals of a very distant province (*Buffalo Commercial Advertiser*), prefaced by a note by the editor, who said that he had seen Toby in person. . . .

. . . Mr. Herman Melville, therefore, hastened to profit by his first success; he quickly wrote a continuation of *Typee*, with the adventures of his poor Toby, and entitled this continuation OMOO. Pretty much the same qualities distinguish the second work ,which had less success; it contains the fragments of the journal of the voyage from which *Typee* had been composed. The reputation of the story-teller was made. Every one allowed that Mr. Herman Melville had an infinite deal of imagination, that he invented the most curious extravagances in the world, and that he excelled, like Cyrano Bergerac, in mystification of the serious kind.

After having read *Typee* and *Omoo*, I had, as I have said, great doubt as to the justice of the opinion which had prevailed in America and in England, and which is expressed in most of the journals and reviews in which the 'romances' of Mr. Melville are analysed. The freshness and profundity of the impressions reproduced in these books astonished me; I saw in their writer one less skilful in amusing himself with a dream, and in playing with a cloud, than constrained by a powerful recollection, which had gained possession of him. A type of the Anglo-American character, living for and by sensation, curious as an infant, adventurous as a savage, the first to throw himself head-foremost into unheard-of adventures, and carrying them through with desperate enthusiasm, I found that Mr. Herman Melville had there depicted himself most faithfully. But who would have dared to affirm the authenticity of Mr. Melville and his veracity? To attack to its face the criticism of the new world and of the old, would have been very immodest. I contented myself with doubting, when chance brought me in contact with one of the most honorable citizens of the United States, a man educated and *spirituel*, well acquainted with the literary affairs of his race: 'Will you,' I said to him, 'tell me the real name of that singular writer who calls himself Herman Melville, and who has published in the United States those curious tales, *Mardi* and *Typee*?'

'Ah!' said he, 'you are too subtle a nation, you look for mischief in everything. Mr. Herman Melville's name is Herman Melville, he is the son of a former Secretary of Legation of our Republic at the Court of St. James. Of a fiery and ardent temperament, he embarked at an early age, and, as we say, *followed the sea*.'

'Did he form part of the *regular navy*, or did he ship in a privateer?'

'He alone can inform you as to that, and if you ever visit Massachusetts, where he is married and settled, I advise you to go and ask him for the information. He is an athletic man, still young, hardy, and enterprising by nature, one of those men all nerve and muscle, who delight in combating waves and storms, men and the seasons. He is married to the daughter of Judge Shaw, one of the most distinguished magistrates of New England, and he now lives in the calm of family life, enjoying a just and singular celebrity, of which he accepts the slightly equivocal side, for he is generally regarded as a narrator of well made up stories, but very day-dreams withal. His family, who know that the adventures related by him are *genuine*, are not flattered by the eulogiums bestowed upon Mr. Herman Melville's imagination at the expense of his morality. His cousin, at whose house I passed last summer, cried out against the obstinacy of readers who would see only fantastic scenes in *Typee* and *Omoo*. My cousin, said he, writes very well, especially when he reproduces exactly what he has seen; not having (fait d'etudes) been a student in the ordinary and accepted sense of the word, he has preserved the freshness of his impressions. It is precisely to this young man's life passed amidst savages that he owes this sincerity, this vigor, this odor of bizarre reality which give him such extraordinary vividness;—he never would have invented the scenes which he describes. The pleasant part of the story is, that charmed by his improvised reputation, he has not contradicted those who attribute to the brilliancy and creative fecundity of his imagination the merit which belongs only to the fidelity of his memory. He would be vexed, if the essential truth of this curious episode in the life of a young sailor should be acknowledged. The re-appearance of his companion Toby or Richard Green provoked him to some extent, by making him descend from the pedestal of the novelist to the ordinary level of a narrator. As for myself, who know what a bad head this Melville has, and the way in which he employed his early years, and who have read his journal, his *Rough Notes*, actually in the hands of his father-in-law, and conversed with Richard Green, his faithful Achates, I laugh at the infatuation of the public. You see falsehood in what is truth, and truth in what is falsehood. Read *Typee* over again, I beg of you; I do not speak of *Omoo*, which is a faint re-impression of the other. Read this book again; no more as a romance, but as bearing the most naive impression of the ideas and manners common to that great Polynesian Archipelago of which we know so little. The new traveller is more faithful than Bougainville, who has turned the thickets of Tahiti into boudoirs à la Pompadour; than Diderot, who avails himself, to color and embellish his material sensualism, of the voluptuous tales of Bougainville. He is more worthy of credence than the Englishmen Ellis and Earle, entirely occupied with a justification of the conduct of the Anglican missionaries in the midst of these populations, authors who want at the same time the poetic and picturesque perception, and the animated style necessary for such scenes. Without doubt Mr. Melville uses too violent colors, but that is not astonishing. At his age, at that time, at that epoch when the first sap and freshness of the life which developes itself, gives a passionate force to its ideas and impressions, he ought to feel a lively emotion, exaggerated if you will, of the novelty of objects, and the singularity of perils. His exuberant style is too ornate, his tints à la Rubens, his warm and violent colors, his predilection for dramatic effect, his efflorescent descriptions shock the taste. Nevertheless, there are scarcely fewer romantic details in the pages of the old Spanish doctor Saaverde de Figueroa, who was the first to describe those voluptuous latitudes, and it would be ridiculous to expect a great sobriety of color from a young American cabin boy, who had the honor to pass four months with MM. the savages, who has partaken of the pleasures of their primitive existence, and been within an ace of being eaten by them. Like all his predecessors, like Don Christoval Saavedra de Figueroa, Captain Cook, and Bougainville, he has written under the charm caused by the prestige of primitive nature and the novelty of habits. The American alone, less seduced by the pleasures of the new Cythera than excited to the search of adventure, shows himself resolute, rough, and vehement; he is a character by himself, which renders this singular work still more worthy of study.'

This authentic information did not surprise me, it only confirmed my previous opinion.* It was therefore as a book of travels and not a dream, as at 'a peep at Polynesian life,' and not an agreeable invention, that I re-perused this book.

—— Here we pause. In our next we shall pursue M. Philarète Chasles' critical sketch of *Mardi*, with a word or so of comment and elucidation of the amusing picture which M. Chasles has drawn of Herman Melville.

(*Concluded from our last.*)

Before we return to Mr. Melville's last work, let us follow the young cabin boy awhile in this unknown valley of the Marquesas Islands, in the midst of a tribe of the interior, scarcely visited by the missionaries, strangers to the half-civilization which European contact has imposed upon the aborigines of the coast, who have become patterns of pretentious barbarity and coquettish ignorance. Mr. Melville does not tell us explicitly by what title he found himself, at so young an age, on board of the American whaler, the Dolly, then on holiday at Nukuheva, in 1842. Neither does he inform us to what circumstances the little favor which he enjoyed from Captain Vangs was attributable, nor the

* My opinion relative to the voyage of Mr. Herman Melville, and the authenticity of the details which he has given, is on record in the columns of the *Journal des Debats* for 1846, numbers from the 20th to the 22d of June. An English journal ridiculed greatly my credulity. I thought I was mistaken, and so made no answer.

motives which decided him on the first opportunity to play traunt, that is to say desert.

(Here follows a translation of the passage descriptive of the entrance to the bay of Tior.)

It is this identical descriptive style, this talent of the colorist, perhaps a little exaggerated, and choosing from preference vivid and brilliant touches, that has obtained for Mr. Melville his reputation as a fanciful writer.

(The critic continues his analysis of *Typee*, accompanied with long extracts. He remarks, after quoting the passage descriptive of the *taboo* rites—)

The situation was not in truth very reassuring, but it must be confessed that we are indebted to it for a narrative that may pass for a model in the art of communicating to the reader vividly-felt sensations, and above all, that nervous thrill which has relation rather with physical instinct than with thought.

★ ★ ★ ★

The real value of these two works consists, as we see, in their vivacity of impression, and lightness of touch of the pencil. Led away by his first success, the author afterwards attempted to write a new humoristic book, *Mardi, and a Voyage Thither*. Irritated by the false reputation for invention which had been bestowed upon him, he took the pains to merit it, he endeavoured to make use of the treasures of the imagination which had been lent to him. We shall see how he has succeeded.

In starting, like a good man of business, he was unwilling to lose the credit which his first speculation with the isle of Tior had brought him, and so did not leave Polynesia, which was the first fault. Then he pretended to be perfectly original, his second error. Originality can hardly be had for the wishing. Criticism is absurd when it reproaches the Americans for being wanting in originality in the arts; originality is a thing which is not to be ordered, and which comes late. Nations and individuals commence by imitation. Originality belongs only to ripe minds, who have a perfect knowledge of their depth and their extent; infancy is never original. This pretension to excessive novelty has in this case resulted only in an awkward and singular mélange of grotesque comedy and fantastic grandeur, which one may look for in vain in any other book. Nothing is so fatiguing as this mingling of the pompous and the vulgar, of the common-place and the unintelligible, of violent rapidity in the accumulation of catastrophes, and emphatic deliberation in the description of landscapes. These discursions, these graces, this flowery style, festooned, twisted into quaint shapes, call to mind the arabesques of certain writing masters, which render the text unintelligible.

A humoristic book is the rarest product of art. It is a voyage without compass on a limitless ocean. Sterne, Jean Paul, and Cervantes have alone been able to accomplish the task; Mr. Melville has certainly not succeeded in it. Although he commences by a fairy tale, continues with a romantic fiction, and afterwards attempts the ironical and symbolical, his ill-compacted implement breaks with a crash under his novice hand. How much study, reflection, and labor, what skill in style, what a power of combination, and what progress in civilization, were necessary to create Rabelais, Swift, or Cervantes! Let us not be surprised that *Mardi* should have all the faults of the rising Anglo-American literature, and let us seek for what it contains that is new and remarkable. Let us observe the curious development of a nationality of a second creation, and let us remember that there are maladies connected with growth, and that men like races do not develope themselves solely by their virtues.

. . . The nocturnal abduction of the boat, the peripatetics of the eighteen days passed upon the sea, the hurricane which follows the calm upon these transparent and unfathomed waters, the examination of the strange tribes (scarcely known by the naturalists) who inhabit this ocean, would have a vivid interest if the author had not stifled life and reality under a luxurious maze of circumlocutions, exclamations, divagations, and hyperboles. To the Americans, as to all nations not yet possessed of an individual literature, it appears that simplicity must be vulgar and truth of detail contemptible. The hyperbole, heaping Ossa upon Pelion, and Pelion upon Ossa, the envelopment in clouds, which destroy the delicacy and severity of the color, is one of the most prevalent vices both of infant and superannuated literatures. To this first fault is to be joined the incorrectness arising from rapidity of execution. Mr. Herman Melville does not use the English language with learned ability, like Wadsworth Longfellow; nor like Bryant, another remarkable poet, with a somewhat timid grace. He misuses the vocabulary, reverses periods, creates unknown adjectives, invents absurd ellipses, and composes new words contrary to all the laws of the old Anglo-Germanic analogy—'Unshadow—tireless—fadeless,' and many other monsters of the same kind.* Nevertheless, in despite of its

* *Un*, which expresses negation like the *a* privative of the Greeks, can only precede adjectives, adverbs, and verbs—*un earthly*, *un willingly*, *untie*. Less, an adverb expressing

unheard of style, the emotions of the sea are admirably rendered. At one time from the deck of the ship, the sailor sees in her the powerful and rebellious steed whom industry, patience, and science have subdued to their will; at another, from his frail shallop, she seems an herculean force which plays with man as the wind tosses about the feather in the air. . . .

The whole of this part of the book save the effort continually manifested by the author to be eloquent, ingenious, and original, is charming and full of life. There is much interest and vigor in the maritime scenes, such as the pictures of the calm, the storm, and above all of the capture of the abandoned brigantine. You would think that you were commencing a recital of probable or actual adventures. No such thing. Scarcely has the author entered these delicious lagunes where spring time is eternal and the night luminous as the day, when he renounces reality, and fairy land and somnambulism commence. . . .

As far as the somnambulism awakened by this part of the book permits the intentions of the American author to be divined, Yillah should represent 'human happiness' sacrificed by the priests. Mr. Melville has an old grudge against the priesthood, and since the missionaries of the *New York Evangelist*, his dislike seems to have been envenomed.

Here commences a symbolic Odyssey of the strangest nature, very clumsily imitated from Rabelais—an odyssey which is to plunge us in a world of extravagant phantoms and allegorical shades. The adventurers visit in turn the chiefs of the small islands of the Archipelago, which have all a symbolic signification. Borabolla the gastronome evidently represents epicureanism; Maramma is the religious world, superstition; Donjalolo is the poetic world; the antiquarian Oh-Oh is the symbol of erudition. One chapter seems to be devoted to the etiquette of the Spaniards, another to the artistic genius of the Italians, a third to French mobility. I think that the island of Pimminy must be the fashionable world, the society of exquisites, of which Mr. Melville makes a sufficiently piquant satire. It is, in two words, young America amusing himself with old Europe. We would not be sorry to receive some lessons from this young infant precocious and robust; our

---

privation (*los* in German, the Gothic *laus*), should only be placed after substantives: *father less*, *penny less*. These principles, emanating from the special genius and inseparable from the logic of the language, govern in all the idioms of the Germanic and Scandinavian stock, the vigorous and extensive formation of compound words. To be unfaithful to these essential laws is to destroy the idiom and sap its roots.

decrepitude has need of them and we are playing very sad comedies, but Mr. Melville has taken a wrong course to indoctrinate or parody us. Of what import to us are the interminable excursions of Melville, Samoah, and Jarl? What have we to do with King Prello and King Xipho, who symbolize feudality and military glory. Those then are not our present terrors. Our nineteenth century has other enemies to combat.

At last a queen, Queen Hautia, who is smitten with the traveller, takes upon herself to abduct the young captain. From time to time Hautia, who seems to be something like voluptuousness, sends three of her *femmes de chambre* to Melville, armed with symbolic flowers, which the hero never fails to send back to her. In the midst of this chaos the old theories of D'Holbach, the already superannuated dogmas of Hegel, the pantheistic algebra of Spinoza, are mixed and pitched together in inextricable confusion. The philosophical commonplaces of the rationalistic schools are veiled under a thousand symbolic folds, which the author seems to consider something grand—let him know that we are completely blaséd by the blasphemies.

The second volume is devoted to this obscure satire of European faiths, and the vague doctrines of a pantheistic scepticism. None of the voyagers has been able to find human happiness (Yillah), they do not accept voluptuousness (Hautia) as sufficient compensation. They then make sail for Mardi, a kind of world in the clouds,—from metaphysical symbolism we pass to transparent allegory.

Mardi is the modern political world. This part is the most piquant of the book. We are curious to learn how a republican of the United States judges the civilization of the present, and resolves the obscure problem of human destinies. Let us pass rapidly over the invention of the strange names with which Europe, France, and America are baptized by our author: they are *Dominora* (England), *Franko* (France), *Ibirie* (Spain), *Romara* (Rome), *Apsburga* (Germany), *Kannida* (Canada). This harlequinade reminds us too much of our own Rabelais, so fruitful in appellations, whose grotesque sound suffices to provoke the *pantagruelian* titillation. Mr. Melville is not a magician of this kind. He has good sense and sagacity, he would make out of them humor, which is not the same thing.

The fantastic vessel upon which a poet, a philosopher, Mr. Melville, and a rabble of fabulous personages of mediocre invention find themselves, touches in turn at the shores of Europe or *Porphyro* (the morning star), and of America, or the Land of Life (*Vivenza*). They visit Germany,

England, Spain, Italy, France. There is a filial respect and profound love in the manner in which the author speaks of Great Britain, worthy of notice, and a thorough Anglo-Saxon severity in the pity which he accords to Ireland. At last he sees France—the year 1848 has just commenced.

It will be seen that our author preserves a very beautiful sang-froid in contemplating our miseries. As soon as he sees American land, this philosophic calm gives place to a very lively exultation.

There are few lyric chants more beautiful than this: the poet is here true as to his proper emotion—true as to that which he expresses. In effect, what will vast America become where each year fleets of various populations arrive to aggregate themselves to the old puritan and calvinistic nucleus of the Anglo-Saxon colony—what will be the genius of this new world as yet scarcely sketched? It is one of the most curious subjects for speculation and conjecture which can offer themselves to the philosopher. What one can affirm with certainty is that, on the one side, America is yet very far from her necessary development; on the other, that she will attain it in the same ratio that will force back Europe into the shade. The Europeans are too enlightened to believe that European civilization comprehends the past and the future of the world. The zones of light change; the march of civilization, that of science, the successive and constant discovery of the truth, can not only no longer be the object of a doubt, but this vast ascendant progression is alone conformed to the divine law and the divine love.

Mr. Melville has therefore had his eyes very wide open to the magnificent future of his country: he predicts what will certainly arrive—the transformation of the whole continent into an immense and renovated Europe. . . .

When Mr. Melville has visited and criticised Europe and America, he turns his course again towards the metaphysical regions, where he admires, without being able to inhabit them, the kingdoms of Alma and the domains of Serenia. Alma represents the Saviour; Serenia is his domain. Yillah, or human happiness, is lost for ever, and Mr. Melville resigns himself to do without it.

Such is the colossal machine invented by Mr. Melville. It might be compared to the gigantic original American panorama, now placarded on the walls of London in these terms: '*Gigantic original American panorama. Now on exhibition in the great American Hall, the prodigious moving panorama of the Gulf of Mexico, the falls of St. Anthony and of the*

Mississippi, painted by J. R. Smith, the illustrious artist of the United States, and covering an extent of canvas four miles long, and representing more than four thousand miles of American scenery.'

In the midst of this puerile and fatiguing confusion, among the many faults of taste and incoherencies which shock the reader, talent and reason, as we have seen, are not wanting to this singular writer. The words which he addresses to the French deserve to be pondered.

[here Chasles concludes with his 'translation' of Melville's putative charge to the French people]

Thus far our Parisian critic.

Of the criticisms of M. Chasles, who, besides being an eminent contributor to the *Revue de Deux Mondes*, in which the above appears as a leading article, and a *feuilletonist*[1] of approved standing in the *Journal des Debats*, occupies the important post of lecturer on the literature of the modern languages at the *Collège de France*, and of whose early days, by the way, we published last week an interesting biographical reminiscence, connected with the sketch of Charles Lamb,—of M. Chasles' criticisms we have to acknowledge the general acuteness and the sympathy which, stretching itself across the Atlantic, solves a point or two on which even English critics have unnecessarily mystified themselves. M. Chasles' sketch of *Mardi* is undoubtedly the nearest approach to a full and fair estimation of that work which has proceeded from any foreign pen, and many critical writers in England—weekly and others—have tried their hands upon it. It gives us pleasure to say this; for it vastly enlarges the motives of an American author, when he can look to an influential European journal on the Continent for so cordial, appreciative a reception. It is something for a young American writer to have the way thus cleared for his introduction to the literary society of the old world—to be read at Paris, St. Petersburgh, and Madrid, as well as London and Edinburgh.

It is natural, of course, that there should be some slight errors in the chance anecdotes of an American author, picked up in conversation in Paris. The alternative of Mr. Melville's being a member of the regular navy or a *privateersman*, is amusing, did we not reflect how unlikely an adventure it would be for the son of a European gentleman to try a voyage or two in the forecastle. There is nothing remarkable in the United States in a young man of education and of good family embarking on the sea as a common sailor. The information of Mr.

[1] *Feuilletonist:* a writer of articles, criticism, etc.

Melville, derived through the medium of the 'cousin,' is as true as such authoritative narratives generally are; and the reference to his early years, with the phrenological indications of his head, as favorable as the appreciation in most families of the youthful book-writer and 'genius' —at least until admiration is forced back upon them by the world at large. The *mauvaise tête*[1] of Herman Melville would, after all, fill a very eulogistic and highly luminous page of Mr. Fowler's magazine, should the author submit to the necessary manipulation. That Mr. Melville is a resident of New York, and not of Boston, is a fact, upon the authenticity of which we have the very best reason to congratulate ourselves. Of his married life, and of the family inspection of his papers, we say nothing, for they are not subjects of public comment. Mr. M. may consider himself fortunate that the *spirituel* gentleman in Paris made no mesmeric revelation of his love-letters, if he ever wrote any. The allusion to the late secretary of legation at London should read the brother of Mr. Melville.

The substantial merit of M. Chasles' criticism is its reliance upon the innate evidence of the books themselves, which leads him at once to distinguish between the actual Typee and the fantastic Mardi. He treats the subject in a philosophical manner, and hits upon the true solution:—

> Truth severe in fairy fiction drest,

would describe all the marvellous descriptions of Melville. There is no exaggeration in the coloring of Titian at Venice. Mr. Melville is matter of fact at the Marquesas.

In one respect he is an inventor, and that from the beginning; in the humor and character which he assigns to the savages. Those are graces borrowed altogether from civilization. Your savage is a dull, stupid fellow; Mr. Melville makes him good company, and the humor which he appears to get out of him, he actually, like an adroit juggler at his tricks, brings along with himself. There are imagination and invention enough in *Typee* and *Omoo* to have saved Mr. M. from his critic's rather hasty observation on the mistake of memory for poetry. It is not worth while, at this stage of a young author's career, to pronounce definitively on his capabilities, but it is safe to say that the invention, fancy, and reflective powers of *Mardi*, are of a high order, and to the reader, who is not deterred by occasional defects, sources of far higher pleasure in his last than in his earlier books. We have so recently given

[1] *Mauvaise tête:* bad head (a phrenological term).

our own 'development' of *Mardi*, that we find no occasion to enter the field again. Mr. Melville has just announced a new book of nautical adventure which will bring us again into his company.

45. William A. Jones, unsigned review, *United States Magazine and Democratic Review*

July 1849, xxv, 44–50

Jones (1817–1900), another of the Young America group and an original member of the Tetractys Club, contributed critical articles to several periodicals during the 1840s. He often wrote on theories of literature and on the relationship between literature and politics.

There are few men whose scope of vision extends over the area of human existence. The view of most is confined to their trade, profession, or sect. Success in the lowest uses of life, in the competitive sphere in which we live, has made this limitation of sight a necessary fact. The boy's advice to the clergyman is too commonly quoted to need explanation, viz.: 'Every one to his trade—you to your preaching, and I to my mouse-traps.' A man cannot be expected to till his farm, build his house, and make his shoes, and his clock. He is a useful member of society, and a man of most respectable acquirements, if he does either one of these things well, and keeps a sharp look-out upon those who engage in the remainder of these occupations, that they do not make poor work, and thus cheat him out of his earnings in his particular vocation; for all must exchange work; and whoso does his work ill steals from his fellows, and is a leech upon the body politic. Competitive industry does not compel this kind of theft, but gives ample allowance for it. There seems a sort of necessity that men should not see all over the field of human economy, or philosophy, when engaged to the limit of their strength, in making pegs, or shoes, heads or points of pins, six days out of the week, and getting a little not very refreshing sleep at church on the seventh, and watching the above-mentioned thieves, who snatch openly, and abstract secretly from their honest labor. And when their sight is thus abridged and confined, it would be gratuitous cruelty to blame them if they do not recognize and accept, as belonging to this mundane sphere, world-pictures made in high places, by the few of far-sight. There is such a thing as being too near for a good view; and bad odors are not perceived by those who live among them. Swedenborg says the devils delight in the fetor of their hells. When men bury money, they walk to all points of the compass, and look back at the spot from each point, that they may know the place from whatever direction they may happen to approach it.

Mr. Melville has given us in his work a sort of retina picture, or inverted view of the world, under the name of *Mardi*. The different countries are represented by different islands in the South Sea. Thus Dominora represents England; and the hump-backed King Bello represents the British monarchy, with the load of the national debt. Those who have not looked at the world, and the kingdoms of it, from all Mr. Melville's points of sight, will not recognize his pictures, and will find no buried treasure. It is not strange that many will not accept this work as a fair showing of their world. What is fetor to the author is fragrance to them; and they have never beheld the view that his pencil has delineated. They could not see it if they would—they would not if they could.

The beginning of the book is accepted by most, perhaps all, readers. It is in the style of *Omoo* and *Typee*—books that made the multitude crazy with delight. These works were to *Mardi* as a seven-by-nine sketch of a sylvan lake, with a lone hunter, or a boy fishing, compared with the cartoons of Raphael.

Once upon a time a certain married couple were litigating for divorce. The lady possessed great literary talent, more artistic skill, was highly accomplished, and, in fine, had almost all sorts of ability. We need not describe the husband, only by calling him a gentleman. Having large sympathy for women and wives, we enquired of a friend as to the character of the husband, hinting that we opined he was no better than he should be. Our friend answered: 'There is nothing to condemn, only the mistake of marriage. There is incompatibility of character—nothing worse. The husband likes a breeze—the wife gets up a storm; he loves a flute—she wants a full orchestra.'

We were reminded of this explanation when we saw those who rejoiced in the flute-like music of Melville's *Typee* and *Omoo*, and had not the slightest conception of the meaning of his magnificent orchestra in *Mardi*. Is it our misfortune, or Sivori's fault, that we do not understand or love the harmonies that he educes with Paganini's bow?

Typee and *Omoo* were written for the multitude, and consequently had no deep philosophy; and, being a true record of simplistic life, had not high harmonic beauty. They were pictures of earth's loveliest vallies, rich with green fields, and flowers, and golden-fruits, with a warm, mellow light glowing over all. The shadows upon the picture were a gross preponderance of the sensual life, occasionally a dead man's head, and the fact that the author was imprisoned in this lap of beauty. We believe it is not in human nature—we *know* it is not in Yankee human nature—to live in heaven, without liberty to leave any hour in the twenty-four, and a night-key in the bargain to make return equally feasible. So we must confess to the slightest possible prejudice against the Paradise of Typee. But we would give all due credit to books that won the plaudits of the people so widely. Now, every one who had read *Typee* and *Omoo*, anxiously expected *Mardi*—and more, they expected a work of similar character. The man who expects and asks for loaf sugar will not be satisfied with marble, though it be built into a palace.

An honest man who had read *Mardi*, expecting another and more beautiful *Omoo*, said to us: 'I am disappointed. I feel much as I did, when, a good many years ago, I came a long distance from the country to see an elephant on the stage, at the Chatham Theatre. I went home *sick*, from disappointment, *for he looked just like any other elephant*.'

The fact that *Mardi* is an allegory that mirrors the world, has thus far escaped the critics, who do notices for the book-table on a large scale. *Pilgrim's Progress* and *Gulliver's Travels* were written so long ago, that they seem to have dropped through the meshes of the memory of critics, and they have ceased to think any reproduction or improvement of that sort of thing possible in the future, because they have forgotten its existence in the past.

The first half of the first volume of *Mardi* is the world of a far-seeking and high-aspiring youth, afloat on the ocean of life, which as yet is lashed by no storms, but bright with the rainbow of hope and beauty. On a green isle he finds his heart's first love, his Yillah, a shadowy sort of semi-divinity, as dreamy, and beautiful, and unsubstantial as the lady love of a boy-poet usually is. At length he comes into this actual world of ours, where he loses his Yillah. It is not quite clear whether she dies as natural a death as such a supernatural could; whether she is translated, or whether she exhales like gems of dew in the morning sun, or fades out of the hardening heart of the young world-wanderer, like other brilliant evanescent fancies. And then he seeks her through all Mardi, and finds wherewithal to make his book.

The manner of the book is unique, and like all new things must take the chance of being considered ugly, because it is uncommon. Some minds delight in mystery. 'Darkness heightens the sublime,' says our old Rhetoric. Nobody asks why; but we venture to say it is because the spirit within us is greater than the world without us, and can create more of beauty and more of terror. The creative spirit is the highest of God's works. The veil of mystery thrown over *Mardi* enhances its beauty to those who have sympathy with the author, and can finish his creation with a corresponding or heightened sublimity.

In these volumes, youth with its pure, deep love, its fervent aspirations, its heavenly visions, is personified. The hard, rugged world, full of politics, trade, and theology, and a good many other things quite as real and unlovely, passes in review before our voyager; and everywhere he seeks that the shine of his Yillah may fall again on his soul. If he loses any of his love for his ideal, which we think he does not, evermore grows more holy his love for humanity. This mighty love that wells up always in his heart, whether his hand guides the knife through the foul fungus of a false religion, or his eye flashes in scorn at the meanness of the men of mark in Mardi, this love is the boon of Heaven to him, and through him to this fellow-men. Whoso wishes to read a romance—a novel of the sentimental or satanic school—has no business in *Mardi*. He need not open the book. But whoso wishes to see the spirit of philosophy and humanity, love and wisdom, showing man to himself as he is, that he may know his evil and folly, and be saved from them, will be reverently thankful for this book. There is an immortality in love. It is indeed the only immortality—and the author, whose heart burns within him like a live coal from God's own altar, need take no care for his fame. Such an one is Herman Melville.

We do not despise criticism, nor do we believe that there is much for sale that a man would care to buy; but there are honest men who are petty in their strictures upon works of genius. They do not believe in poetry unless it is fettered with feet, or with rhymes. Like the old lady, they know that 'poetry begins with capital letters, and has the lines of a length;' and an author who should write a book full of poetic fire, without regard to their rules, is an insubordinate officer, who must be disciplined, or broke, but most likely the latter. To them genius is irregular. It does not corvet according to their patterns, which they assure us are highly ornamental, and very proper. These men would pluck the eagle's quills, and sell them at 'a penny a piece,' and reduce the royal bird to a respectable barn-yard fowl.

We have small respect for authors who are wilful, and cannot be advised; but we reverence a man when God's *must* is upon him, and he does his work in his own and other's spite. Portions of *Mardi* are written with this divine impulse, and they thrill through every fibre of the reader with an electric force. The chapter on dreams is an example.

[quotes chapter 119, complete]

Beside the majestic poetry, which reminds us of the Hebrew, there are in *Mardi* passages of a sweet and gentle beauty, that seem like brief snatches from the melody above.

'Over balmy waves still westward sailing! From dawn to eve, the bright, bright days sped on, chased by the gloomy nights; and in glory dying lent their lustre to the starry skies. So long the radiant dolphins fly before the sable sharks; but seized and torn in flames, die burning. Their last splendor left in sparkling scales that float along the sea.

'The next morning's twilight found us once more afloat. A bright mustering is seen among the myriad white Tartar tents in the Orient; like lines of spears defiling in the upland plain, the sunbeams thwart the sky. And see! amid the blaze of banners, and the pawing of ten thousand golden hoofs, day's mounted Sultan, Xerxes-like, moves on—the dawn his standard, east and west his cymbals.

' "Oh, morning life," cried Yoomy, with a Persian air, "would that all time were a sunrise, and all life a youth." '

There is very sharp satire for the three professions—law, physic, and divinity—and some tough lessons for politicians and republicans. There is a chapter for gold-hunters, one for surgeons, and one for slave-holders. We think they will be about equally acceptable to those for whom they are intended.

We give a few specimens of Mardian proverbs:—

'Fame is an accident—Merit a thing absolute.

'No gold but that comes from dark mines.

'The catalogue of true thoughts is small. They are ubiquitous—no man's property—and unspoken or bruited are the same.

'Fame has dropped more rolls than she displays.

'Freedom is the name for a thing that is not freedom.

'Your Federal Temple of Freedom, sovereign kings, was the handiwork of slaves.

'It is not crown jewels alone that make a people servile.

'Anywhere the wise will lord it over the fool.'

To obtain a clear conception of the character of *Mardi* the book must be read carefully, and by those measurably imbued with the author's philosophy. To those who believe that ours is the best of all possible worlds, this book will be a senseless homily, as impertinent as it is to them untrue. To those who believe that the world is bad, and cannot be made better, and that they have only to take care of themselves and their families, and thus prove that they are orthodox in faith and practice, *Mardi* will have been written in vain. The world is the least of their concerns. They are themselves the centre of gravity.

As an illustration of the style and thought of the work, we give a portion of a chapter, entitled—

ODO AND ITS LORD.

[quotes from chapter 63, 'Time now to enter' to 'mixed with shells.']

The life blood that belongs to the poor of this world, and that now stagnates in the plethora of the rich, must get somewhat of an equalized circulation before sentiments like the above will be thankfully accepted at church or on 'change. Those who are rebuked in this chapter, may be sufficiently shrewd and politic to keep silence, lest they be known to the people, but this is all the grace that can be expected of them.

We claim not perfection for our author—we have a few things against the author of *Mardi* even. He has given us real pictures of a very bad world; and its worthless babble, its vulgar smoking and drinking, appear very natural and life-like in the reflection. Perhaps we ought not to complain of the frequent turning up of the calabashes, any more than of the politics and religion described. Both these are often of a very hard kind; but we get good evidence that the author has little sympathy with either, whilst he describes the drinking and smoking as his own act. We do not believe they are in his actual life, though we confess that there is a little murkiness in *Mardi*, that smells of the smoke of the vile weed. But the pure human love of the great Heart that has conceived and executed this work must, ere long, purify the *whole* life of its author.

We have found much in *Mardi*; we have given due credit for it, and yet we have been saddened that we did not find more. With all his humanity, Mr. Melville seems to lack the absolute faith that God had a purpose in creating the world. He seems to think that the race is in a vicious circle, from which we cannot escape—that what has been must be again forever.

We believe in God, and therefore we cannot accept the doctrine that this world can be a failure. It is a doctrine born out of poverty and want, material and spiritual, and there are enough of both at our present period of progress, to insure a plentiful crop of barren unbelief. Mr. Melville must emerge from this evil state, with those for whom he has labored in bonds, bound with them; for, as he has most truly said, 'to scale great heights we must come out of lowermost depths. The way to heaven is through hell. We need fiery baptisms in the fiercest flames of our own bosoms. We must feel our hearts hot and hissing in us. And ere their fire is revealed, it must burn its way out of us, though it consume us and itself.'

Wherefore these baptisms by fire, if they purify us not? And wherefore is one made strong and washed white, if not for others—for all; and can any *one* be holy and happy until all are? Can the plague-spot live in one heart, or in one spot of earth—can it live here, there, or *anywhere*, and exhale its pestiferous influence, and not affect the whole globe? If we have faith for one, we must have faith for all—African or Caucasian, Italian, American, Jew, or Kalmuck Tartar. There is on the earth but one man. 'We are all members one of another.' For what was this MAN and this EARTH created? Will God save, or destroy his Earth-Son, and the world that he has given for his abode?

46. Henry Cood Watson, unsigned review, New York *Saroni's Musical Times*

29 September 1849, 6

Watson (1818–75) moved from his native London to New York in 1841 where he was hired by Park Benjamin as music critic for the *New World*. He contributed to several periodicals and edited others, most note-worthy the *Broadway Journal*, with Edgar Allan Poe and Charles F. Briggs as co-editors in 1845, and his own *Watson's Weekly Art Journal* from 1864 to 1870.

We proceed to notice this extraordinary production with feelings anything but gentle towards its gifted but excentric author. The truth is, that we have been deceived, inveigled, entrapped into reading a *work* where we had been led to expect only a *book*. We were flattered with the promise of an account of travel, amusing, though fictitious; and we have been compelled to pore over an undigested mass of rambling metaphysics. We had hoped for a pleasant boat-ride among the sunny isles of the tropics; instead of which, we were taken bodily, and immersed into the fathomless sea of Allegory, from which we have just emerged, gasping for breath, with monstrous Types, Myths, Symbols and such like fantastic weeds tangled in our vestments and hair. True, it is the province of the hapless critic to peruse all kinds of books—the good and the bad, or, worse yet, the indifferent—the serious and the grave. But, in his distribution of his task, it is his consoling privilege to appropriate a different season for each class of works—reserving dull trash and all manner of figurative strictures for his hours of penance. There was nothing in the appearance of this work, or the reputation of its author, to cause us to take it up as one of that class. And yet its perusal has proven to us a most unmitigated 'mortification of the flesh.'

For, *Mardi* is the world—partly the actual world parabolically presented, piece-meal—and partly an imaginative world, whereof the original type never existed anywhere save in the fancy of Mr. Melville.

Let the reader, therefore, expect, when he opens this book, first to peruse the life-like incidents of an agreeable sea-romance; and then, just as his interest is fairly enlisted in behalf of its heroes, to be plunged into a cold bath of symbolical ethics, metaphysics and political economy. He will travel figuratively through England, France, Scotland, Italy, etc., and, if he succeed in studying out the riddles under which the author's meaning is disguised, he will be treated to—indifferent rhetoric in the premises. He will be accompanied in his travel by a Demi-God—the only sensible man in the book—a philosopher, a historian and a poet, all discussing various topics by the way; sometimes in a very pleasing, sometimes in a very prolix and tedious manner. He will be often tempted to address the author in the language of one of his own personages: 'I beseech thee, instruct me in thy dialectics that I may embrace thy more recondite lore.' He will often have occasion to admire the genius of our author; and oftener still, he will painfully realize that—to use Mr. Melville's own words: 'Genius is full of trash.'

We do not propose to enter any further into the plan of the work—if it had a plan. Its execution alone, saves it from contemptuous oblivion. Style is its sole redeeming feature. Mr. Melville possesses many of the essentials of poetry—a store of images, a readiness at perceiving analogies and felicitous expressions. Poetic thoughts and turns of phrase occur at every page. Nevertheless, although so poetic in his prose, he is remarkably unfortunate in his verse. The specimens in the work before us are not worth quoting. Whence this anomaly? The explanation which occurs to us might be addressed, in the shape of a warning, to several authors of undoubted talent in our age and country, who strive for originality of metre, and whose unsaleable works throng the shelves of their publishers. The English tongue no longer admits of such experiments; its genius has reached its culminating point; it has nothing to do but to remain at its level or descend. To climb higher is impracticable. After the great works of any language have made their appearance, a certain standard is obtained, from which to depart is to sink. The head waters of composition flowing from a certain ascertained height, there is no principle in the hydraulics of Art that will carry them to a more elevated point. All that subsequent endeavours can compass, is to make them reach the stated altitude. In the age of Virgil—the culminating age of Latin literature—Horace was successful in importing new metres from the poets of Greece. But the Claudians of after periods ventured no such license; or, if they did, just posterity has buried their attempts in the merited oblivion, which will soon cover the works of our cotemporary experimentalists.

Do these writers imagine that metre was instituted by arbitrary rule? No! when the heart of a nation first begins to beat, that nation spontaneously cadences its speech according to its hidden genius. That cadence is metre. Let poets cease contriving new combinations or resuscitating the buried measures of other tongues. Let them study the cadence of their own language as noted down in its earliest works.

Mr. Melville is hard upon the critics. We somewhat question the good taste of his remarks on that topic. The only difference between critics and other readers is that the former *print* their opinions. Oral and published criticisms generally agree, except when injudicious friends abuse the privilege of criticism to write up a book, or when malicious enemies attempt the reverse. In speaking of critics, he says: 'Like mules too from their dunghills, they trample down gardens of roses and deem that crushed fragrance their own.' We will take care not to bring ourselves within the scope of that reproach. Flowers there are many and beautiful in the garden of *Mardi*; but we refrain even from culling a bouquet for the benefit of our readers, partly for want of space, and partly because we shrink from the labor of again toiling through the rank vegetation that hides the roses. Let us not, therefore, be accused of trampling the flowers of Mr. Melville, when we beseech him to weed out the noxious plants whose offensive luxuriance chokes up the fragrant spots in his garden.

47. Unsigned notice, *Southern Quarterly Review*

October 1849, xvi, 260–1

Mr. Melville is well and favorably known as the writer of two very pleasant books of South Sea experience, in which the critic persuaded himself that he found as many proofs of the romancer, as of the historian. Mr. Melville alludes to this doubt and difficulty, and somewhat needlessly warns us that, in the present work, we are to expect nothing but fiction. His fiction takes the form of allegory rather than action or adventure. His book, in fact, is a fanciful voyage about the world in search of happiness. In this voyage the writer gives a satirical picture of most of the deeds and doings of the more prominent nations, under names which preserve the sound of the real word to the ear, while slightly disguising it to the eye. In this progress, which is a somewhat monotonous one, the author gives us many glowing rhapsodies, much epigrammatic thought, and many sweet and attractive fancies; but he spoils every thing to the Southern reader when he paints a loathsome picture of Mr. Calhoun, in the character of a slave driver, drawing mixed blood and tears from the victim at every stroke of the whip. We make no farther comments.

REDBURN

1849

48. From an unsigned review, London *Literary Gazette*

20 October 1849, 776–8

Let any author be only flighty enough, be it in imaginary travels or in poetry, there are sure to be a set of critical writers who can twist systems out of their absurdities, and discover the most recondite lessons of truth in their imbecilities. Like folks sitting round the fire, it is wonderful what extraordinary things they can make out of the bits of coal and cinders, or, like higher speculators, who take the clouds for their 'suggestive' sapience, it is really pleasant to hear them confess the striking resemblances to angels, whales, or aught else in or out of nature. It glorifies a fellow not only to pretend to understand what nobody else comprehends, but even to find in it some astounding purpose and deep philosophical execution that escape all human discernment but their own. And then to explain and demonstrate this in a manner which renders the palpable obscure yet more impenetrably dark, till the awestruck world are half convinced that there must be something immensely profound in the mystery, and, though they cannot see it, that a glorious and immortal light has dawned upon the conscious earth.

A good deal of this sort of interpretation has, we think, been bestowed on Mr. Melville, and wherever he was the most extravagant, his admirers made out that he had the most natural meaning. Thus great has been the fame of his allegories, of which all we shall say for ourselves is, that we could not learn so much from *Typee* as from *Gulliver*, from *Omoo* as from *Lilliput*, nor from *Mardi* as from *Laputa*.

We are glad, therefore, that the author has descended from his sublime, not to the ridiculous, but to common and real life. His sailor boy's first voyage from New York to Liverpool in a merchant vessel (occupying the first of these volumes) is as perfect a specimen of the naval yarn as we ever read. And a new interest is communicated to it by its being the narrative of a mere lad, and not the spinning of an old hand; and farther by his being the child of a good family, whose reminiscences of home afford point and feeling to his 'confessions' whilst enduring the hardships of his seafaring lot. Many of the touches in this kind are very fine, and if the imagination is sometimes pressed, as it were, to seek them out, still there is a naturalness about their exponency which creates much sympathy for the 'Sailor Boy.'

The second volume describes numerous scenes in Liverpool, sailors' haunts and doings, and also a romance in the shape of an excursion to London, the return voyage with an English companion strangely brought about, a picture of Irish emigrants, the devastations of a pestilence, and the final distribution of the parties. It will thus be perceived that the sequel is more desultory than the earlier moiety; but both display much various talent and power, though the first is the most peculiar and novel. The tale opens with an account of Redburn's humble and quiet home on the Hudson, glances back on his parentage, and states the causes which induce him to seek his fortunes on the sea. All this is nicely told, and lays good foundations for what is to come. . . .

. . . His excogitations on circumstances as they occur, his adventures, if they may be called so, his sufferings, and his portraits of his companions, appear to be, and we presume they are, altogether free from fiction, and hardly dressed up beyond the simple truth. They have consequently a higher degree of interest, which is not lessened by the talent which the author has bestowed upon their recital. . . .

The inhabitants of Liverpool will, we imagine, be surprised at some of the minute local revelations of an American visitor; and that he is really an American may be credited by his use of the Yankee words realizing, loaning, and others not yet transferred to the English vocabulary.

49. Unsigned review, *Britannia*

27 October 1849, 683–4

The fierce and swaggering exaggeration of the genuine Yankee style is forcibly and, if truth must be told, unpleasantly conspicuous in this work. It is chiefly descriptive of a voyage to England and of a short residence in Liverpool, which appears to be in these pages quite as strange and queer a place as any that figures in *Omoo* or *Typee*. The author's faculty of representation is similar to that possessed by a bad glass. He distorts whatever he reflects, making nearly every object appear monstrous and unnatural. The first part of the work, relating the childhood of an imaginative and adventurous spirit, is the best, and there are some good salt-water passages in the account of the voyage across the Atlantic of great breadth and power. But the staple of the book is so coarse and horrible, mingled, however, with much that is tediously minute, as to leave anything rather than an agreeable impression on the mind. As a sample of the contents we extract part of the chapter headed

A LIVING CORPSE

[quotes from chapter 48, 'It was destined' to 'eternal condemnation.']

The Jackson mentioned is one of the sailors, a weak character enfeebled by illness, but of a savage temper and reckless courage. His death is told in a manner similar to the above:—

[quotes from chapter 59, 'Before the sailors' to 'deadly had happened.']

The author, from his slap-dash kind of writing, seems to have taken up with the notion that anything will do for the public. We are afraid he has been spoiled by partial success. In this work, as in *Mardi*, his talent seems running to seed from want of careful pruning, and, unless he pays more attention to his composition in future, we think it very unlikely that the announcement of a new work from his pen will excite the slightest desire to peruse it.

50. Unsigned review, *Spectator*

27 October 1849, 1020–1

Mr. Melville's present work is even more remarkable than his stories 'founded on fact' descriptive of native scenery and life in the islands of the Pacific. In *Typee* and *Omoo* there was novelty and interest of subject. Everything was fresh and vigorous in the manners of the people, the character of the country and its vegetation; there were rapidity, variety, and adventure in the story, with enough of nautical character to introduce the element of contrast. In *Redburn his First Voyage* there are none of these sources of attraction; yet, with the exception of some chapters descriptive of commonplace things, the book is very readable and attractive. It has not the reality or more properly the veracity of Dana's *Two Years Before the Mast*, nor the comprehensiveness and truthfulness of delineation which distinguish some of Cooper's novels that only aim at a simple exhibition of a sea life without strange adventures or exciting dangers: *Redburn*, though merely the narrative of a voyage from New York to Liverpool and back, with a description of the characters of officers and crew, is, however, a book both of information and interest. We get a good idea of life at sea, as it appears at first to the boy novice and afterwards to the more experienced seaman. The hardships and privations of the crew, the petty tyranny, the pettier greatness, with the tricks and frauds practised in a common merchant-vessel on the raw hands, are well exhibited, without exaggeration. As Redburn sails in a vessel that carries passengers as well as cargo, the evils resulting from the indifferent regulations of emigration-ships, and the practical disregard at sea of such regulations as exist, are exhibited in a scarcity among the poor emigrants, the effect of a slow passage, and in a fever produced by the scantiness and quality of the diet. Mr. Melville's character as an American is also a source of variety. The scenes on shore at New York, in the pawnbroker's and other places, indicate that the Atlantic cities of the Union are not much freer from vice and profligacy, if they are indeed from distress, than the seaports of Europe. At Liverpool many things are fresh to the American that are common to us, or which we ignore without intending it,—as the low haunts and lodging-houses of sailors.

The plan of the book is well designed to bring out its matter effectively; though the position and reputed character of Redburn as 'the son of a gentleman,' contrived apparently for the sake of contrast and the display of a quiet humour, is not always consistently maintained. At the commencement of the book, Redburn's father is dead, the family reduced, and the hero is cast upon the world to choose a means of living. His father's travels, some sea pieces, and a real glass ship in a glass case, (all rather tediously described,) combine with the enthusiasm and ignorance of youth to determine him to the sea; and he starts for New York, with enough money to pay his passage thither, a letter to a friend, and a gun the gift of his elder brother, who had nothing else to bestow upon him. The friend furnishes Redburn with a day's board and lodging, and gets him a ship, the captain taking him at low wages; he vainly tries to sell his gun, and has at last to pawn it; his wardrobe is none of the amplest, and by no means adapted to marine work; he is utterly ignorant of all that relates to the sea, the ship, or the service. The idea of throwing a simple and innocent-minded lad, just fresh from home, into the midst of the roughness, rudeness, and startling novelty of a ship, may be found in *Peter Simple*; but the circumstances of poor Redburn are so different from those of the well-connected midshipman, and the nautical incidents and characters have so little in common, that the story has the effect of originality. The quiet humour arising from the contrast between the frame of mind of the boy and his position and circumstances, as well as the sharp reflections his freshness and home education induce him to make, bear some resemblance in point of style to Marryat; but it may arise from the nature of the subject.

There is nothing very striking in the incidents of *Redburn*—nothing, in fact, beyond the common probabilities of the merchant service in almost every vessel that sails between Great Britain and America: the characters, or something like them, may doubtless be met in almost every ship that leaves harbour. Nor does Mr. Melville aim at effect by melodramatic exaggeration, except once in an episodical trip to London: on the contrary, he indicates several things, leaving the filling up to the reader's imagination, instead of painting scenes in detail, that a vulgar writer would certainly have done. The interest of *Redburn* arises from its quiet naturalness. It reads like a 'true story'—as if it had all taken place.

The best idea of the book, however, is obtained by extracts. The following are among the hero's earlier experiences.

[quotes from chapter 6, 'By the time' to '*you break owners.*" ']

This account of a first adventure aloft is a piece of truthful and powerful description.

[quotes from chapter 16, 'It happened on' to 'Max the Dutchman.']

Some of the occurrences give rise to reflections or suggestions on nautical matters; and there are some terrible pictures of vice and poverty in Liverpool, pointed by contrast with the American's experience at home, where absolute death by hunger and privation (the Americans say) cannot occur. We will, however, take a different sample to close with,—a case of spontaneous combustion.

[quotes from chapter 48, 'Of the three' to 'happened to others.']

51. From an unsigned review, London *Morning Post*

29 October 1849

The adventures of a sailor-boy during his first voyage in a 'regular trader,' from New York to Liverpool and back, do not, at first thought, seem likely to prove very rife in novel incident, or rich in new descriptive matter. But there is a way of telling old stories and dressing up old objects, and presenting old incidents so as to look quite fresh—at least, fresh enough for the passing entertainment of one who reads for amusement. The author of the work before us possesses this art, and he introduces his readers to a captain, and mates, and sailors in the American merchant vessel the Highlander, all of whom they have peradventure known before, but with whom they have no objection to renew acquaintance. He relates to them also sea-fearing mishaps and shipboard oppressions, and nautical perils, which most likely they have previously heard something of, but which they have much pleasure in again hearing described as he describes them. This is not a novel, for there is neither plot nor love in it; it is simply what it professes to be, the narrative of a voyage from New York to Liverpool and back by a sailor boy. It is a narrative, however, full of interest, and containing many bold portraits of striking individual sea characters, many graphic pictures of life in a 'transient ship,' and some clever sketches of men and manners, and scenes, in Liverpool, such as would naturally impress themselves on the mind of a Yankee boy who visited that great commercial port for the first time.

The details of the horrors aboard such a vessel as the Highlander, when returning to New York with a cargo of poor Irish emigrants, are peculiarly deserving of notice; we believe some amelioration has taken place, and that some care is now taken of these live cargoes of human beings, but still these emigrant vessels require to be closely watched. There were some odd fish aboard the Highlander; one Jack Blunt, an Irishman by birth, but naturalised at Radcliffe Highway, is worth exhibiting as a specimen . . . .

If all the rest of the story be as true as the vision of the '*London Times*,' which words he saw 'boldly printed on the back of the large sheet,' we must conclude that our Yankee sailor-boy draws largely on his imagination for his facts. There is no such paper as the *London Times*. Our transatlantic biographer likewise, we opine, depends upon what he has heard, not what he has seen, when he describes a young English nobleman 'stepping to the open window of a flashy carriage, and throwing himself into an interesting posture with the sole of one boot vertically exposed, so as to show the stamp on it—*a coronet*.' . . .

We said that the sketches taken in Liverpool by the Yankee sailor-boy were spirited, but some of them are rather apocryphal . . . .

Mr. Herman Melville, the author of this work, is already known in the literary world as a writer of great descriptive power and considerable fancy. His romance of *Mardi* gave high promise, which has been fully borne out in *Redburn*, who, we trust, will, ere long, give us another yarn as entertaining as this reminiscence of his first voyage.

52. Unsigned review, London *Daily News*

29 October 1849

This is another 'Voice from the forecastle.' Pleasant as *Two Years before the Mast* in its earnestness of purpose and simplicity, it has not the holiday look or joyous blitheness of Dana, the amateur seaman escaping from the trammels and conventionalities of society. *Redburn's* first voyage is one of hardship and struggling against the difficulties which old seamen put in the way of greenhorns, and is likely to act as a considerable damper to those who, like the hero, feel a vocation for the sea. *Redburn* starts from his humble home on the 'lordly Hudson' with a touch of Chattertonian misanthropy, which colours the first part of the narrative, but wears off as he gets more experienced in sea matters. These he imparts in a clear, simple style, and in the way in which ship and crew are depicted, and are artfully made subservient to the development of character and story, one is reminded of Defoe. The sailors emerge from his ordeal in their genuine rude nature and generous impulses, and the moral of the tale, a true one doubtless, seems to be that sailors, like women, are what their husbands and captains make them.

The first volume brings the crew to Liverpool, of which city and its docks the author gives an elaborate account, of Daguerreotype fidelity and freshness, and after a mysterious rush up to London (he is not at home there) ships a cargo of Irish emigrants, lands them at New York, and is glad to get back to his wigwam on the Hudson.

There is discrepancy felt at first between the author and the biographer. Herman Melville and *Redburn* are two distinct personages; thus when *Redburn* does a silly action, which he does frequently, though he knows better afterwards, we find him enveloping it with rich thought and keen observation. How can we admit the fool in action with 'the wit in mind?'

As in the work of Dana, the forecastle and its inmates afford the richest materials to the limner of sea life. Mr. Melville has made the most of their strange and exceptional existence. The story of the man running up the scuttle hole, and rushing over the bows into the sea, in a fit of *delirium tremens*, is striking. The collision is also fine; a catastrophe now more common since the denizens of the ocean have increased, and too often are found to rush together like fighting elks, with jib-boom to jib-boom, sinking down into the ocean with their antlers locked in death.

We have seldom met with two volumes from which extracts more striking or more powerfully written could be extracted. But these cannot fail to attract the dealers and critics special in light literature. For our part we must be contented with highly lauding a work so much out of the common.

53. Frederick Hardman, from an unsigned review, *Blackwood's Edinburgh Magazine*

November 1849, lxvi, 567–80

Hardman (1814–74), a novelist and journalist, contributed frequently to the 'Magazine' from 1840 on. About 1850 he became a foreign correspondent for *The Times*. This long review, entitled 'Across the Atlantic,' quotes at length from *Redburn* and summarizes the story, with occasional observations regarding particular points.

Another book from the active pen of our American acquaintance, the able seaman. The question having been raised whether Mr Herman Melville has really served before the mast, and has actually, like the heroine of a well-known pathetic ballad, disfigured his lily-white fingers with the nasty pitch and tar, he does his best to dissipate all such doubts by the title-page of his new work, on which, in large capitals, is proclaimed that *Redburn* is '*The Sailor-boy Confessions and Reminiscences of the son of a gentleman in the merchant service;*' and, collaterally, by a dedication to his younger brother, '*now a sailor on a voyage to China.*' An unmerited importance has perhaps been given to the inquiry whether

Mr Melville's voyages were made on quarterdeck or on forecastle, and are genuine adventures or mere Robinsonades. The book, not the writer, concerns the critic; and even as there assuredly are circumstances that might induce a youth of gentle birth and breeding to don flannel shirt, and put fist in tar-bucket as a merchant seaman, so the probably unpleasant nature of those circumstances precludes too inquisitive investigation into them. We accept Mr Melville, therefore, for what he professes to be, and we accept his books, also, with pleasure and gratitude when good, just as we neglect and reject them when they are the contrary. *Redburn*, we are bound to admit, is entitled to a more favourable verdict than the author's last previous work. We do not like it so well as *Typee* and *Omoo*; and, although quite aware that this is a class of fiction to which one cannot often return without finding it pall, by reason of a certain inevitable sameness, we yet are quite sure we should not have liked it so well as those two books, even though priority of publication had brought it to a palate unsated with that particular sort of literary diet. Nevertheless, after a decided and deplorable retrogression, Mr Melville seems likely to go ahead again, if he will only take time and pains, and not over-write himself, and avoid certain affectations and pedantry unworthy a man of his ability. Many of the defects of *Mardi* are corrected in *Redburn*. We gladly miss much of the obscurity and nonsense that abound in the former work. The style, too, of this one is more natural and manly; and even in the minor matter of a title, we find reason to congratulate Mr Melville on improved taste, inasmuch as we think an English book is better fitted with an English-sounding name than with uncouth dissyllables from Polynesia, however convenient these may be found for the purposes of the puff provocative.

Redburn comprises four months of the life of a hardy wrong-headed lad, who ships himself on board a trading vessel, for the voyage from New York to Liverpool and back. As there is no question of shipwreck, storm, pirates, mutiny, or any other nautico-dramatic incidents, during Wellingborough Redburn's voyage out and home; and as the events of his brief abode in England are neither numerous nor (with the exception of one rather far-fetched episode) by any means extraordinary, it is evident that a good deal of detail and ingenuity are necessary to fill two volumes, on so simple and commonplace a theme. . . .

. . . Minute incidents of this kind, reflections, reminiscences, and thoughts of home, occupy many chapters; and, at times, one is inclined to think they are dwelt upon at too great length: but, as before hinted, it is necessary to do something to fill two volumes. A slight inconsistency strikes us in this first portion of the book. Redburn, a sharp enough lad on shore, and who, it has been seen, is altogether precocious in experience of the world's disappointments, seems converted, by the first sniff of salt water, into as arrant a simpleton as ever made mirth in a cockpit. Mr Melville must surely have had Peter Simple in his head, when describing 'Buttons' at his first deck-washing. 'The water began to splash about all over the decks, and I began to think I should surely get my feet wet, and catch my death of cold. So I went to the chief mate and told him I thought I would just step below, till this miserable wetting was over; for I did not have any waterproof boots, and an aunt of mine had died of consumption. But he only roared out for me to get a broom, and go to scrubbing, or he would prove a worse consumption to me than ever got hold of my poor aunt.' Now Redburn, from what has previously been seen of him, was evidently not the lad to care a rush about wet soles, or even about a thorough ducking. On the Hudson river steamer, he had voluntarily walked the deck in a dreary storm till soaked through; and his first night on board the Highlander had been passed uncomplainingly in wet clothes. He has borne hunger and thirst and other disagreeables most manfully, and the impression given of him is quite that of a stubborn hardy fellow. So that this sudden fear of a splashing is evidently introduced merely to afford Mr Melville opportunity of making a little mild fun, and is altogether out of character. Equally so is the elaborate *naïveté* with which Redburn inquires of a sailor whether, as the big bell on the forecastle 'hung right over the scuttle that went down to the place where the watch below were sleeping, such a ringing every little while would not tend to disturb them, and beget unpleasant dreams.' The account of his attempts at intimacy with the captain, although humorous enough, is liable to a similar objection; and, in so sharp a lad, such simple blunders are not sufficiently accounted for by ignorance of sea usages. . . .

. . . As we read, we cannot help a comparison with some former pencillings . . . which, although earlier made, referred to a later voyage. Involuntarily we are carried back to the rat-and-cockroach-haunted hull of the crazy little Jule, and to the strange collection of originals that therein did dwell. We think of bold Jermin and timid Captain Guy, and, above all, of that glorious fellow Doctor Long-Ghost. We remember the easy natural tone, and well-sustained interest of the book in which they figured; and, desirous though we are to praise, we are compelled to admit that, in *Redburn*, Mr Melville comes not up to the mark he himself has made. It is evident that, on his debut, he threw off the rich cream of his experiences, and he must not marvel if readers have thereby been rendered dainty, and grumble a little when served with the skim-milk. *Redburn* is a clever book, as books now go, and we are far from visiting it with wholesale condemnation; but it certainly lacks the spontaneous flow and racy originality of the author's South Sea narration.

[here Hardman devotes three full columns to a summary of the Lancelott's Hey episode]

Mr Melville is, of course, at liberty to introduce fictitious adventure into what professes to be a narrative of real events; the thing is done every day, and doubtless he largely avails of the privilege. He has also a clear right to deal in the lugubrious, and even in the loathsome, if he thinks an occasional dash of tragedy will advantageously relieve the humorous features of his book. But here he is perverting truth, and leading into error the simple persons who put their faith in him.

[Hardman next discusses at length the characterization of Harry Bolton]

Now all this sort of thing, we can assure its author, is in the very stalest style of minor-theatre melodrama. We perfectly remember our intense gratification when witnessing, at country fairs in our boyish days, a thrilling domestic tragedy, in which the murderer rushes on the stage with a chalked face and a gory carving-knife, howling for 'Brandy! Brandy!!' swallows a goblet of strong toast and water, and is tranquillised. But surely Mr Melville had no need to recur to such antiquated traditions. Nor had he any need to introduce this fantastical gambling episode, unless it were upon the principle of the old cakes of roses in the apothecary's shop—to make up a show. We unhesitatingly qualify the whole of this London expedition as utter rubbish, intended evidently to be very fine and effective, but which totally misses the mark. Why will not Mr Melville stick to the ship? There he is at home. The worst passages of his sea-going narrative are better than the best of his metropolitan experiences. In fact, the introduction at all of the male brunette is quite impertinent. Having got him, Mr Melville finds it necessary to do something with him, and he is greatly puzzled what that is to be. Bolton's character is full of inconsistencies. . . .

If it be possible (we are aware that it is very difficult) for an author to form a correct estimate of his own productions, it must surely have struck Mr Melville, whilst glancing over the proof-sheets of *Redburn*, that plain, vigorous, unaffected writing of this sort is a far superior style of thing to rhapsodies about Italian boys and hurdy-gurdies, to gairish descriptions of imaginary gambling-houses, and to sentimental effusions about Harry Bolton, his 'Bury blade,' and his 'Zebra,' as he called him—the latter word being used, we suppose, to indicate that the young man was only one remove from a donkey. We can assure Mr Melville he is most effective when most simple and unpretending; and if he will put away affectation and curb the eccentricities of his fancy, we see no reason for his not becoming a very agreeable writer of nautical fictions. He will never have the power of a Cringle, or the sustained humour and vivacity of a Marryat, but he may do very well without aspiring to rival the masters of the art.

Redburn is not a novel; it has no plot; the mysterious visit to London remains more or less an enigma to the end. . . .

When this review of his last work meets the eye of Mr Herman Melville, which probably it will do, we would have him bear in mind that, if we have now dwelt upon his failings, it is in the hope of inducing him to amend them; and that we have already, on a former occasion, expended at least as much time and space on a laudation of his merits, and many undeniable good qualities, as a writer. It always gives us pleasure to speak favourably of a book by an American author, when we conscientiously can do so. First, because Americans, although cousins, are not *of the house;* although allied by blood, they are in some sort strangers; and it is an act of more graceful courtesy to laud a stranger than one of ourselves. Secondly, because we hope thereby to encourage Americans to the cultivation of literature—to induce some to write, who, having talent, have not hitherto revealed it; and to stimulate those who have already written to increased exertion and better things. For it were false modesty on our part to ignore the fact, that the words of Maga have much weight and many readers throughout the whole length and breadth of the Union—that her verdict is respectfully heard, not only in the city, but in the hamlet, and even in those remote backwoods where the law of Lynch prevails. And, thirdly, we gladly praise an American book because we praise none but good books, and we desire to see many such written in America, in the hope that she will at last awake to the advantages of an international copyright. For surely it is little creditable to a great country to see her men of genius and talent, her Irvings and Prescotts, and we will also say her Coopers and Melvilles, publishing their works in a foreign capital, as the sole means of obtaining that fair remuneration which, although it should never be the sole object, is yet the legitimate and honourable reward of the labourer in literature's paths.

54. Evert Duyckinck, from an unsigned review, *Literary World*

17 November 1849, 418–20

In our last number we called Mr. Melville the De Foe of the Ocean. It is an honourable distinction, to which we think he is fairly entitled by the life-like portraiture of his characters at sea, the strong relishing style in which his observations are conveyed, the fidelity to nature, and, in the combination of all these, the thorough impression and conviction of reality. The book belongs to the great school of nature. It has no verbosity, no artificiality, no languor; the style is always exactly filled by the thought and material. It has the lights and shades, the mirth and melancholy, the humor and tears of real life. . . .

There were some little articles to be disposed of for the outfit, 'a dismal rainy day' to be passed on the wharves, and then came a bit of gentle initiation into the duties of ship-craft, in the business of 'cleaning out the pig-pen and slushing down the topmast.' The first impressions of a boy of spirit, but of tender nurture, are very naturally conveyed through these and similar scenes. There are some touching incidents, too, which will strike home to the hearts of mothers as they read, and excite, peradventure, in old sea-captains, a revival of old memories at which they will pause for a moment before hurrying to the next chapter. The meal of 'raw carrots' is one of those touches of nature (homely, of little import in a world of great things, but so true in itself and the relation) which have caused us to think of De Foe. Raw novelties and hardships, however, soon become familiarity and insensibility, and the green hand turns in and out, as the various nautical duties arise, with the confirmed feelings of a sailor. A gentleman in the forecastle would be simply a subject for caricature; the son of a gentleman turned sailor, and writing his report, is a character which old Montaigne, or any other philosophic lover of his kind, would study with delight. The forecastle of any ship is the world in miniature. You will find all the governments of the world represented there in individuals—nautical Louis Bonapartes, Pope Pius, and the Emperor Nicholas. The tyrant of the crew was one Jackson, perhaps the most remarkable specimen of portraiture in the book. . . .

At Liverpool we have the same fidelity of description, which, if we mistake not, will add to the English critics' wonderment over the author of the Tale of Types. A Sailor's Boarding House is finished in a style worthy of Smollett. We have the dock scenes, gentlemanly explorations of the town, low life sufferings, pictures of traffic, of quackery, of vice, all reeking with life.

At this stage of the narrative we are introduced to a fancy young gentleman who gets up with Redburn a hurried, romantic night visit to London, which is enveloped in the glare of a splendid gambling establishment. The parties, however, soon get back to duty, and find nothing whatever lurid or romantic in the discipline under Captain Riga. The steerage on the homeward voyage has become with its multitude of inhabitants a new source of interest. We are introduced to its new-world population of future states, but there is little grandeur at that period of progress. A little newspaper item, such as we have often read this last season, is filled out in its terrible details—for every death at sea, be sure, is a tragedy. To sickness and death succeeds famine; but the harbor is gained and the voyage accomplished.

A book of incident and detail cannot be described in an article, but we have suggested to the reader the main outlines of *Redburn*.

In the filling up there is a simplicity, an ease, which may win the attention of a child, and there is reflection which may stir the profoundest depths of manhood. The talk of the sailors is plain, direct, straightforward; where imagery is employed the figure being vivid and the sense unmistakable. This sailor's use of language, the most in the shortest compass, may be the literary school which has rescued Herman Melville from the dull verbosity of many of his contemporaries. If some of our writers were compelled to utter a few words occasionally through the breathings of a gale of wind it might benefit their style. There is also much sound judgment united with good feeling in *Redburn*—a knowledge of sailor's life unobtrusively conveyed through a narrative which has the force of a life current from the writer's own heart.

55. Charles Gordon Greene, unsigned review, Boston *Post*

20 November 1849

It gives us pleasure to be able to praise this book, for we feared that the author had exhausted his vein, and that he might follow up his *Mardi* with others of similar sort, to disgust rather than to amuse the public. In noticing the first two of Mr Melville's productions, we especially pointed out their Crusoe-like naturalness, and this first of all qualities in fiction, assuming to be truth, is the distinguishing excellence of *Redburn*. We are now satisfied that *Mardi* was the offspring of that unaccountable insanity which sometimes possesses minds of undoubted ability and experience, as with a legion of devils—depriving them of all common sense and critical acumen, and causing them to believe the merest trash, if of their own making, to be surpassingly excellent. But in *Redburn*, no glimmer of the levity, coxcombry, affectation, inconsistency and *hodge-podge* of *Mardi* is visible. Every thing, or nearly every thing, is done properly and in order—the author assumes the virtues if he have them not, and speaks in an artificial character. The book is intensely interesting, and yet is reared on a basis apparently insufficient. The first voyage of a green hand to and from Liverpool furnishes all the incidents—the hero and narrator being a sort of American Peter Simple. But the great charm of the work is its realness. It seems to be *fact* word for word, bating a little that is melo-dramatic and exaggerated in the hero, at the outset. With this exception, the tale is told simply and without the least pretension; and yet, within its narrow bounds, are flashes of genuine humor, strokes of pure pathos, and real and original characters. The captain, the mate, Max the Dutchman, Harry Bolton, Jackson the sailor, the O'Brien and O'Regan boys, and the story-teller himself, are as well individualised as if volumes had been devoted to each. We know not of a nicer or more vivid sketch than that of the two Irish mothers and their boys, and we should be puzzled to turn to a more heart-rending and terrible picture than Mr Melville presents to us in the Emigrant Ship, filled with filth, disease, famine and passengers. The highest praise we can give him is our opinion, that could he and

Defoe but change their generations, Mr Melville would deserve all the honors awarded to the latter for his *Robinson Crusoe*, while Defoe would not receive so much praise as Mr Melville now does, for his *Typee*, *Omoo* and *Redburn*. Indeed, in *Robinson Crusoe* there is no character-painting to be named with that in the books we have named, while in truthfulness and vividness of detail it is not greatly superior. *Redburn* is a *Robinson Crusoe modernised*—it has a breadth, purpose, elevation, of which Defoe, by the nature of things, could never have dreamed; for since he wrote, have shone forth Scott, and Bulwer and Dickens and a host of lesser but shining lights, developing phrases of human nature, in a style and tone, and of which even the many-sided Shakspeare seems not to have been cognizant. But Mr Melville, for great fame, has lived a century too late; and while he undoubtedly equals, and, in some respects, excels the greatest masters in his peculiar work, he must be content with the name of having written some very clever books, and be overjoyed if thereby he put money in his purse.

56. William Young, from an unsigned review, *Albion*

24 November 1849, 561

The *Albion* had published a long extract from *Redburn* in its 17 November issue.

The *alias* that figures upon the title-page of this volume has, in our eyes, no especial value. It runs thus—'being the Sailor-boy confessions and reminiscences of the son of a gentleman, in the merchant service.' Now the term 'gentleman' appears, in this quarter of the globe, to be reserved for designating that very useful and often estimable class of persons, with whom, on board steam vessels, passengers are invited to 'walk up and settle'; obliging conductors of rail-way trains being also sometimes admitted into the category. But Redburn's father does not seem to have belonged to this privileged set; nor was it necessary to proclaim that the work was autobiographical, inasmuch as this fact is revealed in the very first page. Still, as Redburn's occasional sneers at *noble* birth are balanced by his open claim to gentility, this slight difficulty is not worth further allusion.

Ships, the sea, and those that plough it, with their belongings on shore—these subjects are identified with Herman Melville's name; for he has most unquestionably made them his own. No writer, not even Marryat himself, has observed them more closely, or pictured them more impressively. Indeed, in one respect, Melville, to our thinking, has shown more talent than many of his predecessors in telling tales of the sea. They have generally chosen the picturesque side of nautical life. He often selects those views of it which, apart from his clever treatment, would be uninteresting, if not repulsive. The stately frigate and the rakish privateer, the man-of-war's man and the pirate, are obviously clothed with an interest, on which we need not dwell; Mr. Melville has painted us pictures of the emigrant ship and the whaler, the crimp and the cabin-boy, so truthfully and so vividly, that one forgets the unpromising nature of his subjects in consideration of his skill in treating them. The Oliver Twists of ocean life are his best *dramatis personæ*—not the Pelhams. He will be read and judged accordingly.

Redburn's 'First Voyage,' described in the book before us, was to and from Liverpool, as boy on board a transient ship. His ship-mates, from the captain to the cook, both as a class and as individuals, are described with remarkable skill. Whether brought only once before us, or re-appearing at intervals, they stand out boldly and impressively, and though altogether wanting in the romance that other writers throw around their *heroes*, they become *characters* in Mr. Melville's hands. We should, however, go beyond our limits, and fail into the bargain, if we attempted to make sketches from his portraits. The extract we gave last week showed something of his simple and effective style; and we shall make room for one or two more specimens. Before doing so, we must notice the exceeding and unusual gravity of the book, since fun and frolic seem, according to custom, to be part and parcel of any nautical tale. Occasional samples we have here of a quiet, subdued humour, but the mode of thought is serious, and even the incidents described are almost entirely cast in the same mould. Ashore—with slight variations—we have poverty, vice, and degradation: afloat, the horrors of an emigrant ship's voyage across the Atlantic are made to rival the awful scenes of the 'middle passage' in a slaver. Several chapters are devoted to Liverpool—not as it is generally described to, and often seen by, American tourists, but as the sailor-boy finds it when transferred from the forecastle of his ship to the loathsome haunts of his shipmates. Persons of very delicate nerves will recoil from some of the details here given of the destitution and degradation prevalent in that abode of merchant princes. Poor little Redburn's Liverpool is not associated in his reminiscences with the Adelphi Hotel, and grand civic entertainments, and a trip to Eaton Hall. He lives as Jack lives, ashore; and he tells us of scenes and social systems that must startle, if they produce no further effect. Passing by these local sketches, we select a passage touching the general condition of seamen, which strikes us much. Mr. Melville sees evil with an observant eye, but does not adopt the pretentious style of those fault-finders who have remedies cut and dried for every evil under the sun. . . .

There is some spinning out of the material of this book in lengthened lucubrations about Liverpool in the olden time; and Mr. Melville egregiously fails when he goes out of his own peculiar walk. A flying visit to a London gambling-house, made by the sailor-boy under absurdly improbable circumstances, does but show the author's inability to paint scenes of this sort. There is a dash of romance thrown into this part of the volume; and a chance reader stumbling thereon would have little idea of the intrinsic value of what precedes and what follows it. Neptune forbid that Herman Melville should quit the sea, and add another to the long list of feeble dabblers in romances of high life! We cannot spare him, and rate him too highly on his own peculiar element. Give us a few more graphic views of life afloat, but be warned off in time from the regions of parks and palaces! Even Charles Dickens cuts a very sorry figure when he enters therein.

57. Nathaniel Parker Willis, from an unsigned review, New York *Home Journal*

24 November 1849

Willis (1806–67) was a popular poet and playwright as well as a critic and editor. Two years after his graduation from Yale College in 1827, he started the *American Monthly Magazine*, and when it failed in 1831, he joined the New York *Mirror*. His observations on English life in the *Mirror* brought on verbal attacks in the Tory press. Willis responded to an attack by Captain Frederick Marryat —a retired naval officer and writer of sea fiction often compared to Melville's—by challenging him to a duel. Willis directed the *Home Journal* from 1846 almost to the time of his death.

Rousseau, Lamartine, and now Melville, have given us their 'Confessions' and, of all these partial autobiographies, the last will not be found the least interesting to most readers. We will not attempt to make any comparison between them, or, what some may perhaps think more necessary, strive to show points of similarity. Sufficient will it be for the present to say, that in amplicity of style, warmth and openness of heart, and in general truthfulness of manner, the last named of the trio will not be found inferior to the illustrious persons that we have by chance named in connection with him.

Melville is most truly a remarkable man. But a few years have passed, since his first book, *Typee*, set the world agog. A simple history of events that had actually occurred, the incidents perhaps somewhat heightened—which had often been told to attentive though uncultivated listeners in the forecastle of a whaler—which had beguiled the long winter hours of his own home circle—printed at their request—has found equally delighted readers, both in the old and new world.

But a short interval elapses, and *Omoo* appears in the same happy vein, but the attentive reader will observe traces of that vigorous intellect, which in *Mardi* reminds one of the departed great. Allegory, irony, sarcasm, innuendo, wit, feeling, simplicity, all and more combined—the work startled the community. Even now, months after its publication, it is read and re-read with interest, and may we say with doubt as to its purpose.

Redburn is not a bit as we expected. We could have easily believed that the author of *Mardi* could write a *Tale of a Tub* or *Pantagruel*, but not *Redburn*. The work is just what its title indicates—a narrative of the events and feelings of a youth who has left a kind home for the hardships of a sailor's life. The life-like manner in which every event is brought to the reader is most astonishing. One actually thinks, when arising from the perusal, that of these occurrences he was actually a witness, so vividly is the mind impressed with their truthfulness. . . .

. . . A chapter in London is very dramatical. The deep feeling which breathes out through the entire work—the love of home, family, affection, that which will be most admired, can be least described. We feel elevated even while reading scenes in low life, and we arise from the perusal better and with nobler intentions. The popularity of this work we think will far exceed any of the previous ones, though it will not perhaps raise the author's literary reputation from the pinnacle where *Mardi* placed it.

58. Herrman S. Saroni, unsigned review, *Saroni's Musical Times*

24 November 1849, 97

Saroni founded this magazine in early 1849, and it failed three years later. He was known as a composer of classical and popular music—in 1848 he set to music William Cullen Bryant's poem 'The Saw Mill'—and as an author and translator of works on musical theory.

Thanks to Marryat, Cooper, Dana and others, the sea, as a stage for dramatic action has become quite familiar to most of our readers. Indeed it furnishes nearly as inexhaustible a source of topics as *terra firma* itself. In the novel now before us, Mr. Melville, without troubling himself about a plot, merely follows up an inexperienced youth, fresh from the privacy and happiness of a refined domestic circle, through the hardships of his initiatory trip at sea. In selecting this nowise novel theme, the author has trusted almost entirely to the boundless suggestiveness of the subject, to his own intimate knowledge of it and to his genius, to make Redburn's first voyage interesting. And he has succeeded. The beginning of the work is particularly lively. The poor lad's complete ignorance of nautical affairs, his wonder and amazement at the many new scenes he enters upon, the wrath of the officers at his amusing blunders, his first ascent in the rigging, and his unsophisticated awkwardness, furnish opportunities for racy anecdote of which Mr. Melville has taken advantage with much wit and humor.

No one who has been to sea can help smiling when Redburn proposes to pay the captain a social call in the cabin, when he gets cheated of his *burgoo*, when he presumes to offer the mate a 'chaw' out of his tortoise-shell box. As the story is told in the first person, Redburn's account of the gradual ripening of his 'greenness,' given in a style of appropriate candor and simplicity, is extremely entertaining. He soon grows 'too wise for that foolish kind of talk,' and the reader, we must say, has cause to regret the questionable improvement.

Fortunately when he lands at Liverpool he proves as ignorant of English affairs as he was of the sea when he first embarked; his account of British soil derives most of its interest from that circumstance. After availing himself, *to the utmost*, of his hero's peculiar position, to give us a rather lengthy description of the English Manhattan, the author, fearful probably of sliding from extreme simplicity into languor, here introduces a slight element of romance. This, though not personal to the hero of the book, carries us very pleasantly through the remaining chapters.

Of the incidents of the return passage, the most striking is the description of a contagious disease which breaks out among the steerage passengers. This scene is painted in the most plain yet vigorous colors. Our talented yet eccentric writer never lapses into sentimentalism when he has something truly tragical to relate. Withal, he is so completely at home on shipboard, he 'knows the ropes so well,' that the book we are engaged in noticing is full as instructive as it is amusing. But now that Redburn has grown wiser from his first voyage, let us hope that his next will prove rather more fertile in incidents.

59. George Ripley, initialled review, New York *Tribune*

1 December 1849

Mr. Melville has not worked himself entirely free from the affectations and pretensious spirit by which *Mardi* has gained such an unlucky notoriety. Nor does this work exhibit the freshness, the gayety, the natural frolicsomeness, which gave such a charm to the fragrant descriptions of *Typee*, and to a certain extent, to the off-hand, picturesque sketches of *Omoo*. It has something about it which savours more of the bookmaker by profession, and shows that it is not the product of any innate necessity. The writer never seems to be entirely at his ease, never so much lost in the reality of his story as to be indifferent to the effect of his readers. He reminds us of a certain facetious gentleman of our acquaintance, who, after saying a good thing, always looks round for the laugh. Still, this book is a decided improvement on *Mardi*. Mr. Melville shows his good sense, or his respect for public opinion, by leaving the vein of mystic allegory and this transcendental, glittering soap-bubble speculation which he has 'done to death' in that ambitious composition.

Redburn is a genuine tale of the sea. It has the real briny flavor. The writer is equally at home on the deck or in the forecastle. His pictures of life on the ocean are drawn from nature, and no one can doubt their identity. His pages smell of tarred ropes and bilge water. With some occasional exaggerations, his descriptions have all the fidelity of a Dutch painting. Nor is he less skillful in his delineations of a sailor's life in port. The interior of the boarding house in Liverpool, the scenes of destitution and misery about the docks, the impressions of low life in a commercial city on the mind of an untrammelled rustic just landing from his first voyage are depicted with a minute fidelity of touch that is hardly surpassed by the dark and lurid coloring of Crabbe.

Redburn can scarcely fail of an extensive popularity. It is idle to compare its author with Defoe or even with some modern writers in the same line. But he is an artist of unparalleled merit in his own right. He has the true kind of 'stuff' in him, and writes with an original power, when in his best vein, that will always keep his productions before the public eye. If he would trust more entirely to the natural play of his own fine imagination without goading it on to a monstrous activity, his work would stand a better chance of obtaining a healthy and lasting reputation.

60. Unsigned notice, *Graham's Magazine*

January 1850, xxxvi, 94–5

Mr. Melville has been called the 'De Foe of the Ocean,' and we can hardly conceive of a compliment more flattering, and, on the whole, more appropriate. He has De Foe's power of realizing the details of a scene to his own imagination, and of impressing them on the imaginations of others, but he has also a bit of deviltry in him which we do not observe in De Foe, however much raciness it may lend to Melville. The present work, though it hardly has the intellectual merit of *Mardi*, is less adventurous in style, and more interesting. It can be read through at one sitting, with continued delight, and we see no reason why it should not be one of the most popular of all the books relating to the romance of the sea. The fact that it narrates the adventures of a 'green hand,' will make it invaluable to a large class of youthful sailors. The style sparkles with wit and fancy, but its great merit is a rapidity of movement, which bears the reader along, almost by main force from the commencement to the conclusion of the volume.

61. Charles F. Briggs, unsigned review, *Holden's Dollar Magazine*

January 1850, v, 55–6

Briggs (1804–77) himself had sailed 'before the mast' to Europe and South America, experience that provided material for his popular *Adventures of Harry Franco* (1831) and gave him a special perspective on *Redburn*. He edited, with Edgar Allan Poe and Henry Cood Watson, the *Broadway Journal* in 1845 and was later editor of *Putnam's Monthly Magazine*, which published much of Melville's writings in the 1850s.

Setting aside the mere style of this book, it is not an easy matter to pronounce an accurate judgment on its merits. In *Typee* and *Omoo*, Mr. Melville professed to give us nothing more than his personal experiences; in *Mardi* he avowed his design to try his hand at a romance, which turned out a romantic allegory or satire; but in *Redburn* we have neither a romance, a satire nor a narrative of actual events, but a hodge podge of all three different kinds of literary composition. There are many real events narrated which must have befallen the author; then there are a good many forecastle traditions familiar to every sailor, which the author claims as his own, that tend to create a suspicion of the actuality of the occurrences which really befel him; then there are a few palpable inventions—the story of the London Hell for instance—that do not give us a very exalted idea of Mr. Melville's imaginative capacities; then there are a few rhapsodies such as the rigmarole about the hand organ at sea, that distract the attention from the chief interest of the work; and in addition to these are the sober descriptions such as the account of Liverpool, which are the most valuable and interesting portions of the book.

If Mr. Melville had confined himself to a simple record of facts, after the manner of Dana in his *Two Years Before the Mast*, or after the manner of *Typee* he might not have made so large a book as he has done, but he would have produced one which would have been more profitable not only to himself but to his readers. But, it is not for us to say what an author should have done; all that we are allowed to say is what he has done; and we can with entire sincerity confess that Mr. Melville's last work is an exceedingly interesting one, even with all its faults. All the incidents narrated are common place; but, clothed in the fresh and poetic style of the author, the incidents of his first voyage charm us more than novelties would in a less beautiful dress. Redburn is the juvenile hero of *Typee*. He is the son of a gentleman's widow in reduced circumstances; he quits the maternal roof and comes to New York attired in a shooting jacket and with a fowling piece in his hand for the purpose of trying his fortune at sea. He has no fitting out, nor even money enough in his pocket to pay his passage to New York; he ships as a green hand on board a ship bound to Liverpool, receives no advance wages, raises a few shillings by pawning his fowling piece at a pawn shop in Chatham street, subsisting during two or three days on air and raw carrots, makes the voyage to Liverpool and back without clothes or money, is paid off with a few shillings and, in the end, goes on his whaling voyage which resulted in *Typee* and *Omoo* and a literary reputation. We are accustomed, on the stage to see heroes pass through a series of years without stopping to change their fancy dresses or once taking a nap, but in a narrative we expect our heroes to live like other mortals, and we are puzzled to conceive how Redburn contrived to 'skim slicks' on ship board without a change of clothing or a bed to lie upon.

Many of the notices of *Redburn* that we have seen, speak of him as a second De Foe, but there is hardly an English writer he so little resembles as the author of *Robinson Crusoe*. The charm of De Foe is his simplicity of style, and artistic accuracy of description; the author of *Redburn* on the contrary is, at times, ambitiously gorgeous in style, and at others coarse and abrupt in his simplicity. But his style is always copious, free and transparent. His chief defect is an ambitious desire to appear fine and learned which causes him to drag in by the head and shoulders remote images that ought not to be within a thousand miles of the reader's thoughts.

The descriptions of Liverpool are, as we have said, the best part of the book; he notices precisely those objects that must first strike the eye of a sailor boy on arriving at that port, and none others; hence the honesty and beauty which are so apparent in the descriptions of the sailor-boarding house; Launcelot's Hay; the church-yard of St. Nicholas; the Docks; Nelson's Monument; the salt barges; Castle street, and above all, the walk into the country. Had the book contained nothing but these, the descriptions of his companions on ship board, and the incidents that actually befell him, it would have been one of the raciest books of sea adventure with which the English language is enriched. There is nothing in Falconer, or Cooper, or Marryatt finer than the portraiture of Jackson, the sailor friend, whose end is so fit and so tragic. We have not space to quote more than this admirable description of the last act in an old sailor's life:

[quotes from chapter 59, 'The breeze was stiff' to 'from the mate.']

62. Unsigned notice, *Southern Quarterly Review*

April 1850, (n.s.) i, 259–60

A volume in direct contrast with *Mardi*, being rather cold and prosaic, while that was wild, warm and richly fanciful. *Redburn*, however, is much more than *Mardi*, within the range of the popular sympathies. It is a book fashioned somewhat after the school of Defoe and Marryatt, partaking of the simplicity and employing the numerous details which constituted the striking features of these writers. But 'Redburn,' as a character, is not symmetrically drawn. He forgets his part at times; and the wild, very knowing and bold boy ashore, becomes a sneak, and a numbskull aboard ship. The portraiture is thus far faulty. There is another defect in the book. All that foreign graffing, which shows us the scion of nobility at a gaming house in London, and subsequently, as a sailor-boy, in sundry fantastic scenes, is by no means proper to such a story. But the truth is, the author has an imagination which naturally becomes restive in the monotonous details of such a career as that of 'Redburn;' and, in breaking away from bonds self-imposed, does not suffer him to see how much hurt is done to his previous labors. The transition was quite too rapid from *Mardi* to *Redburn*, wild, improbable and fantastic as was that allegorical production, it is more in proof of real powers in reserve, than either of the books of this author.

WHITE-JACKET

1850

63. Henry F. Chorley, from an unsigned review, *Athenæum*

2 February 1850, 123–5

Though it might have been thought that the world on shore has heard enough of the world in man-of-war or merchantman—and that the incidents and combinations of both have been practically, romantically and facetiously exhausted by such writers as Basil Hall, Cooper, Marryat, and the host of their imitators—*White Jacket* will probably tell another story; and find (since it deserves to find) many animated and interested readers. Mr. Melville stands as far apart from any past or present marine painter in pen and ink as Turner does from the magnificent artist vilipended by Mr. Ruskin for Turner's sake—Vandervelde. We cannot recall another novelist or sketcher who has given the poetry of the Ship—her voyages and her crew—in a manner at all resembling his. No ingratitude is hereby meant to the memory of *Tom Coffin*—no disrespect to the breathless *coup de théâtre*[1] at the close of *The Pirate*, when the huge man-of-war is seen cleaving the fog. But the personage and the picture referred to are both theatrical; whereas Mr. Melville's sea-creatures, calms and storms, belong to the more dreamy tone of 'The Ancient Mariner,' and have a touch of serious and suggestive picturesqueness appertaining to a world of art higher than the actor's or the scene-painter's. In *Mardi* it will be recollected that this humour ran riot. Yet we felt as we read even that absurd *extravaganza* that to Melville (and not to Marryat) should the legend of Vanderdecken, the Flying Dutchman, have fallen. In *White Jacket* our author has brought his familiar into capital, practical, working order; and throwing, as his Jack o'Lantern does, a new light on the

[1] *Coup de théâtre:* dramatic surprise.

coarse, weather-beaten shapes and into the cavernous corners of a man-of-war, the author's pages have a tone and a relish which are alike individual and attractive.

Mr. Melville's 'yarn' receives its baptismal appellation from a certain shirt which, owing to necessity perhaps, he was obliged to 'fit up' for duty in place of the rougher average *grego* which the sailor takes with him by way of blanket, watch-box, anti-fog, and what not, when he is bound for a voyage round 'the Cape of Storms.' Surely neither Mr. Nicoll's novelist nor the many minstrels of Moses ever threw a livelier interest around their *alpaca* wares, or other of the thousand pieces of clothing which they praise with so various a magniloquence, than the author of *Typee* imparts to *his* garment. . . .

We had marked other passages, sad, serious and shrewd; some bearing a close coincidence to the revelations which gave Mr. Dana's real sea-journal so painful an interest—others further to exhibit the writer's peculiar manner of description;—but no room is left to us. To conclude, then,—with a thousand faults, which it were needless here to point out, Mr. Melville possesses, also, more vivacity, fancy, colour and energy than ninety-nine out of the hundred who undertake to poetize or to prate about 'sea monsters or land monsters;' and we think that, with only the commonest care, he might do brilliant service by enlarging the library of fictitious adventure.

64. From an unsigned review, *Britannia*

2 February 1850, 122

The sketches of which this work is composed are worked up with the skill and power of a practised pen; but, nevertheless, the want of continuity of interest is painfully felt as the reader proceeds from one chapter to another. Mr. Melville, while exhibiting all the phases of sea life during a long voyage, exhibits, too, something of its monotony, until at last we get tired of the careless dashing of the waves, the groaning of the masts, and the creaking of the bulk-headings. The faces of the crew weary us in like manner; we see too much of them; and heartily long for land and change of company. Unless he changes his style, his popularity, at least with those who read for amusement, will not survive the issue of another *White Jacket.*

The work, besides, labours under the defect of want of motive. The elaborate descriptions lead to no end. There is not enough of the true spirit of art in them to show that the intellect was thoughtful as well as active which produced them. They are wanting in that quality which in painting we term composition, which is one great source of pleasure to the eye and mind, and the want of which is instinctively felt even when its absence is not distinctly detected.

In this respect Mr. Melville resembles the great majority of his countrymen who aspire to literary eminence. They imagine everything depends on mental vigour, and nothing on mental discipline. Their aim is to astonish and horrify rather than to elevate and please. They revel in exaggeration of all kinds; and even when they deal with simple nature they know not how to select and combine, so that its representation shall at once give an impression of truth and a sentiment of delight. . . .

Mr. Melville has strength, but he is not skillful in the use of it; he has fancy, but he knows not how to restrain and guide it. His genius requires the direction of taste. Perhaps the opposite fault may be detected in our literature. But at present it is sufficient for the instruction of Mr. Melville and other American writers of his class to insist on the principle that even nature, to be pleasing, must be represented by art, and that the coarse exaggeration which aims at improving nature is but a miserable substitute for that skill which can make it, in its truth and simplicity, the most delightful object of contemplation.

The book, however, apart from its literary merits and defects, deserves some attention for the incidental notices scattered through it of the state and discipline of the American navy. . . .

The author advocates a complete reform in naval discipline, and certainly from his account reform is much needed, though one wonders how the monstrous abuses and horrible tyranny he relates could have arisen under the jealous eye of Republican rule. From his description of an American frigate it must be a floating hell. In this, as in other parts of the work, there may possibly be exaggeration, but no doubt can exist, from what is said, that under the free institutions of the freest of Republics the commanders in the American navy are not unfrequently brutal tyrants, and the men degraded slaves.

65. From an unsigned review, *John Bull*

2 February 1850, 74–5

It were the height of injustice to deny that Mr. Herman Melville is an improving and a vastly improved writer. He is no longer the wanton boy that used to give the rein to his wit and fancy, indulging in refined licentiousness of description, more seductive and mischievous than open violations of decorum, and in that smart dare-devil style of remark which perverts, while it dazzles, the mind, inducing habits of levity and irreverence of thought. Whether it be through the maturing influence of time, through the salutary castigation of criticism, through the chastening experience of life, or through the severe conflict of a better principle within, struggling against, and subduing, the wildness and flightiness of youth, matters not—the pleasing fact remains that the rattling youngster has grown into a thoughtful man, who, without any abatement of his rich and ever sparkling wit, has obtained the mastery of his own fancy, and fills life's log with sober entries, instead of defacing it with broad caricatures and sketches of still more questionable propriety.

In the convenient form of a fragment of a sailor's autobiography,—the narrative of a homeward-bound voyage from the Pacific, round Cape Horn, in the United States frigate *Neversink*, *White Jacket* contains a picture of the American Naval service, so minutely graphic, that he who has spent a few hours as a reader in this 'World in a Man-of-War,' is as much at home in the ways and manners of the Yankee Navy, as if he had himself served his time under Commodore Bougee and Captain Claret. Every arrangement of an American man-of-war, every feature of the American service, is brought under notice; the dryness of professional discussion is so felicitously palliated by the incidents in connexion with which each point is introduced, that a work which is in its substance a caustic *critique* upon the American Navy, assumes the form, and possesses all the attraction, of a first rate sea-novel, while, at the same time, it embodies the author's philosophy of life. The characters which are brought upon the stage are admirable life-pictures, exhibiting, by the magic effect of a few masterly touches, each man in the complete individuality of his person and his office;

from the Commodore, who as he paces the quarter-deck covers up his deficiency in the qualities necessary for command by the unbending starchness of official etiquette, down to the meanest specimen of the genus 'loblolly-boy.' . . .

. . . we cannot, however, forbear taking a hasty glance at the religious appointments of the American navy, which are, singularly enough, and, in this instance at least, happily for the poor sailors, as great an infringement upon the Constitution of the Republic, as its social etiquette and its penal code. Whereas the fundamental articles of the Constitution declare a religious establishment inadmissible, the men-of-war are all supplied with Naval Chaplains. On the *Neversink*, the Chaplain was an Episcopalian, whose spiritual charge, nevertheless, extended over Baptists and all manner of sectarians, non-conformity, which on shore is a right and a virtue in the Model Republic, being strictly forbidden when afloat. The external arrangements of the 'Established Church' of the United States navy are, it seems, but of an indifferent character; . . .

But it is time to take leave of the *Neversink*, and of her crew,—even of *White Jacket* himself,—and return to Mr. Herman Melville. Of the ability of this his latest,—we sincerely trust not his last, nor his best,—performance, we have already spoken. The versatility of his genius and brilliancy of his wit are rare gifts, which he has moreover had the wisdom to display in a manner peculiarly his own, and far from infelicitous. It is all the more to be regretted, therefore, that his religious views are of a character so little calculated either to satisfy himself, or to edify his readers. Occasionally, it is true, traces, hopeful symptoms, of a better mind and a truer view are not wanting; still there is far too great a freedom in touching upon sacred subjects, and, deeper and more dangerous still, there is running through the whole of his views a philosophy which ill accords with the truth of revelation. . . .

66. Unsigned review, *Spectator* Supplement

2 February 1850, 3–4

In form, this is the narrative of a homeward voyage from Callao to New York in an American frigate; but as general rather than particular incidents, characters, and nautical manners, are professed to be delineated, *White Jacket* has some of the properties of fiction. Strictly, however, it is an illustration of life and economy in the naval service of the United States, accompanied by the author's disquisitions on those topics which the incidents may be said to embody. Thus, a flogging gives rise to several essays on naval punishments, the power regularly granted to naval officers, and the unconstitutional power they usurp. The arrival of the Neversink frigate at Rio, and some complimentary visits paid and received, with the ceremonies attendant upon them, occasion a discussion on the formal etiquette still maintained in the navy. The rumours of a war about the Oregon dispute, and the different manner in which they are received by the sailors, who can look for nothing but hard knocks, and the officers, who hope for glory, promotion, and prize-money, introduces a sensible discussion on the honours and inequalities of war, with several anecdotes and remarks on the combats between English and American vessels during the contest of 1812. By such means, the interior life in a man-of-war is pretty well exhibited in the form of sketch, and its moral pretty fully expounded, according to Mr. Melville's views.

Those views are of the Peace Congress and Democratic kind, but possessing more force and more logic than we are accustomed to in the platform orators at home. Mr. Melville has served in a man-of-war himself. He practically understands the evils of the system, as well as the evils which a stern discipline must keep down. His tone is more sober, his views are more sensible than the tone and views of the platform sophists, who would not only have lectured Hannibal on the art of war, but Columbus on navigation, Newton on gravitation, or Cook on nautical hygiene. Neither is there always a ready answer to his religious, legal, or constitutional logic; except upon the plea of necessity in the case of law and constitution, or the general neglect of true Christian humility, and the avoidance of certain topics in the pulpit, on shore as well as afloat. In his quiet ridicule of many ceremonies and customs of the service, apparently useless, he seems to forget the necessity of forming habits of obedience, readiness, activity, vigilance. It is true of many things what Napier remarks on the daily inspection of arms, that it is not necessary pro hac vice. As regards the arms and other matters, less frequent and rigid rules would suffice for the thing, but not for the discipline of the men. Gun exercises, sham fights, and piping all hands in the dead of night to clear the ship for action, are vexatious and troublesome; but they are surely necessary. The skill must be acquired, and having been acquired must be retained; or what would happen when the real occasion arrived? As for the 'constitution,' the essence of war is a state of violence, and the preparation for it is the same. The martial codes of all countries are more severe than their civil laws; though it is probable that the codes would be better for a revision adapted to the opinion of the times, and that the practice may be frequently too severe (as may be the case with municipal laws between civilians on shore): but it is only necessary to read Mr. Melville's terrible description of the villanies and vices on shipboard to be satisfied that the 'law's delay' would not do for a man-of-war. The following remarks, and some others on chaplains, prayers, and matters connected therewith, are also true enough.

[quotes from chapter 38, 'The accommodations of' to 'to that instrument.']

To the theory of this there can be no answer. Practically, the presence even of a merely decorous chaplain is admitted to have its advantages; but to have chaplains for all the denominations on board a frigate or ship of the line, is obviously impossible. As little would it answer to allow common sailors to absent themselves from a solemn congregation, on the hypocritical plea of conscience. Nor, in fact, need any one absent himself from any Christian service on conscientious grounds, unless perhaps a Protestant from the Romanist mass.

There is nothing like a continuous story in *White Jacket;* nor are the incidents so striking in themselves as they might have been made, or always very fresh. Some interest will be found in the English-like picture furnished of the American navy,—the same terms, the same customs, the same tunes, the same songs; though Mr. Melville considers the American discipline more severe, the generality of the officers more tyrannical, and there appears as much interest and corruption going on as at home, when the comparatively smaller numbers are considered.

Subject to the remarks already made, the disquisitions may be pronounced judicious; and the book conveys a good idea of the economy and character of the United States navy.

Of the fictitious topics that vary, and indeed often introduce the disquisitions, we will take a short specimen.

[quotes from chapter 14, 'It was during this' to 'before daylight obtruded.']

67. From an unsigned review, *Atlas*

9 February 1850, 90–1

Great has been the company of the captains who have unfolded to the gentle readers, 'who stay at home at ease,' the mysteries of life on board ship. Basil Hall, Marryatt, Chamier, Cooper, and many another epauletted author have written out their logbooks in narratives and descriptions of admirable minuteness, and anatomatised the wooden walls which form the seaman's home, and the sturdy tars the inmates thereof, until we fancy that we know every rope and spar in the ship better than we do the nooks and corners of our own library. At times we even fancy that ourselves have 'suffered a sea-change,' and pass on side by side with the mariner from bell to bell—*littorally*, half-hour to half-hour—throughout the livelong day.

But all these pictures were sketched from the quarter deck. Even when the common seaman was made the apparent portrait-painter, his perspective referred invariably to that sacred spot where he himself dare not utter a grumbling word, or show a wrinkle of discontent. Mr. Melville draws the same subject, but with the forecastle for his point of sight. The outline is here very different, the colouring harsher, and the resulting impression less pleasant; though, we fear, much more true. We are now admitted behind the scenes; we see the seamy side of the canvas; we can count the tar-buckets, the oil lamps, the dangling ropes and grimy workmen, whose services are tasked to form the *tableaux*, that look so agreeably to the spectators standing aft. The captain, as he emerges from his cabin at sunrise, may pride himself on the tautness of the rigging and the immaculate purity of the decks of his 'tight little frigate.' The foretopman tells us how the mathematical trim of the yards has been secured by remorseless 'coltings' inflicted on all laggers at the lifts and braces; and how the sleepy sailors were piped out of their hammocks long before it was necessary, in order to spend the chilliest hours of the twenty-four in slushing, scrubbing, and holy-stoning every plank in the ship.

Many of the wonders of the 'world of a man-of-war' are now revealed to us for the first time, as they could only have been revealed by an occupant of the 'berth deck.' . . .

The prevailing tone of the book is one of discontent. Mr. Melville depicts the seaman's life as full of anything but *agrémens*.[1] . . .

As for glory, the author thinks he has settled the question when he tells us that the common sailor is never mentioned in the *Gazette* nor buried in Westminster Abbey. He seems conscious of no influence in the thought of duties gallantly and silently performed. There are no memories of past triumphs that will stir his enthusiasm; no names of dead heroes that rouse him to admire and emulate. We know well that of all sources of pride those derived from the bloodstained trophies of war are the least to be cherished. But they are not without their value even as a substitute for coarser and more barbarous stimulus. The captain may unbend his sternness, and the boatswain's mate stow away the cat, with a crew whose hearts will respond involuntarily to a Dibdin chorus, or leap at the repetition of that signal which immortalised, even more than the victory which it heralded, the morning of Trafalgar.

There are worse characteristics than those hinted at by Mr. Melville. We hear of secret and murderous revenge practised upon the master at arms—the policeman of the man-of-war—by punished criminals; and of the disgraceful extent to which smuggling is carried for the sake of enriching, at the expense of the hard-working men, some of the officers who are appointed to retrain and protect them. Can these be true, the stories we are here told of brandy brought stealthily on board by some of the superiors and sold at twelve dollars a bottle to the sailors—of a purser making 50,000 dollars in a single cruise—and of the scant residuum of a single thousand dollars paid as the three years' wages of eighty men on board one ship; all the rest, amounting to perhaps twenty-

[1] *Agrémens:* pleasurable.

five thousand dollars, being stopped for articles, and chiefly for spirits, supplied to them during the voyage? We must leave to professional judges to decide as to the truth of these tales; but their very publication involves the suspicion of disorders from which we are happy to believe our own navy to be *almost*, if not quite, exempt.

'White Jacket's' own story is that he enlisted in the United States frigate Neversink, while she was lying in a harbour of the Pacific, and served in her for a twelve-month during her voyage round the South American continent and home to New York to be paid off. The anecdotes he gives of the cruise are, he tells us, strictly veritable, except as to the names—and we believe him. His whole narrative is, indeed, marked by all the sobriety of truth; and, though enlivened by the sparkling and racy style which characterises the author in his happiest moments, are full of those homely and trivial details which bear with them the conviction that the scene is sketched from the life. Here and there 'White Jacket' indulges in descriptive flights, which remind us of *Mardi*, and with one of these we must close our remarks. . . .

[quotes from chapter 25, 'Colder and colder' to 'the arteries himself.']

68. Evert Duyckinck, from 'Mr. Melville's *White Jacket*,' unsigned review, *Literary World*

16 March 1850, 271–2

The keen sense of outward life, mingled with the growing weight of reflection which cheers or burdens the inner man, observable in Mr. Melville's later volumes, keep us company in the present. It is this union of culture and experience, of thought and observation, the sharp breeze of the forecastle alternating with the mellow stillness of the library, books and work imparting to each other mutual life, which distinguishes the narratives of the author of *Typee* from all other productions of their class. He is not a bookish sailor or a tar among books; each character is separate and perfect in its integrity, but he is all the better sailor for the duty and decision which books teach, all the better reader for the independence and sharpness of observation incidental to the objective life of the sea. It is very seldom that you can get at the latter from this point of view. Your men of choice literature and of educated fancy, your Sternes, Jean Pauls, Southeys, and Longfellows, are not likely to acquire the practical experiences of the tar bucket. The sea of course attracts them with its materials for poetic illustration, but they copy from the descriptions of others. To have the fancy and the fact united is rare in any walk, almost unknown on the sea. Hence to Herman Melville, whose mind swarms with tender, poetic, or humorous fancies, the ship is a new world, now first conquered. No one has so occupied it. Sailors have been described and well described, as sailors, and there has been a deal of brilliant and justly admired nautical writing, from the quarter-deck; but the sailor as a man, seen with a genial philosophy and seen from the forecastle, has been reserved for our author. The effect is novel and startling. It is a new dish *en matelote*[1] brought upon our epicurean over-civilized tables. Is Jack to be recognised, you ask, with all this embroidery of reading and reflection about him and his tarry ways? Yes! for Jack is a man, and his ways, tarry as they are, point as indexes to the universal nature among all surely as any gilded duties or elegances on shore.

Mr. Melville is true to his title, the *world* in a man-of-war: there is no difficulty in finding it there; it may be concentrated in less space with fewer subjects. And it is a sound humanitarian lesson which he teaches, or rather that life teaches, which he records. There is no sentimentality, no effort to elevate the 'people' or degrade the commodores; his characters are not thrust out of their ordinary positions or range of ideas; he does not sew any finery upon them, but they are all heroes nevertheless, interesting while they are on the stage, one and all, as genuine Shakspearean, that is human personages.

Open the book, this *White Jacket*, which is simply a clear reflecting mirror, in a quaintly-cased gold frame, of a twelve months' voyage in a United States frigate, of an 'ordinary seaman,' and see what company you are in.

Here is a fellow with the salt on him. Chaucer could not have seen him with brighter eyes:—

[quotes from chapter 8, 'the man who' to 'the main-topsail-yard?'

[1] *En matelote*: in a wine sauce with various vegetables and spices.

describing 'Mad Jack.' Also quotes from descriptions of two other characters]

But we cannot stop at this great portrait-gallery of the man-of-war. They are all there, from the inhabitants of the main-top to the old men of the cock-pit. Truly is it a world, the frigate, with its thousand picked men, the contribution of every state of life, of every stage of civilization, of each profession, of all arts and callings, but—of one sex. And therein is a significant key to the peculiar position of the 'Navy' in the affairs of the race. The man-of-war is divorced from civilization,—we will not repeat the stale phrase, from the progress of humanity,— but from humanity itself. *How* thus divorced, through all the windings and intricacies of the artificial system, *White Jacket* will show.

Herman Melville tests all his characters by their manhood. His book is thoroughly American and democratic. There is no patronage in his exhibition of a sailor, any more than in his portraits of captains and commodores. He gives all fair play in an impartial spirit. There is no railing, no scolding; he never loses his temper when he hits hardest. A quaint, satirical, yet genial humor is his grand destructive weapon. It would be a most dangerous one (for what is there which cannot be shaken with ridicule?), were it not for the poetic element by which it is elevated. Let our author treasure this as his choicest possession, for without it his humor would soon degenerate into a sneer, than which there is nothing sadder, more fatal. In regarding, too, the spirit of things, may he not fall into the error of undervaluing their forms, lest he get into a bewildering, barren, and void scepticism!

We have intimated Herman Melville is a poet, and such he is, though, perhaps, 'lacking the accomplishment of verse.' Let this old main-mast-man prove it:—

'The *main-mast-man* of the Neversink was a very aged seaman, who well deserved his comfortable berth. He had seen more than half a century of the most active service, and through all had proved himself a good and faithful man. He furnished one of the very rare examples of a sailor in a green old age; for, with most sailors, old age comes in youth, and Hardship and Vice carry them on an early bier to the grave.

'As in the evening of life, and at the close of day, old Abraham sat at the door of his tent, biding his time to die, so sits our old mast-man on the *coat of the mast*, glancing round him with patriarchal benignity. And that mild expression of his sets off very strangely a face that has been burned almost black by the torrid suns that shone fifty years ago—a face that is seamed with three sabre cuts. You would almost think this old mast-man had been blown out of Vesuvius, to look alone at his scarred, blackened forehead, chin, and cheeks. But gaze down into his eye, and though all the snows of Time have drifted higher and higher upon his brow, yet deep down in that eye you behold an infantile, sinless look, the same that answered the glance of this old man's mother when first she cried for the babe to be laid by her side. That look is the fadeless, ever infantile immortality within.' . . .

And the whole book is written with this abounding life and freshness—from the first page to the last.

We have but indicated some of its general characteristics. The speciality of the book, its particular treatment of the 'service:' its views on the naval reform questions which are now prominently before the public, afford matter for another article. We shall return to 'The World in a Man-of-War,' in our next.

It is, we should add, a book essentially of personal observation, the author claiming this in the few lines prefixed of preface, in which he refers to 1843 as the date of his 'experiences.'

69. Herrman S. Saroni, from an unsigned review, *Saroni's Musical Times*

30 March 1850, 317–18

The bustling little world of a Man-of-war has often been described, but never before in the truthful colors of Mr. Melville's picture now lying before us. Our accounts of man-of-war's-men heretofore have been written in the melodramatic style: heroic sailors and epic quarter-deck characters, romantic incidents and stirring sea scenes have furnished the staple of naval romances. But no one had yet lifted the veil which covers the man-of-war's real 'life below stairs.' We hope that our naval acquaintance will pardon us for the expression 'stairs' as here applied, nor argue from its insertion that we 'don't know the ropes.' Ever since we have resumed our 'long togs,' sailor talk no longer comes 'natural' to us any more than to Mr. Melville.

The author of *Mardi* has not deemed it worth while on this occasion to bind his recollections of the sea with any thread of fiction. The identity of 'White-Jacket' himself furnishes the sole unity of interest. Whatever may be with others the result of this want of artifice, it nowise detracts from the merit of the book in our eyes. To us personally this last work of Mr. Melville presents a very intense interest still heightened by the personal recollections it awakens. We too, lured by highly wrought descriptions of life on board ship, have done long and grievous penance in a man-of-war. We too, have measured the length and breadth of the popular deception and learned to a certainty, according to the sailor's proverb, *whither* may 'go for pastime' those who 'go to sea for pleasure.' It is this our own experience which we find set down in *White-Jacket*; and, but for the immeasurable talent displayed, as well as for a very few propositions wherein we do not wholly acquiesce, we might think that we ourself had written the book and not Melville.

How remorselessly and truthful he tears the veil of romance which has been cast over the 'world in a man-of-war;' how eloquently he strips our jolly tars of their proverbial attributes, our quarter-deck dignitaries of their pompous chivalry of 'longshore' demeanor. Not that he has written his book in a cynical spirit; for much he has softened down which would have furnished texts for endless anti-naval harangues. Dark as the picture appears in some parts, the author must acknowledge that he has left much the darkest colors untouched upon the pallet. Let *White-Jacket* be printed thousands of thousands of times, let a copy be attached to every village library wherever the English language is spoken, nay, let a polyglot edition be spread all over the world, in order that adventurous youths, who meditate the rash experiment which has already ruined so many, may awake from their day-dreams of 'spicy islands' and 'moonlit waters' and other fairy-like incidents of 'a life on the ocean-wave.' If after reading *White-Jacket*, they be still bent upon 'shipping,' they will then sign the roll with their eyes wide open. . . .

Would you know well the farcical struttings of those who wield a little brief authority in a man-of-war, whenever they are pleased to 'ship their quarter deck faces?' Would you know how 'the people' (authoritative for 'common sailors') manage with a little hard philosophy to beguile the sad hours of their tedious slavery? Then consult 'White-Jacket' *passim*. He is an oracle that speaks truth.

'White-Jacket' discourses most eloquently on the popular side of the question, which is now attracting so much attention, the question of flogging in the Navy. We neither approve nor absolutely dissent. We rather wonder at the boldness with which he begs the principle, or storms it, to speak more truly. We are not prepared to say that he is wrong—wiser heads than ours argue fiercely on both sides. We merely surmise that carried away by his very natural sympathy, he has substituted rhetoric for logic, and has viewed the question from one side only. . . .

70. Unsigned notice, *United States Magazine and Democratic Review*

April 1850, xxvi, 384

Mr. Melville is again before the world with his inimitable sea scenes. A note to the present volume states briefly, 'In the year 1843 I shipped as "ordinary seaman" on board of a United States frigate, then lying in a harbor of the Pacific Ocean.' He remained a year, and was discharged. His experience are embraced in the present volume, and most agreeably are sketched the manners and customs of these 'wooden walls.' It is, however, evidently manufactured for the English market—all the seamen heroes are Britons, and all the admirals of England are the oracles and text-books. Although the accomplished author thanks God that he is free from national invidiousness, he nevertheless betrays the fact, that London pays him better for his copy-right than New-York; and the puffs for English officers, with the left-handed compliments to the American service, doubtless had their value with Bentley. The book is highly interesting, and we can afford to wink at the author's weakness. He was threatened with a rope's-end in the service, and is now apparently approaching the end of his rope.

71. George Ripley, from an initialled review, New York *Tribune*

5 April 1850

Never has there been a more memorable White Jacket than this which gives the name to Mr. Melville's glowing log-book of a year's cruise in a United States frigate. . . .

The White Jacket is made the emblem and 'sweet remembrancer' of all Mr. Melville's perilous and comic experiences, while immured in the floating prison—to use the mildest term—of a public man-of-war. He here finds ample materials for an entertaining book, and has worked them up into a narrative of great power and interest. He always tells a story well, and a plenty are related in this volume. If he had confined himself to repeating what he had heard and seen, his book would have been more valuable, for the moral and metaphysical reflections he sets forth in bad Carlylese, are only incumbrances to the narrative, and often become intolerable.

Mr. Melville has performed an excellent service in revealing the secrets of his prison-house, and calling the public attention to the indescribable abominations of the naval life, reeking with the rankest corruption, cruelty, and blood.

He writes without ill-temper, or prejudice, with no distempered, sentimental philanthropy, but vividly portraying scenes of which he was the constant witness, and in many instances suggesting a judicious remedy for the evils which he exhibits. His remarks on the discipline of our public vessels, are entitled to great consideration, and coincide with the prevailing tendencies of the public mind. It is not often that an observer of his shrewdness and penetration is admitted behind the scenes, and still less often that the results of personal experience are presented in such high-wrought pictures. A man of Melville's brain and pen is a dangerous character in the presence of a gigantic humbug, and those who are interested in the preservation of rotten abuses had better stop that 'chiel from taking notes.'

72. Charles Gordon Greene, from an unsigned review, Boston *Post*

10 April 1850

All the notices that we have seen of this book regard it in a literary light only. They speak of the power and vividness of its descriptions, of its wit, its humor, its character-painting, &c., &c., and they make quotations embracing such and such a marked incident or personage. In fine, they treat *White-Jacket* like the 'last new novel.' But the truth is that the literary feature of the book is its least prominent, and, it may be added, its least presuming one. It certainly has many a passage of excellent writing, and here and there peep forth the qualities mentioned by the critics; but on the whole, *White-Jacket* assumes to be a didactic rather than an ornamental book—a description of fact rather than a romance of fiction. Its purpose is, as it were, to portray the entire *physique* and *morale* of a man-of-war, and all but a fraction of its matter is devoted to the consideration of the actual duties, practices, habits, manners, faults, virtues and oppressions of the sailor, to a description of almost every portion of the ship, to the discussion of the laws, usages and fashions by which an armed vessel is, or should be governed. Such, upon the whole, is *White-Jacket*; and it will be perceived that although such a book may be well written in all the points whereon the man of genius and talent—the writer of sea-novels—may properly stand, its didactic portions may be marked by crudities and puerilities that would disgrace a school-boy. For it is unfortunately true, that because a man produces a spirited and beautiful romance like *Typee*, or an autobiography like *Redburn*, running over with a Defoe naturalness and verisimilitude, it does not follow that he is competent to discuss the fitness or unfitness of the 'Articles of War,' the propriety or impropriety of 'Flogging in the Navy,' or the whole system of government and ceremonials of our 'National Marine.' The discussion of these great practical subjects requires practical men—men of character, wisdom and experience—not men of theories, fancies and enthusiasm. The cobbler of old, who so justly criticised the foot of the statue, but who, embolded by success, made himself utterly ridiculous in finding fault with the nobler portions of the work, should be remembered by the man of genius as well as by the fool. The mind as well as the body is subject to the 'Division of Labor,' and, in most cases, those gifts and acquirements which enable one to produce a good romance unfit him for the calm, comprehensive and practical consideration of questions of jurisprudence or policy. And a forgetfulness of the 'cobbler of old,' is the rock, we think, on which *White-Jacket* has split.

Mr Melville seems to have been determined or impelled to make a tremendous spluttering among 'Naval Abuses' of all sorts—to produce a marked and strong book at any rate—and the result is that he has 'run a muck' against almost every thing that IS in our navy, at this present moment. More than this, he abuses things so *very* heartily, as to make one doubt the soundness and knowledge of such a wholesale reformer, such a venomous upholder of abstract right, against that singular mixture of right and wrong, which always has prevailed, and ever must prevail, to some extent, in the administration of terrestrial affairs, whether of religion or government, of ships or armies. The true and wise philanthropist, it may be remarked, seeks only to make this 'singular mixture of right and wrong' contain as much of the former and as little of the latter ingredient as possible, and does not hope, indeed, to utterly annihilate an evil. But Mr Melville goes for abstractions and perfections—nay, discharges his heaviest batteries, time and time again, against war, the navy, heroic glory, &c., &c., in the midst of argument and fine writing, for the proper government of the marine. It is true that he has a right to his opinion, and even to the expression of it, but being ourselves a sincere and zealous advocate of naval reform, we are sorry to see any man make himself and the good cause ridiculous, by going so far into theoreticals. . . .

In conclusion, we would insinuate a hope that Mr Melville will now try his hand at something else beside the sea. The theme is a stale one at the best, and we cannot perceive why he may not give as brilliant, spirited and truthful sketches and descriptions of 'land rats' as of 'water rats.' It cannot be that his scanty experience of two or three voyages has driven from his imagination all terrors, sublimities and glories but those of ocean. Moreover, we would hope that he may take time for his next book, and learn to criticise as well as to write. Such stuff as *Jack Chase* in the book in hand addresses to the captain and commodore is outrageous, as the discourse of anything but a stage-sailor, and that of the most bombastic kind. And still further, we would hope that Mr

Melville may select some subject and style of treatment which may not require what we must term 'autobiographical twaddle.' This constant attempt to be smart, witty and entertaining on no capital, becomes dreadfully tedious to the reader ere he 'achieves' the end of a book of 465 pages. A little of it is very well, but as poured out by Mr Melville, in his stupid invention of a white-jacket, it appears to be a stream of egotism, vapidness and affectation, with, here and there, a fragment of amber on its waters.

73. Frederick Swartwout Cozzens, unsigned review, *Knickerbocker*

May 1850, xxxv, 448

Cozzens (1818–69) contributed to the *Knickerbocker* from 1847 to 1855 and wrote a number of humorous pieces, including *The Sparrowgrass Papers* (1856). Part of this work first appeared in *Putnam's* in 1854 at the same time as the magazine was publishing Melville's *Israel Potter* serially.

Well, we are glad to find the author of *Typee* on the right ground at last. When we read his *Mardi*, or rather *tried* to read it, for we never could get quite through it, we feared that the author had mistaken his bent, like a comic actor with a 'penshong' for tragedy, and that we were thenceforth to hear from him in a pseudo-philosophical *rifacciamento*[1] of CARLYLE and EMERSON. *Redburn* reässured us; and now comes *White-Jacket*, to reïnstate the author in the best good-graces of the reading public. Not a page of this last work has escaped us; and so strong was the *continuous* interest which it excited, a quality not always encountered even in the most popular works of our time, that we accomplished its perusal in two 'sittings,' unavoidably protracted,

[1] *Rifacciamento:* rifacimento, remaking.

we may remark, for we could not leave the work, while there was yet a page unread. Without the aid of much imagination, but with a daguerreotype-like naturalness of description of all which the writer saw and felt himself, and all which he saw others feel, Mr. MELVILLE has given us a volume which, in its evident truthfulness and accuracy of personal and individual delineation, reminds us continually of that admirable and justly popular work, the *Two Years Before the Mast* of the younger DANA. A vein of sly humor percolates through the book; and a sort of unctuous toying with verbal double-meanings, is once in a while to be met with, which go far to indicate, that if the author had lived in the 'City of *Brotherly Love*,' (church-burners, firemen-fighters, assassins, and rowdies, excuse the implied exceptions!) he might, with a little proper instruction, have become as celebrated as 'a Philadelphia lawyer,' that preëminent model of a pun-hunter. We had intended to present several extracts from *White-Jacket*, which we had pencilled for that purpose in the perusal; but the universal prevalence of the book itself, at this late period, would doubtless make them 'twice-told tales' to the great majority of our readers. We would call especial attention, as a matter of present public interest, to the chapters descriptive of an instance of almost indiscriminate flogging on board a man-of-war, and the consequences of such inconsistent punishment, in the case of each offender. The force of public opinion, and the example of certain humane officers in the highest rank of the American navy, would seem to indicate that the time is not distant when corporeal punishment, if not mainly abolished, will at least be hereafter less frequently resorted to than formerly, and greatly lessened in its severity. The 'signs of the times' would seem to point unerringly to this result.

MELVILLE'S JUDGMENTS

1850–1

74. From 'Hawthorne and His Mosses. By a Virginian Spending His Summer in Vermont,' *Literary World*

17, 24 August 1850, 125–7, 145–7

Melville probably wrote this article very soon after meeting Hawthorne for the first time and spending the day of 5 August with him, Evert Duyckinck, Cornelius Matthews, Oliver Wendell Holmes, and others important in the American literary scene of the time. They climbed Monument Mountain in the Berkshires and dined at nearby Stockbridge, Massachusetts. Much of the conversation that day had to do with a comparison of things English and American, which was to be one of the keynotes of Melville's essay when it appeared later in the month.

. . . I know not what would be the right name to put on the title-page of an excellent book; but this I feel, that the names of all fine authors are fictitious ones, far more so than that of Junius; simply standing, as they do, for the mystical, ever-eluding spirit of all beauty, which ubiquitously possesses men of genius. Purely imaginative as this fancy may appear, it nevertheless seems to receive some warranty from the fact, that on a personal interview no great author has ever come up to the idea of his reader. But that dust of which our bodies are composed, how can it fitly express the nobler intelligences among us? With reverence be it spoken, that not even in the case of one deemed more than man, not even in our Saviour, did his visible frame betoken anything of the augustness of the nature within. Else, how could those Jewish eyewitnesses fail to see heaven in his glance!

It is curious how a man may travel along a country road, and yet miss the grandest or sweetest of prospects by reason of an intervening hedge, so like all other hedges, as in no way to hint of the wide landscape beyond. So has it been with me concerning the enchanting landscape in the soul of this Hawthorne, this most excellent Man of Mosses. His 'Old Manse' has been written now four years, but I never read it till a day or two since. I had seen it in the book-stores—heard of it often—even had it recommended to me by a tasteful friend, as a rare, quiet book, perhaps too deserving of popularity to be popular. But there are so many books called 'excellent,' and so much unpopular merit, that amid the thick stir of other things, the hint of my tasteful friend was disregarded; and for four years the Mosses on the Old Manse never refreshed me with their perennial green. It may be, however, that all this while the book, likewise, was only improving in flavor and body. At any rate, it so chanced that this long procrastination eventuated in a happy result. . . .

What a wild moonlight of contemplative humor bathes that Old Manse!—the rich and rare distilment of a spicy and slowly-oozing heart. No rollicking rudeness, no gross fun fed on fat dinners, and bred in the lees of wine,—but a humor so spiritually gentle, so high, so deep, and yet so richly relishable, that it were hardly inappropriate in an angel. It is the very religion of mirth; for nothing so human but it may be advanced to that. The orchard of the Old Manse seems the visible type of the fine mind that has described it—those twisted and contorted old trees, 'that stretch out their crooked branches, and take such hold of the imagination, that we remember them as humorists and odd-fellows.' And then, as surrounded by these grotesque forms, and hushed in the noon-day repose of this Hawthorne's spell, how aptly might the still fall of his ruddy thoughts into your soul be symbolized by 'the thump of a great apple, in the stillest afternoon, falling without a breath of wind, from the mere necessity of perfect ripeness!' . . .

But he has still other apples, not quite so ruddy, though full as ripe; —apples, that have been left to wither on the tree, after the pleasant autumn gathering is past. The sketch of 'The Old Apple-Dealer' is conceived in the subtlest spirit of sadness; he whose 'subdued and nerveless boyhood prefigured his abortive prime, which, likewise, contained within itself the prophecy and image of his lean and torpid age.' Such touches as are in this piece cannot proceed from any common heart. They argue such a depth of tenderness, such a boundless sympathy with all forms of being, such an omnipresent love, that we must needs say that this Hawthorne is here almost alone in his generation,—at least, in the artistic manifestation of these things. Still more. Such touches as these,—and many, very many similar ones, all through his chapters—furnish clues whereby we enter a little way into the intricate, profound heart where they originated. And we see that suffering, some time or other and in some shape or other,—this only can enable any man to depict it in others. All over him, Hawthorne's melancholy rests like an Indian-summer, which, though bathing a whole country in one softness, still reveals the distinctive hue of every towering hill and each far-winding vale.

But it is the least part of genius that attracts admiration. Where Hawthorne is known, he seems to be deemed a pleasant writer, with a pleasant style,—a sequestered, harmless man, from whom any deep and weighty thing would hardly be anticipated—a man who means no meanings. But there is no man, in whom humor and love, like mountain peaks, soar to such a rapt height as to receive the irradiations of the upper skies;—there is no man in whom humor and love are developed in that high form called genius; no such man can exist without also possessing, as the indispensable complement of these, a great, deep intellect, which drops down into the universe like a plummet. Or, love and humor are only the eyes through which such an intellect views this world. The great beauty in such a mind is but the product of its strength. What, to all readers, can be more charming than the piece entitled 'Monsieur du Miroir;' and to a reader at all capable of fully fathoming it, what, at the same time, can possess more mystical depth of meaning?—yes, there he sits and looks at me,—this 'shape of mystery,' this 'identical Monsieur du Miroir.' 'Methinks I should tremble now, were his wizard power of gliding through all impediments in search of me, to place him suddenly before my eyes.'

How profound, nay appalling, is the moral evolved by the Earth's Holocaust; where—beginning with the hollow follies and affectations of the world,—all vanities and empty theories and forms are, one after another, and by an admirably graduated, growing comprehensiveness, thrown into the allegorical fire, till, at length, nothing is left but the all-engendering heart of man; which remaining still unconsumed, the great conflagration is naught.

Of a piece with this, is the 'Intelligence Office,' a wondrous symbolizing of the secret workings in men's souls. There are other sketches still more charged with ponderous import.

'The Christmas Banquet,' and 'The Bosom Serpent,' would be fine subjects for a curious and elaborate analysis, touching the conjectural parts of the mind that produced them. For spite of all the Indian-summer sunlight on the hither side of Hawthorne's soul, the other side —like the dark half of the physical sphere—is shrouded in a blackness, ten times black. But this darkness but gives more effect to the ever-moving dawn, that for ever advances through it, and circumnavigates his world. Whether Hawthorne has simply availed himself of this mystical blackness as a means to the wondrous effects he makes it to produce in his lights and shades; or whether there really lurks in him, perhaps unknown to himself, a touch of Puritanic gloom,—this, I cannot altogether tell. Certain it is, however, that this great power of blackness in him derives its force from its appeals to that Calvinistic sense of Innate Depravity and Original Sin, from whose visitations, in some shape or other, no deeply thinking mind is always and wholly free. For, in certain moods, no man can weigh this world without throwing in something, somehow like Original Sin, to strike the uneven balance. At all events, perhaps no writer has ever wielded this terrific thought with greater terror than this same harmless Hawthorne. Still more: this black conceit pervades him through and through. You may be witched by his sunlight,—transported by the bright gildings in the skies he builds over you; but there is the blackness of darkness beyond; and even his bright gildings but fringe and play upon the edges of thunder-clouds. In one word, the world is mistaken in this Nathaniel Hawthorne. He himself must often have smiled at its absurd misconception of him. He is immeasurably deeper than the plummet of the mere critic. For it is not the brain that can test such a man; it is only the heart. Yet cannot come to know greatness by inspecting it; there is no glimpse to be caught of it, except by intuition; you need not ring it, you but touch it, and you find it is gold.

Now, it is that blackness in Hawthorne, of which I have spoken, that so fixes and fascinates me. It may be, nevertheless, that it is too largely developed in him. Perhaps he does not give us a ray of his light for every shade of his dark. But however this may be, this blackness it is that furnishes the infinite obscure of his back-ground,—that background, against which Shakspeare plays his grandest conceits, the things that have made for Shakspeare his loftiest but most circumscribed renown, as the profoundest of thinkers. For by philosophers Shakspeare is not adored as the great man of tragedy and comedy.—'Off with his head; so much for Buckingham!' This sort of rant, interlined by another hand, brings down the house,—those mistaken souls, who dream of Shakspeare as a mere man of Richard-the-Third humps and Macbeth daggers. But it is those deep far-away things in him; those occasional flashings-forth of the intuitive Truth in him; those short, quick probings at the very axis of reality;—these are the things that make Shakspeare, Shakspeare. Through the mouths of the dark characters of Hamlet, Timon, Lear, and Iago, he craftily says, or sometimes insinuates the things which we feel to be so terrifically true, that it were all but madness for any good man, in his own proper character, to utter, or even hint of them. Tormented into desperation, Lear, the frantic king, tears off the mask, and speaks the sane madness of vital truth. But, as I before said, it is the least part of genius that attracts admiration. And so, much of the blind, unbridled admiration that has been heaped upon Shakspeare, has been lavished upon the least part of him. And few of his endless commentators and critics seem to have remembered, or even perceived, that the immediate products of a great mind are not so great as that undeveloped and sometimes undevelopable yet dimly-discernible greatness, to which those immedate products are but the infallible indices. In Shakspeare's tomb lies infinitely more than Shakspeare ever wrote. And if I magnify Shakspeare, it is not so much for what he did do as for what he did not do, or refrained from doing. For in this world of lies, Truth is forced to fly like a scared white doe in the woodlands; and only by cunning glimpses will she reveal herself, as in Shakspeare and other masters of the great Art of Telling the Truth,—even though it be covertly and by snatches.

But if this view of the all-popular Shakspeare be seldom taken by his readers, and if very few who extol him have ever read him deeply, or perhaps, only have seen him on the tricky stage (which alone made, and is still making him his mere mob renown)—if few men have time, or patience, or palate, for the spiritual truth as it is in that great genius;—it is then no matter of surprise, than in a contemporaneous age, Nathaniel Hawthorne is a man as yet almost utterly mistaken among men. Here and there, in some quiet armchair in the noisy town, or some deep nook among the noiseless mountains, he may be appreciated for something of what he is. But unlike Shakspeare, who was forced to the contrary course by circumstances, Hawthorne (either from simple disinclination, or else from inaptitude) refrains from all the popularizing noise and show of broad farce and blood-besmeared tragedy; content with the still, rich utterance of a great intellect in repose, and which sends few thoughts into circulation, except they be arterialized at his large warm lungs, and expanded in his honest heart.

Nor need you fix upon that blackness in him, if it suit you not. Nor, indeed, will all readers discern it; for it is, mostly, insinuated to those who may best understand it, and account for it; it is not obtruded upon every one alike.

Some may start to read of Shakspeare and Hawthorne on the same page. They may say, that if an illustration were needed, a lesser light might have sufficed to elucidate this Hawthorne, this small man of yesterday. But I am not willingly one of those who, as touching Shakspeare at least, exemplify the maxim of Rochefoucault, that 'we exalt the reputation of some, in order to depress that of others;'—who, to teach all noble-souled aspirants that there is no hope for them, pronounce Shakspeare absolutely unapproachable. But Shakspeare has been approached. There are minds that have gone as far as Shakspeare into the universe. And hardly a mortal man, who, at some time or other, has not felt as great thoughts in him as any you will find in Hamlet. We must not inferentially malign mankind for the sake of any one man, whoever he may be. This is too cheap a purchase of contentment for conscious mediocrity to make. Besides, this absolute and unconditional adoration of Shakspeare has grown to be a part of our Anglo-Saxon superstitions. The Thirty-Nine articles are now Forty. Intolerance has come to exist in this matter. You must believe in Shakspeare's unapproachability, or quit the country. But what sort of a belief is this for an American, a man who is bound to carry republican progressiveness into Literature as well as into Life? Believe me, my friends, that men, not very much inferior to Shakspeare, are this day being born on the banks of the Ohio. And the day will come when you shall say, Who reads a book by an Englishman that is a modern? The great mistake seems to be, that even with those Americans who look forward to the coming of a great literary genius among us, they somehow fancy he will come in the costume of Queen Elizabeth's day; be a writer of dramas founded upon old English history or the tales of Boccaccio. Whereas, great geniuses are parts of the times, they themselves are the times, and possess a correspondent coloring. It is of a piece with the Jews, who, while their Shiloh was meekly walking in their streets, were still praying for his magnificent coming; looking for him in a chariot, who was already among them on an ass. Nor must we forget that, in his own lifetime, Shakspeare was not Shakspeare, but only Master

William Shakspeare of the shrewd, thriving, business firm of Condell, Shakspeare & Co., proprietors of the Globe Theatre in London; and by a courtly author, of the name of Chettle, was looked at as an 'upstart crow,' beautified 'with other birds' feathers.' For, mark it well, imitation is often the first charge brought against real originality. Why this is so, there is no space to set forth here. You must have plenty of sea-room to tell the Truth in; especially when it seems to have an aspect of newness, as America did in 1492, though it was then just as old, and perhaps older than Asia, only those sagacious philosophers, the common sailors, had never seen it before, swearing it was all water and moonshine there.

Now I do not say that Nathaniel of Salem is a greater than William of Avon, or as great. But the difference between the two men is by no means immeasurable. Not a very great deal more, and Nathaniel were verily William.

This, too, I mean, that if Shakspeare has not been equalled, give the world time, and he is sure to be surpassed, in one hemisphere or the other. Nor will it at all do to say, that the world is getting grey and grizzled now, and has lost that fresh charm which she wore of old, and by virtue of which the great poets of past times made themselves what we esteem them to be. Not so. The world is as young to-day as when it was created; and this Vermont morning dew is as wet to my feet, as Eden's dew to Adam's. Nor has nature been all over ransacked by our progenitors, so that no new charms and mysteries remain for this latter generation to find. Far from it. The trillionth part has not yet been said; and all that has been said, but multiplies the avenues to what remains to be said. It is not so much paucity as superabundance of material that seems to incapacitate modern authors.

Let America, then, prize and cherish her writers; yea, let her glorify them. They are not so many in number as to exhaust her good-will. And while she has good kith and kin of her own, to take to her bosom, let her not lavish her embraces upon the household of an alien. For believe it or not, England, after all, is in many things an alien to us. China has more bonds of real love for us than she. But even were there no strong literary individualities among us, as there are some dozens at least, nevertheless, let America first praise mediocrity even, in her own children, before she praises (for everywhere, merit demands acknowledgment from everyone) the best excellence in the children of any other land. Let her own authors, I say, have the priority of appreciation. I was much pleased with a hot-headed Carolina cousin of mine, who once said,—'If there were no other American to stand by, in literature, why, then, I would stand by Pop Emmons and his 'Fredoniad,' and till a better epic came along, swear it was not very far behind the Iliad.' Take away the words, and in spirit he was sound.

Not that American genius needs patronage in order to expand. For that explosive sort of stuff will expand though screwed up in a vice, and burst it, though it were triple steel. It is for the nation's sake, and not for her authors' sake, that I would have America be heedful of the increasing greatness among her writers. For how great the shame, if other nations should be before her, in crowning her heroes of the pen! But this is almost the case now. American authors have received more just and discriminating praise (however loftily and ridiculously given, in certain cases) even from some Englishmen, than from their own countrymen. There are hardly five critics in America; and several of them are asleep. As for patronage, it is the American author who now patronizes his country, and not his country him. And if at times some among them appeal to the people for more recognition, it is not always with selfish motives, but patriotic ones.

It is true, that but few of them as yet have evinced that decided originality which merits great praise. But that graceful writer, who perhaps of all Americans has received the most plaudits from his own country for his productions,—that very popular and amiable writer, however good and self-reliant in many things, perhaps owes his chief reputation to the self-acknowledged imitation of a foreign model, and to the studied avoidance of all topics but smooth ones. But it is better to fail in originality, than to succeed in imitation. He who has never failed somewhere, that man cannot be great. Failure is the true test of greatness. And if it be said, that continual success is a proof that a man wisely knows his powers,—it is only to be added, that, in that case, he knows them to be small. Let us believe it, then, once for all, that there is no hope for us in these smooth, pleasing writers that know their powers. Without malice, but to speak the plain fact, they but furnish an appendix to Goldsmith, and other English authors. And we want no American Goldsmiths: nay, we want no American Miltons. It were the vilest thing you could say of a true American author, that he were an American Tompkins. Call him an American and have done, for you cannot say a nobler thing of him. But it is not meant that all American writers should studiously cleave to nationality in their writings; only this, no American writer should write like an Englishman or a Frenchman; let him write like a man, for then he will be sure to write like an American. Let us away with this leaven of literary flunkeyism towards

England. If either must play the flunkey in this thing, let England do it, not us. While we are rapidly preparing for that political supremacy among the nations which prophetically awaits us at the close of the present century, in a literary point of view, we are deplorably unprepared for it; and we seem studious to remain so. Hitherto, reasons might have existed why this should be; but no good reason exists now. And all that is requisite to amendment in this matter, is simply this: that while fully acknowledging all excellence everywhere, we should refrain from unduly lauding foreign writers, and, at the same time, duly recognise the meritorious writers that are our own;—those writers who breathe that unshackled, democratic spirit of Christianity in all things, which now takes the practical lead in this world, though at the same time led by ourselves—us Americans. Let us boldly contemn all imitation, though it comes to us graceful and fragrant as the morning; and foster all originality, though at first it be crabbed and ugly as our own pine knots. And if any of our authors fail, or seem to fail, then, in the words of my Carolina cousin, let us clap him on the shoulder, and back him against all Europe for his second round. The truth is, that in one point of view, this matter of a national literature has come to such a pass with us, that in some sense we must turn bullies, else the day is lost, or superiority so far beyond us, that we can hardly say it will ever be ours.

And now, my countrymen, as an excellent author of your own flesh and blood,—an unimitating, and, perhaps, in his way, an inimitable man—whom better can I commend to you, in the first place, than Nathaniel Hawthorne. He is one of the new, and far better generation of your writers. The smell of your beeches and hemlocks is upon him; your own broad prairies are in his soul; and if you travel away inland into his deep and noble nature, you will hear the far roar of his Niagara. Give not over to future generations the glad duty of acknowledging him for what he is. Take that joy to yourself, in your own generation; and so shall he feel those grateful impulses on him, that may possibly prompt him to the full flower of some still greater achievement in your eyes. And by confessing him you thereby confess others; you brace the whole brotherhood. For genius, all over the world, stands hand in hand, and one shock of recognition runs the whole circle round. . . .

But my chief business now, is to point out a particular page in this piece, having reference to an honored guest, who under the name of 'The Master Genius,' but in the guise 'of a young man of poor attire, with no insignia of rank or acknowledged eminence,' is introduced to the man of Fancy, who is the giver of the feast. Now, the page having reference to this 'Master Genius,' so happily expresses much of what I yesterday wrote, touching the coming of the literary Shiloh of America, that I cannot but be charmed by the coincidence; especially, when it shows such a parity of ideas, at least in this one point, between a man like Hawthorne and a man like me.

And here, let me throw out another conceit of mine touching this American Shiloh, or 'Master Genius,' as Hawthorne calls him. May it not be, that this commanding mind has not been, is not, and never will be, individually developed in any one man? And would it, indeed, appear so unreasonable to suppose, that his great fullness and overflowing may be, or may be destined to be, shared by a plurality of men of genius? Surely, to take the very greatest example on record, Shakspeare cannot be regarded as in himself the concretion of all the genius of his time; nor as so immeasurably beyond Marlow, Webster, Ford, Beaumont, Jonson, that these great men can be said to share none of his power? For one, I conceive that there were dramatists in Elizabeth's day, between whom and Shakspeare the distance was by no means great. Let any one, hitherto little acquainted with those neglected old authors, for the first time read them thoroughly, or even read Charles Lamb's Specimens of them, and he will be amazed at the wondrous ability of those Anaks of men, and shocked at this renewed example of the fact, that Fortune has more to do with fame than merit,—though, without merit, lasting fame there can be none.

Nevertheless, it would argue too ill of my country were this maxim to hold good concerning Nathaniel Hawthorne, a man, who already, in some few minds, has shed 'such a light, as never illuminates the earth save when a great heart burns as the household fire of a grand intellect.'

The words are his,—'in the Select Party;' and they are a magnificent setting to a coincident sentiment of my own, but ramblingly expressed yesterday, in reference to himself. Gainsay it who will, as I now write, I am Posterity speaking by proxy—and after times will make it more than good, when I declare, that the American, who up to the present day has evinced, in literature, the largest brain with the largest heart, that man is Nathaniel Hawthorne. Moreover, that whatever Nathaniel Hawthorne may hereafter write, 'The Mosses from an Old Manse' will be ultimately accounted his master-piece. For there is a sure, though a secret sign in some works which proves the culmination of the powers (only the developable ones, however) that produced them. But I am by no means desirous of the glory of a prophet. I pray Heaven that Hawthorne may *yet* prove me an impostor in this prediction. Especially, as I somehow cling to the strange fancy, that, in all men, hiddenly reside certain wondrous, occult properties—as in some plants and minerals—which by some happy but very rare accident (as bronze was discovered by the melting of the iron and brass at the burning of Corinth) may chance to be called forth here on earth; not entirely waiting for their better discovery in the more congenial, blessed atmosphere of heaven.

Once more—for it is hard to be finite upon an infinite subject, and all subjects are infinite. By some people this entire scrawl of mine may be esteemed altogether unnecessary, inasmuch 'as years ago' (they may say) 'we found out the rich and rare stuff in this Hawthorne, whom you now parade forth, as if only *yourself* were the discoverer of this Portuguese diamond in our literature.' But even granting all this—and adding to it, the assumption that the books of Hawthorne have sold by the five thousand,—what does that signify? They should be sold by the hundred thousand; and read by the million; and admired by every one who is capable of admiration.

75. From a letter to Nathaniel Hawthorne

1[?] June 1851

Written at the height of their friendship, this letter reveals Melville's attitudes about literature and criticism as well as about more general philosophical subjects. He believed that in Hawthorne he had the perfect audience for his deepest thoughts and feelings.

. . . It seems an inconsistency to assert unconditional democracy in all things, and yet confess a dislike to all mankind—in the mass. But not so.—But it's an endless sermon,—no more of it. I began by saying that the reason I have not been to Lenox is this,—in the evening I feel completely done up, as the phrase is, and incapable of the long jolting to get to your house and back. In a week or so, I go to New York, to bury myself in a third-story room, and work and slave on my 'Whale' while it is driving through the press. *That* is the only way I can finish it now,—I am so pulled hither and thither by circumstances. The calm, the coolness, the silent grass-growing mood in which a man *ought* always to compose,—that, I fear, can seldom be mine. Dollars damn me; and the malicious Devil is forever grinning in upon me, holding the door ajar. My dear Sir, a presentiment is on me,—I shall at last be worn out and perish, like an old nutmeg-grater, grated to pieces by the constant attrition of the wood, that is, the nutmeg. What I feel most moved to write, that is banned,—it will not pay. Yet, altogether, write the *other* way I cannot. So the product is a final hash, and all my books are botches. I'm rather sore, perhaps, in this letter; but see my hand!—four blisters on this palm, made by hoes and hammers within the last few days. It is a rainy morning; so I am indoors, and all work suspended. I feel cheerfully disposed, and therefore I write a little bluely. Would the Gin were here! If ever, my dear Hawthorne, in the eternal times that are to come, you and I shall sit down in Paradise, in some little shady corner by ourselves; and if we shall by any means be able to smuggle a basket of champagne there (I won't believe in a Temperance Heaven), and if we shall then cross our celestial legs in the celestial grass that is forever tropical, and strike our glasses and our heads together, till both musically ring in concert,—then, O my dear fellow-mortal, how shall we pleasantly discourse of all the things manifold which now so distress us,—when all the earth shall be but a reminiscence, yea, its final dissolution an antiquity. Then shall songs be composed as when wars are over; humorous, comic songs,—'Oh, when I lived in that queer little hole called the world,' or, 'Oh, when I toiled and sweated below,' or, 'Oh, when I knocked and was knocked in the fight'—yes, let us look forward to such things. Let us swear that, though now we sweat, yet it is because of the dry heat which is indispensable to the nourishment of the vine which is to bear the grapes that are to give us the champagne hereafter.

But I was talking about the 'Whale.' As the fishermen say, 'he's in his flurry' when I left him some three weeks ago. I'm going to take him by his jaw, however, before long, and finish him up in some fashion or other. What's the use of elaborating what, in its very essence, is so short-lived as a modern book? Though I wrote the Gospels in this century, I should die in the gutter.—I talk all about myself, and this is selfishness and egotism. Granted. But how help it? I am writing to you; I know little about you, but something about myself. So I write about myself,—

at least, to you. Don't trouble yourself, though, about writing; and don't trouble yourself about visiting; and when you *do* visit, don't trouble yourself about talking. I will do all the writing and visiting and talking myself.—By the way, in the last 'Dollar Magazine' I read 'The Unpardonable Sin.' He was a sad fellow, that Ethan Brand. I have no doubt you are by this time responsible for many a shake and tremor of the tribe of 'general readers.' It is a frightful poetical creed that the cultivation of the brain eats out the heart. But it's my *prose* opinion that in most cases, in those men who have fine brains and work them well, the heart extends down to hams. And though you smoke them with the fire of tribulation, yet, like veritable hams, the head only gives the richer and the better flavor. I stand for the heart. To the dogs with the head! I had rather be a fool with a heart, than Jupiter Olympus with his head. The reason the mass of men fear God, and *at bottom dislike* Him, is because they rather distrust His heart, and fancy Him all brain like a watch. (You perceive I employ a capital initial in the pronoun referring to the Deity; don't you think there is a slight dash of flunkeyism in that usage?) Another thing. I was in New York for four-and-twenty hours the other day, and saw a portrait of N.H. And I have seen and heard many flattering (in a publisher's point of view) allusions to the 'Seven Gables.' And I have seen 'Tales,' and 'A New Volume' announced, by N.H. So upon the whole, I say to myself, this N.H. is in the ascendant. My dear Sir, they begin to patronize. All Fame is patronage. Let me be infamous: there is no patronage in *that*. What 'reputation' H.M. has is horrible. Think of it! To go down to posterity is bad enough, any way; but to go down as a 'man who lived among the cannibals'! When I speak of posterity, in reference to myself, I only mean the babies who will probably be born in the moment immediately ensuing upon my giving up the ghost. I shall go down to some of them, in all likelihood. *Typee* will be given to them, perhaps, with their gingerbread. I have come to regard this matter of Fame as the most transparent of all vanities. I read Solomon more and more, and every time see deeper and deeper and unspeakable meanings in him. I did not think of Fame, a year ago, as I do now. My development has been all within a few years past. I am like one of those seeds taken out of the Egyptian Pyramids, which, after being three thousand years a seed and nothing but a seed, being planted in English soil, it developed itself, grew to greenness, and then fell to mould. So I. Until I was twenty-five, I had no development at all. From my twenty-fifth year I date my life. Three weeks have scarcely passed, at any time between then and now, that I have not unfolded within myself. But I feel that I am now come to the inmost leaf of the bulb, and that shortly the flower must fall to the mould. It seems to me now that Solomon was the truest man who ever spoke, and yet that he a little *managed* the truth with a view to popular conservatism; or else there have been many corruptions and interpolations of the text. . . .

MOBY-DICK

1851

76. From an unsigned review, London *Morning Advertiser*

24 October 1851

To convey an adequate idea of a book of such various merits as that which the author of *Typee* and *Omoo* has here placed before the reading public, is impossible in the scope of a review. High philosophy, liberal feeling, abstruse metaphysics popularly phrased, soaring speculation, a style as many-coloured as the theme, yet always good, and often admirable; fertile fancy, ingenious construction, playful learning, and an unusual power of enchaining the interest, and rising to the verge of the sublime, without overpassing that narrow boundary which plunges the ambitious penman into the ridiculous: all these are possessed by Herman Melville, and exemplified in these volumes.

In the first chapter, bearing the title of 'Loomings,' we are introduced to the author, who on its threshold desires us to call him Ishmael. The very name being significant of a propensity to wander, we are prepared for an adventurer's acquaintance.

We have said that the writer is philosophically playful, and we will back his opening chapter, descriptive of New York, with its disquisitions on men's motives, the sea, nay water in the abstract as well as the concrete, against the same amount of prose in any book of fiction for the last dozen years, with a couple of exceptions, which we shall keep to ourselves. . . .

We remember reading in the life of Whitefield, a story of his power over the passions of uncultivated hearers. The anecdote runs that he was preaching to a congregation of seamen on the perils of sin and of the judgment-day, when he so worked upon them by his vivid description of the perils of a storm, that, maddened with the reality of the sinking ship thus word-painted before them, the entire auditory jumped up, and in reply to his question:—'Oh my brethren, what will you do then?' shouted out, 'Take to the long-boat!' The unsophisticated reply was well used by the preacher. Let those who would read such a sermon as that which we have lost of Whitefield's, turn to the 9th chapter of this book, and he may realise the idea by a perusal of the discourse of Father Mapple. . . .

. . . As a sample of Herman Meville's learning, we may refer to the chapter headed 'Cetology,' in the second volume; and that we have not overrated his dramatic ability for producing a prose poem, read the chapter on the 'whiteness of the whale,' and the scene where Ahab nails the doubloon to the mast, as an earnest of the reward he will give to the seaman, who just 'sights' 'Moby Dick,' the white whale, the object of his burning and unappeasable revenge. Then come whale adventures wild as dreams, and powerful in their cumulated horrors. Now we have a Carlylism of phrase, then a quaintness reminding us of Sir Thomas Brown, and anon a heap of curious out-of-the-way learning after the fashion of the Burton who 'anatomised' 'melancholy.' Mingled with all this are bustle, adventure, battle and the breeze. In brief the interest never palls, although we are free to confess that in the later scenes of Ahab's fierce madness we were fain to exclaim, 'Somewhat too much of this!' . . .

Did space permit us we might be tempted to the injustice of giving more of the defence; as it is, we can only again refer the reader to the volumes, than which three more honourable to American literature, albeit issued in London, have not yet reflected credit on the country of Washington Irving, Fenimore Cooper, Dana, Sigourney, Bryant, Longfellow, and Prescott.

77. Henry F. Chorley, from an unsigned review, *Athenæum*

25 October 1851, 1112–13

This is an ill-compounded mixture of romance and matter-of-fact. The idea of a connected and collected story has obviously visited and abandoned its writer again and again in the course of composition. The style of his tale is in places disfigured by mad (rather than bad) English; and its catastrophe is hastily, weakly, and obscurely managed. The second title—'Moby Dick'—is the name given to a particular sperm whale, or white sea monster, more malignant and diabolical even than the sperm whale in general is known to be. This ocean fiend is invested with especial horrors for our ship's crew;—because, once upon a time, a conflict with him cost their Captain a limb. Captain Ahab had an ivory leg made,—took an oath of retribution,—grew crazy,—lashed himself up into a purpose of cruising in quest of his adversary,—and bound all who sailed with him to stand by him in his wrath. With this cheerful Captain, on such a wise and Christian voyage of discovery, went to sea Ishmael, the imaginary writer of this narrative.

Frantic though such an invention seems to be, it might possibly have been accepted as the motive and purpose of an *extravaganza* had its author been consistent with himself. Nay, in such a terrible cause—when Krakens and Typhoons and the wonders of Mid-Ocean, &c. &c. were the topics and toys to be arranged and manoeuvred—we might have stretched a point in admission of electrical verbs and adjectives as hoarse as the hurricane. There is a time for everything in imaginative literature;—and, according to its order, a place—for rant as well as for reserve; but the rant must be good, honest, shameless rant, without flaw or misgiving. The voice of 'the storm wind Euroclydon' must not be interrupted by the facts of Scoresby and the figures of Cocker. Ravings and scraps of useful knowledge flung together salad-wise make a dish in which there may be much surprise, but in which there is little savour. The real secret of this patchiness in the present case is disclosed in Mr. Melville's appendix; which contains such an assortment of curious quotations as Southey might have wrought up into a whale-chapter for

'The Doctor,'—suggesting the idea that a substantial work on the subject may have been originally contemplated. Either Mr. Melville's purpose must have changed, or his power must have fallen short. The result is, at all events, a most provoking book,—neither so utterly extravagant as to be entirely comfortable, nor so instructively complete as to take place among documents on the subject of the Great Fish, his capabilities, his home and his capture. Our author must be henceforth numbered in the company of the incorrigibles who occasionally tantalize us with indications of genius, while they constantly summon us to endure monstrosities, carelessnesses, and other such harassing manifestations of bad taste as daring or disordered ingenuity can devise.

The opening of this wild book contains some graphic descriptions of a dreariness such as we do not remember to have met with before in marine literature. . . .

We have little more to say in reprobation or in recommendation of this absurd book,—having detailed its leading incident. Mr. Melville has been on former occasions characterized by us as one who thoroughly understands the tone of sea superstition. There is a wild humorous poetry in some of his terrors which distinguishes him from the vulgar herd of fustian-weavers. For instance, his interchapter on 'The Whiteness of the Whale' is full of ghostly suggestions for which a Maturin or a Monk Lewis would have been thankful. Mr. Melville has to thank himself only if his horrors and his heroics are flung aside by the general reader, as so much trash belonging to the worst school of Bedlam literature,—since he seems not so much unable to learn as disdainful of learning the craft of an artist.

78. Unsigned review, *John Bull*

25 October 1851, 687

Of all the extraordinary books from the pen of Herman Melville this is out and out the most extraordinary. Who would have looked for philosophy in whales, or for poetry in blubber. Yet few books which professedly deal in metaphysics, or claim the parentage of the muses, contain as much true philosophy and as much genuine poetry as the tale of the *Pequod's* whaling expedition. Hardly has the ship set sail from Nantucket than it is, with its strangely assorted crew on board, isolated from the rest of creation; wholly engulphed, as it were, in the world of whales, a world peculiar to itself, and, as the reader of these volumes will find, as brimful of matters of deepest interest as any other sublunary world. In that wonderful world the most extravagant specimens of the genus *homo*, the offspring of Herman Melville's wild and grotesque fancy, are pursuing their career of adventure and of danger with an energy not unlike that of the whale himself; their chieftain, Captain Ahab, being a perfect match in every way for his foe-whale Moby Dick.

To give anything like an outline of the narrative woven together from materials seemingly so uncouth, with a power of thought and force of diction suited to the huge dimensions of its subject, is wholly impossible. Those who seek acquaintance with 'the whale' must needs embark on board the venturesome craft, and bear company to her commander with the ivory leg and the heart of steel. They must be prepared, however, to hear much on board that singularly-tenanted ship which grates upon civilized ears; some heathenish, and worse than heathenish talk is calculated to give even more serious offence. This feature of Herman Melville's new work we cannot but deeply regret. It is due to him to say that he has steered clear of much that was objectionable in some of his former tales; and it is all the greater pity, that he should have defaced his pages by occasional thrusts against revealed religion which add nothing to the interest of his story, and cannot but shock readers accustomed to a reverent treatment of whatever is associated with sacred subjects.

All that is idiomatically American in the tone of his sentiments, and in the slang which runs through his discourse, we are most willing to forgive him. These things belong to the individuality of the author and the book. The perfect Yankee, surrounded as he is, in reality no less than in Mr. Melville's fiction, with savage and demi-savage life, is a picture which, like everything that is true to nature, possesses a charm of its own, though it may not fall within the ordinary canons of beauty. The exhibition of it is both a novelty, and a study; and the artist is entitled to his meed of praise; even though his subject should in itself be of a somewhat repulsive character. And in the present case that praise is the more abundantly due, because the artist has succeeded in investing objects apparently the most unattractive with an absorbing fascination. The flashes of truth, too, which sparkle on the surface of the foaming sea of thought through which the author pulls his readers in the wake of the whale-ship,—the profound reflections uttered by the actors in the wild watery chase in their own quaint forms of thought and speech,—and the graphic representations of human nature in the startling disguises under which it appears on the deck of the *Pequod*,—all these things combine to raise *The Whale* far beyond the level of an ordinary work of fiction. It is not a mere tale of adventures, but a whole philosophy of life, that it unfolds.

We are unwilling to part with a book so intensely interesting without placing before our readers at least a leaf or two from the sketch-book of 'Ishmael,' the spinner of this wonderful whale yarn. One of the finest scenes of the tale is that in which the half-crazy Captain, intent on the pursuit of Moby Dick, threatens to shoot the chief mate for attempting by his advice to interfere with his authority.

[quotes from chapter 109, 'Starbuck found Ahab' to 'out in the main-hold." ']

As a sample of the manner in which the author extracts lessons of life from the carcass of a dead whale, we give the following passage:—

[quotes from chapter 68, 'A word or two' to 'vast at the whale!']

We shall conclude our extracts with the following apostrophe, addressed by the whaling Captain to the head of a captured whale lashed to his ship's side:—

[quotes from chapter 70, ' "Speak, thou vast' to 'longing arms!']

79. Unsigned review, *Spectator*

25 October 1851, 1026–7

This sea novel is a singular medley of naval observation, magazine article writing, satiric reflection upon the conventionalisms of civilized life, and rhapsody run mad. So far as the nautical parts are appropriate and unmixed, the portraiture is truthful and interesting. Some of the satire, especially in the early parts, is biting and reckless. The chapter-spinning is various in character; now powerful from the vigorous and fertile fancy of the author, now little more than empty though sounding phrases. The rhapsody belongs to wordmongering where ideas are the staple; where it takes the shape of narrative or dramatic fiction, it is phantasmal—an attempted description of what is impossible in nature and without probability in art; it repels the reader instead of attracting him.

The elements of the story are a South Sea whaling voyage, narrated by Ishmael, one of the crew of the ship Pequod, from Nantucket. Its 'probable' portions consist of the usual sea matter in that branch of the industrial marine; embracing the preparations for departure, the voyage, the chase and capture of whale, with the economy of cutting up, &c., and the peculiar discipline of the service. This matter is expanded by a variety of digressions on the nature and characteristics of the sperm whale, the history of the fishery, and similar things, in which a little knowledge is made the excuse for a vast many words. The voyage is introduced by several chapters in which life in American seaports is rather broadly depicted.

The 'marvellous' injures the book by disjointing the narrative, as well as by its inherent want of interest, at least as managed by Mr. Melville. In the superstition of some whalers, (grounded upon the malicious foresight which occasionally characterizes the attacks of the sperm fish upon the boats sent to capture it,) there is a *white* whale which possesses supernatural power. To capture or even to hurt it is beyond the art of man; the skill of the whaler is useless; the harpoon does not wound it; it exhibits a contemptuous strategy in its attacks upon the boats of its pursuers; and happy is the vessel where only loss of limb, or of a single life, attends its chase. Ahab, the master of the Pequod—a mariner of long experience, stern resolve, and indomitable courage, the high hero of romance, in short, transferred to a whale-ship—has lost his leg in a contest with the white whale. Instead of daunting Ahab, the loss exasperates him; and by long brooding over it his reason becomes shaken. In this condition he undertakes the voyage; making the chase of his fishy antagonist the sole object of his thoughts, and, so far as he can without exciting overt insubordination among his officers, the object of his proceedings.

Such a groundwork is hardly natural enough for a regular-built novel, though it might form a tale, if properly managed. But Mr. Melville's mysteries provoke wonder at the author rather than terror at the creation; the soliloquies and dialogues of Ahab, in which the author attempts delineating the wild imaginings of monomania, and exhibiting some profoundly speculative views of things in general, induce weariness or skipping; while the whole scheme mars, as we have said, the nautical continuity of story—greatly assisted by various chapters of a bookmaking kind.

Perhaps the earliest chapters are the best, although they contain little adventure. Their topics are fresher to English readers than the whale-chase, and they have more direct satire. One of the leading personages in the voyage is Queequeg, a South Sea Islander, that Ishmael falls in with at New Bedford, and with whom he forms a bosom friendship.

[quotes from chapter 12, 'Queequeg was a native' to 'die a Pagan.']

The strongest point of the book is its 'characters.' Ahab, indeed, is a melodramatic exaggeration, and Ishmael is little more than a mouthpiece; but the harpooners, the mates, and several of the seamen, are truthful portraitures of the sailor as modified by the whaling service. The persons ashore are equally good, though they are soon lost sight of. The two Quaker owners are the author's means for a hit at the religious hypocrisies. Captain Bildad, an old sea-dog, has got rid of everything pertaining to the meeting-house save an occasional 'thou' and 'thee.' Captain Peleg, in American phrase 'professes religion.' The following extract exhibits the two men when Ishmael is shipped.

[quotes from chapter 16, 'I began to think' to 'fiery pit, Captain Peleg." ']

It is a canon with some critics that nothing should be introduced into a novel which it is physically impossible for the writer to have known:

thus, he must not describe the conversation of miners in a pit if they *all* perish. Mr. Melville hardly steers clear of this rule, and he continually violates another, by beginning in the autobiographical form and changing ad libitum into the narrative. His catastrophe overrides all rule: not only is Ahab, with his boat's-crew, destroyed in his last desperate attack upon the white whale, but the Pequod herself sinks with all on board into the depths of the illimitable ocean. Such is the go-ahead method.

80. 'A. B. R.,' from 'Town Talk And Table Talk,' review, *Illustrated London News*

1 November 1851, 539

The excitement of the Exhibition over, the disturbed publishing trade is beginning to resume its activity, and a fair outburst of works of all classes is announced. Railway books hold a conspicuous place in the list—the growing habit of wiling away the hours upon the rail by reading being apparently likely to exercise as much, and I hope a more, salutary effect upon popular literature than even circulating libraries. The peculiarity of railway books is that they must be pithy, short, and cheap; and, if I am not much mistaken, they will speedily give the spun-out thirty-shilling three-volume novels a blow which will greatly accelerate the downward progress which has been observable for some time in the class of books in question. Among the works of travel announced, Hungarian adventures take the lead; and all opinions about the late revolution and its champions will, no doubt, find their advocates. As to the works of fancy, two, in two very different departments, seem to be attracting most attention—one a controversial and pro-Catholic novel called *Cecile*, and understood to be the production of the Count de Jarnac, under the *nom-de-guerre*[1] of Sir Charles Rockingham; and the

[1] *Nom-de-guerre:* pseudonym.

other Herman Melville's last and best and most wildly imaginative story, *The Whale*. The controversial novel is remarkable for fairness, good temper, and good humour—most rare qualities in books of the kind; and the personages are so conceived as to be types of the principal different parties and classes into which the late Aggression agitation split up the community. Mr. Melville's romance will worthily support his reputation for singularly vivid and reckless imaginative power—great aptitude for quaint and original philosophical speculation, degenerating, however, too often into rhapsody and purposeless extravagance—an almost unparalleled power over the capabilities of the language. . . .

81. From an unsigned review, *Britannia*

8 November 1851, 714–15

The Whale is a most extraordinary work. There is so much eccentricity in its style and in its construction, in the original conception and in the gradual development of its strange and improbable story, that we are at a loss to determine in what category of works of amusement to place it. It is certainly neither a novel nor a romance, although it is made to drag its weary length through three closely printed volumes, and is published by Bentley, who, *par excellence*, is the publisher of the novels of the fashionable world, for who ever heard of novel or romance without a heroine or a single love scene? The plot of the narrative is scarcely worthy of the name, as it hangs entirely on the inveterate pursuit by a monomaniac old Captain after a certain humpbacked whale, who in some previous voyage had bitten off one of his legs, and whose destruction he had bound himself and his crew by terrible oaths to accomplish, in revenge for the injury he had himself sustained. The tragical catastrophe, which innumerable signs, omens, and superstitious warnings are constantly predicting to the infatuated commander, is the wreck of the ship, and the loss of the whole crew in the frantic attack that is made upon the invincible white whale.

The story has merit, but it is a merit *sui generis*,[1] and does not consist in the work either when viewed as a whole or with reference to the arrangement of its separate parts. The plot is meagre beyond comparison, as the whole of the incident might very conveniently have been comprised in half of one of these three interminable volumes. Nevertheless, in his descriptions of character, in his analysis of the motives of actions, and in the novelty of the details of a whaling expedition, the author has evinced not only a considerable knowledge of the human heart, combined with a thorough acquaintance with the subject he is handling, but a rare versatility of talent. The crew of the Pequod, the inharmonious name given to the whaler, is composed of mariners of all countries and all colours, from the civilised British sailor to the savage and cannibal harpooner of the South Sea Islands. In describing the idiosyncrasies of all these different castes of men our author has evinced acuteness of observation and powers of discrimination, which would alone render his work a valuable addition to the literature of the day. . . .

. . . These original sketches constitute as we have said the principal merit of the work, but in the latter half of the third volume, the action of the story, which had halted considerably through the preceding chapters, assumes all at once an exciting interest, which is as gratifying as it is unexpected. . . .

The first and second volumes are spun out with long descriptions of the various cetacious tribes, which do now, and have at different periods of time inhabited the ocean. The information these chapters convey may be important to naturalists or whalers, but will have little interest for the general reader. Bating a few Americanisms, which sometimes mar the perspicuity and the purity of the style, the language of the work is appropriate and impressive; and the stirring scenes with which the author concludes are abundant evidence of the power he possesses of making his narrative intensely interesting.

[1] *Sui generis:* in a class by itself; peculiar.

82. From an unsigned review, London *Leader*

8 November 1851, 1067–9

Want of originality has long been the just and standing reproach to American literature; the best of its writers were but second-hand Englishmen. Of late some have given evidence of originality; not *absolute* originality, but such genuine outcoming of the American intellect as can be safely called national. Edgar Poe, Nathaniel Hawthorne, Herman Melville are assuredly no British offshoots; nor is Emerson—the *German* American that he is! The observer of this commencement of an American literature, properly so called, will notice as significant that these writers have a wild and mystic love of the supersensual, peculiarly their own. To move a horror skilfully, with something of the earnest faith in the Unseen, and with weird imagery to shape these Phantasms so vividly that the most incredulous mind is hushed, absorbed—to do this no European pen has apparently any longer the power—to do this American literature is without a rival. What *romance* writer can be named with Hawthorne? Who knows the terrors of the seas like Herman Melville?

The Whale—Melville's last book—is a strange, wild, weird book, full of poetry and full of interest. To use a hackneyed phrase, it is indeed 'refreshing' to quit the old, wornout pathways of romance, and feel the sea breezes playing through our hair, the salt spray dashing on our brows, as we do here. One tires terribly of ballrooms, dinners, and the incidents of town life! One never tires of Nature. And there is Nature here, though the daring imagery often grows riotously extravagant.

Then the ghostly terrors which Herman Melville so skilfully evokes, have a strange fascination. In vain Reason rebels. Imagination is absolute. Ordinary superstitions related by vulgar pens have lost their power over all but the credulous; but Imagination has a credulity of its own respondent to power. So it is with Melville's superstitions: we believe in them imaginatively. . . .

. . . The book is not a romance, nor a treatise on Cetology. It is something of both: a strange, wild work with the tangled overgrowth and luxuriant vegetation of American forests, not the trim orderliness of an English park. Criticism may pick many holes in this work; but no criticism will thwart its fascination. . . .

83. Unsigned notice, Hartford, Connecticut, *Daily Courant*

15 November 1851

Melville's stories are decidedly interesting and graphic, and, as he writes, he improves in the minor details of incident, management, and style. There is always one singular character about them—you don't know whether they are truth or fiction. There is the same want of unity of subject—of a regular beginning and end—of the form and shape and outline of a well built novel—which we find in real life. But there is a little too much romance and adventure, of 'imminent perils' and hair-breadth escapes, to be any thing but fiction. The present story is the most interesting and the best told of any of the group. There is in it the same happy carelessness of style and the same abandonment to all the easy slipshod luxuries of story telling. It is well worth reading as a book of amusement, and well worth a place on the book shelf from the beautiful style of its publication.

84. Evert Duyckinck, from an unsigned review, *Literary World*

15, 22 November 1851, 381–3, 403–4

The review opens with an account of a whale ramming and sinking a whale ship—the *Ann Alexander* of New Bedford, Mass., under the command of Captain John S. Deblois—in the Pacific on 20 August 1851.

By a singular coincidence this extreme adventure is, even to very many of the details, the catastrophe of Mr. Melville's new book, which is a natural-historical, philosophical, romantic account of the person, habits, manners, ideas of the great sperm whale; of his haunts and of his belongings; of his associations with the world of the deep, and of the not less remarkable individuals and combinations of individuals who hunt him on the oceans. Nothing like it has ever before been written of the whale; for no man who has at once seen so much of the actual conflict, and weighed so carefully all that has been recorded on the subject, with equal powers of perception and reflection, has attempted to write at all on it—the labors of Scoresby covering a different and inferior branch of the history. To the popular mind this book of Herman Melville, touching the Leviathan of the deep, is as much of a discovery in Natural History as was the revelation of America by Christopher Columbus in geography. Let any one read this book with the attention which it deserves, and then converse with the best informed of his friends and acquaintances who have not seen it, and he will notice the extent and variety of treatment; while scientific men must admit the original observation and speculation.

Such an infuriated, resolute sperm whale as pursued and destroyed the Ann Alexander is the hero, Moby Dick, of Mr. Melville's book. The vengeance with which he is hunted, which with Capt. Deblois was the incident of a single, though most memorable day, is the leading passion and idea of Captain Ahab of the Pequod for years, and throughout the seas of the world. Incidentally with this melo-dramatic action and spiritual development of the character of Ahab, is included a full, minute, thorough investigation, and description of the whale and its fishery. Such is a short-hand account of this bulky and multifarious volume.

It opens, after a dedication to Nathaniel Hawthorne, with a preliminary flourish in the style of Carlyle and the 'Doctor' of etymology, followed by a hundred or so of extracts of 'Old Burton,' passages of a quaint and pithy character from Job and King Alfred to Miriam Coffin; in lieu of the old style of Scott, Cooper, and others, of distributing such flourishes about the heads of chapters. Here they are all in a lump, like the grace over the Franklin barrel of pork, and may be taken as a kind of bitters, a whet and fillip to the imagination, exciting it to the curious, ludicrous, sublime traits and contemplations which are to follow.

It is some time after opening with Chapter I. before we get fairly afloat, but the time is very satisfactorily occupied with some very strange, romantic, and, withal, highly humorous adventures at New Bedford and Nantucket. A scene at the Spouter Inn, of the former town, a night in bed with a Pacific Islander, and a mid-ocean adventure subsequently with a Frenchman over some dead whales in the Pacific, treat the reader to a laugh worthy of Smollet. . . .

A difficulty in the estimate of this, in common with one or two other of Mr. Melville's books, occurs from the double character under which they present themselves. In one light they are romantic fictions, in another statements of absolute fact. When to this is added that the romance is made a vehicle of opinion and satire through a more or less opaque allegorical veil, as particularly in the latter half of *Mardi*, and to some extent in this present volume, the critical difficulty is considerably thickened. It becomes quite impossible to submit such books to a distinct classification as fact, fiction, or essay. Something of a parallel may be found in Jean Paul's German tales, with an admixture of Southey's *Doctor*. Under these combined influences of personal observation, actual fidelity to local truthfulness in description, a taste for reading and sentiment, a fondness for fanciful analogies, near and remote, a rash daring in speculation, reckless at times of taste and propriety, again refined and eloquent, this volume of *Moby Dick* may be pronounced a most remarkable sea-dish—an intellectual chowder of romance, philosophy, natural history, fine writing, good feeling, bad sayings—but over which, in spite of all uncertainties, and in spite of the author himself, predominates his keen perceptive faculties, exhibited in vivid narration.

There are evidently two if not three books in *Moby Dick* rolled into one. Book No. I. we could describe as a thorough exhaustive account admirably given of the great Sperm Whale. The information is minute, brilliantly illustrated, as it should be—the whale himself so generously illuminating the midnight page on which his memoirs are written—has its level passages, its humorous touches, its quaint suggestion, its incident usually picturesque and occasionally sublime. All this is given in the most delightful manner in 'The Whale.' Book No. 2 is the romance of Captain Ahab, Queequeg, Tashtego, Pip & Co., who are more or less spiritual personages talking and acting differently from the general business run of the conversation on the decks of whalers. They are for the most part very serious people, and seem to be concerned a great deal about the problem of the universe. They are striking characters withal, of the romantic spiritual cast of the German drama; realities of some kinds at bottom, but veiled in all sorts of poetical incidents and expressions. As a bit of German melodrama, with Captain Ahab for the Faust of the quarter-deck, and Queequeg with the crew, for Walpurgis night revellers in the forecastle, it has its strong points, though here the limits as to space and treatment of the stage would improve it. Moby Dick in this view becomes a sort of fishy moralist, a leviathan metaphysician, a folio Ductor Dubitantium, in fact, in the fresh water illustration of Mrs. Malaprop, 'an allegory on the banks of the Nile.' After pursuing him in this melancholic company over a few hundred squares of latitude and longitude, we begin to have some faint idea of the association of whaling and lamentation, and why blubber is popularly synonymous with tears.

The intense Captain Ahab is too long drawn out; something more of *him* might, we think, be left to the reader's imagination. The value of this kind of writing can only be through the personal consciousness of the reader, what he brings to the book; and all this is sufficiently evoked by a dramatic trait or suggestion. If we had as much of Hamlet or Macbeth as Mr. Melville gives us of Ahab, we should be tired even of their sublime company. Yet Captain Ahab is a striking conception, firmly planted on the wild deck of the Pequod—a dark disturbed soul arraying itself with every ingenuity of material resources for a conflict at once natural and supernatural in his eye, with the most dangerous extant physical monster of the earth, embodying, in strongly drawn lines of mental association, the vaster moral evil of the world. The pursuit of the White Whale thus interweaves with the literal perils of the fishery—a problem of fate and destiny—to the tragic solution of which Ahab hurries on, amidst the wild stage scenery of the ocean. To this end the motley crew, the air, the sky, the sea, its inhabitants are idealized throughout. It is a noble and praiseworthy conception; and though our sympathies may not always accord with the train of thought, we would caution the reader against a light or hasty condemnation of this part of the work.

Book III., appropriating perhaps a fourth of the volume, is a vein of moralizing, half essay, half rhapsody, in which much refinement and subtlety, and no little poetical feeling, are mingled with quaint conceit and extravagant daring speculation. This is to be taken as in some sense dramatic; the narrator throughout among the personages of the Pequod being one Ishmael, whose wit may be allowed to be against everything on land, as his hand is against everything at sea. This piratical running down of creeds and opinions, the conceited indifferentism of Emerson, or the run-a-muck style of Carlyle is, we will not say dangerous in such cases, for there are various forces at work to meet more powerful onslaught, but it is out of place and uncomfortable. We do not like to see what, under any view, must be to the world the most sacred associations of life violated and defaced.

We call for fair play in this matter. Here is Ishmael, telling the story of this volume, going down on his knees with a cannibal to a piece of wood, in the second story fireplace of a New-Bedford tavern, in the spirit of amiable and transcendent charity, which may be all very well in its way; but why dislodge from heaven, with contumely, 'long-pampered Gabriel, Michael and Raphael.' Surely Ishmael, who is a scholar, might have spoken respectfully of the Archangel Gabriel, out of consideration, if not for the Bible (which might be asking too much of the school), at least for one John Milton, who wrote *Paradise Lost*.

Nor is it fair to inveigh against the terrors of priestcraft, which, skilful though it may be in making up its woes, at least seeks to provide a remedy for the evils of the world, and attribute the existence of conscience to 'hereditary dyspepsias, nurtured by Ramadans'—and at the same time go about petrifying us with imaginary horrors, and all sorts of gloomy suggestions, all the world through. It is a curious fact that there are no more bilious people in the world, more completely filled with megrims and head shakings, than some of these very people who are constantly inveighing against the religious melancholy of priestcraft.

So much for the consistency of Ishmael—who, if it is the author's object to exhibit the painful contradictions of this self-dependent, self-torturing agency of a mind driven hither and thither as a flame in a whirlwind, is, in a degree, a successful embodiment of opinions, without securing from us, however, much admiration for the result.

With this we make an end of what we have been reluctantly compelled to object to this volume. With far greater pleasure, we acknowledge the acuteness of observation, the freshness of perception, with which the author brings home to us from the deep, 'things unattempted yet in prose or rhyme,' the weird influences of his ocean scenes, the salient imagination which connects them with the past and distant, the world of books and the life of experience—certain prevalent traits of manly sentiment. These are strong powers with which Mr. Melville wrestles in this book. It would be a great glory to subdue them to the highest uses of fiction. It is still a great honor, among the crowd of successful mediocrities which throng our publishers' counters, and know nothing of divine impulses, to be in the company of these nobler spirits on any terms.

85. Unsigned notice, Springfield, Massachusetts, *Republican*

17 November 1851

'Moby Dick' is the name of a fabulous white whale of the Northern regions of the Pacific, and in this, his last book Mr Melville has woven around this cumbrous bulk of romance, a large and interesting web of narrative, information, and sketches of character and scenery, in a quaint though interesting style, and with an easy, rollicking freedom of language and structure, characteristic of himself. What the author does not know about the sea, is not worth knowing, and there is not an experience of sea life, but he has the happy power of surrounding with romance. This book, and all hitherto written by the author, are as much superior to the sea books of Marryatt, as are the latter to those of the blanket weeklies. But there is one painful thought connected with the tale. There is no Fayaway in it. Alas! fickle and forgetful Melville, that thou should'st ever forget the gentle native who gave herself to thee in her far-off, savage home, and take to wantoning with 'the monsters of the bubbling deep!'

86. Unsigned notice, New Bedford, Massachusetts, *Daily Mercury*

18 November 1851

This is a bulky, queer looking volume, in some respects 'very like a whale' even in outward appearance. We have had before volume upon volume of narratives of whaling voyages, and adventures with the leviathans of the deep, but never before a work combining so much of natural history of Moby-Dick, nor in so attractive guise as the volume before us. After some introductory chapters of luminous etymological illustrations, etc., we find our author quitting the good city of old Manhatto, 'for Cape Horn and the Pacific,' and in due time arriving in New Bedford on a Saturday night in December, on his way to Nantucket—having made up his mind to sail in no other than a Nantucket craft; for though New Bedford, as he says, has of late been gradually monopolizing the business of whaling, and though in this matter poor old Nantucket is yet much behind her, yet Nantucket was her great original—the place where the first dead American whale was stranded. His adventures in New Bedford are extended through several pages, and are followed by others of greater importance. Although as a whole the book is made to serve as a 'tub for the whale,' the characters and subjects which figure in it are set off with artistic effect, and with irresistible attraction to the reader. . . .

87. Unsigned notice, New York *Evangelist*

20 November 1851, 188

Mr. Melville grows wilder and more untameable with every adventure. In *Typee* and *Omoo*, he began with the semblance of life and reality, though it was often but the faintest kind of semblance. As he advanced, he threw off the pretense of probability, and wandered from the verisimilitude of fiction into the mist and vagueness of poetry and fantasy, and now in this last venture, has reached the very limbo of eccentricity. From first to last, oddity is the governing characteristic. The extraordinary descriptive powers which *Typee* disclosed, are here in full strength. More graphic and terrible portraitures of hair-breadth 'scapes we never read. The delineation of character, too, is exquisitely humorous, sharp, individual and never-to-be forgotten. The description of Father Mapple's sermon is a powerful piece of sailor-oratory; and passages of great eloquence, and artistic beauty and force, are to be found everywhere. It will add to Mr. Melville's repute as a writer, undoubtedly, and furnishes, incidentally, a most striking picture of sea life and adventures.

88. William Young, from an unsigned review, *Albion*

22 November 1851, 561

This mere announcement of the book's and the author's name will prepare you in a measure for what follows; for you know just as well as we do that Herman Melville is a practical and practised sea-novelist, and that what comes from his pen will be worth the reading. And so indeed is *Moby-Dick*, and not lacking much of being a great work. How it falls short of this, we shall presently endeavour to show. Let us in the first place briefly describe it.

It treats then mainly of whales, whaling, whalers, and whaling-men—incidentally it touches on mythology, sharks, religion, South Sea islanders, philosophy, cannibalism and curiosity shops. The writer uses the first person in narrating his tale, without however any attempt at making himself its hero. He was (or says he was, which is the same thing) but a seaman on board the vessel whose voyage he relates, and a consequent eye-witness of the strange characters on board her. Foremost amongst these is the Captain, in the conception of whose part lies the most original thought of the whole book, stamping it decidedly as the production of a man of genius. . . .

The idea of even a nautical Don Quixote chasing a particular fish from ocean to ocean, running down the line of the Equator, or rushing from Torrid to Temperate zones—this may seem intolerably absurd. But the author clearly shows the *possibility* of such a search being successful, which is more than sufficient motive. . . .

A deadly strife, then, between Capt. Ahab and Moby-Dick, is the vein of romance woven through the varied wanderings of the good ship *Pequod* and her crew, and to which the reader is brought back from matter-of-fact details of the fishery, from abstruse and sceptical and comical speculations on men and things, from hand-breadth escapes, and from thrilling adventures. The book opens with the writer's personal search for a berth on ship-board, at New Bedford and Nantucket, and closes with the total loss of the *Pequod* in the Pacific, the fated vessel being deliberately run into by Moby-Dick, just as the *Ann Alexander* was lately sunk in the same seas by a malicious sperm whale, as mentioned in our columns a few weeks since. It is a singular coincidence that Mr. Melville should have wound up with this catastrophe, and that its truthfulness should have met such sad and immediate confirmation. Be it further noted that *Moby-Dick* was published in London, before the fate of the *Ann Alexander* could have been known there.

Not only is there an immense amount of reliable information here before us; the *dramatis personæ*, mates, harpooners, carpenters, and cooks, are all vivid sketches done in the author's best style. What they do, and how they look, is brought to one's perception with wondrous elaborateness of detail; and yet this minuteness does not spoil the broad outline of each. It is only when Mr. Melville puts words into the mouths of these living and moving beings, that his cunning fails him, and the illusion passes away. From the Captain to the Cabin-boy, not a soul amongst them talks pure seaman's lingo; and as this is a grave charge, we feel bound to substantiate it—not by an ill-natured selection of isolated bits, but by such samples as may be considered an average. . . .

But there is no pleasure in making these extracts; still less would there be in quoting anything of the stuff and nonsense spouted forth by the crazy Captain; for so indeed must nine-tenths of his dialogue be considered, even though one bears in mind that it has been compounded in a maniac's brain from the queer mixture of New England conventicle phraseology with the devilish profanity too common on board South-Sea Whalers. The rarely-imagined character has been grievously spoiled, nay altogether ruined, by a vile overdaubing with a coat of book-learning and mysticism; there is no method in his madness; and we must needs pronounce the chief feature of the volume a perfect failure, and the work itself inartistic. There is nevertheless in it, as we have already hinted, abundant choice reading for these who can skip a page now and then, judiciously; and perhaps, when one's mind is made up to disregard the continuous interest, the separate portions may be better relished. . . .

Mr. Melville has crowded together in a few prefatory pages a large collection of brief and pithy extracts from authors innumerable, such as one might expect as headings for chapters. We do not like the innovation. It is having oil, mustard, vinegar, and pepper served up as a dish, in place of being scientifically administered sauce-wise.

89. Horace Greeley, from an unsigned review, New York *Tribune*

22 November 1851

Everybody has heard of the tradition which is said to prevail among the old salts of Nantucket and New-Bedford, of a ferocious monster of a whale, who is proof against all the arts of harpoonery, and who occasionally amuses himself with swallowing down a boat's crew without winking. The present volume is a 'Whaliad,' or the Epic of that veritable old leviathan, who 'esteemeth iron as straw, and laughs at the spear, the dart, and the habergeon,' no one being able to 'fill his skin with a barbed iron, or his head with fish-hooks.' Mr. Melville gives us not only the romance of his history, but a great mass of instruction on the character and habits of his whole race, with complete details of the wily stratagems of their pursuers. . . .

The narrative is constructed in Herman Melville's best manner. It combines the various features which form the chief attractions of his style, and is commendably free from the faults which we have before had occasion to specify in this powerful writer. The intensity of the plot is happily relieved by minute descriptions of the most homely processes of the whale fishery. We have occasional touches of the subtle mysticism, which is carried to such an inconvenient excess in *Mardi*, but it is here mixed up with so many tangible and odorous realities, that we always safely alight from the excursion through mid-air upon the solid deck of the whaler. We are recalled to this world by the fumes of 'oil and blubber,' and are made to think more of the contents of barrels than of allegories. The work is also full of episodes, descriptive of strange and original phases of character. . . .

Here we will retire from the chase, which lasts three days, not having a fancy to be in at the death. We part with the adventurous philosophical Ishmael, truly thankful that the whale did not get his head, for which we are indebted for this wildly imaginative and truly thrilling story. We think it the best production which has yet come from that seething brain, and in spite of its lawless flights, which put all regular criticism at defiance, it gives us a higher opinion of the author's originality and power than even the favorite and fragrant first-fruits of his genius, the never-to-be-forgotten *Typee*.

90. George Ripley, unsigned review, *Harper's New Monthly Magazine*

December 1851, iv, 137

A new work by HERMAN MELVILLE, entitled *Moby Dick; or, The Whale*, has just been issued by Harper and Brothers, which, in point of richness and variety of incident, originality of conception, and splendor of description, surpasses any of the former productions of this highly successful author. *Moby Dick* is the name of an old White Whale; half fish and half devil; the terror of the Nantucket cruisers; the scourge of distant oceans; leading an invulnerable, charmed life; the subject of many grim and ghostly traditions. This huge sea monster has a conflict with one Captain Ahab; the veteran Nantucket salt comes off second best; not only loses a leg in the affray, but receives a twist in the brain; becomes the victim of a deep, cunning monomania; believes himself predestined to take a bloody revenge on his fearful enemy; pursues him with fierce demoniac energy of purpose; and at last perishes in the dreadful fight, just as he deems that he has reached the goal of his frantic passion. On this slight framework, the author has contrasted a romance, a tragedy, and a natural history, not without numerous gratuitous suggestions on psychology, ethics, and theology. Beneath the whole story, the subtle, imaginative reader may perhaps find a pregnant allegory, intended to illustrate the mystery of human life. Certain it is that the rapid, pointed hints which are often thrown out, with the keenness and velocity of a harpoon, penetrate deep into the heart of things, showing that the genius of the author for moral analysis is scarcely surpassed by his wizard power of description.

In the course of the narrative the habits of the whale are fully and ably described. Frequent graphic and instructive sketches of the fishery, of sea-life in a whaling vessel, and of the manners and customs of strange nations are interspersed with excellent artistic effect among the thrilling scenes of the story. The various processes of procuring oil are explained with the minute, painstaking fidelity of a statistical record, contrasting strangely with the weird, phantom-like character of the plot, and of some of the leading personages, who present a no less unearthly appearance than the witches in *Macbeth*. These sudden and decided transitions form a striking feature of the volume. Difficult of management, in the highest degree, they are wrought with consummate skill. To a less gifted author, they would inevitably have proved fatal. He has not only deftly avoided their dangers, but made them an element of great power. They constantly pique the attention of the reader, keeping curiosity alive, and presenting the combined charm of surprise and alternation.

The introductory chapters of the volume, containing sketches of life in the great marts of Whalingdom, New Bedford and Nantucket, are pervaded with a fine vein of comic humor, and reveal a succession of portraitures, in which the lineaments of nature shine forth, through a good deal of perverse, intentional exaggeration. To many readers, these will prove the most interesting portions of the work. Nothing can be better than the description of the owners of the vessel, Captain Peleg and Captain Bildad, whose acquaintance we make before the commencement of the voyage. The character of Captain Ahab also opens upon us with wonderful power. He exercises a wild, bewildering fascination by his dark and mysterious nature, which is not at all diminished when we obtain a clearer insight into his strange history. Indeed, all the members of the ship's company, the three mates, Starbuck, Stubbs, and Flash, the wild, savage Gayheader, the case-hardened old blacksmith, to say nothing of the pearl of a New Zealand harpooner, the bosom friend of the narrator—all stand before us in the strongest individual relief, presenting a unique picture gallery, which every artist must despair of rivaling.

The plot becomes more intense and tragic, as it approaches toward the denouement. The malicious old Moby Dick, after long cruisings in pursuit of him, is at length discovered. He comes up to the battle, like an army with banners. He seems inspired with the same fierce, inveterate cunning with which Captain Ahab has followed the traces of his mortal foe. The fight is described in letters of blood. It is easy to foresee which will be the victor in such a contest. We need not say that the ill-omened ship is broken in fragments by the wrath of the weltering fiend. Captain Ahab becomes the prey of his intended victim. The crew perish. One alone escapes to tell the tale. Moby Dick disappears unscathed, and for aught we know, is the same 'delicate monster,' whose power in destroying another ship is just announced from Panama.

91. Unsigned review, *Literary Gazette*

6 December 1851, 841–2

Thrice unlucky Herman Melville! Three goodly volumes has he written, with the main purpose of honouring the Cachalot, and disparaging the *Mysticete*, and his publisher has sent them into the world in brilliant covers of blue and white, with three Greenland whales stamped in gold on their binding. How they spout! Three unmistakeable Mysticeti, sloping heads, and jaws fringed with long combs of baleen. Shade of extinguished spermaceti, how thy light has been put out by the bookbinders!

This is an odd book, professing to be a novel; wantonly eccentric; outrageously bombastic; in places charmingly and vividly descriptive. The author has read up laboriously to make a show of cetalogical learning. He has turned over the articles Whale, Porpoise, Cachalot, Spermaceti, Baleen, and their relatives, in every Encyclopædia within his reach. Thence he has resorted to the original authorities—a difficult and tedious task, as every one who has sought out the sources of statements set forth without reference in Cyclopædias knows too well. For our own part, we believe that there must have been some old original Cyclopædia, long since lost or destroyed, out of which all the others have been compiled. For when one is compared with another, it becomes too plain that one or other is a barefaced pillage and extract from a secondhand source. Herman Melville is wise in this sort of wisdom. He uses it as stuffing to fill out his skeleton story. Bad stuffing it makes, serving only to try the patience of his readers, and to tempt them to wish both him and his whales at the bottom of an unfathomable sea. If a man will light his lamp with whale oil, when gas and camphine are at hand, he must be content with a dull illumination.

The story of this novel scarcely deserves the name. The supposed author, a young sailor, resolves to join the whalers. He falls in with a strange bedfellow at starting, a picturesque savage, one Queequeg, a New Zealand prince, who has abdicated his dignities in order to see the world, and who moves through nautical society with a harpoon in his hand and a wooden god in his pocket. Mr. Melville cannot do without savages so he makes half of his *dramatis personæ* wild Indians, Malays, and other untamed humanities. Queequeg and the writer become sworn friends. They join a whale-ship, commanded by a strange one-legged Captain Ahab, who cherishes a mysterious purpose—no less than the intention of pursuing to death a ferocious white spermaceti whale, who has knocked no end of ships to pieces, and chewed off any number of legs, arms, and heads of whale-fishers. Ahab peregrinates the ocean in search of his enemy, for it was Moby Dick—that is the name of the whale—who abbreviated the Captain's lower extremities. What the author's original intention in spinning his preposterous yarn was, it is impossible to guess; evidently, when we compare the first and third volumes, it was never carried out. He seems to have despaired of exciting interest about a leviathan hero and a crazy whale-skipper, and when he found his manuscript sufficient for the filling up of three octavos, resolved to put a stop to whale, captain, crew, and savages by a *coup de main*.[1] Accordingly, he sends them down to the depths of ocean all in a heap, using his milk-white spermaceti as the instrument of ruthless destruction. How the imaginary writer, who appears to have been drowned with the rest, communicated his notes for publication to Mr. Bentley is not explained. The whole affair would make an admirable subject for an Easter entertainment at Astley's.

Having said so much that may be interpreted as censure, it is right that we should add a word of praise where deserved. There are sketches of scenes at sea, of whaling adventures, storms, and ship-life, equal to any we have ever met with. A single extract will serve as an illustration. It is a description of an attack upon a whale during a squall, and the fearful consequences of the rash exploit:—

[quotes from chapter 48, 'Our sail was now' to 'or a lance pole.']

Mr. Herman Melville has earned a deservedly high reputation for his

[1] *Coup de main:* sudden movement.

performances in descriptive fiction. He has gathered his own materials, and travelled along fresh and untrodden literary paths, exhibiting powers of no common order, and great originality. The more careful, therefore, should he be to maintain the fame he so rapidly acquired, and not waste his strength on such purposeless and unequal doings as these rambling volumes about spermaceti whales.

92. William T. Porter, from an unsigned review, New York *Spirit of the Times*

6 December 1851, 494

Porter (1809–58) was the editor of the *Spirit of the Times*, America's first sporting journal, from 1831 to 1856 and an associate editor after that. His interest in fishing and hunting led to his publishing many humorous sketches of Southern and Western life that touched on those sports.

Our friend Melville's books begin to accumulate. His literary family increases rapidly. He had already a happy and smiling progeny around him, but lo! at the appointed time another child of his brain, with the accustomed signs of the family, claims our attention and regard. We bid the book a hearty welcome. We assure the 'happy father' that his 'labors of love' are no 'love's labor lost.'

We confess an admiration for Mr. Melville's books, which, perhaps, spoils us for mere criticism. There are few writers, living or dead, who describe the sea and its adjuncts with such true art, such graphic power, and with such powerfully resulting interest. *Typee*, *Omoo*, *Redburn*, *Mardi*, and *White Jacket*, are equal to anything in the language. They are things of their own. They are results of the youthful experience on the ocean of a man who is at once philosopher, painter, and poet. This is not, perhaps, a very unusual mental combination, but it is not usual to find such a combination 'before the mast.' So far Mr. Melville's early experiences, though perhaps none of the pleasantest to himself, are infinitely valuable to the world. We say *valuable* with a full knowledge of the terms used; and, not to enter into details, which will be fresh in the memory of most of Mr. Melville's readers, it is sufficient to say that the humanities of the world have been quickened by his works. Who can forget the missionary *expose*—the practical good sense which pleads for 'Poor Jack,' or the unsparing but just severity of his delineations of naval abuses, and that crowning disgrace to our navy—flogging? Taken as matters of art these books are amongst the largest and the freshest contributions of original thought and observation which have been presented in many years. Take the majority of modern writers, and it will be admitted that however much they may elaborate and rearrange the stock of ideas pre-existant, there is little added to the 'common fund.' Philosophers bark at each other—poets sing stereotyped phrases—John Miltons re-appear in innumerable 'Pollock's Courses of Time'—novelists and romancers stick to the same overdone incidents, careless of the memories of defunct Scotts and Radcliffs, and it is only now and then when genius, by some lucky chance of youth, ploughs deeper into the soil of humanity and nature, that fresher experiences—perhaps at the cost of much individual pain and sorrow—are obtained; and the results are books, such as those of Herman Melville and Charles Dickens. Books which are living pictures, at once of the practical truth, and the ideal amendment: books which mark epochs in literature and art.

It is, however, not with Mr. Melville generally as a writer that we have now to deal, but with *Moby Dick, or the Whale*, in particular; and at first let us not forget to say that in 'taking titles' no man is more felicitous than our author. Sufficiently dreamy to excite one's curiosity, sufficiently explicit to indicate some main and peculiar feature. 'Moby Dick' is perhaps a creation of the brain—'The Whale' a result of experience; and the whole title a fine polished result of both. A title may be a truth or a lie. It may be clap-trap, or true art. A bad book may have a good title, but you will seldom find a good book with an inappropriate name.

Moby Dick, or the Whale, is all whale. Leviathan is here in full amplitude. Not one of your museum affairs, but the real, living whale, a bona-fide, warm-blooded creature, ransacking the waters from pole to pole. His enormous bulk, his terribly destructive energies, his habits, his food, are all before us. Nay, even his lighter moods are exhibited. We are permitted to see the whale as a lover, a husband, and the head of a family. So to speak, we are made guests at his fire-side; we set our mental legs beneath his mahogany, and become members of his interesting social circle. No book in the world brings together so much whale. We have his history, natural and social, living and dead. But Leviathan's natural history, though undoubtedly valuable to science, is but a part of the book. It is in the personal adventures of his captors, their toils, and, alas! not unfrequently their wounds and martyrdom, that our highest interest is excited. This mingling of human adventure with new, startling, and striking objects and pursuits, constitute one of the chief charms of Mr. Melville's books. His present work is a drama of intense interest. A whale, 'Moby Dick'—a dim, gigantic, unconquerable, but terribly destructive being, is one of the persons of the drama. We admit a disposition to be critical on this character. We had doubts as to his admissibility as an actor into dramatic action, and so it would seem had our author, but his chapter, 'The Affidavit,' disarms us; all improbability or incongruity disappears, and 'Moby Dick' becomes a living fact, simply doubtful at first, because he was so new an idea, one of those beings whose whole life, like the Palladius or the Sea-serpent, is a romance, and whose memoirs unvarnished are of themselves a fortune to the first analist or his publisher.

Moby Dick, or the Whale, is a 'many-sided' book. Mingled with much curious information respecting whales and whaling there is a fine vein of sermonizing, a good deal of keen satire, much humor, and that too of the finest order, and a story of peculiar interest. As a romance its characters are so new and unusual that we doubt not it will excite the ire of critics. It is not tame enough to pass this ordeal safely. Think of a monomaniac whaling captain, who, mutilated on a former voyage by a particular whale, well known for its peculiar bulk, shape, and color—seeks, at the risk of his life and the lives of his crew, to capture and slay this terror of the seas! It is on this idea that the romance hinges. The usual staple of novelists is entirely wanting. We have neither flinty-hearted fathers, designing villains, dark caverns, men in armor, nor anxious lovers. There is not in the book any individual, who, at a certain hour, '*might have been seen*' ascending hills or descending valleys, as is usual. The thing is entirely new, fresh, often startling, and highly dramatic, and with those even, who, oblivious of other fine matters, scattered with profusest hand, read for the sake of the story, must be exceedingly successful.

. . . we must conclude by strongly recommending *Moby Dick, or the Whale*, to all who can appreciate a work of exceeding power, beauty, and genius.

93. William A. Butler, from an unsigned review, Washington, D.C., *National Intelligencer*

16 December 1851

Butler (1825–1902) was a lawyer, satirical poet, and biographer of public figures, including Evert Duyckinck, who was a friend of his. The review of *Moby-Dick* opens with a long attack on critics—'a set of literary jackals' having nothing more than 'a negative influence on the literature of the day'—and a discussion of the critic's role as Devil's Advocate in assessing the worth of authors.

If we were disposed on the present occasion to follow the example thus set us by our betters, we should forthwith proceed, taking *Moby Dick, or the Whale*, as our text, to indite a discourse on cetology. Such, however, is not our intention. Nor do we propose, like a veritable devil's advocate, to haul Mr. Herman Melville over the coals for any offences committed against the code of Aristotle and Aristarchus: we have nothing to allege against his admission among the few writers of the present day who give evidence of some originality; but, while disposed to concede to Mr. Melville a palm of high praise for his literary excellencies, we must enter our decided protest against the querulous and cavilling innuendoes which he so much loves to discharge, like barbed and poisoned arrows, against objects that should be shielded from his irreverent wit. On this point we hope it is unncessary to enlarge in terms of reprehension, further than to say that there are many passages in his last work, as indeed in most that Mr. Melville has written, which 'dying he would wish to blot.' Neither good taste nor good morals can approve the 'forecastle scene,' with its maudlin and ribald orgies, as contained in the 40th chapter of *Moby Dick*. It has all that is disgusting in Goethe's 'Witches' Kitchen,' without its genius.

Very few readers of the lighter literature of the day have forgotten, we presume, the impression produced upon their minds of Mr. Melville's earlier publications—*Typee* and *Omoo*. They opened to all the circulating library readers an entirely new world. His 'Peep at Polynesian Life,' during a four months' residence in a valley of the Marquesas, as unfolded in *Typee*, with his rovings in the 'Little Jule' and his rambles through Tahiti, as detailed in *Omoo*, abound with incidents of stirring adventure and 'moving accidents by flood and field,' replete with all the charms of novelty and dramatic vividness. He first introduced us to cannibal banquets, feasts of raw fish and *poee-poee*; he first made us acquainted with the sunny glades and tropical fruits of the Typee valley, with its golden lizards among the spear-grass and many colored birds among the trees; with its groves of cocoa-nut, its tattooed savages, and temples of light bamboo. Borne along by the current of his limpid style, we sweep past bluff and grove, wooded glen and valley, and dark ravines lighted up far within by wild waterfalls, while here and there in the distance are seen the white huts of the natives, nestling like birdsnests in clefts gushing with verdure, while off the coral reefs of each sea-girt island the carved canoes of tattooed chieftains dance on the blue waters. Who has forgotten the maiden Fayaway and the faithful Kory-Kory, or the generous Marheyo, or the Doctor Long Ghost, that figure in his narratives? So new and interesting were his sketches of life in the South Sea islands that few were able to persuade themselves that his story of adventure was not authentic. We have not time at present to renew the inquiry into their authenticity, though we incline to suspect they were about as true as the sketches of adventures detailed by De Foe in his *Robinson Crusoe*. The points of resemblance between the inimitable novel of De Foe and the production of Mr. Melville are neither few nor difficult to be traced. In the conduct of his narrative the former displays more of naturalness and *vraisemblance*;[1] the latter more of fancy and invention; and while we rather suspect that Robinson's man Friday will always remain more of a favorite than Kory-Kory among all readers 'in their teens,' persons of maturer judgment and more cultivated taste will prefer the mingled *bonhommie*,[2] quiet humor, and unstrained pathos which underlie and pervade the graphic narratives of Mr. Melville. Still we are far from considering Mr. Melville a greater artist than Daniel De Foe in the general design of his romantic pictures; for is it not a greater proof of skill in the use of language to be able so to paint the scenes in a narration as to make us forget the narrator in the interests of his subjects? In this, as we think, consists the charm of

[1] *Vraisemblance:* verisimilitude.
[2] *Bonhommie*: good nature.

Robinson Crusoe—a book which every boy reads and no man forgets; the perfect naturalness of the narrative, and the transparent diction in which it is told, have never been equalled by any subsequent writer, nor is it likely that they will be in an age fond of point and pungency.

Mr. Melville is not without a rival in this species of romance-writing, founded on personal adventure in foreign and unknown lands. Dr. Mayo, the author of *Kaloolah* and other works, has opened to us a phantasmagorical view of life in Northern Africa similar to the 'peep' which Mr. Melville has given us of the South Sea Islands through his kaleidoscope. Each author has familiarized himself with the localities in which his dramatic exhibition of men and things is enacted, and each have doubtless claimed for themselves a goodly share of that invention which produced the Travels of Gulliver and the unheard-of adventures and exploits of the Baron Munchausen. Framazugda, as painted by Dr. Mayo, is the Eutopia of Negrodom, just as the Typee valley has been called the Eutopia of the Pacific Islands, and Kaloolah is the 'counterfeit presentment' of Fayaway.

Moby-Dick, or the Whale, is the narrative of a whaling voyage; and, while we must beg permission to doubt its authenticity in all respects, we are free to confess that it presents a most striking and truthful portraiture of the whale and his perilous capture. We do not imagine that Mr. Melville claims for this his latest production the same historical credence which he asserted was due to *Typee* and *Omoo*; and we do not know how we can better express our conception of his general drift and style in the work under consideration than by entitling it a prose Epic on Whaling. In whatever light it may be viewed, no one can deny it to be the production of a man of genius. The descriptive powers of Mr. Melville are unrivalled, whether the scenes he paints reveal 'old ocean into tempest toss'd,' or are laid among the bright hillsides of some Pacific island, so warm and undulating that the printed page on which they are so graphically depicted seems almost to palpitate beneath the sun. Language in the hands of this master becomes like a magician's wand, evoking at will 'thick-coming fancies,' and peopling the 'chambers of imagery' with hideous shapes of terror or winning forms of beauty and loveliness. Mr. Melville has a strange power to reach the sinuosities of a thought, if we may so express ourselves; he touches with his lead and line depths of pathos that few can fathom, and by a single word can set a whole chime of sweet or wild emotions into a pealing concert. His delineation of character is actually Shakspearean—a quality which is even more prominently evinced in *Moby Dick* than in any of his antecedent efforts. Mr. Melville especially delights to limn the full-length portrait of a savage, and if he is a cannibal it is all the better; he seems fully convinced that the highest type of man is to be found in the forests or among the anthropophagi of the Fejee Islands. Brighter geniuses than even his have disported on this same fancy; for such was the youthful dream of Burke, and such was the crazy vision of Jean Jacques Rosseau.

The humor of Mr. Melville is of that subdued yet unquenchable nature which spreads such a charm over the pages of Sterne. As illustrative of this quality in his style, we must refer our readers to the irresistibly comic passages scattered at irregular intervals through *Moby Dick*; and occasionally we find in this singular production the traces of that 'wild imagining' which throws such a weird-like charm about the Ancient Mariner of Coleridge; and many of the scenes and objects in *Moby Dick* were suggested, we doubt not, by this ghastly rhyme. The argument of what we choose to consider as a sort of prose epic on whales, whalers, and whaling may be briefly stated as follows: . . .

On such a slender thread hangs the whole of this ingenious romance, which for variety of incident and vigor of style can scarcely be exceeded.

94. From an unsigned review, London *Morning Chronicle*

20 December 1851

When the author of *Omoo* and *Typee* appeared, we were happy to hail a new and bright star in the firmament of letters. There was vast promise in these finely imagined fictions. Sea stories had been gradually waning in attraction. A vast number of respectable sailors, who never ought to have had their hands blacked in any fluid save tar, were discolouring them in ink. Cooper was not much imitated, but Marryat had a shoal of clumsy followers, who believed that the public liked to read of the most ordinary naval manœuvers told in technical language, and who imagined and let loose upon the world a swarm of *soi-disant*[1] naval characters, who were either weak and conventional, or wildly extravagant and clumsily caricatured. Herman Melville was a man of different mettle: originality—thorough originality—was stamped upon every line he wrote. There never was a fresher author. He took up a new subject, and treated it in a new fashion. Round his readers he flung a new atmosphere, and round his fictions a new light. Herman Melville, in fact, gave the world a new sensation: springing triumphantly away from the old scenes of naval romances, abjuring the West Indies, and the English Channel, and the North Sea; recognising as classic ground neither the Common Hard nor Portsmouth Point—treating us to no exciting frigate battles—absolutely repudiating all notion of daring cuttings out of French luggers moored under batteries of tremendous power—never chasing slavers, and never being chased by pirates—inventing no mysterious corsairs, and launching no renowned privateers, Herman Melville flung himself entirely into a new naval hemisphere. The Pacific, with its eternally sunny skies and tranquil seas—the great ocean of the world—with its mysterious inhabitants—its whales, to which the whales of Greenland are babies, and its ships—worn, battered, warped, and faded ships, cruising for months and months, and years and years in that great illimitable flood—its glorious isles, too—ocean Edens—the very gardens of the south, coral girt and palm crowned, set in sparkling surf, smiled over by everlasting summer skies, and fanned by never-dying summer breezes—the birthplace of a happy, mirthful, Epicurean race, living in the balmy air and the tepid seas—pure and beautiful in their wildness, loving and kind, simple and truthful—such was the semi-fairy world into the gorgeous midst of which Herman Melville, like a potent and beneficent magician, hurled his readers. The power and the skill of the new literary enchanter were at once admitted. With a bursting imagination, and an intellect working with muscles which seemed not likely soon to tire, Herman Melville bid high for a high place among the spirits of the age. There never was an author more instinct with the flush of power and the pride of mental wealth. He dashed at his pages and overflowed them with the rushing fulness of his mind. A perception of the picturesque and of the beautiful—equally powerful and equally intense—an imagination of singular force, and capable of calling up the wildest, most vivid, and most gorgeous conceptions, and a genuine, hearty, warm, and genial

[1] *Soi-disant:* self-styled; would-be.

earnestness—in all he imagined, and in all he wrote—marked Herman Melville, not for a man of talent and a clever writer, but for a genius. And his style was just as thoroughly characteristic. Its strength, its living energy, its abounding vitality, were all his own. He seemed to write like a giant refreshed. He bounded on and on, as if irresistibly impelled by the blast of his own inspiration, and the general happiness of phrase, and the occasional flash of thought rendered in the most deliciously perfect words, were subsidiary proofs of the genuineness of the new powers which addressed the world.

But still, even in the best parts of the best books of the American sailor, there lurked an ominous presence which we hoped would disappear, but which, as we feared, has increased and multiplied. We could not shut our eyes to the fact that constantly before us we saw, like a plague spot, the tendency to rhapsody—the constant leaning towards wild and aimless extravagance, which has since, in so melancholy a degree, overflown, and, so to speak, drowned the human interest—the very possibility of human interest—in so great a portion of Herman Melville's works. First, indeed, there was but a little cloud the size of a man's hand. Unhappily it has overspread the horizon, and the reader stumbles and wanders disconsolately in its gloom. It was in *Mardi* that the storm of extravagance burst fairly forth. The first volume was charming. What could be more poetic, yet life-like, than the picture of the sea-worn whaler, with her crew yearning again for a sight of a clod of dry green land—what finer than the canoe voyage—what more strangely thrilling, yet truth-like, than the falling in with the island schooner, with her grass ropes and cotton sails, drifting with two savages along the sea? So far Melville had held his fine imagination in curb. It had worked legitimately, and worked right well. It had proceeded by the eternal rules of art and the unchanging principles of the truthful and the symmetrical. But with the second volume the curb of judgment is removed. Common sense, which Herman Melville can depose or keep enthroned at will, was driven out by one *coup d'état*,[1] and the two last volumes are melancholy rhodomontade—half raving, half babble—animated only by the outlines of a dull cold allegory, which flits before the reader like a phantom with a veiled face, and a form which is but the foldings of vapour wreaths. You yearn for the world again—for sea and sky and timber—for human flesh, white or brown—for the solid wood of the ship and the coarse canvass of the sail—as did the whaler's crew for land and grass. What are these impalpable shadows to you?

[1] *Coup d'état:* overthrow of the existing government.

What care you for these misty phantoms of an indefinite cloud-land? You want reality—you want truth—you want *vraisemblance*.[1] Close the book—there are none in the last two volumes of *Mardi*.

Next, if we remember rightly, came a three-volume series of sketches called *White Jacket*. They depicted life on board an American frigate in the Pacific—the severe, and in many points brutal, discipline of a Transatlantic ship of war, elaborated with such daguerreotype exactitude and finish, so swarming with the finest and minutest details, and so studded with little points never to be imagined, that you are irresistibly impelled to the conclusion that, from the first word to the last, every syllable is literal, downright truth. Here Herman Melville rushes into the other extreme from *Mardi*. In one he painted visions, in the other he engraves still life. The first is all broad, vague dashes—the second all carefully finished lines. You look at one book, as it were, through a hazy telescope with many coloured glasses—at the other, through a carefully cleaned microscope, which shows you every infinitesimal blister of the tar in the ship's seams—every fibre in a topsail haul-yard, and every hair in a topman's whisker. And yet, every now and then, even in the midst of all this Dutch painting, comes a dash at the old fashion of raving. Every now and then a startling chapter lugs you from the forecastle, or the cock-pit, or the cable-tiers, or the very run, up into the highest, bluest Empyrean—you are snatched up from bilge-water to the nectar of the Gods—you are hurried from the consideration of maggots in biscuits, to that of the world beyond the stars or the world before the flood: in one chapter there is a horrifying account of the amputation of a man's leg—in the next you are told how the great mountain peaks of the Andes raised all their organ notes to peal forth hallelujahs on the morning when the world was born.

One other work by Herman Melville divides his wildly extravagant *Mardi* from the little less extravagant fiction before us. It is called, if we remember right, *My First Voyage*, and is the literally and strongly told experiences of a sailor boy on his first trip from New York to Liverpool. The work smacks strongly of reality, but it is written in a lower, less buoyant, and less confident key than the earlier fictions. It seemed to us, also, as we read it, that some, at all events, of the virtue of the author had departed, and that he knew it. He walked feebly and groped. The inward sunshine was wanting, and the strong throb of the vigorous brain was neither so full nor so steady as before.

Here, however—in *The Whale*—comes Herman Melville, in all his

[1] *Vraisemblance*: verisimilitude.

pristine powers—in all his abounding vigour—in the full swing of his mental energy, with his imagination invoking as strange and wild and original themes as ever, with his fancy arraying them in the old bright and vivid hues, with that store of quaint and out-of-the-way information—we would rather call it reading than learning—which he ever and anon scatters around, in, frequently, unreasonable profusion, with the old mingled opulence and happiness of phrase, and alas! too, with the old extravagance, running a perfect muck throughout the three volumes, raving and rhapsodising in chapter after chapter—unchecked, as it would appear, by the very slightest remembrance of judgment or common sense, and occasionally soaring into such absolute clouds of phantasmal unreason, that we seriously and sorrowfully ask ourselves whether this can be anything other than sheer moonstruck lunacy. . . .

. . . in fact the entire book, except the portions we have mentioned, reads like a ghost story done with rare imaginative power and noble might of expression. The captain of the Pequod—Captain Ahab—is a mystery of mysteries. He looms out of a halo of terrors—scents prophecies, omens, and auguries. He is an ancient mariner—an ancient whaler—and there seems on him a doom and a curse. . . .

The personages introduced as the author's shipmates are even more phantom-like, un-human, and vaguely uninteresting than the Captain. There are three mates—Starbuck, Stubb, and Flash—mere talking shadows—and rare rhapsodies of nonsense they sometimes talk. Queequeg, the Pagan harpooner, is the only flesh and blood like portraiture, and he is little save an animal. A cook and a carpenter, and a half-witted negro called Pip, are absolutely shadows. The voyage out to the whaling grounds is told with all those extraordinary plunges into all manner of historical, allegorical, and metaphysical disquisitions and rhapsodies which distinguish the author; but, mixed up with these, there are very many chapters devoted to the natural history of the whale, containing, in our view, some of the most delightful pages in the book. Herman Melville, we believe, knows more about whales than any man alive, or who ever lived. . . .

. . . To form anything like an idea of this strange conglomeration of fine description, reckless fancy, rhapsodic mistiness, and minute and careful Dutch painting, the book itself must be referred to. We can only give a faint and outlined idea of its strange contents. . . .

95. Unsigned notice, *Southern Quarterly Review*

January 1852, v, 262

In all those portions of this volume which relate directly to the whale, his appearance in the oceans which he inhabits; his habits, powers and peculiarities; his pursuit and capture; the interest of the reader will be kept alive, and his attention fully rewarded. We should judge, from what is before us, that Mr. Melville has as much personal knowledge of the whale as any man living, and is better able, than any man living, to display this knowledge in print. In all the scenes where the whale is the performer or the sufferer, the delineation and action are highly vivid and exciting. In all other respects, the book is sad stuff, dull and dreary, or ridiculous. Mr. Melville's Quakers are the wretchedest dolts and drivellers, and his Mad Captain, who pursues his personal revenges against the fish who has taken off his leg, at the expense of ship, crew and owners, is a monstrous bore, whom Mr. Melville has no way helped, by enveloping him in a sort of mystery. His ravings, and the ravings of some of the tributary characters, and the ravings of Mr. Melville himself, meant for eloquent declamation, are such as would justify a writ *de lunatico* against all the parties.

96. Unsigned review, *United States Magazine and Democratic Review*

January 1852, xxx, 93

Mr. Melville is evidently trying to ascertain how far the public will consent to be imposed upon. He is gauging, at once, our gullibility and our patience. Having written one or two passable extravagancies, he has considered himself privileged to produce as many more as he pleases, increasingly exaggerated and increasingly dull. The field from which his first crops of literature were produced, has become greatly impoverished, and no amount of forcing seems likely to restore it to its pristine vigor. In bombast, in caricature, in rhetorical artifice—generally as clumsy as it is ineffectual—and in low attempts at humor, each one of his volumes has been an advance upon its predecessors, while, in all those qualities which make books readable, it has shown a decided retrogression from former efforts. Mr. Melville never writes naturally. His sentiment is forced, his wit is forced, and his enthusiasm is forced. And in his attempts to display to the utmost extent his powers of 'fine writing,' he has succeeded, we think, beyond his most sanguine expectations.

The truth is, Mr. Melville has survived his reputation. If he had been contented with writing one or two books, he might have been famous, but his vanity has destroyed all his chances of immortality, or even of a good name with his own generation. For, in sober truth, Mr. Melville's vanity is immeasurable. He will either be first among the book-making tribe, or he will be nowhere. He will centre all attention upon himself, or he will abandon the field of literature at once. From this morbid self-esteem, coupled with a most unbounded love of notoriety, spring all Mr. Melville's efforts, all his rhetorical contortions, all his declamatory abuse of society, all his inflated sentiment, and all his insinuating licentiousness.

Typee was undoubtedly a very proper book for the parlor, and we have seen it in company with *Omoo*, lying upon tables from which Byron was strictly prohibited, although we were unable to fathom those niceties of logic by which one was patronized, and the other proscribed. But these were Mr. Melville's triumphs. *Redburn* was a stupid failure, *Mardi* was hopelessly dull, *White Jacket* was worse than either; and, in fact, it was such a very bad book, that, until the appearance of *Moby Dick*, we had set it down as the very ultimatum of weakness to which its author could attain. It seems, however, that we were mistaken.

We have no intention of quoting any passages just now from *Moby Dick*. The London journals, we understand, 'have bestowed upon the work many flattering notices,' and we should be loth to combat such high authority. But if there are any of our readers who wish to find examples of bad rhetoric, involved syntax, stilted sentiment and incoherent English, we will take the liberty of recommending to them this precious volume of Mr. Melville's.

PIERRE

1852

97. Melville, from *Pierre*, book XVII, 'Young America in Literature'

1852

Melville's satirical attack in book XVII of *Pierre* on the literary establishment in general and on the critics in particular may have grown out of his displeasure with the reviews of *Moby-Dick*, especially that by Evert Duyckinck in the *Literary World* (No. 84). Books XVIII, XXI, XXII, and XXV contain more of Melville's thoughts on authorship.

But it still remains to be said, that Pierre himself had written many a fugitive thing, which had brought him, not only vast credit and compliments from his more immediate acquaintances, but the less partial applauses of the always intelligent, and extremely discriminating public. In short, Pierre had frequently done that, which many other boys have done—published. Not in the imposing form of a book, but in the more modest and becoming way of occasional contributions to magazines and other polite periodicals. His magnificent and victorious *debut* had been made in that delightful love-sonnet, entitled 'The Tropical Summer.' Not only the public had applauded his gemmed little sketches of thought and fancy, whether in poetry or prose; but the high and mighty Campbell clan of editors of all sorts had bestowed upon him those generous commendations, which, with one instantaneous glance, they had immediately perceived was his due. They spoke in high terms of his surprising command of language; they begged to express their wonder at his euphonious construction of sentences; they regarded with reverence the pervading symmetry of his general style. But transcending even this profound insight into the deep merits of Pierre, they looked infinitely beyond, and confessed their complete inability to restrain their unqualified admiration for the highly judicious smoothness and genteelness of the sentiments and fancies expressed. 'This writer,' said one,—in an ungovernable burst of admiring fury—'is characterized throughout by Perfect Taste.' Another, after endorsingly quoting that sapient, suppressed maxim of Dr. Goldsmith's, which asserts that whatever is new is false, went on to apply it to the excellent productions before him; concluding with this: 'He has translated the unruffled gentleman from the drawing-room into the general levee of letters; he never permits himself to astonish; is never betrayed into any thing coarse or new; as assured that whatever astonishes is vulgar, and whatever is new must be crude. Yes, it is the glory of this admirable young author, that vulgarity and vigor—two inseparable adjuncts—are equally removed from him.'

A third, perorated a long and beautifully written review, by the bold and startling announcement—'This writer is unquestionably a highly respectable youth.'

Nor had the editors of various moral and religious periodicals failed to render the tribute of their severer appreciation, and more enviable, because more chary applause. A renowned clerical and philological conductor of a weekly publication of this kind, whose surprising proficiency in the Greek, Hebrew, and Chaldaic, to which he had devoted by far the greater part of his life, peculiarly fitted him to pronounce unerring judgment upon works of taste in the English, had unhesitatingly delivered himself thus:—'He is blameless in morals, and harmless throughout.' Another, had unhesitatingly recommended his effusions to the family-circle. A third, had no reserve in saying, that the predominant end and aim of this author was evangelical piety.

A mind less naturally strong than Pierre's might well have been hurried into vast self-complacency, by such eulogy as this, especially as there could be no possible doubt, that the primitive verdict pronounced by the editors was irreversible, except in the highly improbable event of the near approach of the Millennium, which might establish a different dynasty of taste, and possibly eject the editors. It is true, that in view of the general practical vagueness of these panegyrics, and the circumstance that, in essence, they were all somehow of the prudently indecisive sort; and, considering that they were panegyrics, and nothing but panegyrics, without any thing analytical about them; an elderly friend of a literary turn, had made bold to say to our hero—'Pierre, this is very high praise, I grant, and you are a surprisingly young author to receive it; but I do not see any criticisms as yet.'

'Criticisms?' cried Pierre, in amazement; 'why, sir, they are all criticisms! I am the idol of the critics!'

'Ah!' sighed the elderly friend, as if suddenly reminded that that was true after all—'Ah!' and went on with his inoffensive, non-committa cigar.

98. Charles Gordon Greene, unsigned review, Boston *Post*

4 August 1852

Mr Melville has received considerable attention from those whose hard fate it is, to 'notice' new books; and as emanating from the writer of *Typee*, Mr Melville's subsequent works, ranging from fair to execrable, have been held worthy of lengthy critiques, while critics have been at some pains to state, in detail and by means of extracts, their various merits and defects. But we think it full time to stop this mode of treatment. The author of one good book more than offsets the amusement derived from it by the reading public, when he produces a score of trashy and crazy volumes; and in the present case, and after the delivery of such stuff as *Mardi* and the *White Whale*, are not disposed to stand upon much ceremony. Mr Melville's latest books, we are pleased to say, fell almost stillborn from the press, and we opened the volume under notice with the hope and almost the expectation that he would not again abuse the great gift of genius that has been bestowed upon him. We hoped and almost expected that he had sown his literary wild oats, and had now come forth, the vivid and brilliant author that he might be, if he chose to criticise himself, and lop off the puerility, conceit, affectation and insanity which he had previously exhibited. But we reckoned without our host. *Pierre; or the Ambiguities* is, perhaps, the craziest fiction extant. It has scenes and descriptions of unmistakeable power. The characters, however false to nature, are painted with a glowing pencil, and many of the thoughts reveal an intellect, the intensity and cultivation of which it is impossible to doubt. But the amount of utter trash in the volume is almost infinite—trash of conception, execution, dialogue and sentiment. Whoever buys the book on the strength of Melville's reputation, will be cheating himself of his money, and we believe we shall *never* see the man who has endured the reading of the whole of it. We give the story of the book in a few sentences. Pierre Glendinning and his proud but loving mother are living together, surrounded by everything the world, intellect, health and affection can bestow. The son is betrothed to a beautiful girl of equal position and fortune, and everything looks brightly as a summer morning. All at once, Pierre learns that his father has left an illegitimate daughter, who is in poverty and obscurity. His conscience calls upon him to befriend and acknowledge her—although, by the way, his proof of the fact that the girl is his father's offspring is just nothing at all. On the other hand, he will not discover to the world or to his mother the error of his (supposed) sainted father, and he adopts the novel expedient of carrying off the girl, and giving out that he has married her. His mother discards him and soon dies of wounded love and pride, and his betrothed is brought to the brink of the grave. She finally recovers somewhat, and strange to say, invites herself to reside with Pierre and his sister, who, as far as the world and herself were concerned, are living as husband and wife. The relatives of Lucy, as a matter of course, try to regain her, and brand Pierre with every bad name possible. The latter finally shoots his cousin who had become the possessor of the family estate and a pretender to the hand of Lucy—is arrested and taken to prison. There he is visited by the two ladies, the sister and the betrothed. Lucy falls dead of a broken heart and Pierre and his sister take poison and also give up the ghost. This tissue of unnatural horrors is diversified a little, by the attempts of the hero to earn his living by authorship, and by the 'ambiguous' love between Pierre and his natural sister.

Comment upon the foregoing is needless. But even this string of nonsense is equalled by the nonsense that is strung upon it, in the way of crazy sentiment and exaggerated passion. What the book means, we know not. To save it from almost utter worthlessness, it must be called a prose poem, and even then, it might be supposed to emanate from a lunatic hospital rather than from the quiet retreats of Berkshire. We say it with grief—it is too bad for Mr Melville to abuse his really fine talents as he does. A hundred times better if he kept them in a napkin all his natural life. A thousand times better, had he dropped authorship with *Typee*. He would then have been known as the writer of one of the pleasantest books of its class in the English language. As it is, he has produced more and sadder trash than any other man of undoubted ability among us, and the most provoking fact is, that in his bushels of chaff, the 'two grains of wheat' are clearly discernible.

99. Unsigned notice, Springfield, Massachusetts, *Republican*

16 August 1852

Dedicated in form to the mountain 'Greylock,' is this last work of Melville. Dedicated in spirit to the mystical Greylock, is the tangled skein of narrative which the work developes. Of mist-caps, and ravines, and sky piercing peaks, and tangled underwoods, and barren rocks of language and incident, the book is made. Genteel hifalutin, painful, though ingenious involutions of language, and high-flown incidental detail, characterize the work, to the uprooting of our affection for the graceful and simple writer of *Omoo* and *Typee*. Melville has changed his style entirely, and is to be judged as a new author.—We regret the change, for while the new Melville displays more subtleness of thought, more elaborateness of manner, (or mannerism), and a higher range of imagination, he has done it at a sad sacrifice of simplicity and popular appreciation. His present story, although possessing the characteristics we have ascribed to it, is readable to all those who, like us, possess a forgiving spirit, and who entertain the hope that the author, seeing his exceeding sinfulness, will return to the simple and beautiful path of authorship so graced by his early footsteps.

100. Unsigned notice, Washington, D.C., *National Era*

19 August 1852, 134

Truly is there 'but one step from the sublime to the ridiculous,' and as truly hath Mr. Melville herein accomplished it. Such a mass of incongruities, 'ambiguities,' heterogeneities, absurdities, and absolute impossibilities, as the two covers of this volume enfold, it has rarely been our fortune to light upon. Now and then we strike upon something that reminds us of *Typee*, *Omoo*, &c., but it is speedily swallowed up in the slough of metaphysical speculation, which constitutes the largest portion of the work. The characters are absurdly paradoxical and greatly overdrawn; the incidents are impossible, in real life, and the whole book is utterly unworthy of Mr. Melville's genius. It unquestionably contains a vast deal of power, but it amounts to nothing, and accomplishes nothing but a climax too horribly unnatural to be thought of.

Mr. M. has evidently taken hold of a subject which has mastered *him*, and led him into all manner of vagaries. He is more at home in the manifold intricacies of a ship's rigging than amid the subtleties of psychological phenonema.

101. William Young, from an unsigned review, *Albion*

21 August 1852, 405

Ambiguities there are, not a few, in this new work by a popular author; but very little doubt can there be, touching the opinion which the public will entertain of its merits. It must, we regret to say, be pronounced a dead failure, seeing that neither in design or execution does it merit praise, or come within any measurable distance of Mr. Melville's well-deserved reputation. And sorely goes it against the grain with us to venture so harsh a judgment; but whilst we would pass lightly over the errors and short-comings of unknown writers, with whom it is sufficient punishment that their books drop still-born from the press, we deem it the bounden duty of an honest critic to speak out the plain truth when public favourites go palpably astray. Such is now the case; *Pierre* is an objectionable tale, clumsily told. Let us try to sketch briefly its contents. . . .

Now the candid reader will probably agree with us (and we are quite serious) that the situations so far are wrought up cleverly enough. What a fine dramatic starting point would this have been for the hero of a play! Imagine Pierre having to choose between all this contrarity of duties, and feelings, and interests. Just think of an attempt to reconcile his respect for his living mother, his jealousy for his dead father's good repute, his passion for his intended Lucy, and his sense of duty to his new-found sister Isabel, to say nothing of the infallible loss of his inheritance, which has been left at his mother's disposal. A clash and a catastrophe are foreseen at the moment. Would that Mr. Melville had hit upon a less Frenchified mode of carrying us through the one, and bringing about the other! What fatality could have tempted him to call upon the spirit of Eugène Sue, to help him in such extreme emergency! For, what doth the romantic Master Pierre? He determines to pass off Isabel as his already secretly married wife, and to live with her *nominally* as her husband. Good bye to astounded Mrs. Glendinning, who of course turns him out of doors, maddened into speedy death by her son's dishonest breach of faith with Lucy and his presumed degrading match with a low-born substitute! Adieu to the gentle Lucy herself, who should have quite died outright of a broken heart, instead of being reserved to add another absurdity to the monstrous conclusion of the tale! Farewell to the ancestral mansion, and to the esteem of men, and to all cheerful ways of life, to all usefulness, to all honour, to all happiness. Pierre, with his sham-wife and the Magdalen Delly, hies him to New York. There he passes through scenes of poverty and wretchedness, physical and moral, such as you can scarcely read without thanking God that if woe and want do produce unutterable misery, such additions to it as Master Pierre voluntarily made can scarcely have existence, save in the diseased brain of a romancer. . . . Reader, we have not been sketching a Porte St. Martin tragedy, but condensing the newest work of one of our favourite novelists. We wish we could close here, but we regret to add that in several places the ambiguities are still further thickened by hints at that fearfullest of all human crimes, which one shrinks from naming, but to which the narrative alludes when it brings some of its personages face to face with a copy of the Cenci portrait.

In noticing that bold, original work *Moby-Dick*, we remember showing that Mr. Melville never could make his characters talk. It is the same here. Almost every spoken word reminds you of the chorus of the old Greek Tragedies. With the exception of some few sentences very naturally suited to the mouth of the Revd. Mr. Falsgrave, a sleek, smooth-tongued clergyman, there is scarcely a page of dialogue that is not absurd to the last degree. It would really pain us to give extracts, and we decline doing so; but the truth is as we state it. We allow the greatest stretch to the imagination of an author, so far as situations and persons are concerned; but if they can't speak as such men and women would be likely to speak, under such and such circumstances, the reader cannot sympathise with them. We repeat our opinion that this is an objectionable tale, clumsily told; and if we had any influence with Mr. Melville, we would pray him to wash out the remembrance of it by writing forthwith a fresh romance of the Ocean, without a line of dialogue in it. Thereon is he at home; thereon he earned his literary laurels; thereon may he regain his literary standing, which he must have perilled by this crazy rigmarole. Do, Sir, give us something fresh from the sea; you have power, earnestness, experience, and talent. But let it be either truthful or fanciful; not an incoherent hodge-podge. Peter Simple is worth a ship-load of your Peter the Ambiguous.

102. Evert or George Duyckinck, from an unsigned review, *Literary World*

21 August 1852, 118–20

The purpose of Mr. Melville's story, though vaguely hinted, rather than directly stated, seems to be to illustrate the possible antagonism of a sense of duty, conceived in the heat and impetuosity of youth, to all the recognised laws of social morality; and to exhibit a conflict between the virtues. . . .

Mr. Melville may have constructed his story upon some new theory of art to a knowledge of which we have not yet transcended; he evidently has not constructed it according to the established principles of the only theory accepted by us until assured of a better, of one more true and natural than truth and nature themselves, which are the germinal principles of all true art.

The pivot of the story is the pretended marriage of Pierre with his sister, in order to conceal her illegitimacy and protect his father's memory. Pierre, to carry out his purpose, abandons mother, home, his betrothed, all the advantages of his high social position, wealth and its appointments of ease and luxury and respect, and invites poverty, misery, infamy, and death. Apart from the very obvious way of gaining the same object at an infinitely smaller cost, is it natural that a loving youth should cast away the affection of his mother and his betrothed and the attachment of home to hide a dim stain upon his father's memory and to enjoy the love of an equivocal sister? Pierre not only acts thus absurdly, but pretends to act from a sense of duty. He is battling for Truth and Right, and the first thing he does in behalf of Truth is to proclaim to the whole world a falsehood, and the next thing he does is to commit in behalf of Right, a half a dozen most foul wrongs. The combined power of New England transcendentalism and Spanish Jesuitical casuistry could not have more completely befogged nature and truth, than this confounded Pierre has done. It is needless to test minutely the truth and nature of each character. In a word, Pierre is a psychological curiosity, a moral and intellectual phenomenon; Isabel, a lusus naturæ;[1] Lucy, an

[1] *Lusus naturæ:* joke of nature.

incomprehensible woman; and the rest not of the earth nor, we may venture to state, of heaven. The object of the author, perhaps, has been, not to delineate life and character as they are or may possibly be, but as they are not and cannot be. We must receive the book, then, as an eccentricity of the imagination.

The most immoral *moral* of the story, if it has any moral at all, seems to be the impracticability of virtue; a leering demoniacal spectre of an idea seems to be speering at us through the dim obscure of this dark book, and mocking us with this dismal falsehood. Mr. Melville's chapter on 'Chronometricals and Horologicals,' if it has any meaning at all, simply means that virtue and religion are only for gods and not to be attempted by man. But ordinary novel readers will never unkennel this loathsome suggestion. The stagnant pool at the bottom of which it lies, is not too deep for their penetration, but too muddy, foul, and corrupt. If truth is hid in a well, falsehood lies in a quagmire.

We cannot pass without remark, the supersensuousness with which the holy relations of the family are described. Mother and son, brother and sister are sacred facts not to be disturbed by any sacrilegious speculations. Mrs. Glendenning and Pierre, mother and son, call each other brother and sister, and are described with all the coquetry of a lover and mistress. And again, in what we have termed the supersensuousness of description, the horrors of an incestuous relation between Pierre and Isabel seem to be vaguely hinted at.

In commenting upon the vagueness of the book, the uncertainty of its aim, the indefiniteness of its characters, and want of distinctness in its pictures, we are perhaps only proclaiming ourselves as the discoverers of a literary mare's nest; this vagueness, as the title of the 'Ambiguities' seems to indicate, having been possibly intended by the author, and the work meant as a problem of impossible solution, to set critics and readers a wool-gathering. It is alone intelligible as an unintelligibility.

In illustration of the manner of the book, we give this description of a gloomy apparition of a house, such as it was conjured up by the vague confused memory of Isabel. There is a spectral, ghost-like air about the description, that conveys powerfully to the imagination the intended effect of gloom and remote indistinctness:—

[quotes from book VI, part iii, 'My first dim life-thoughts' to 'cup of water by me.']

All the male characters of the book have a certain robust, animal force and untamed energy, which carry them through their melodramatic parts—no slight duty—with an effect sure to bring down the applause of the excitable and impulsive. Mr. Melville can think clearly, and write with distinctness and force—in a style of simplicity and purity. Why, then, does he allow his mind to run riot amid remote analogies, where the chain of association is invisible to mortal minds? Why does he give us incoherencies of thought, in infelicities of language? . . . Such infelicities of expression, such unknown words as these, to wit: 'human*ness*,' 'heroic*ness*,' 'patriarchal*ness*,' 'descended*ness*,' 'flushful*ness*,' 'amaranthi*ness*,' 'instantaneous*ness*,' 'leapingly acknowledging,' 'fateful frame of mind,' 'protecting*ness*,' 'young*ness*,' 'infantile*ness*,' 'visible*ness*,' *et id genus omne!*[1]

The author of *Pierre; or, the Ambiguities*; the writer of a mystic romance, in which are conjured up unreal nightmare-conceptions, a confused phantasmagoria of distorted fancies and conceits, ghostly abstractions and fitful shadows, is certainly but a spectre of the substantial author of *Omoo* and *Typee*, the jovial and hearty narrator of the traveller's tale of incident and adventure. By what *diablerie*,[2] hocus-pocus, or thimble-rigging, 'now you see him and now you don't' process, the transformation has been effected, we are not skilled in necromancy to detect. Nor, if it be a true psychological development, are we sufficiently advanced in transcendentalism to lift ourselves skywards and see clearly the coming light with our heads above the clouds. If this novel indicates a chaotic state of authorship,—and we can distinguish fragmentary elements of beauty—out of which is to rise a future temple of order, grace, and proportion, in which the genius of Mr. Melville is to enshrine itself, we will be happy to worship there; but let its foundation be firmly based on *terra firma*, or, if in the heavens, let us not trust our common sense to the flight of any waxen pinion. We would rejoice to meet Mr. Melville again in the hale company of sturdy sailors, men of flesh and blood, and, strengthened by the wholesome air of the outside world, whether it be land-breeze or sea-breeze, listen to his narrative of a traveller's tale, in which he has few equals in power and felicity.

[1] *Et id genus omne:* and all of that kind.
[2] *Diablerie:* witchcraft.

103. Lampoon, from 'The Editor's Shanty,' *Anglo-American Magazine*

September 1852, i, 273

The speakers in the 'Editor's Shanty' section of this Toronto, Canada, monthly are set up as types to present varied points of view regarding the works under discussion.

THE LAIRD.—I say lads, hae ony o' ye read Herman Melville's new wark?

THE DOCTOR.—You mean *Pierre; or the Ambiguites* I presume?

THE LAIRD.—Just sae! I saw it on Scobie's counter this morning, and wad ha'e coft it if I had had sillar eneuch in my spleuhan!

THE DOCTOR.—It was just as lucky, that your exchequer was at so low an ebb, else thou might have been a practical illustration of the old saw which declares that a fool and his money are soon parted!

THE LAIRD.—You astonish me! I wad ha'e judged that in this age o' commonplace, a production frae the pen o' the author o' *Mardi* wad ha'e been a welcome addition to the stores o' our booksellers!

THE DOCTOR.—Melville unquestionably is a clever man, but in the present instance he has sadly mistaken his walk. *Pierre* from beginning to end is a gigantic blunder, with hardly one redeeming feature.

THE MAJOR.—What is the nature of the story?

THE DOCTOR.—You might as well ask me to analyse the night-mare visions of an Alderman who after dining upon turtle and venison had wound up by supping upon lobsters and toasted cheese! The hero is a dreamy spoon, alike deficient in heart and brains, who like Hamlet drives a gentle confiding maiden crazy by his flatulent caprices, and finally winds up by drinking poison in prison to save his neck from a hempen cravat!

THE MAJOR.—The affair, I presume belongs to the German school?

THE DOCTOR.—Yes! *Pierre* is a species of New York Werter, having all the absurdities and none of the beauties of Goethe's juvenile indiscretion!

THE MAJOR.—Strange that a really able man like Herman Melville should have compromised himself so egregiously by giving birth to such a production!

THE DOCTOR.—'Tis passing strange!

THE SQUIREEN.—Men of genius will occasionally be guilty of such freaks. I remember Liston once playing Richard III. for his benefit in the Theatre Royal, Dublin, and though his most tragic passages were received with shrieks of laughter from box, pit, and gallery, the besotted comedian could not be convinced that it was with himself and not the public where the error lay!

104. John R. Thompson, unsigned review, *Southern Literary Messenger*

September 1852, xviii, 574–5

Thompson (1823–73) was 'editor and proprietor' of this Richmond, Virginia, monthly bought for him by his father in 1847. He was a spokesman in England for the Southern cause during the American Civil War. In 1867 he went to New York and became literary editor of the *Evening Post*.

We know not what evil genius delights in attending the literary movements of all those who have achieved great success in the publication of their first book; but that some such companion all young and successful authors have, is placed beyond dispute by the almost invariable inferiority of their subsequent writings. With strong intellects, there is little danger that the influence of this unhappy minister will be lasting, but with far the greater number it continues until their reputation is wholly gone, or as the phrase runs.—*they have written themselves out*. Mr. Melville would really seem to be one of this class. Few books ever rose so rapidly and deservedly into popular favor as *Typee*. It came from the press at a time when the public taste wearied and sickened of didactic novels and journals of travel through fields explored many hundred times before. It presented us with fresh and delightful incidents from beyond the seas, over which was thrown an atmosphere soft and glowing as that hung above the youthful lovers in the enchanting story of St. Pierre. In a word, it was a novelty, and a novelty in literature, when it offends not against rule, is always to be commended. But from the time that *Typee* came from Mr. Melville's portfolio, he seems to have been writing under an unlucky star. The meandering nonsense of *Mardi* was but ill atoned for even by the capital sea-pieces of *Redburn* and *White Jacket*; *Moby Dick* proved a very tiresome yarn indeed, and as for the *Ambiguities*, we are compelled to say that it seems to us the most aptly titled volume we have met with for years.

The purpose of the *Ambiguities*, (if it have any, for none is either avowed or hinted,) we should take to be the illustration of this fact—that it is quite possible for a young and fiery soul, acting strictly from a sense of duty, and being therefore in the right, to erect itself in direct hostility to all the universally-received rules of moral and social order. At all events, such is the course of Pierre the hero of the story, from the opening chapter, without one moment's deviation, down to the 'bloody work' of the final catastrophe. And our sympathies are sought to be enlisted with Pierre for the reason that throughout all his follies and crimes, *his sense of duty* struggles with and overcomes every law of religion and morality. It is a battle of the virtues, we are led to think, and the supreme virtue prevails.

To show how curiously Mr. Melville proceeds in his purpose, (supposing him to have one,) it will be necessary for us to give some hurried sketch of the story. Pierre, then, the hero, is the sole male representative of the family of Glendinning, a sprig of American Aristocracy, the idol of his proud and accomplished mother and the plighted lover of Lucy Tartan, who is every thing that she should be, either in or out of a story-book. The course of true love runs without a ripple for these pleasant young people, until one day there appears an obstacle in the person of a fair unknown, with eyes of jet and tress of raven hue, who demonstrates to the entire conviction of Pierre that she is his sister—the illegitimate offspring of the paternal Glendinning. To Pierre, then, here was a dreadful disclosure—a bar sinister upon the family escutcheon—an indisputable and living reproach upon the memory of a sainted father. Pierre was therefore perplexed. How to reconcile the obligation which rested upon him to protect his father's fame with the equally binding obligation to love his newly found sister, was indeed a puzzle, and one which he proceeded to solve in a very extraordinary manner. Pierre affects to marry the darkeyed one, the sister, by name Isabel; by which agreeable device he accomplishes three things—

1st. He drives his mother to the horrors of lunacy, in a paroxysm of which she dies.

2nd. He brings upon himself and sister penury and anguish, while endeavoring to live by literary labor; and

3rd. He involves in wholesale assassination by pistols, poison and other diabolical means, the rest of the characters, making as much work for the Coroner as the fifth act of *Romeo and Juliet*, or the terrific melodrama of the *Forty Thieves*.

This latter state of things is thus brought about. Pierre having been driven off by his relatives, sets up a small establishment of his own. Lucy Tartan, recovering from the earliest burst of grief into which she had been thrown by Pierre's pretended marriage, and still, most unaccountably, clinging to the belief that Pierre is not wholly unfaithful, determines to live in his presence at all hazards. But her brother, and a new suitor to her hand, a cousin of Pierre, attempt to wrest her by violence from Pierre's household. Frustrated in this, they write to Pierre, calling him some rather hard names, such as liar and seducer, whereupon Pierre,—in no very good humor from having received a communication from his publishers, declining to purchase his last novel, —arms himself, seeks his cousin, and kills him several times with two pistols. But Pierre is 'no sooner out than taken by the watch' and escorted to jail. Here he is visited by Isabel and Lucy, and the latter discovering that Isabel is the sister and not the mistress of Pierre, there ensues a fainting scene, after which these amiable ladies, for no adequate motive that we can see, proceed to drink each other's healths in prussic acid, though not exactly with the air of Socrates pouring off his hemlock to immortality. Her fitly ends the volume, for surely in its 'shocking department' we have 'supped full of horrors,' and yet the tragic effect of its perusal does *not* end here, for Lucy's fate, and supposed infamy 'leave to the imagination of the reader' any desired quantity of despair among the surviving relatives.

Such is the outline of the *Ambiguities* hurriedly given. The observant reader will see at once the absurdity of the principle upon which it has been constructed. Pierre discovers a sister whose very existence is evidence of a father's sin. To treat that sister with kindness and to cover over the father's shame, is without doubt a most laudable thing. But to accomplish it, Pierre is led to do things infinitely worse than it would be to neglect it. He not only acts like a fool in severing the most sacred ties and making the dearest sacrifices to purchase what he might have obtained at a much lighter expense, but he justifies his conduct by a sense of duty, false in the extreme. He wishes to uphold the just and true, and to do this he commences by stating a lie—his marriage with Isabel. It is in the cause of affection and consanguinity that he is content to suffer, and for this cause, he breaks off the closest and holiest bond that exists on earth, the bond of filial love, thus causing the mother that bore him to die a maniac. For every duty he performs, he is compelled to commit a dozen outrages on the moral sense, and these are committed without hesitancy or compunction. The truth is, Mr. Melville's theory is wrong. It should be the object of fiction to delineate life and character either as it is around us, or as it ought to be. Now, Pierre never did exist, and it is very certain that he never ought to exist. Consequently, in the production of Pierre, Mr. Melville has deviated from the legitimate line of the novelist. But badly as we think of the book as a work of art, we think infinitely worse of it as to its moral tendency. We have not space left us to enter upon this view of the volume, and we must therefore leave it with the remark that if one does not desire to look at virtue and religion with the eye of Mephistopheles, or, at least, through a haze of *ambiguous* meaning, in which they may readily be taken for their opposites, he had better leave *Pierre or the Ambiguities* unbought on the shelves of the bookseller.

105. Unsigned review, New York *Herald*

18 September 1852

Ambiguities, indeed! One long brain-muddling, soul-bewildering ambiguity (to borrow Mr. Melville's style), like Melchisedeck, without beginning or end—a labyrinth without a clue—an Irish bog without so much as a Jack-o' th'-lantern to guide the wanderer's footsteps—the dream of a distempered stomach, disordered by a hasty supper or half-cooked pork chops. Verily, books spring into life, now a days, by a strange Cæsarean process. Our ancestors, simple folks, used to fancy it incumbent on an author to nurse the germ in his fecundated brain till the fœtus assumed a definite shape, and could be marsalled into existence, safe from the brand of monstrosity. Modern writers miscarry 'ere the embryo hath shapen limb or nerve, or blood, and mid-wives and doctors in droves pledge their willing faith that it will live. Potent elixirs and cordials elicit some reluctant spark of animation; but reaction soon follows, and 'mid the feigned astonishment of foster-mothers and wet-nurses, the emasculated bantling expires a miserable death.

What can be more conclusive evidence of immature conception than the planting on the social stage of this nineteenth century, of a man like Pierre—brimful of noble passions—silly weaknesses—lordly power of mind and warmth of heart—the petted child of a tender mother, who, yielding to her son's craving after sisterly love, calls him 'brother'—thrusting him into contact with a timid, fragile girl, who turns out to be an illegitimate daughter of his father's, and firing him with such a chivalrous devotion for this new found sister, *par la main gauche*,[1] that he resigns, without a pang, home, mother, betrothed, rank, and even the necessaries of life, to roam the world, knight-errant like, in her company; reversing, with less show of reason, Abraham's white lie, and proclaiming publicly that the daughter of his is his wife! Where did Mr. Melville find an original for the portrait of Isabel? Where for Mrs. Glendinning? or where for the fond, but unwomanly Lucy? Alas! those pork chops! Sore must have been the grapple between the monster indigestion and the poor suffering epigastrium. Frantic the struggle between the fiend nightmare and our unfortunate friend the author.

[1] *Par la main gauche:* by the left hand.

We do not object to a canvas well laid with weird horrors, fantastic sprites gushing from out some misty cloud, and playful imps, dancing and chattering in the foreground, to the ruin of the composition of the picture, and to the speechless agony of the severe classic. But good Mr. Melville, your dream has overstepped the bounds of our impressibility. We long to give you one good shake, to have you rub your eyes, and favor us with the common sense word of the enigma. Is Pierre really a candidate for the distinguished honor of a latticed chamber at the Battleborough asylum? Would a mild infusion of hellebore, and a judicious course of treatment in some sunny vale, calm his phrenzy, and cool his calcined brain? or are his erratic habits—his wondrous *épanchement*[1] for a full-blown sister—his reckless disregard of filial duty, plighted love, and public esteem—mere forms of eccentricity, outward symptoms of the genius latent within? We confess that we should like to be correctly informed on these points. We own to a speaking partiality for Pierre, rough and unnatural as he is, and share his fiery rebellion against the yoke of conventional proprieties, and the world's cold rules of esteem. Weep we, too, with gentle Isabel; poor bud, blighted by a hereditary canker. And, need we blush to avow that our pulse beat faster than our physician in ordinary would have sanctioned, when the heartless Stanly disclaimed his poverty-stricken cousin, and strove to wrest his reluctant bride from the arms of her chosen lover? But that shot—was it manly? was it honorable? was it fair? to requite a hasty blow, well warranted, *du reste*[2]—for who would not strike to the earth one who passed for the seducer of his mistress?—with a pistol ball fired from an arm's length on a defenceless man? This, Mr. Melville, is murder. For a murderer in cold blood—a wretch who coolly loads his arms, rams the charge home, and sallies forth with the set purpose of taking the life of his rival—we have no thrill of sympathy, no bowels of compassion. Let him hang like a dog! A harmless madman in the first chapter, he is a dangerous poet in the last. Let him hang! And those ill starred girls! Ill became it their pure maidenhood to drench the fatal phial, and drown the spark of heavenly virtue and earthly sense in one corroding draught of poisonous passion. Sadly, too sadly—but, as we said, we cannot wholly eradicate every trace of compassion for the erring impulse of confiding girlhood—do we see Lucy relax her hold of the flask, and reeling forward, fall heavily across the prostrate form of her lover. These three—the murderer, the child of fractious whim and

[1] *Épanchement:* outpouring (of emotion).

[2] *Du reste:* besides.

ungovernable passion, the self denying woman, to whom infamy is pleasant, so it be the price of her lover's society—the pariah, clinging, cerement-like, to the only hand that has ever clasped hers in friendly grasp—stiffening horridly in the rack of death, and clenching, in the last throe, the hem of each other's garment—oh! 'tis a mournful, a sickening picture!

Why did Mr. Melville desert 'that bright little isle of his own,' in the blue waters of the Pacific? Is Polynesia used up? Has the vulgar herd of authors penetrated the fastnesses of those primitive tribes, whose taboo has become naturalized among us, and whose aquatic nymphs have fired the imagination of many a future Bouganville or Cook? Is there not a solitary whale left, whose cetaceous biography might have added another stone to the monumental fame of the author of *Moby-Dick*? If our senses do not deceive us, Mr. Melville will rue his desertion of the forecastle and the virgin forest, for the drawing room and the modest boarding-house chamber. The former was the scene of victories of which no young author need be ashamed; the latter, we fear, has some defeats to witness. Social life is not, perhaps, more difficult to paint than pleasant excursions into Mahomet's paradise; but it requires a different order of talent. Mere analytical description of sentiment, mere wordy anatomy of the heart is not enough for a novel to-day. Modern readers wish to exercise some little judgment of their own; deeds they will have, not characters painted in cold colors, to a hairbreadth or a shade. We are past the age when an artist superscribed his *chef d'oeuvre*[1] with the judicious explanation, 'this is a horse.' Mr. Melville longs for the good old times when the chorus filled the gaps between the acts with a well-timed commentary on the past, and a shrewd guess at the future.

But we have a heavier charge than this to advance. Mr. Herman Melville, the author of *Typee* and *Omoo*, we know; but who is Mr. Herman Melville, the copyist of Carlyle? Most men begin by treading in the wake of a known author, and timidly seeking for shelter under the cover of his costume. Mr. Melville ventured his first flight on his own unaided pinions, and now that their strength has been fully tested, voluntarily descends to the nursery, and catches at leading-strings. No book was ever such a compendium of Carlyle's faults, with so few of his redeeming qualities, as this *Pierre*. We have the same German English—the same transcendental flights of fancy—the same abrupt starts—the same incoherent ravings, and unearthly visions. The depth of thought—the unerring accuracy of eye—the inflexible honesty of purpose, are

[1] *Chef d'oeuvre:* masterpiece.

wanting, at least, nothing outwardly reveals their presence. Like many other people, Mr. Melville seems to have attributed a large share of Carlyle's popularity to his bad English; whereas, in point of fact, his defects of form have always proved a drawback to his success, and nothing short of his matchless excellence of matter, would have introduced him into literary society. A much higher rank would have been held to-day by the author of *Sartor Resartus*, had he clad his striking and brilliant ideas in a less barbarous garb. The fault was original and 'catching.' Herds of pretenders to literary fame have ranged themselves under the banner of the Edinburgh reviewer, and, fancying they were establishing a Carlyle-ist school, have borrowed their master's hump, without stealing a single ray from the flashing of his eye, or a single tone from the harmony of his tongue. Sorry, indeed, are we to class Mr. Melville among these. Could he but sound the depths of his own soul, he would discover pearls of matchless price, that 'twere a sin and a shame to set in pinchbeck finery. Let him but study the classic writers of his own language—dissect their system—brood over their plain, honest, Saxon style—not more French than German—the search would soon convince him that he might still be attractive, though clad in his homely mother tongue. *Soyons de notre pays*,[1] says the poet-philosopher of Passy, it will satisfy our wants, without borrowing tinsel imagery of a Lamartine, or the obscure mysticism of a Goethe or a Kant.

Yet a single admonition. Nature, Mr. Melville, is the proper model of every true artist. Fancy must be kept within proper bounds, and the eye must never be suffered to wander from the reality we are striving to paint. No poetical license can justify such departures from the style of ordinary dialogue as abound in this book. The Tireis-and-Phillis tone of conversation is long since dead and buried; trouble not its ashes. Passion can excuse incoherency, but not fine drawn mannerism, or gaudy *conceits*. For instance, what can be in worse taste than the following reply of Isabel, when Pierre entreats her not to demur to Lucy's living with them?

'Thy hand is the castor's ladle, Pierre, which holds me entirely fluid. Into thy forms and slightest moods of thought thou pourest me; and I there solidify to that form, and take it on, and thenceforth wear it, till once more thou mouldest me anew. If what thou tellest me be thy thought, how can I help its being mine?'

How false this coloring! How far from the sweet simplicity with which Sterne or Tennyson would have robed the timid Isabel!

[1] *Soyons de notre pays:* Let us be of our country.

As we said above, we can trace many of the faults of the book to the deleterious influence of deep, untempered draughts of Carlyle. This particular one may perhaps be laid to the charge of a man who has done no good to our literature—Martin Farquhar Tupper. We want no such *réchauffé*,[1] though the hot dish were, at its first appearance on table, worthy the palate of an epicure; we want our own author, in his own unborrowed garb, adorned with his own jewels, and composing his features into that countenance and expression which nature intended they should wear.

106. Unsigned notice, *Godey's Magazine and Lady's Book*

October 1852, xlv, 390

We really have nothing to add to the severity of the critical notices which have already appeared in respect to this elegantly printed volume; for, in all truth, all the notices which we have seen have been severe enough to satisfy the author, as well as the public, that he has strangely mistaken his own powers and the patience of his friends in presuming to leave his native element, the ocean, and his original business of harpooning whales, for the mysteries and 'ambiguities' of metaphysics, love, and romance. It may be, however, that the heretofore intelligible and popular author has merely assumed his present transcendental metamorphosis, in order that he may have range and scope enough to satirize the ridiculous pretensions of some of our modern literati. Under the supposition that such has been his intention, we submit the following notice of his book, as the very best off-hand effort we could make in imitation of his style: Melodiously breathing an inane mysteriousness, into the impalpable airiness of our unsearchable sanctum, this wonderful creation of its ineffable author's sublime-winging imagination has been fluttering its snow-like-invested pinions upon our multi-

[1] *Réchauffé:* warmed-over dish.

tudinous table. Mysteriously breathing an inane melody, it has been beautifying the innermost recesses of our visual organs with the luscious purpleness and superb goldness of its exterior adornment. We have listened to its outbreathing of sweet-swarming sounds, and their melodious, mournful, wonderful, and unintelligible melodiousness has 'dropped like pendulous, glittering icicles,' with soft-ringing silveriness, upon our never-to-be-delighted-sufficiently organs of hearing; and, in the insignificant significancies of that deftly-stealing and wonderfully-serpentining melodiousness, we have found an infinite, unbounded, inexpressible mysteriousness of nothingness.

107. Unsigned notice, *Graham's Magazine*

October 1852, xli, 445

This work is generally considered a failure. The cause of its ill-success is certainly not to be sought in its lack of power. None of Melville's novels equals the present in force and subtlety of thinking and unity of purpose. Many of the scenes are wrought out with great splendor and vigor, and a capacity is evinced of holding with a firm grasp, and describing with a masterly distinctness, some of the most evanescent phenomena of morbid emotions. But the spirit pervading the whole book is intolerably unhealthy, and the most friendly reader is obliged at the end to protest against such a provoking perversion of talent and waste of power. The author has attempted seemingly to combine in it the peculiarities of Poe and Hawthorne, and has succeeded in producing nothing but a powerfully unpleasant caricature of morbid thought and passion. Pierre, we take it, is crazy, and the merit of the book is in clearly presenting the psychology of his madness; but the details of such a mental malady as that which afflicts Pierre are almost as disgusting as those of physical disease itself.

108. George Washington Peck, from an unsigned review, *American Whig Review*

November 1852, xvi, 446–54

A bad book! Affected in dialect, unnatural in conception, repulsive in plot, and inartistic in construction. Such is Mr. Melville's worst and latest work.

Some reputations seem to be born of accident. There are commonplace men who on some fine day light, unknown to themselves, upon a popular idea, and suddenly rise on the strength of it into public favor. They stride the bubble for a little while, but at last its prismatic hues begin to fade; men see that the object of their applause has after all but an unsubstantial basis, and when at length the frail foundation bursts, they fall back into their original obscurity, unheeded and unlamented. Mr. Melville has experienced some such success. A few years back, he gave to the world a story of romantic adventure; this was untrue in its painting, coarse in its coloring, and often tedious and prolix in its descriptive passages. But there was a certain air of rude romance about it, that captivated the general public. It depicted scenes in a strange land, and dealt with all the interests that circle around men whose lives are passed in peril. Nor were appeals to the grosser instincts of humanity wanting. Naked women were scattered profusely through the pages, and the author seemed to feel that in a city where the ballet was admired, *Typee* would be successful.* Mr. Melville thought he had hit the key-note to fame. His book was reprinted in all directions, and people talked about it, as much from the singularity of its title as from any intrinsic merit it possessed.

This was encouraging, and Mr. Melville evidently thought so, for he immediately issued a series of books in the same strain. *Omoo*, *Mardi*, *White-Jacket*, *Redburn*, followed one another in quick succession; and the foolish critics, too blind to perceive that the books derived their chief interest from the fact of the scenes being laid in countries little known, and that the author had no other stock in trade beyond tropical scenery and

* Mr. Cornelius Mathews was, we believe, the first to designate this prurient taste under the happy and specific head of 'the ballet-feeling.'

eccentric sailors, applauded to the very echo. This indiscriminating praise produced its usual effect. Mr. Melville fancied himself a genius, and the result of this sad mistake has been—*Pierre.*

As a general rule, sea-stories are very effective, and to those versed in nautical lore, very easy writing. The majority of the reading public are landsmen, and the events of an ocean-life come to them recommended by the charm of novelty. They cannot detect the blunders, and incongruity passes with them for originality. The author can make his vessel and his characters perform the most impossible feats, and who, except the favored few that themselves traverse the sea professionally, will be one bit the wiser? The scope for events is also limited, and this very limitation renders the task of writing a sea-tale more simple. A storm, a wreck, a chase and a battle, a mutiny, desertions, and going into and leaving port, with perhaps a fire at sea, form the principal 'properties' of a salt-water artist. Considerable descriptive powers are, we admit, necessary to the management of these materials. The storm must be wild, the battle fierce, and the fire terrible; but these, after all, are broad outlines, and require little delicacy of handling to fill them in. Sometimes, as in the *Pilot*, one finds a veil of pathetic tenderness and grace flung over the characters, but as a general rule in nautical fictions, the wit is coarse, the pathos clumsy, and the most striking characters are invariably unnatural.

It is when a writer comes to deal with the varied interests of a more extended life; when his hand must touch in harmonious succession the numberless chords of domestic sorrows, duties and affections, and draw from each the proper vibration; when he has to range among the ever-changing relations of every-day humanity, and set each phase of being down in its correct lineaments; it is then he discovers that something more is necessary for the task than a mere arrangement of strong words in certain forms,—or the trick of painting nature, until, like a ranting actress, she pleases certain tastes according as she deviates from truth.

Mr. Melville's previous stories, all sea-born as they were, went down the public throat because they were prettily gilt with novelty. There are crowds of people who will run after a new pill, and swallow it with avidity, because it is new, and has a long Greek name. It may be made of bread, or it may be made of poison; the novelty of the affair renders all considerations of its composition quite immaterial. They learn the name, eat the bolus, and pay the doctor. We have a shrewd suspicion that the uncouth and mysterious syllables with which Mr. Melville baptized his books had much to do with their success. Like Doctor Dulcamara, he gave his wares an exciting title, and trusted to Providence for the rest. The enchantment worked. The mystic cabala of 'OMOO, *by the author of* TYPEE,' was enough in itself to turn any common novel-reader's brain, and the books went off as well as a collection of magic rings would in Germany, or the latest batch of *Agnus Deis*[1] in an Italian village. People had little opportunity of judging of their truth. Remote scenes and savage actors gave a fine opportunity for high coloring and exaggerated outline, of which Mr. Melville was not slow to avail himself, and hence Fayaway is as unreal as the scenery with which she is surrounded.

We do not blame Mr. Melville for these deviations from truth. It is not much matter if South Sea savages are painted like the heroes of a penny theatre, and disport themselves amid pasteboard groves, and lakes of canvas. We can afford Mr. Melville full license to do what he likes with *Omoo* and its inhabitants; it is only when he presumes to thrust his tragic *Fantoccini*[2] upon us, as representatives of our own race, that we feel compelled to turn our critical Ægis upon him, and freeze him into silence.

Pierre aims at something beyond the mere records of adventure contained in *Mardi* and *Omoo*. The author, doubtless puffed up by the very false applause which some critics chose to bestow upon him, took for granted that he was a genius, and made up his mind to write a fine book; and he has succeeded in writing a fine book with a vengeance. Our experience of literature is necessarily large, but we unhesitatingly state, that from the period when the Minerva press was in fashion, up to the present time, we never met with so turgid, pretentious, and useless a book as *Pierre*. It is always an unpleasant and apparently invidious statement for a critic to make, that he can find nothing worthy of praise in a work under consideration; but in the case of *Pierre* we feel bound to add to the assertion the sweeping conclusion, that there we find every thing to condemn. If a repulsive, unnatural and indecent plot, a style disfigured by every paltry affectation of the worst German school, and ideas perfectly unparalleled for earnest absurdity, are deserving of condemnation, we think that our already expressed sentence upon *Pierre* will meet with the approval of every body who has sufficient strength of mind to read it through.

Mr. Pierre Glendinning, the hero of the book, and intended by the author to be an object of our mournful admiration, supports in the course of the story the arduous characters of a disobedient son, a dishonest

[1] *Agnus Deis:* wax disks stamped with the figure of a lamb and blessed by the pope.
[2] *Fantoccini:* puppets.

lover, an incestuous brother, a cold-blooded murderer, and an unrepentant suicide. This *repertoire* is agreeably relieved by his playing the part of a madman whenever he is not engaged in doing any thing worse.

This agreeable young gentleman is the only son of a widow lady of large fortune, who coquets in her old age with suitors about the same age as Pierre. And to render the matter still more interesting, Pierre by mutual consent sinks the son, and deports himself by word and look towards his mother as a lover; while she, charming coquette of fifty that she is, readily imitates this delightful *abandon*. . . .

. . . Mr. Melville has done a very serious thing, a thing which not even unsoundness of intellect could excuse. He might have been mad to the very pinnacle of insanity; he might have torn our poor language into tatters, and made from the shreds a harlequin suit in which to play his tricks; he might have piled up word upon word, and adjective upon adjective, until he had built a pyramid of nonsense, which should last to the admiration of all men; he might have done all this and a great deal more, and we should not have complained. But when he dares to outrage every principle of virtue; when he strikes with an impious, though, happily, weak hand, at the very foundations of society, we feel it our duty to tear off the veil with which he has thought to soften the hideous features of the idea, and warn the public against the reception of such atrocious doctrines. If Mr. Melville had reflected at all—and certainly we find in him but few traces of reflection—when he was writing this book, his better sense would perhaps have informed him that there are certain ideas so repulsive to the general mind that they themselves are not alone kept out of sight, but, by a fit ordination of society, every thing that might be supposed to even collaterally suggest them is carefully shrouded in a decorous darkness. Nor has any man the right, in his morbid craving after originality, to strip these horrors of their decent mystery. But the subject which Mr. Melville has taken upon himself to handle is one of no ordinary depravity; and however he may endeavor to gloss the idea over with a platonic polish, no matter how energetically he strives to wrap the mystery in a cloud of high-sounding but meaningless words, the main conception remains still unaltered in all its moral deformity. We trust that we have said enough on this topic. It is a subject that we would gladly not have been obliged to approach, and which we are exceedingly grieved that any gentleman pretending to the rank of a man of letters should have chosen to embody in a book. Nor can we avoid a feeling of surprise, that professedly moral and apparently respectable publishers like the Messrs. Harper should have ever consented to issue from their establishment any book containing such glaring abominations as *Pierre*. . . .

Previous to entering more closely upon the singular merits of this book, we have endeavored, we fear but feebly, to give the reader some idea of the ground-work on which Mr. Melville has strung his farrago of words. If we have succeeded, so much the better, for our readers will perhaps appreciate more fully our approaching remarks. If we have not, it matters but little, for the reader will have lost nothing that is worth a regret.

We have already dismissed the immorality of Mr. Melville's book, which is as horrible in its tendency as Shelley's *Cenci*, without a ray of the eloquent genius that lights up the deformity of that terrible play; but we have yet another and less repulsive treat in store for the reader. Mr. Melville's style of writing in this book is probably the most extraordinary thing that an American press ever beheld. It is precisely what a raving lunatic who had read Jean Paul Richter *in a translation* might be supposed to spout under the influence of a particularly moonlight night. Word piled upon word, and syllable heaped upon syllable, until the tongue grows as bewildered as the mind, and both refuse to perform their offices from sheer inability to grasp the magnitude of the absurdities. Who would have believed that in the present day a man would write the following, and another be found to publish it?

> 'Now Pierre began to see mysteries interpierced with mysteries, and mysteries eluding mysteries; and began to seem to see the mere imaginariness of the so supposed solidest principle of human association. Fate had done this for them. Fate had separated brother and sister, till to each other they somehow seemed so not at all.'—Page 193.

There, public! there's a style for you! There, Mr. Hawthorne, you who rely so much upon the quiet force of your language, read that and profit by it! And you, Mr. Longfellow, who love the Germans, and who in 'Hyperion' have given us a sample of an ornate and poetical style, pray read it too, and tell us if it is a wise thing to bind 495 pages of such stuff together, and palm it off upon the public as a book! But here is a string of assertions that we think are not to be surpassed; it is positively refreshing to read them:

> 'Of old Greek times, before man's brain went into doting bondage, and bleached and beaten in Baconian fulling mills, his four limbs lost their barbaric tan and beauty; when the round world was fresh, and rosy, and spicy as a new-plucked apple; all's wilted now! In those bold times, the great dead were not,

turkey-like, dished in trenchers, and set down all garnished in the ground to glut the damned Cyclop like a cannibal; but nobly envious Life cheated the glutton worm, and gloriously burned the corpse; so that the spirit uppointed, and visibly forked to heaven!'—Page 269.

. . . A perfectly plain and pure style is the only one which we cannot properly analyze. Its elements are so equally combined that no one preponderates over the other, and we are not able to discover the exact boundary line that separates the art of the author from the nature of the man. But who writes such a style now-a-days? We feel convinced that echo will *not* answer, 'Mr. Melville.'

The author of *Omoo* has his own pecularities. The English language he seems to think is capable of improvement, but his scheme for accomplishing this end is rather a singular one. Carlyle's compound words and Milton's latinic ones sink into insignificance before Mr. Melville's extraordinary concoctions. The gentleman, however, appears to be governed by a very distinct principle in his eccentricities of composition, and errs systematically. The essence of this great eureka, this philological reform, consists in 'est' and 'ness,' added to every word to which they have no earthly right to belong. Feeling it to be our duty to give currency to every new discovery at all likely to benefit the world or literature, we present a few of Mr. Melville's word-combinations, in the hope that our rising authors will profit by the lesson, and thereby increase the richness and intelligibility of their style:

Flushfulness,	page 7	Solidest,	page 193
Patriarchalness,	,, 12	Uncapitulatable,	,, 229
Humanness,	,, 16	Ladylikeness,	,, 235
Heroicness,	,, do.	Electricalness,	,, 206
Perfectest,	,, 41	Ardentest,	,, 193
Imaginariness,	,, 193	Unsystemizable,	,, 191
Insolubleness,	,, 188	Youngness,	,, 190
Recallable,	,, 186	Unemigrating,	,, 470
Entangledly,	,, 262	Unrunagate,	,, do.
Intermarryingly,	,, 151	Undoffable,	,, do.
Magnifiedly,	,, 472		

After such a list, what shall we say? Shall we leave Mr. Melville to the tender mercies of the Purists, or shall we execute vengeance upon him ourselves? We would gladly pursue the latter course if we only knew how to accomplish it. As to destroying or abusing the book, we cannot make it appear worse than it is; and if we continue our remarks upon it, it is simply because we have a duty to perform by every improper work, which we have no right to leave unfinished. . . .

Perhaps one of the most remarkable features in *Pierre*, is the boldness of the metaphors with which it is so thickly studded. Mr. Melville's imagination stops at nothing, and clears a six-barred simile or a twenty-word antithesis with equal dexterity and daring. It is no light obstacle that will bring him up in his headlong course, and he scoffs alike at the boundaries of common sense and the limits of poetical propriety. We have just caught an image which will serve our purpose, and transfix it, butterfly-like, on our critical pin, for the admiration of scientific etymologists. It is a fine specimen, and quite perfect of its kind. Fortunately for the world, however, the species is very rare:

'An infixing stillness now thrust a long rivet through the night, and fast nailed it to that side of the world!'—Page 219.

This is a grand and simple metaphor. To realize it thoroughly, all we have to do is to imagine some Titantic upholsterer armed with a gigantic nail, and hammer to match, hanging one hemisphere with black crape. . . .

We have been so far particular in pointing out Mr. Melville's faults. We have attached a certain degree of importance to each of them, from the fact that we are obliged to look upon him in the light of an experienced author, and cannot allow him that boyish license which we are always ready to grant to tyros who lose themselves for the first time amid the bewildering paths of literature. Mr. Melville has written good books, and tasted largely of success, and he ought to have known better. We regret that we are not able to temper our criticism with some unalloyed praise. Critics too often gain the reputation of deriving pleasure from the depreciation of others, but it is those who are ignorant of the art that say so. The true critic rejoices with a boyish enthusiasm when he meets with a work worthy of his admiration. The very nature of his avocation enhances the pleasure he feels at the recognition of original beauty. He that has been travelling for many a weary day over dry and dusty tracks of letter-press, strewn thickly with withered commonplaces, and enlivened only with newly-feathered platitudes, must experience a thrill of strange delight when he suddenly emerges from the desolate path he has been pursuing, and comes upon a rich and pleasant pasture of thought. Believe not, fair Public, that this weary critic will not do the fresh mead justice. Believe rather that in his wild pleasure at lighting upon this pure untrodden ground, where things do not smell of second-hand nature, he will rush madly into the extreme of praise, and search as sedulously for the hidden flowers of beauty as he did before for faults. Critics are not envious or malicious—they are simply just; and being just, they are obliged to condemn three fourths of the books that are submitted to their notice. It is not by any means with a view of proving our magnanimity that we quote the following passage from *Pierre* as a specimen of Mr. Melville's better genius. Even this very passage is disfigured by affectations and faults, which, in any other book, would condemn it to exclusion; but in a work like *Pierre*, where all else is so intensely bad, and this is probably the only passage in it that could be extracted with advantage, we feel that we would be doing our author an injustice if, after setting forth all his sins so systematically, we did not present to our readers some favorable specimen of his powers. The passage we subjoin is a description of old Pierre Glendinning, the grandfather of the young Pierre, our ambiguous hero:

[quotes from book II, part iii, 'Now, this grand old' to 'had reined before.']

We have dwelt long enough upon these 'Ambiguities.' We fear that if we were to continue much longer, we should become ambiguous ourselves. We have, we think, said sufficient to show our readers that Mr. Melville is a man wholly unfitted for the task of writing wholesome fictions; that he possesses none of the faculties necessary for such work; that his fancy is diseased, his morality vitiated, his style nonsensical and ungrammatical, and his characters as far removed from our sympathies as they are from nature.

Let him continue, then, if he must write, his pleasant sea and island tales. We will be always happy to hear Mr. Melville discourse about savages, but we must protest against any more Absurdities, misnamed 'Ambiguities.'

109. From an unsigned review, *Athenæum*

20 November 1852, 1265–6

The brilliant success of some recent American fictionists makes us turn with more than common interest to any new work coming from transatlantic authors. This volume is a would-be utterance of 'Young Yankee' sentimentalism:—but beyond that its writer may be a subject of the States, we can discern nothing either American or original in its pages. It reads like an 'upsetting' into English of the first novel of a very whimsical and lackadaisical young student at

the U—
niversity of Gottingen.

It is one of the most diffuse doses of transcendentalism offered for a long time to the public. When he sat down to compose it, the author evidently had not determined what he was going to write about. Its plot is amongst the inexplicable 'ambiguities' of the book,—the style is a prolonged succession of spasms,—and the characters are a marrowless tribe of phantoms, flitting through dense clouds of transcendental mysticism. 'Be sure,' said Pope to a young author, 'when you have written any passage that you think particularly fine—*to erase it*.' If this precept were applied to *Pierre; or, the Ambiguities*,—its present form would shrink into almost as many pages as there are now chapters. German literature with its depths and shallows is too keenly appreciated in this country for readers to endure Germanism at second hand. We take up novels to be amused—not bewildered,—in search of pleasure for the mind—not in pursuit of cloudy metaphysics; and it is no refreshment after the daily toils and troubles of life, for a reader to be soused into a torrent rhapsody uttered in defiance of taste and sense. . . .

That many readers will not follow 'the moody way' of Pierre, is in our apprehension not amongst the 'ambiguities' of the age. The present chaotic performance has nothing American about it, except that it reminds us of a prairie in print,—wanting the flowers and freshness of the savannahs, but almost equally puzzling to find a way through it.

GENERAL ESTIMATES

1853

110. Fitz-James O'Brien, from 'Our Young Authors—Melville,' unsigned article, *Putnam's Monthly Magazine*

February 1853, i, 155–64

O'Brien (1828–62), Irish-born author and critic, contributed poems and short stories as well as critical pieces to the *American Review*, *Putnam's*, *Harper's*, and *Vanity Fair*. He died while fighting for the Union side in the American Civil War.

When *Typee* first appeared, great was the enthusiasm. The oddity of the name sets critics a wondering. Reviewers who were in the habit of writing an elaborate review of a work, from merely glancing over the heads of the chapters, and thinking a little over the title-page, were completely at fault. *Typee* told nothing. It had no antecedents. It might have been an animal, or it might have been a new game, or it might have been a treatise on magic. Did they open the book, and look over the chapters, they were not much wiser. Barbarous congregations of syllables, such as Kory-Kory, Nukuheva, Moa Artua, met their eyes. The end of it was, that the whole tribe of London and American critics had to sit down and read it all, before they dared speak of a book filled with such mysterious syllables. From reading they began to like it. There was a great deal of rich, rough talent about it. The scenes were fresh, and highly colored; the habits and manners described had the charm of novelty; and the style, though not the purest or most elegant, had a fine narrative facility about it, that rendered it very pleasurable reading, after the maudlin journeys in Greece—travels in the Holy

Land, full of Biblical raptures, and yacht-tours in the Mediterranean, where monotonous sea-dinners and vulgar shore-pleasures were faithfully chronicled, with such like trash that had been inundating the literary market for years previous. *Typee* was successful. It could scarcely be otherwise. Prosy to the last degree, in some portions, there yet were scenes in it full of exquisite description, and novel characters, who, like Fayaway, were in themselves so graceful, that we could not help loving them. Mr. Melville found that he had opened a fertile field, which he was not slow to work. Sea novels had, as it were, been run into the ground by Marryatt, Chamier, and Cooper. People were growing weary of shipwrecks and fires at sea. Every possible incident that could occur, on board men-of-war, privateers, and prizes, had been described over and over again, with an ability that left nothing to be desired. The whole of a sailor's life was laid bare to us. We knew exactly what they ate, what they drank, and at what hours they ate and drank it. Their language, their loves, their grievances, and their mutinies, were as familiar as the death of Cock Robin. Even staid, sober, land-lubbering people, who got sea-sick crossing in a Brooklyn ferry-boat, began to know the names of ropes and spars, and imagined no longer that a 'scupper' was one of the sails. Mr. Melville came forward with his books, to relieve this state of well informed dulness. By a happy mixture of fresh land scenery, with some clever ship-life, he produced a brilliant amalgam, that was loudly welcomed by the public. Who does not relish Dr. Long-ghost all the better, for leaving the Julia, albeit prisoner-wise, and going ashore to that funny Calabooza Beretance where he has epileptic fits, in order to get a good dinner, and makes a fan out of a paddle, to keep off the mosquitoes. Does not the wild voluptuous dance of the 'back-sliding girls,' in the Valley of Martair, contrast magnificently with that terrible night off Papeetee, when the Mowree tried to run 'Little Jule' ashore upon the coral breakers. In this contrast, which abounds in Mr. Melville's books, lies one of his greatest charms. Sea and shore mingling harmoniously together, like music-chords. Now floating on the wide blue southern seas—the sport of calms and hurricanes—the companion of the sullen Bent, the Doctor and Captain Guy. Anon clasping to our bosoms those jaunty, impassioned creatures, yclept Day-born, Night-born, and the Wakeful; or watching Fayaway laving her perfect, shining form in the cool lake, by whose green bank the cocoa sheds its fruit, and the bread-fruit tree towers. All this is delicious, to those who have been playing vulgar midshipman's tricks with Chamier and Marryatt, and comes to us pleasantly even after

Cooper's powerful and tender sea-tales.

It is no easy matter to pronounce which of Mr. Melville's books is the best. All of them (and he has published a goodly number, for so young an author) have had their own share of success, and their own peculiar merits, always saving and excepting *Pierre*—wild, inflated, repulsive that it is.

For us there is something very charming about *Mardi*, all the time fully aware of its sad defects in taste and style. Of course, we give Mr. Melville every credit for his deliberate plagiarisms of old Sir Thomas Browne's gorgeous and metaphorical manner. Affectation upon affectation is scattered recklessly through its pages. Wild similes, cloudy philosophy, all things turned topsy-turvy, until we seem to feel all earth melting away from beneath our feet, and nothing but *Mardi* remaining. . . .

. . . From forms, and forms alone does Melville take his text. He looks out of himself, and takes a rich outline view of what he sees. He is essentially exoterical in feeling. Matter is his god. His dreams are material. His philosophy is sensual. Beautiful women, shadowy lakes, nodding, plumy trees, and succulent banquets, make Melville's scenery, unless his theme utterly preclude all such. His language is rich and heavy, with a plating of imagery. He has a barbaric love of ornament, and does not mind much how it is put on. Swept away by this sensual longing, he frequently writes at random. One can see that he uses certain words only because they roll off the pen lusciously and roundly, just as a child, who is entirely the sport of sense, grasps at the largest apple. In *Mardi* is this peculiarly obvious. A long experience of the South sea islanders has no doubt induced this. The languages of these groups are singularly mellifluous and resonant, vowels enter largely into the composition of every word, and dissyllabled words are rare. Mr. Melville has been attracted by this. Whenever he can use a word of four syllables where a monosyllable would answer just as well, he chooses the former. A certain fulness of style is very attractive. Sir Thomas Browne, from whom Mr. Melville copies much that is good, is a great friend of magnificent diction. And his tract on urn burial is as lofty and poetical as if Memnon's statue chanted it, when the setting sun fell aslant across the Pyramids. But we find no nonsense in Sir Thomas. In every thing he says there is a deep meaning, although sometimes an erroneous one. We cannot always say as much for Mr. Melville. In his latest work he transcended even the jargon of Paracelsus and his followers. The Rosetta stone gave up its secret, but we believe that to the end of time *Pierre* will remain an ambiguity.

Mardi, we believe, is intended to embody all the philosophy of which Mr. Melville is capable, and we have no hesitation in saying that the philosophical parts are the worst. We do not for a moment pretend to say that we understand the system laid down by the author. Whether there be a system in it at all, is at least somewhat problematical, but when Mr. Melville does condescend to be intelligible, what he has to say for himself in the way of philosophy, is so exceedingly stale and trite, that it would be more in place in a school-boy's copy-book, than in a romance otherwise distinguished for splendor of imagery, and richness of diction. The descriptive painting in this wild book is gorgeous and fantastic in the extreme. It is a tapestry of dreams, worked with silken threads, dyed in the ocean of an Eastern sunset. Nothing however strange startles us as we float onwards through this misty panorama. . . .

All these characters flit before us in *Mardi*, and bring with them no consciousness of their unreality and deception. As shadows they come to us, but they are sensual shades. Their joys thrill through us. When they banquet in drowsy splendor—when they wander upon beaches of pearls and rubies—when they wreath their brows with blossoms more fragrant and luscious than the buds that grow in Paradise, our senses twine with theirs, and we forget every thing, save the vision of their gorgeous pleasures. It is this sensual power that holds the secret of Mr. Melville's first successes. No matter how unreal the scenery, if the pleasure be but truly painted, the world will cry 'bravo!' We draw pictures of Gods and Goddesses, and hang them on our walls, but we take good care to let their divinity be but nominal. Diana, Juno, Venus, are they known, but they loom out from the canvas, substantial, unadulterated women. Seldom does there live an Ixion who loves to embrace clouds. Call it a cloud if you will, and if it have the appearance of flesh and blood, the adorer will be satisfied. But we doubt if there is to be found any man enthusiast enough to clasp a vapor to his heart, be it schirri-shaped or cumulous, and baptized with the sweetest name ever breathed from the Attic tongue. Mr. Melville therefore deals in vapors, but he twines around them so cunningly all human attributes, and pranks them out so lusciously with all the witcheries of sense, that we forget their shadowy nomenclatures, and worship the substantial incarnation.

It must not be imagined from this, that Mr. Melville is incapable of dealing with the events of more matter-of-fact life. He is averse to it, no doubt, and if we may judge by Pierre, is becoming more averse to it as he grows older. But he sometimes takes the vulgar monster by the shoulders and wields it finely. . . .

Typee, the first and most successful of Mr. Melville's books, commands attention for the clearness of its narrative, the novelty of its scenery, and the simplicity of its style, in which latter feature it is a wondrous contrast to *Mardi*, *Moby Dick*, and *Pierre*. . . .

White Jacket is a pure sea-book, but very clever. It is a clear, quiet picture of life on board of a man-of-war. It has less of Mr. Melville's faults than almost any of his works, and is distinguished for clear, wholesome satire, and a manly style. There is a scene describing the amputation of a sailor's leg by a brutal, cold-blooded surgeon, Patella, that Smollett might have painted. We would gladly quote it, but that it rather exceeds the limits usually afforded in an article so short as ours.

There is one chapter in which the hero details the loss of the White Jacket, from wearing which, he and the book take their name, that strikes us as a very fine piece of descriptive writing. We give it entire.

[quotes chapter 92, complete]

This is fine. We have often met with descriptions, some well painted enough, of dizzy aerial adventures, but never one like this. Our ears tingle as we read it. The air surges around us as we fall from that fearful height. The sea divides, the green mist flashes into a thousand hues, and we sit for an instant a stride of Death's balance. Weight, unutterable weight presses upon our shoulders, and we seem as if about to be crushed into nothingness. Then a sudden change. A revulsion which is accompanied with soft, low music; and we float upwards. We seem gliding through an oiled ocean, so smoothly do we pass. It breaks, it parts above our head. The next moment we shoot out from a cloud of feathers, and are battling with the waves.

In *Redburn*, we find an account of the death of a sailor, by spontaneous combustion. Well described, poetically described, fraught with none of the revolting scenery which it is so easy to gather round such an end. In the last number of *Bleak House*, Mr. Dickens has attempted the same thing. He has also performed what he attempted. But, if ever man deserved public prosecution for his writing, he does, for this single passage. A hospital student could not read it without sickening. A ghoul, who had lived all his days upon the festering corruption of the graveyard, could have written nothing more hideously revolting than the death of Krook. It is as loathsome to read it as to enter one of the charnels in London city. We do not believe that a woman of sensitive nerves could take it up without fainting over the details. For ourselves, we fling the book away, with an anathema on the author that we should be sorry for him to hear.

Mr. Melville does not improve with time. His later books are a decided falling off, and his last scarcely deserves naming; this however we scarce believe to be an indication of exhaustion. Keats says beautifully in his preface to 'Endymion,' that 'The imagination of a boy is healthy, and the mature imagination of a man is healthy, but there is a space of life between, in which the soul is in a ferment, the character undecided, the way of life uncertain, the ambition thick-sighted.'

Just at present we believe the author of *Pierre* to be in this state of ferment. *Typee*, his first book, was healthy; *Omoo* nearly so; after that came *Mardi*, with its excusable wildness; then came *Moby Dick*, and *Pierre* with its inexcusable insanity. We trust that these rhapsodies will end the interregnum of nonsense to which Keats refers, as forming a portion of every man's life; and that Mr. Melville will write less at random and more at leisure, than of late. Of his last book we would fain not speak, did we not feel that he is just now at that stage of author-life when a little wholesome advice may save him a hundred future follies. When we first read *Pierre*, we felt a strong inclination to believe the whole thing to be a well-got-up hoax. We remembered having read a novel in six volumes once of the same order, called *The Abbess*, in which the stilted style of writing is exposed very funnily; and, as a specimen of unparalleled bombast, we believed it to be unequalled until we met with *Pierre*. In *Mardi* there is a strong vein of vague, morphinized poetry, running through the whole book. We do not know what it means from the beginning to the end, but we do not want to know, and accept it as a rhapsody. Babbalanja philosophizing drowsily, or the luxurious sybaritical King Media, lazily listening to the hum of waters, are all shrouded dimly in opiate-fumes, and dream-clouds, and we love them only as sensual shadows. Whatever they say or do; whether they sail in a golden boat, or eat silver fruits, or make pies of emeralds and rubies, or any thing else equally ridiculous, we feel perfectly satisfied that it is all right, because there is no claim made upon our practical belief. But if Mr. Melville had placed Babbalanja and Media and Yoomy in the Fifth Avenue, instead of a longitude and latitude less inland; if we met them in theatres instead of palm groves, and heard Babbalanja lecturing before the Historical Society instead of his dreamy islanders, we should feel naturally rather indignant at such a tax upon our credulity. We would feel inclined to say with the Orientals, that Mr. Melville had been laughing at our beards, and Pacha-like condemn on the instant to a literary bastinado. Now *Pierre* has all the madness of *Mardi*, without its vague, dreamy, poetic charm. All Mr. Melville's many affectations of style and thought are here crowded together in a mad mosaic. Talk of Rabelais's word-nonsense! there was always something queer, and odd, and funny, gleaming through his unintelligibility. But *Pierre* transcends all the nonsense-writing that the world ever beheld.

Thought staggers through each page like one poisoned. Language is drunken and reeling. Style is antipodical, and marches on its head. Then the moral is bad. Conceal it how you will, a revolting picture presents itself. A wretched, cowardly boy for a hero who from some feeling of mad romance, together with a mass of inexplicable reasons which, probably, the author alone fathoms, chooses to live in poverty with his illegitimate sister, whom he passes off to the world as his wife, instead of being respectably married to a legitimate cousin. Everybody is vicious in some way or other. The mother is vicious with pride. Isabel has a cancer of morbid, vicious, minerva-press-romance, eating into her heart. Lucy Tartan is viciously humble, and licks the dust beneath Pierre's feet viciously. Delly Ulver is humanly vicious, and in the rest of the book, whatever of vice is wanting in the remaining characters, is made up by superabundant viciosities of style.

Let Mr. Melville stay his step in time. He totters on the edge of a precipice, over which all his hard-earned fame may tumble with such another weight as *Pierre* attached to it. He has peculiar talents, which may be turned to rare advantage. Let him diet himself for a year or two on Addison, and avoid Sir Thomas Browne, and there is little doubt but that he will make a notch on the American Pine.

111. 'Sir Nathaniel,' 'American Authorship. No. IV.—Herman Melville,' article, *New Monthly Magazine*

July 1853, xcviii, 300–8

The Muses, it was once alleged by Christopher North, have but scantly patronised sea-faring verse: they have neglected ship-building, and deserted the dockyards,—though in Homer's days they kept a private yacht, of which he was captain. 'But their attempts to re-establish anything like a club, these two thousand years or so, have miserably failed; and they have never quite recovered their nerves since the loss of poor Falconer, and their disappointment at the ingratitude shown to Dibdin.' And Sir Kit adds, that though they do indeed now and then talk of the 'deep blue sea,' and occasionally, perhaps, skim over it like sea-plovers, yet they avoid the quarter-deck and all its discipline, and decline the dedication of the cat-o'-nine-tails, in spite of their number.

By them, nevertheless, must have been inspired—in fitful and irregular afflatus—some of the prose-poetry of Herman Melville's sea-romances. Ocean breezes blow from his tales of Atlantic and Pacific cruises. Instead of landsman's grey goose quill, he seems to have plucked a quill from skimming curlew, or to have snatched it, a fearful joy, from hovering albatross, if not from the wings of the wind itself. The superstition of life on the waves has no abler interpreter, unequal and undisciplined as he is—that superstition almost inevitably engendered among men who live, as it has been said, 'under a solemn sense of eternal danger, one inch only of plank (often worm-eaten) between themselves and the grave; and who see for ever one wilderness of waters.'* His intimacy with the sights and sounds of that wilderness, almost entitles him to the reversion of the mystic 'blue cloak' of Keats's submarine greybeard, in which

——every ocean form
Was woven with a black distinctness; storm,
And calm, and whispering, and hideous roar

* Thomas de Quincey.

Were emblem'd in the woof; with every shape
That skims, or dives, or sleeps 'twixt cape and cape.*

A landsman, somewhere observes Mr. Tuckerman, can have no conception of the fondness a ship may inspire, before he listens, on a moonlight night, amid the lonely sea, to the details of her build and workings, unfolded by a complacent tar. Moonlight and midseas are much, and a complacent tar is something; but we 'calculate' a landsman *can* get some conception of the true-blue enthusiasm in question, and even become slightly inoculated with it in his own *terra firma* person, under the tuition of a Herman Melville. This graphic narrator assures us, and there needs no additional witness to make the assurance doubly sure, that his sea adventures have often served, when spun as a yarn, not only to relieve the weariness of many a night-watch, but to excite the warmest sympathies of his shipmates. Not that we vouch for the fact of his having experienced the adventures in literal truth, or even of being the pet of the fo'castle as yarn-spinner extraordinary. But we do recognise in him and in his narratives (the earlier ones, at least) a 'capital' fund of even untold 'interest,' and so richly veined a nugget of the *ben trovato*[1] as to 'take the shine out of' many a golden *vero*.[2] Readers there are, who, having been enchanted by a perusal of *Typee* and *Omoo*, have turned again and rent the author, when they heard a surmise, or an assertion, that his tales were more or less imagination. Others there are, and we are of them, whose enjoyment of the history was little affected by a suspicion of the kind during perusal (which few can evade), or an affirmation of it afterwards. 'And if a little more romantic than truth may warrant, it will be no harm,' is Miles Coverdale's morality, when projecting a chronicle of life at Blithedale. Miles *a raison.*

But to Mr. Melville. And in a new, and not improved aspect. *Exit Omoo; enter Mardi.* And the cry is, *Heu! quantum mutatus ab illo*—

Alas, how changed from him,
This vein of Ercles, and this soul of whim—

changed enough to threaten an *exeunt omnes* of his quondam admirers. The first part of *Mardi* is worthy of its antecedents; but too soon we are hurried whither we would not, and subjected to the caprices, *velut ægri somnia*,[3] of one who, of malice aforethought,

* 'Endymion,' Book III.

[1] *Ben trovato:* well found; well invented.

[2] *Vero:* truth.

[3] *Velut ægri somnia:* just as the dreams of a sick man.

Delphinum silvis appingit, fluctibus aprum[1]—

the last clause signifying that he *bores* us with his 'sea of troubles,' and provokes us to take arms against, and (if possible) by opposing, end them. Yet do some prefer his new shade of marine blue, and exult in this his 'sea-change into something rich and strange.' And the author of *Nile Notes* defines *Mardi*, as a whole, to be unrhymed poetry, rhythmical and measured—the swell of its sentences having a low, lapping cadence, like the dip of the sun-stilled, Pacific waves,—and sometimes the grave music of Bacon's Essays! Thou wert right, O Howadji, to add, 'Who but an American could have written them.' Alas, Cis-Atlantic criticism compared them to Foote's 'What, no soap? So he died, and she very imprudently married the barber,'—with the wedding concomitants of the Picninnies and Great Panjandrum and gunpowder-heeled terpsichorics—Foote being, moreover, preferred to Melville, on the score of superiority in sense, diversion, and brevity. Nevertheless, subsequent productions have proved the author of *Mardi* to plume himself on his craze, and love to have it so. And what will he do in the end thereof?

In tone and taste *Redburn* was an improvement upon *Mardi*, but was as deficient as the latter was overfraught with romance and adventure. Whether fiction or fact, this narrative of the first voyage of Wellingborough Redburn,* a New York merchant's son, as sailor-boy in a merchant-vessel, is even prosy, bald, and eventless; and would be dull beyond redemption, as a story, were not the author gifted with a scrutinising gaze, and a habit of taking notes as well as 'prenting' them, which ensures his readers against absolute common-place. It is true, he more than once plunges into episodic extravaganzas—such as the gambling-house frenzy of Harry Bolton—but these are, in effect, the dullest of all his moods; and tend to produce, what surely they are inspired by, blue devils. Nor is he over chary of introducing the repulsive,—notwithstanding his disclaimer, 'Such is the fastidiousness of some readers, that, many times, they must lose the most striking incidents in a narrative like mine:'† for not only some, but most readers, are too fastidious to enjoy such scenes as that of the starving, dying mother and children in a Liverpool cellar, and that of the dead mariner, from whose lips darted

* The hero himself is a sort of amalgam of Perceval Keene and Peter Simple—the keenness strangely antedating the simplicity.

† *Redburn*, vol. ii., ch. 27.

[1] *Delphinum . . . aprum:* paints a dolphin in a forest or a wild boar in the waves. Horace, *Ars Poetica*, 30.

out, when the light touched them 'threads of greenish fire, like a forked tongue,' till the cadaverous face was 'crawled over by a swarm of worm-like flames'—a hideous picture, as deserving of a letter of remonstrance on æsthetic grounds, as Mr. Dickens' spontaneous combustion case (Krook) on physical.* Apart from these exceptions, the experiences of Redburn during his 'first voyage' are singularly free from excitement, and even incident. . . .

Next came *White Jacket; or, the World in a Man-of-War*. The hero's *soubriquet*[1] is derived from his—shirt, or 'white duck frock,' his only wrap-rascal—a garment patched with old socks and old trouser-legs, bedarned and bequilted till stiff as King James's cotton-stuffed and dagger-proof doublet—provided, moreover with a great variety of pockets, pantries, clothes-presses, and cupboards, and 'several unseen recesses behind the arras,'—insomuch, exclaims the proud, glad owner, 'that my jacket, like an old castle, was full of winding stairs, and mysterious closets, crypts, and cabinets; and like a confidential writing-desk, abounded in snug little out-of-the-way lairs and hiding-places, for the storage of valuables.' The adventures of the adventurous proprietor of this encyclopædic toga, this cheap magazine of a coat, are detailed with that eager vivacity, and sometimes that unlicensed extravagance, which are characteristic of the scribe. Some of the sea-pictures are worthy of his highest mood—when a fine imagination over-rides and represses the chaos of a wanton fancy. Give him to describe a storm on the wide waters—the gallant ship labouring for life and against hope—the gigantic masts snapping almost under the strain of the top-sails—the ship's bell dismally tolling, and this at murk midnight—the rampant billows curling their crests in triumph—the gale flattening the mariners against the rigging as they toil upwards, while a hurricane of slanting sleet and hail pelts them in savage wrath: and he will thrill us quiet landsmen who dwell at home at ease.

For so successful a trader in 'marine stores' as Mr. Melville, *The Whale* seemed a speculation every way big with promise. From such a master of his harpoon might have been expected a prodigious hit. There was about blubber and spermaceti something unctuously suggestive, with him for whaleman. And his three volumes entitled *The Whale* undoubtedly contain much vigorous description, much wild power, many striking details. But the effect is distressingly marred throughout by an extravagant treatment of the subject. The style is maniacal—mad as a

* See G. H. Lewes' Two Letters.

[1] *Soubriquet:* nickname.

March hare—mowing, gibbering, screaming, like an incurable Bedlamite, reckless of keeper or strait-waistcoat. Now it vaults on stilts, and performs *Bombastes Furioso* with contortions of figure, and straining strides, and swashbuckler fustian, far beyond *Pistol* in that Ancient's happiest mood. Now it is seized with spasms, acute and convulsive enough to excite bewilderment in all beholders. When he pleases, Mr. Melville can be so lucid, straightforward, hearty, and unaffected, and displays so unmistakable a shrewdness, and satirical sense of the ridiculous, that it is hard to suppose that *he* can have indited the rhodomontade to which we allude. Surely the man is a Doppelganger—a dual number incarnate (singular though he be, in and out of all conscience):—surely he is two single gentlemen rolled into one, but retaining their respective idiosyncrasies—the one sensible, sagacious, observant, graphic, and producing admirable matter—the other maundering, drivelling, subject to paroxysms, cramps, and total collapse, and penning exceeding many pages of unaccountable 'bosh.' So that in tackling every new chapter, one is disposed to question it beforehand, 'Under which king, Bezonian?'—the sane or the insane; the constitutional and legitimate, or the absolute and usurping? Writing of Leviathan, he exclaims, 'Unconsciously my chirography expands into placard capitals. Give me a condor's quill! Give me Vesuvius' crater for an inkstand! Friends, hold my arms!' Oh that his friends had obeyed that summons! They might have saved society from a huge dose of hyperbolical slang, maudlin sentimentalism, and tragi-comic bubble and squeak.

His Yankeeisms are plentiful as blackberries. 'I am tormented,' quoth he, 'with an everlasting itch for things remote.' Remote, too frequently, from good taste, good manners, and good sense. We need not pause at such expressions as 'looking a sort of diabolically funny;'—'beefsteaks done rare;'—'a speechlessly quick chaotic bundling of a man into eternity;'—'bidding adieu to circumspect life, to exist only in a delirious throb.' But why wax fast and furious in a thousand such paragraphs as these:—'In landlessness alone resides the highest truth, indefinite as the Almighty . . . . Take heart, take heart, O Bulkington! Bear thee grimly, demi-god! Up from the spray of thy ocean-perishing—straight up, leaps thy apotheosis!'—'Thou [*scil.* Spirit of Equality] great God! who didst not refuse to the swart convict, Bunyan, the pale, poetic pearl; Thou who didst clothe with doubly hammered leaves of finest gold the stumped and paupered arm of old Cervantes; Thou who didst pick up Andrew Jackson from the pebbles; who didst hurl him upon a war-horse; who didst thunder him higher than a throne!'—'If such a furious trope may stand, his [Capt. Ahab's] special lunacy stormed his general sanity, and carried it, and turned all its concentrated cannon upon its own mad mark . . . . then it was, that his torn body and gashed soul bled into one another; and so interfusing made him mad.'—'And the miser-merman, Wisdom, revealed [to a diving negro][1] his hoarded heaps; and among the joyous, heartless, ever-juvenile eternities, Pip saw the multitudinous, God-omnipresent, coral insects, that out of the firmament of waters heaved the colossal orbs. He saw God's foot upon the treadle of the loom, and spoke it; and therefore his shipmates called him mad.'

The story itself is a strange, wild, furibund thing—about Captain Ahab's vow of revenge against one Moby Dick. And who is Moby Dick? A fellow of a whale, who has made free with the captain's leg; so that the captain now stumps on ivory, and goes circumnavigating the globe in quest of the old offender, and raves by the hour in a lingo borrowed from Rabelais, Carlyle, Emerson, newspapers transcendental and transatlantic, and the magnificent proems of our Christmas pantomimes. Captain Ahab is introduced with prodigious efforts at preparation; and there is really no lack of rude power and character about his presentment—spoiled, however, by the Cambyses' vein in which he dissipates his vigour. His portrait is striking—looking 'like a man cut away from the stake, when the fire has overrunningly wasted all the limbs without consuming them, or taking away one particle from their compacted aged robustness'—a man with a brow gaunt and ribbed, like the black sand beach after some stormy tide has been gnawing it, without being able to drag the firm thing from its place. Ever since his fell encounter with Moby Dick, this impassioned veteran has cherished a wild vindictiveness against the whale, frantically identifying with him not only all his bodily woes, but all his feelings of exasperation—so that the White Whale swims before him 'as the monomaniac incarnation of all those malicious agencies which some deep men feel eating in them, till they are left living on with half a heart and half a lung.' The amiable cannibal Queequeg occasions some stirring and some humorous scenes, and is probably the most reasonable and cultivated creature of the ship's company. Starbuck and Stubb are both tiresome, in different ways. The book is rich with facts connected with the natural history of the whale, and the whole art and process of whaling; and with spirited descriptions of that process, which betray an intense straining at effect.

[1] Brackets are the reviewer's.

The climax of the three days' chase after Moby Dick is highly wrought and sternly exciting—but the catastrophe, in its whirl of waters and fancies, resembles one of Turner's later nebulous transgressions in gamboge.

Speaking of the passengers on board Redburn's ship *Highlander*, Mr. Melville significantly and curtly observes, 'As for the ladies, I have nothing to say concerning them; for ladies are like creeds; if you cannot speak well of them, say nothing.' He will pardon us for including in this somewhat arbitrary classification of forms of beauty and forms of faith, his own, last, and worst production, *Pierre; or, the Ambiguities.*

O author of *Typee* and *Omoo*, we admire so cordially the proven capacity of your pen, that we entreat you to doff the 'non-natural sense' of your late lucubrations—to put off your worser self—and to do your better, real self, that justice which its 'potentiality' deserves.

ISRAEL POTTER

1855

112. Unsigned notice, New Bedford, Massachusetts, *Daily Mercury*

12 March 1855

The wide circle of habitual readers of *Putnam's Monthly Magazine*, will be glad that this very pleasant 'autobiography,' dedicated to 'His Highness The Bunker Hill Monument,' is rescued from its fragmentary state, and has a permanent identity of form and style of Mr. Putnam's best. Mr. Melville's works are unequal, but none of them can be charged with dullness, and he is especially at home on his native soil, with a keen sense of the rugged but abounding picturesqueness and beauty of its scenery, and of the peculiarities of the Yankee character at the revolutionary period. Among the famous, Benjamin Franklin, and Capt. Paul Jones, have a part to play in this veritable history, which is a mixture of fun, gravity, romance and reality very taking from beginning to end. It will take its place among the best of its predecessors, and may certainly be said to belong to *American* literature. For sale in this city by C. Taber & Co.

113. Charles Gordon Greene, unsigned review, Boston *Post*

15 March 1855

Israel Potter is well known to the readers of *Putnam's Magazine*. It is now published as the work of Herman Melville, whose earlier productions placed him high among our writers of fiction, but whose late works have been unsatisfactory, not to say ridiculous. *Israel Potter* is based upon the actual biography of a man who fought at Bunker Haill and with Paul Jones in the war of the revelution, but who, by a complication of accidents, afterwards lived in London in extreme poverty for more than forty years, and finally reached his native land which he had served so well, to die, the neglected survivor of a dead generation. Mr. Melville has made a most interesting book from the facts at his command—a book, not great, not remarkable for any particular in it, but of a curt, manly, independent tone, dealing with truth honestly, and telling it feelingly. Its *Paul Jones* and *Benjamin Franklin*, to be sure, are not without a spice of Melville's former 'humors,' as they used to be called; but upon the whole, its style, sentiment, and construction are so far above those of *Pierre* and some of its predecessors, that we dislike to say one word against it. It is a readable book, with passages and descriptions of power. We trust its successor will be quite as sensible, but be of wider scope and a larger subject.

114. William Young, unsigned review, *Albion*

17 March 1855, 129

A downright good book, though *five* years, in place of *fifty*, would have been a more appropriate title, seeing that forty-five of them are shuffled off in a few pages at the close. But that's a trifle. There is in it a masculine vigour, and even a certain fantastical ruggedness, that separate it from the herd of smoothly-written tales, and give it, so to speak, a distinctness and raciness of flavour.

Israel Potter, a Massachusetts youth, fought at Bunker Hill; and was soon afterwards captured, and carried prisoner to England. He escaped from durance, underwent all sorts of hardships, carried letters between Horne Tooke and Dr. Franklin then in Paris, sailed under Paul Jones, and appeared to be in a fair way to see his native land ere the close of the war, but Fate and Mr. Herman Melville otherwise ordered it. They chose to set him astride a ship's spanker-boom at an inauspicious moment (in a fashion that we shan't explain, lest we spoil a spirited story); and so poor Israel had to wend his way back to the land of his foes, and to lead a wretched dodging sort of a life there, of about the same duration as the Israelitish wanderings in the Desert, until Mr. Melville kindly let him return home.—Franklin and Paul Jones are admirable sketches of character; but our author, as we know of old, is on his own special element when he deals with the sea and its belongings. The fight between the *Serapis* and the *Bonhomme Richard* is a masterpiece of writing; albeit some may deem its imagery too fanciful and far-fetched. Perhaps it is—but it helps the description wonderfully. Here's just the briefest bit of it, but with a terrible closeness.

> The wind now acting on the sails of the *Serapis* forced her, heel and point, her entire length, cheek by jowl, alongside the *Richard*. The projecting cannon scraped; the yards interlocked; but the hulls did not touch. A long lane of darkling water lay wedged between, like that narrow canal in Venice which dozes between two shadowy piles, and high in air is secretly crossed by the Bridge of Sighs. But where the six yard-arms reciprocally arched overhead, three bridges of sighs were both seen and heard, as the moon and wind kept rising.

Into that Lethean canal—pond-like in its smoothness as compared with the sea without—fell many a poor soul that night; fell, forever forgotten.

Of course, the Revolutionary War, in its principle, as in the details that come under notice, is not touched up to the exact taste of some British readers. But Mr. Melville, though American enough to be a Know-Nothing, has a plain way of speaking. Thus, he says:

> Sharing the same blood with England, and yet her proved foe in two wars—not wholly inclined at bottom to forget an old grudge—intrepid, unprincipled, reckless, predatory, with boundless ambition, civilized in externals but a savage at heart, America is, or may yet be, the Paul Jones of nations.

Just contrast this short but expressive passage, with the terms wherein the famous 'Ostend Conference' recently heralded a scheme of spoliation, with a set of fine phrases about 'conscious rectitude' and 'approbation of the world.' Mr. Melville comes to the point.

115. Unsigned notice, *Christian Examiner*

May 1855, lviii, 470–1

Mr. Melville's new volume, we think, scarcely sustains the reputation which he won by the earlier productions of his pen. In them he entered upon a comparatively uncultivated field; and by the freshness of his manner and the romantic interest of his narrative he at once gathered a rich harvest of popularity among readers of every degree of culture. But in his later works (and especially in the volume before us) he has dealt with another and very different class of characters, and placed them in circumstances very different from those which gave interest to his earlier volumes; and here his success has been much less apparent. *Israel Potter*, indeed, notwithstanding some fine passages and some skilful descriptions, is rather heavy reading. Its style is, in the main, flowing and graceful, and its tone genial and healthy; and yet the author fails to interest us very much in the fortunes of his hero. His character, in truth, lacks those elements which arrest and enchain the reader's sympathies; and, at the best, it is only a feeble delineation of a very commonplace person. Nor are the other characters portrayed with greater skill. In our author's delineation, Dr. Franklin's homely wisdom and shrewd philosophy degenerate into ridiculous cant and officious imbecility; and the portraiture of Paul Jones seems almost equally infelicitous. There are, however, some vigorous descriptions of the exploits of this remarkable man on the coasts of Scotland and Ireland, which constitute, perhaps, the ablest and most interesting part of the volume. But from this praise we would exlude the account of the battle between the Bon Homme Richard and the Serapis. A battle so sanguinary and brutal in its whole character cannot form an attractive episode in a work of high art; and it is to be regretted that Mr. Melville should have dwelt so minutely upon its details.

116. Unsigned review, *Leader*

5 May 1855, 428

This is a curiously unequal book. The subject—the adventures of a Yankee prisoner in England at the time of the American War—is an admirable one; and the treatment, for a little more than the first half of the volume, shows such vigour, freshness, and artist-like skill, that as we read on to the Fourteenth Chapter, we felt disposed to rank *Israel Potter* as incomparably the best work that Mr. Melville had yet written. The characters introduced—including, besides minor celebrities, George the Third and Doctor Franklin—were conceived and developed with such genuine dramatic feeling; the incidents were all so striking, and many of them so original; and the style, bating an occasional Americanism, was so hearty and graphic that it was quite refreshing to read the book, after the trash we have had to examine lately, in the vain hope of discovering something worthy to be recommended to our readers. After the Fourteenth Chapter, however, we were sadly disappointed to find that the work began to decline steadily in literary merit, and, excepting one or two detached scenes, to grow duller and duller the nearer it got to the end. The main causes of this curious falling off we found to be obvious enough. In the first place, the least successful character in the biographical story—Paul Jones—is the character which is most fully developed in the latter portions of it. In the second place, Mr. Melville follows his hero's fortunes, from the time of his being taken prisoner by the English, with great minuteness in the beginning and middle of the book, and then suddenly generalises towards the end for the sake of getting to the death of 'Israel Potter,' without exceeding the compass of one small volume. This is a fatal mistake in Art. An author who ceases to be general and becomes particular, is certain of exciting his readers' interest. But an author who ceases to be particular and becomes general, in all cases where the drawing of human character is in question, is sure to lose his hold of the reader in the most disastrous manner. Mr. Melville may urge truly enough, that in writing of 'Fifty Years of Exile' in a man's life, it was absolutely necessary for him to generalise somewhere. We have only to answer that he had better have generalised anywhere rather than in the latter portions of the story. If he had left his hero's life in London and death in America for another volume, and if he had drawn his pen through at least half the sea-scenes in which Paul Jones figures, he would have given us, not only his best book, but the best book that any American author has written for a long time past. As it is, *Israel Potter* is the work of an original thinker and vigorous writer, damaged by want of constructive ability—or, in plainer and shorter words, by want of Art.

Defective, however, as it may be, we can honestly recommend our readers to buy this book, if only for the sake of reading the interesting and powerfully-written chapters which describe the American prisoner's early career in England—and especially that particular chapter which narrates his interview with Doctor Franklin. We should feel tempted to extract some part of this latter passage in the story if we had space enough to do the author justice. The scene between 'Israel' and George the Third is shorter, and we can, therefore, give it at full length, first explaining that the Yankee has escaped from the English soldiers, has met with a kind friend, and has got into snug quarters as one of the assistants in the Royal Gardens at Kew. Here is the interview that follows between

THE REBEL AND THE KING.

[quotes from chapter 5, 'As he was one day' to 'magnanimous lion departed.']

This is neatly and dramatically written. It is by no means the best passage in the book; but it will do to whet the reader's appetite, and to make him follow the example of Master Oliver Twist, and—'ask for more.'

117. Unsigned notice, *Athenæum*

2 June 1855, 643

Mr. Melville's books have been from the outset of his career somewhat singular,—and this is not the least so of the company. Whether Israel Potter belongs to the family of *Mrs. Harris*, or was an actual *bonâ fide* American who took despatches in the heels of his boots to Franklin at Paris, and who sailed with that buccaneer hero, Paul Jones, we confess our inability to decide. Some 'Noter' or 'Querist,' well versed in the minor history of the American War, may perhaps oblige us with the facts, if facts there be. But whether Israel Potter be man or myth, he is here set in a strange framework. Mr. Melville tries for power and commands rhetoric,—but he becomes wilder and wilder, and more and more turgid in each successive book. Take as a specimen, the following passage concerning the Thames, which makes part of his picture of London:—'Hung in long, sepulchral arches of stone, the black, be-smoked bridge seemed a huge scarf of crape, festooning the river across. Similar funeral festoons spanned it to the west, while eastward, towards the sea, tiers and tiers of jetty colliers lay moored, side by side, fleets of black swans. The Thames, which far away, among the green fields of Berks, ran clear as a brook, here, polluted by continual vicinity to man, curdled on between rotten wharves, one murky sheet of sewerage. Fretted by the ill-built piers, while it crested and hissed, then shot balefully through the Erebus arches, desperate as the lost souls of the harlots, who, every night, took the same plunge. Meantime, here and there, like awaiting hearses, the coal-scows drifted along, poled broadside, pell-mell to the current.'—Benjamin Franklin, it is true, is painted in less peculiar colours than those employed to blacken the 'City of Dis.' But the philosophical printer, however available for the purposes of such a nice observer and delicate delineator as Mr. Thackeray, retains neither bone, blood, nor muscle when dealt with by such a proficient in the 'earthquake' and 'alligator' style as Mr. Melville. He is selfish in his prudence, and icy in his calmness,—rather weak and very tiresome. Such, we take it, was not the real Franklin. On the other hand, Paul Jones is a melo-dramatic caricature—an impossible mixture of a Bayard and a bully; and in a book were scene-painting has been tried for, we have encountered few scenes less real than the well-known attempt to burn Whitehaven, and the descent on St. Mary's Isle, as told in *Israel Potter*. Mr. Melville, to conclude, does not improve as an artist,—yet his book, with all its faults, is not a bad shilling's worth for any railway reader, who does not object to small type and a style the glories of which are nebulous.

GENERAL ESTIMATES

1855–6

118. Evert A. and George L. Duyckinck, from 'Herman Melville,' *Cyclopædia of American Literature*

New York, 1855, 672–6

The article opens with a discussion of Melville's ancestry and early life and closes with an extract from *Redburn* (chapter 14) as the one example of Melville's writing.

This voyaging in the merchant, whaling, and naval service rounded Melville's triple experience of nautical life. It was not long after that he made his appearance as an author. His first book, *Typee*, a narrative of his Marquesas adventure, was published in 1846, simultaneously by Murray in London* and Wiley and Putnam in New York. The spirit and vigorous fancy of the style, and the freshness and novelty of the incidents, were at once appreciated. There was, too, at the time, that undefined sentiment of the approaching practical importance of the Pacific in the public mind, which was admirably calculated for the reception of this glowing, picturesque narrative. It was received everywhere with enthusiasm, and made a reputation for its author in a day. The London *Times* reviewed it with a full pen, and even the staid *Gentleman's Magazine* was loud in its praises.

Mr. Melville followed up this success the next year with *Omoo, a Narrative of Adventures in the South Seas*, which takes up the story with

* It was brought to the notice of Mr. Murray in London by Mr. Gansevoort Melville, then Secretary of Legation to the Minister, Mr. Louis McLane. Mr. Gansevoort Melville was a political speaker of talent. He died suddenly in London of an attack of fever in May, 1846.

the escape from the Typees, and gives a humorous account of the adventures of the author and some of his ship companions in Tahiti. For pleasant, easy narrative, it is the most natural and agreeable of his books. In his next book, in 1849—*Mardi, and a Voyage Thither*—the author ventured out of the range of personal observation and matter-of-fact description to which he had kept more closely than was generally supposed,* and projected a philosophical romance, in which human nature and European civilization were to be typified under the aspects of the poetical mythological notions and romantic customs and traditions of the aggregate races of Polynesia. In the first half of the book there are some of the author's best descriptions, wrought up with fanciful associations from the quaint philosophic and other reading in the volumes of Sir Thomas Browne, and such worthies, upon whose pages, after his long sea fast from books and literature, the author had thrown himself with eager avidity. In the latter portions, embarrassed by his spiritual allegories, he wanders without chart or compass in the wildest regions of doubt and scepticism. Though, as a work of fiction, lacking clearness, and maimed as a book of thought and speculation by its want of sobriety, it has many delicate traits and fine bursts of fancy and invention. Critics could find many beauties in *Mardi* which the novel-reading public who long for amusement have not the time or philosophy to discover. Mr. Melville, who throughout his literary career has had the good sense never to argue with the public, whatever opportunities he might afford them for the exercise of their disputative faculties, lost no time in recovering his position by a return to the agreeable narrative which had first gained him his laurels. In the same year he published *Redburn; his First Voyage, being the Sailor-boy Confessions and Reminiscences of the Son of a Gentleman, in the Merchant Service.* In the simplicity of the young sailor, of which the pleasant adventure of leaving the forecastle one day and paying his respects to the captain in the cabin, is an instance, this book is a witty reproduction of natural incidents. The lurid London episode, in the melo-dramatic style, is not so fortunate. Another course of Melville's nautical career, the United States naval service, furnished the subject of the next book—*White Jacket, or the World in a Man-of-war*, published in 1850. It is a

* Lt. Wise in his lively, dashing book of travels—*An Inside View of Mexico and California, with Wanderings in Peru, Chili, and Polynesia*—pays a compliment to Melville's fidelity: 'Apart from the innate beauty and charming tone of his narratives, the delineations of island life and scenery, from my own personal observation, are most correctly and faithfully drawn.'

vivid daguerreotype of the whole life of the ship. The description is everywhere elevated from commonplace and familiarity by the poetical associations which run through it. There is many a good word spoken in this book, as in the author's other writings, for the honor and welfare of Poor Jack. Punishment by flogging is unsparingly condemned.

In 1851 *Moby-Dick, or the Whale*, appeared, the most dramatic and imaginative of Melville's books. In the character of Captain Ahab and his contest with the whale, he has opposed the metaphysical energy of despair to the physical sublime of the ocean. In this encounter the whale becomes a representative of moral evil in the world. In the purely descriptive passages, the details of the fishery, and the natural history of the animal, are narrated with constant brilliancy of illustration from the fertile mind of the author.*

Pierre, or the Ambiguities, was published in 1852. Its conception and execution were both literary mistakes. The author was off the track of his true genius. The passion which he sought to evolve was morbid or unreal, in the worst school of the mixed French and German melodramatic.

Since the publication of this volume, Mr. Melville has written chiefly for the magazines of Harper and Putnam. In the former, a sketch, entitled *Cock-a-doodle doo!* is one of the most lively and animated productions of his pen; in the latter, his *Bartleby the Scrivener*, a quaint, fanciful portrait, and his reproduction, with various inventions and additions, of the adventures of *Israel Potter*,† an actual character of the Revolution, have met with deserved success.

Mr. Melville having been married in 1847 to a daughter of Chief Justice Shaw of Boston, resided for a while at New York, when he took up his residence in Berkshire, on a finely situated farm, adjacent to the old Melville House, in which some members of the family formerly lived; where, in the immediate vicinity of the residence of the poet Holmes, he overlooks the town of Pittsfield and the intermediate territory, flanked by the Taconic range, to the huge height of Saddle-back.

* Just at the time of publication of this book its catastrophe, the attack of the ship by the whale, which had already good historic warrant in the fate of the Essex of Nantucket, was still further supported by the newspaper narrative of the Ann Alexander of New Bedford, in which the infuriated animal demonstrated a spirit of revenge almost human, in turning upon, pursuing, and destroying the vessel from which he had been attacked.

† *The Life and Adventures of Israel R. Potter (a native of Cranston, Rhode Island), who was a soldier in the American Revolution*, were published in a small volume at Providence, in 1824. The story in this book was written from the narrative of Potter, by Mr. Henry Trumbull, of Hartford, Ct.

Gray-lock, cloud girdled, from his purple throne,
  A voice of welcome sends,
And from green sunny fields, a warbling tone
  The Housatonic blends.*

In the fields and in his study, looking out upon the mountains, and in the hearty society of his family and friends, he finds congenial nourishment for his faculties, without looking much to cities, or troubling himself with the exactions of artificial life. In this comparative retirement will be found the secret of much of the speculative character engrafted upon his writings.

* 'Ode for the Berkshire Jubilee,' by Fanny Kemble Butler.

119. From 'A Trio of American Sailor-Authors,' unsigned article, *Dublin University Magazine*

January 1856, xlvii, 47–54

America has produced three authors, who, having acquired their knowledge of sea-life in a practical manner, have written either nautical novels or narratives of the highest degree of excellence. We allude to Fenimore Cooper, R. H. Dana, jun., and Herman Melville, each of whom has written at least one book, which is, in our estimation, decidedly A 1. Our task here happily is not to institute a critical comparison of the respective merits of American and English sea-novelists and writers; but we do not hesitate incidentally to admit that, to say the very least, America worthily rivals us in this department of literature. Taking Cooper, for instance, all in all, we question greatly whether any English author excels him as a sea-novelist. Our two best are Marryat and Michael Scott ('Tom Cringle'), but they are in some respects essentially inferior to Cooper; and although they both have very great distinctive merits of their own, in what shall we deliberately pronounce them superior to the great American? Turn to Dana, and where is the English author, living or dead, who has written a book descriptive of real foremast life worthy to be compared with *Two Years before the Mast*? Again, to select only a single work by Herman Melville, where shall we find an English picture of man-of-war life to rival his marvellous *White-Jacket*? Tastes and opinions of course vary, and there may be, and doubtless are, able and intelligent critics who will dissent from our verdict; but we may be permitted to say that we believe very few works of nautical fiction and narrative (by either English or American authors) exist, with which we are not familiar.

Ere proceeding to consider the peculiar and distinguishing excellencies of our three American sailor-authors, we would observe that, as regards sea-novels, not one realises our idea of what this species of literature ought to be. A sea-novel, to which we can appeal as a standard by which to judge the general artistic merits of similar compositions, is yet, and will, we fear, long continue to be, a desideratum. In many so-called naval fictions, two-thirds or more of the scenes are described as occurring on shore, and the actors are more frequently landsmen than sailors; and even in the very best works of the class we find not a few chapters occupied by scenes and characters which have no connexion whatever with the sea. A genuine sea story should be evolved afloat from first to last; its descriptions should be confined to the ocean and its coasts—to ships and their management; its characters should exclusively be seamen (unless a fair heroine be introduced on shipboard); its episodes and all its incidental materials should smack of sea-life and adventure—the land, and all that exclusively pertains thereto, should as much as possible be *sunk* and forgotten! But, it will be asked, has a book of this kind yet been written? No, it has not. And if the most eminent naval novelists have not attempted such a performance, does not that prove that they considered the idea one that could not be practically carried out? So at least it would appear, and very successful nautical writers explicitly give their testimony against our theory. . . .

Herman Melville completes our Trio. A friend has informed us that 'Herman Melville' is merely a *nom de plume*, and if so, it is only of a piece with the mystification which this remarkable author dearly loves to indulge in from the first page to the last of his works. We think it highly probable that the majority of our readers are only familiar with his earliest books; but as we have read them all carefully (excepting his last production, *Israel Potter*, which is said to be mediocre) we shall briefly refer to their subjects seriatim, ere we consider the general characteristics of his style. His first books were *Omoo* and *Typee*, which quite startled and puzzled the reading world. The ablest critics were for some time unable to decide whether the first of these vivid pictures of life in the South Sea Islands was to be regarded as a mere dexterous fiction, or as a narrative of real adventures, described in glowing, picturesque, and romantic language; but when the second work appeared, there could no longer exist any doubt, that although the author was intimately acquainted with the Marquesas and other islands, and might introduce real incidents and real characters, yet that fiction so largely entered into the composition of the books, that they could not be regarded as matter-of-fact narratives. Both these works contain a few opening chapters, descriptive of foremast-life in whaling-ships, which are exceedingly interesting and striking.

Melville's next work was entitled *Redburn*, and professed to be the autobiographical description of a sailor-boy's first voyage across the

Atlantic. It contains some clever chapters, but very much of the matter, especially that portion relative to the adventures of the young sailor in Liverpool, London, &c., is outrageously improbable, and cannot be read either with pleasure or profit. This abortive work—which neither obtained nor deserved much success—was followed by *Mardi; and a Voyage Thither*. Here we are once more introduced to the lovely and mysterious isles of the vast Pacific, and their half-civilised, or, in some cases, yet heathen and barbarous aborigines. The reader who takes up the book, and reads the first half of volume one, will be delighted and enthralled by the original and exceedingly powerful pictures of sea-life, of a novel and exciting nature, but woful will be his disappointment as he reads on. We hardly know how to characterise the rest of the book. It consists of the wildest, the most improbable, nay, impossible, series of adventures amongst the natives, which would be little better than insane ravings, were it not that we dimly feel conscious that the writer intended to introduce a species of biting, political satire, under grotesque and incredibly extravagant disguises. Moreover, the language is throughout gorgeously poetical, full of energy, replete with the most beautiful metaphors, and crowded with the most brilliant fancies, and majestic and melodiously sonorous sentences. But all the author's unrivalled powers of diction, all his wealth of fancy, all his exuberance of imagination, all his pathos, vigour, and exquisite graces of style, cannot prevent the judicious reader from laying down the book with a weary sigh, and an inward pang of regret that so much rare and lofty talent has been wilfully wasted on a theme which not anybody can fully understand, and which will inevitably repulse nine readers out of ten, by its total want of human interest and sympathy. It is, in our estimation, one of the saddest, most melancholy, most deplorable, and humiliating perversions of genius of a high order in the English language.

Next in order—if we recollect rightly as to the date of publication—came *White Jacket; or the World in a Man-of-war*. This is, in our opinion, his very best work. He states in the preface that he served a year before-the-mast in the United States frigate, Neversink, joining her at a port in the Pacific, where he had been left by—or deserted from, for we do not clearly comprehend which—a whaling-ship, and that the work is the result of his observations on board, &c. We need hardly say that the name Neversink is fictitious, but from various incidental statements we can easily learn that the real name of the frigate is the United States—the very same ship that captured our English frigate Macedonian in the year 1812. The Macedonian, we believe, is yet retained in the American navy. *White Jacket* is the best picture of life-before-the-mast in a ship of war ever yet given to the world. The style is most excellent—occasionally very eccentric and startling, of course, or it would not be Herman Melville's, but invariably energetic, manly, and attractive, and not unfrequently noble, eloquent, and deeply impressive. We could point out a good many instances, however, where the author has borrowed remarkable verbal expressions, and even incidents, from nautical books almost unknown to the general reading public (and this he does without a syllable of acknowledgment). Yet more, there are one or two instances where he describes the frigate as being manœuvred in a way that no practical seaman would commend—indeed, in one case of the kind he writes in such a manner as to shake our confidence in his own practical knowledge of seamanship. We strongly suspect that he can handle a pen much better than a marlingspike—but we may be wrong in our conjecture, and shall be glad if such is the case. At any rate, Herman Melville himself assures us that he has sailed before the mast in whalers, and in a man-of-war, and it is certain that his information on all nautical subjects is most extensive and accurate. Take it all in all, *White Jacket* is an astonishing production, and contains much writing of the highest order.

The last work we have to notice is a large one, entitled *The Whale*, and it is quite as eccentric and monstrously extravagant in many of its incidents as even *Mardi*; but it is, nevertheless, a very valuable book, on account of the unparalleled mass of information it contains on the subject of the history and capture of the great and terrible cachalot, or sperm-whale. Melville describes himself as having made more than one cruise in a South-sea-whaler; and supposing this to have been the fact, he must nevertheless have laboriously consulted all the books treating in the remotest degree on the habits, natural history, and mode of capturing this animal, which he could obtain, for such an amazing mass of accurate and curious information on the subject of the sperm-whale as is comprised in his three volumes could be found in no other single work—or perhaps in no half-dozen works—in existence. We say this with the greater confidence, because we have written on the sperm-whale ourselves, and have consequently had occasion to consult the best works in which it is described. Yet the great and undeniable merits of Melville's book are obscured and almost neutralised by the astounding quantity of wild, mad passages and entire chapters with which it is interlarded. Those who have not read the work cannot have any conception of the reckless, inconceivable extravagancies to which we allude. Nevertheless, the work is throughout splendidly written, in a literary sense; and some of the early chapters contain what we know to be most truthful and superlatively-excellent sketches of out-of-the-way life and characters in connexion with the American whaling trade. . . .

Perhaps we have so far indicated our opinion of the merits and demerits of Herman Melville in the course of the foregoing remarks, that it is hardly necessary to state it in a more general way. Yet, in conclusion, we may sum up our estimate of this singular author in a few short sentences. He is a man of genius—and we intend this word to be understood in its fullest literal sense—one of rare qualifications too; and we do not think there is any living author who rivals him in his peculiar powers of describing scenes at sea and sea-life in a manner at once poetical, forcible, accurate, and, above all, original. But it is his *style* that is original rather than his *matter*. He has read prodigiously on all nautical subjects—naval history, narratives of voyages and shipwrecks, fictions, &c.—and he never scruples to deftly avail himself of these stores of information. He undoubtedly is an original thinker, and boldly and unreservedly expresses his opinions, often in a way that irresistibly startles and enchains the interest of the reader. He possesses amazing powers of expression—he can be terse, copious, eloquent, brilliant, imaginative, poetical, satirical, pathetic, at will. He is never stupid, never dull; but, alas! he is often mystical and unintelligible—*not* from any inability to express himself, for his writing is pure, manly English, and a child can always understand what he *says*, but the ablest critic cannot always tell what he really *means*; for he at times seems to construct beautiful and melodious sentences only to conceal his thoughts, and irritates his warmest admirers by his provoking, deliberate, wilful indulgence in wild and half-insane conceits and rhapsodies. These observations apply mainly to his latter works, *Mardi* and *The Whale*, both of which he seems to have composed in an opium dream; for in no other manner can we understand how they could have been written.

Such is Herman Melville! a man of whom America has reason to be proud, with all his faults; and if he does not eventually rank as one of her greatest giants in literature, it will be owing not to any lack of innate genius, but solely to his own incorrigible perversion of his rare and lofty gifts.

THE PIAZZA TALES

1856

120. Unsigned notice, *Southern Literary Messenger*

June 1856, xxii, 480

For some time the literary world has lost sight of Herman Melville, whose last appearance as an author, in *Pierre or the Ambiguities*, was rather an unfortunate one, but he 'turns up' once more in *The Piazza Tales* with much of his former freshness and vivacity. Of the series of papers here collected, the preference must be given to the *Encantadas, or the Enchanted Islands* in which he conducts us again into that 'wild, weird clime, out of space, out of time,' which is the scene of his earliest and most popular writings. 'The Lightning Rod Man' is a very flat recital which we should never have suspected Melville of producing, had it not been put forth under the sanction of his name.

121. Unsigned notice, New Bedford, Massachusetts, *Daily Mercury*

4 June 1856

The author of *Typee* and *Omoo*, is so well known to the public, that something good is expected by it, when his name appears on the title-page of a book.—not only expected but in the case of the present work, the *Piazza Tales*, is realized. Mr. Melville tells us very pleasantly in his introduction all about his piazza on his house, how and why he built it, and describes in an exceedingly pleasant manner the scenery that he saw therefrom. But he does not tell us that this house was on the edge of the beautiful town of Pittsfield, one of the most lovely of all the Berkshire towns, and that his piazza looked out upon the Berkshire hills, in the midst of all that wonderful scenery. Such, however, is the fact. In the *Piazza Tales*, there are stories of all descriptions, tales of the sea and of the city, some of which are told with due gravity, like that of 'Benito Cereno,' and others, such as 'the Encantadas' with that copiousness of fancy and gentility of imagination, which resemble Melville more nearly to Charles Brockden Brown, the great novelist than to either of our other American story-tellers. Hawthorne is more dry, prosaic and detailed, Irving more elegant, careful and popular, but MELVILLE is a kind of wizard; he writes strange and mysterious things that belong to other worlds beyond this tame and everyday place we live in. Those who delight in romance should get the *Piazza Tales*, who love strange and picturesque sentences, and the thoughtful truth of a writer, who leaves some space for the *reader* to try his own ingenuity upon,—some rests and intervals in the literary voyage. Sold by C. Taber & Co.

122. Unsigned notice, Boston *Evening Transcript*

6 June 1856

The numerous friends of Mr. Melville will peruse this volume with great pleasure. The 'Piazza' is a very charming sketch, and is followed by 'Bartleby,' 'Bonito Cereno,' 'The Lightening Rod Man,' the 'Encantadas, or Enchanted Isles,' and 'The Bell Tower.' Each tale is peculiar in its way, and the author's great powers of description appear to admirable advantage in this work. *The Piazza Tales* must have wide circulation in cultivated circles, and be a favorite book at the watering places and in the rural districts this season.

123. Unsigned notice, Newark, New Jersey, *Daily Advertiser*

18 June 1856

This book is in the real *Omoo* and *Typee* vein. One reads them with delight and with rejoicing that the author has laid his rhapsoding aside, which savored too much of Swift, Rabelais and other such works, as suggest that they were the fruits of his reading rather than of his imagination. But this book evinces that he has neither 'run out' or been overpraised, for the same freshness, geniality and beauty are as flourishing as of old.

124. Unsigned notice, New York *Tribune*

23 June 1856

In these stories, to which the readers of *Putnam's Magazine* will need no introduction, we find the peculiar traits of the author's genius, though in a [less] decided form, than in most of his previous compositions. They show something of the boldness of invention, brilliancy of imagination, and quaintness of expression which usually mark his writings, with not a little of the apparent perversity and self-will, which serve as a foil to their various excellences. 'Bartleby,' the scrivener, is the most original story in the volume, and as a curious study of human nature, possesses unquestionable merit. 'Benito Cereno,' and 'The Encantadas,' are fresh specimens of Mr. Melville's sea-romances, but cannot be regarded as improvements on his former popular productions in that kind. 'The Lightning-Rod Man' and 'The Bell Tower,' which complete the contents of the volume, are ingenious rhapsodies.

125. Unsigned notice, New York *Times*

27 June 1856

HERMAN MELVILLE'S *Piazza Tales*, taken as a whole, will not augment his high reputation. 'Benito Cereno' is melodramatic, *not* effective. The sketches of the 'Encantadas' are the best in the volume. The opening sketch is full of freshness and beauty. The author of *Typee* should do something higher and better than Magazine articles.

126. Unsigned notice, Springfield, Massachusetts, *Republican*

9 July 1856

The Piazza Tales of Herman Melville, published in New York by Dix & Edwards, form one of the most delightful books of the season. Marked by a delicate fancy, a bright and most fruitful imagination, a pure and translucent style, and a certain weirdness of conceit, they are not unlike, and seem to us not inferior, to the best things of Hawthorne. The introduction is one of the most graceful specimens of writing we have seen from an American pen. It is a poem—essentially a poem—lacking only rhythm and form. The remainder of the volume is occupied by fine stories, respectively entitled 'Bartleby,' 'Benito Cereno,' 'The Lightning-rod Man,' 'The Encantadas' and 'The Bell-Tower.' It can be obtained of Chapin, Bridgman & Co.

127. Unsigned notice, *Athenæum*

26 July 1856, 929

That the Americans excel in short tales, the mention of Irving, Poe, Hawthorne, will remind our readers. That Mr. Melville might deserve to be added to the list is also possible; but in these *Piazza Tales* he gives us merely indications, not fulfilment. Under the idea of being romantic and pictorial in style, he is sometimes barely intelligible; as, for instance, in the following passage, which opens the last Piazza tale, that of 'The Bell-Tower':—'In the south of Europe, nigh a once frescoed capital, now with dank mould cankering its bloom, central in a plain, stands what, at distance, seems the black mossed stump of some immeasurable pine, fallen, in forgotten days, with Anak and the Titan. As all along where the pine tree falls, its dissolution leaves a mossy mound—last flung shadow of the perished trunk; never lengthening, never lessening; unsubject to the fleet falsities of the sun; shade immutable, and true gauge which cometh by prostration—so westward from what seems the stump, one steadfast spear of lichened ruin veins the plain. From that tree-top, what birded chimes of silver throats had rung. A stone pine; a metallic aviary in its crown: the Bell-Tower, built by the great mechanician, the unblest foundling, Bannadonna.'—The author who 'flames amazement' in the eyes of his readers by putting forth such grand paragraphs as the above must content himself with a very young public. Elder folk, however tolerant of imagery, and alive to the seductions of colour, will be contented with a few such pages and phrases, and lay by the rhapsody and the raving in favour of something more temperate. The legends themselves have a certain wild and ghostly power; but the exaggeration of their teller's manner appears to be on the increase.

128. Unsigned notice, *Knickerbocker*

September 1856, xlviii, 330

This series of stories, though partaking of the marvellous, are written with the author's usual felicity of expression, and minuteness of detail. The tale entitled 'Benito Cereno,' is most painfully interesting, and in reading it we became nervously anxious for the solution of the mystery it involves. The book will well repay a perusal.

129. Unsigned notice, *United States Democratic Review*

September 1856, xxxviii [n.s. vii], 172

The author of *Typee* and *Omoo* requires none of 'the tricks of the trade' to secure a favorable audience for a collection of tales upon which he seems to have lavished even more than his usual care. As criticism is exhausted, and too much eulogy does not suit our taste, we shall confine ourselves as briefly as possible to an enumeration of the dishes, adapted to various palates, and disagreeable to none, which the purchasers of this book will find set forth before them. The book takes its name from the first story of six, which are here re-collected from the magazines in which they originally appeared. They are called respectively 'The Piazza,' 'Bartleby,' 'Benito Cereno,' 'The Lightning-rod Man'—a story which excited great attention when originally published in *Putnam's Monthly*—'The Encantadas; or, Enchanted Islands,' and the 'Bell Tower.' All of them exhibit that peculiar richness of language, descriptive vitality, and splendidly sombre imagination which are the author's characteristics. Perhaps the admirers of Edgar Poe will see, or think they see, an imitation of his concentrated gloom in the wild, weird tale, called 'Bartleby:' in the 'Bell Tower,' as well, there is a broad tinge of German mysticism, not free from some resemblance to Poe. As a companion for the sultry summer months, and a country residence, we can fancy no volume more agreeable: the tales are perfect in themselves, and would each form the feast of a long summer's noon.

GENERAL ESTIMATE

1857

130. Fitz-James O'Brien, from 'Our Authors and Authorship. Melville and Curtis,' unsigned article, *Putman's Monthly Magazine*

April 1857, ix, 384–93

George William Curtis (1824–92), who often wrote under the pseudonym of 'Howadji,' was well known for his books of travel and for his sketches of 'the vices and the follies, the odious and facetious aspects of American society,' as O'Brien put it in this article. Curtis spent two years at Brook Farm and was influenced strongly by Emerson.

One can imagine a world in which there should be no bad books, and no indifferent authors—a paradise of critics and of readers, in which the writing of a review would be as exhilarating an occupation as the chanting of a pæan, and men would cut the leaves of a new volume with the same sweet certainty of anticipation with which they now pare a ripe round orange. A pleasant world, indeed, that would be for all of us, and the very thought of such delicious possibilities throws a momentary glow upon the page as we write. For what a very different world is this world of actual authorship and actual criticism, in which we live! . . .

The first duty of a critic, then, is to remember that, behind every book, there is a man—or rather, that there is a man *in* every book. He is to reflect that the mighty names, which ring through the trumpets of foreign or of antique fame, and thrill his fancy with their sounding music, are the names of men, and indicate the measure of the concentrated influences of character and intellect upon the nations of which they are the boast. And when he considers the literature of his own times, he is to examine first into the value of the personalities which inspire that literature, and pass judgment upon the present, and prophesy for the future, according to the results of that examination. . . .

How does our own literature bear the test of such criticism?

Writers we have always had, because we have been always in some degree, at least, an educated people, and education, if it cannot guarantee inspiration, at least continues the traditions of literary ambition, and the phantoms of an interest in literature. But of authors—of men who communicated themselves to mankind, because there was something in themselves to communicate—our nation has not been so abundantly prolific. From the settlement of the colonies, down to the epoch of our independence, only two men detach themselves from the multitude of cisatlantic scribes, as emphatic individualities, expressing themselves through the written word. Jonathan Edwards and Benjamin Franklin are, as it seems to us, the two permanent realities contributed by colonial America to the literary history of the English race. . . .

Sparks of true fire flashed for a moment from the words of other men who yet drew back from the path of glory, because uncheered by cordial criticism, and unwelcomed by a public which had not yet accommodated itself to all the necessities, nor accustomed itself to all the privileges, of its new national position. As time went on, and the American nationality gathered vigor and consistency, the literature of America began to assume more respectable proportions; and, within the last ten or twelve years, it has developed with a rapidity and a reality which certainly afforded us no reasons for despondent views of the future. A generation of writers is giving way to a generation of authors, and though it is, of course, a very distressing thing that we have not yet produced an authentic and unquestionable Shakespeare, nor even an admitted Pope, we may yet take some small comfort, surely, from the fact, that we have given birth to a certain number of artists in words, whose touch the world has recognised as betraying the individuality of genius, and the reality of manhood. . . .

But it must be confessed that our public criticism is not wholly worthy of our actual rank in the world of letters. Its defects are not sure to be of a mean or malicious kind. We are, happily, not cursed with much of that petty spirit of clique and starveling ill-will, which degrade and make worthless the minor criticism of the London press. But our criticism too commonly wants dignity and sincerity. We deal our praise out very lightly, with a kind of good-natured *nonchalance*, as if it didn't matter much after all, and it was better for all parties, on the whole, to 'laugh than look sad.' If life were only one long alternation of dinings and digestions, the philosophy of this jovial old adage would be as sound as it is cheery; but we must not be vexed if a man, who has a serious and intense interest in his art, grows rather sad than merry when all his efforts are rewarded with an undiscriminating salvo of applause, or a patronizing nod of encouragement. Welcome to the true author's soul is the strong, cordial voice which recognizes his honesty and his manliness, and mingles, with sincere praise of that which is beautiful in his work, sturdy reprobation of that which is *not* beautiful, and a distinct intimation of that which is *less* than beautiful.

Who can tell how much good Alfred Tennyson gained from that stout, straightforward, large-hearted paper in which old Christopher North took him so smartly to task for his early follies, and commended, with such a fond and generous warmth, his immortal gifts—his works of real beauty already achieved? Heaven send you such a critic of that first book which you now profoundly meditate, dear and aspiring young friend! You will bless his memory when your laurels are greenest.

If there ever was an author who deserved such a critic, and needed such an one, alike for praise and blame, it is our old acquaintance and esteemed prose-poet, Herman Melville. . . .

Mr. Melville was not only a young man, but a young American, and a young American educated according to the standard of our day and country. He had all the metaphysical tendencies which belong so eminently to the American mind—the love of antic and extravagant speculation, the fearlessness of intellectual consequences, and the passion for intellectual legislation, which distinguish the cleverest of our people. It was inevitable that he should have stamped himself pretty clearly on his book, and his book was all the more interesting that he had so stamped himself upon it. Still we waited anxiously for number two. It came, and with it came more than we had anticipated of the metaphysics of *Typee*, and less than we had hoped of its poetry. Had not Mr. Melville been impelled to a good deal of sharp, sensible writing in *Omoo*, by his wrath against the missionaries, it is clear, we think, that he would have plunged headlong into the vasty void of the obscure, the oracular, and the incomprehensible. But a little wholesome indignation is a capital stimulus to good writing, and the beneficial effects of it were never more clearly apparent than in this very book. We trembled for its successor, and we trembled with reason; for, when *Mardi* came, or rather when we came to 'Mardi,' our 'voyage thither' affected us much as it would to be literally knocked into the middle of next week.

We frankly own here, and now, and once for all, that we have not, and never expect to have, the faintest notion of why we took a voyage to 'Mardi,' nor of what we found when we reached 'Mardi,' if we ever did reach it, nor of how we got away from 'Mardi' again, if we ever did get away from that enchanted, mysterious place. We would just as soon undertake to give anybody a connected and coherent account of the *Mardi gras* of Paris, on coming out of the *Bal de l'Opéra* at three in the morning, as criticise, or describe, or analyze the *Mardi* of our friend Mr. Melville. Do we believe, then, that Mr. Melville meant nothing by taking us to 'Mardi'—that he had no purpose at all in his mind, but was *carnivalizing* when he wrote the book? Not a bit of it; for, dull of perception, and still more dull of instinct must the critic be who does not recognize in every page of Mr. Melville's writings, however vague, and obscure, and fantastic, the breathing spirit of a man of genius, and of a passionate and earnest man of genius. It is precisely because we are always sure that Mr. Melville *does* mean something, and something intrinsically manly and noble, too, that we quarrel with him for hiding his light under such an impervious bushel.

Mr. Melville is not a *dilettante* in metaphysics. If he is fantastically philosophical in his language, it is because he wants to say something subtle and penetrating which he has discerned, or *thinks he has* discerned, and takes this to be the most effective way of saying it. And this is just the issue we have to make with him. We made it when we read *Mardi*; we have been obliged to make it, again and again, in reading his subsequent books. What, for instance, did Mr. Melville mean when he wrote *Moby Dick*? We have a right to know; for he carried us floundering on with him after his great white whale, through all manner of scenes, and all kinds of company—now perfectly exhausted with fatigue and deafened with many words whereof we understood no syllable, and then suddenly refreshed with a brisk sea breeze and a touch of nature kindling as the dawn. There was so much truth in the book that we knew the author must have meant to give us more, and we were excessively vexed with him for darkening his counsel by words which we could not but esteem to be words without knowledge. Is it not a hard case, O sympathizing reader? Here is a man of distinct and unquestionable genius; a man who means righteously and thinks sensibly; a man whose aims do honor to himself and to his country; a man who wishes to understand life himself, and to help other people to understand it; a man, too, who has proved not once only but fifty, yea, a hundred times, that he can write good English—good, strong, sweet, clear English—a man who has music in his soul, and can ring fair chimes upon the silver bells of style—and this man will persist in distorting the images of his mind, and in deodorizing the flowers of his fancy; a man born to create, who resolves to anatomize; a man born to see, who insists upon speculating.

The sum and substance of our fault-finding with Herman Melville is this. He has indulged himself in a trick of metaphysical and morbid meditations until he has almost perverted his fine mind from its healthy productive tendencies. A singularly truthful person—as all his sympathies show him to be—he has succeeded in vitiating both his thought and his style into an appearance of the wildest affectation and untruth. His life, we should judge, has been excessively introverted. Much as he has seen of the world, and keen as his appreciation is of all that is true and suggestive in external life, he has turned away habitually, of late years, at least, to look in upon his own imaginations, and to cultivate his speculative faculties in a strange, loose way. We do not know a more curious and instructive spectacle than some of his books afford, of the conflict between resolute nature and stubborn cultivation.

Nature says to Herman Melville, 'You shall tell the world what you have seen and see, in a warm, quick, nervous style, and bring the realities of life and man before your readers in such a way that they shall know your mind without calling on you to speak it. You shall be as true as Teniers or Defoe, without the coarseness of the Fleming or the bluntness of the Englishman.'

Obstinate cultivation rejoins: 'No! you shall dissect and divide; you shall cauterize and confound; you shall amaze and electrify; you shall be as grotesquely terrible as Callot, as subtly profound as Balzac, as formidably satirical as Rabelais.' . . .

The two latest published books of our author differ considerably from their predecessors, in the degree in which they exhibit the characteristics of the classes of writing to which they respectively belong. *Israel Potter* is a comparatively reasonable narrative, embodying a story of the national war of independence, which may almost be considered a national legend. In the main, it is a coherent story, and is told with considerable clearness and force, but it lacks the animation that pervades those writings of Mr. Melville which, in other respects, it resembles. Two characters of a somewhat fantastic strain figure in it,

Benjamin Franklin being represented as one of the prosiest possible old maxim-mongers, though the epoch of his life selected for the story is just that time at which he was living brilliantly at Paris, and cracking rather irreverent jokes with the Abbé Morellet; and Paul Jones comes and goes through the story—a veritable hero of melo-drama—sullen, scornful, unappeasable, and impracticable.

The *Confidence Man*, on the contrary, belongs to the metaphysical and Rabelaistical class of Mr. Melville's works, and yet Mr. Melville, in this book, is more reasonable, and more respectful of probabilities, possibilities, and the weak perceptions of the ordinary mind than he usually is when he wraps his prophetic mantle about him. The *Confidence Man* is a thoroughly American story; and Mr. Melville evidently had some occult object in his mind, which he has not yet accomplished, when he began to paint the 'Masquerades' of this remarkable personage.

The 'Confidence Man' comes into the book, a mute, on board of a Mississippi steam-boat. He is 'a man in cream-colors, whose cheek was fair, whose chin downy, and whose hair flaxen, and whose hat was of white fur with a long, fleecy nap.' But for the fact that this singular being is presented to us as quite *dumb*, one might suppose that Mr. Melville meant to give us the portrait of a distinguished metropolitan editor, and, in this way, to suggest some clue to his purpose in the story. But this theory, of course, cannot be advanced for a moment, and the cream-colored man in the white hat goes off again into space at the end of this part (for the volume already published only begins the work) just as much masked as when he came.

In the interval, he does a great many very odd and rather reprehensible things. He comes and goes very mysteriously, and assumes new shapes, though he always betrays himself by a certain uniformity in the style of his thoughts and his machinations, which also communicates itself to the conduct and the conversation of the parties whom he meets. From the barber on the Mississippi boat to the Methodist minister, who believes in the sword of the Lord, there is not a character in the book who does not talk very much like all the others. Save for its greater reasonableness and moderation, the *Confidence Man* ought to be ranked with *Moby Dick* and *Mardi*, as one of those books which everybody will buy, many persons read, and very few understand.

Ought Mr. Melville to write such books? Will he continue to write such books always? We do not hesitate to return an emphatic 'No!' to both these questions. Mr. Melville has rare gifts; he has a sound hearts a warm and lively, though not now healthy, imagination, a vigorou, intellect—somewhat given to crooked courses—and a brilliant reputation, which is also a gift, as enabling a man to work his best work to the best advantage. We expect much from him. To use the emphatic words of a Winnebago chief, who dissented from the missionary doctrine of the goodness of Providence, on the ground that the Winnebagoes invariably had more rain in their country than they wanted, while the Sacs and Foxes had more cattle than they could eat, we expect, from Mr. Melville, 'more beef and less thunder.' We desire him to give up metaphysics and take to nature and the study of mankind. We rejoice, therefore, to know that he is, at this moment, traveling in the Old World, where, we hope, he will enjoy himself heartily, look about him wisely, and come home ready to give us pictures of life and reality. It cannot be possible, that a man of Mr. Melville's genius is to go on forever producing books which shall deserve such praise as was bestowed upon *Mardi* by a bewildered French critic in the *Revue des Deux Mondes*—books which resemble 'the dream of a badly-educated midshipman, drunk on hasheesh, and swinging asleep at the mast-head of a ship in a warm, tropical night!'

The thing is absurd; and Maga, who loves her step-son Melville, as if he were wholly her own, knows perfectly well that he is destined to do her and his country much honor and much good.

Honor and good, too, Maga expects from Mr. Melville's younger brother in letters, Mr. George William Curtis. For he, too, has an individuality of his own, and has won for himself a distinct place in our young literature.

If the five volumes, which bear his name, and lie before us now, cannot be taken as the measure of their author's capacity, they do, at least, indicate very fairly the qualities of his mind. A stronger contrast than they afford to the works of Mr. Melville it would be hard to find. Both writers are, evidently, men who wish to be thought and felt to be in earnest; but Mr. Melville takes as much pains to protest his earnestness as Mr. Curtis takes to conceal his. Mr. Melville is always as grave in his gayeties as Mr. Curtis is gay in his gravities. Mr. Melville has so much fancy and so little taste that he goes about accompanied by a grotesque troop of notions, whose preposterous attire more provokes the laugh than their numbers excite the respect of the world. Mr. Curtis has not so much fancy, but a great deal of fine instinctive grace, and the ideas which he introduces always do him credit by their style and accoutrements. Neither of these writers is natural enough, and enough at his ease to do himself full justice; for, while Mr. Melville throws himself off his balance by an over-eagerness to be prophetic and impressive, Mr. Curtis loses his through an over-anxiety to be moderate, judicious, and experienced.

The same kind of mischief which has been done to Mr. Melville, by his study of Rabelais, has been done to Mr. Curtis by his admiration of Thackeray. In the one case, as in the other, we cannot but commend the fanaticism whose effects we deplore and try to point out; for a good, hearty, unreasonable love of anything or anybody is an excellent thing for body and soul, and we shall never quarrel with it. But, in the one case as in the other, we wish to see the admirers shake themselves free of their admiration so far as to find out that it is leading them astray. . . .

THE CONFIDENCE-MAN

1857

131. Unsigned review, New York *Dispatch*

5 April 1857

When we meet with a book written by Herman Melville, the fascinations of *Omoo* and *Typee* recur to us, and we take up the work with as much confidence in its worth, as we should feel in the possession of a checque drawn by a well-known capitalist. So much greater is the disappointment, therefore, when we find the book does not come up to our mark. Mr. Melville cannot write badly, it is true, but he appears to have adopted a quaint, unnatural style, of late, which has little of the sparkling vigor and freshness of his early works. In fact we close this book—finding nothing concluded, and wondering what on earth the author has been driving at. It has all the faults of style peculiar to *Mardi*, without the romance which attaches itself to that strange book. The Confidence Man goes on board a Mississippi steamboat and assumes such a variety of disguises, with an astonishing rapidity, that no person could assume without detection, and gets into the confidence of his fellow-passengers in such a manner as would tend to show that the passengers of a Mississippi steamboat are the most gullible people in the world, and the most ready to part with their money. A deaf mute; a deformed negro; a Herb Doctor; a Secretary of a coal-mining company; a Collector for an Indian Charity, and a sort of crazy cosmopolitan philanthropist, are among the disguises he assumes; though why he appears in the character of a deaf and dumb man, we are unable to divine, unless to prepare the expected dupes for his extortions, and to exort them to charity, by means of moral sentences written on a slate and held up to view; and what is intended by the rigmarole of the cosmopolitan, we find it impossible to surmise, being left quite in the dark, with the simple information that 'something further may follow of this masquerade.' In the last number of *Putnam's Magazine*, there is an article on authors, in which the genius of Melville is duly acknowledged, and his faults frankly spoken of. We noticed the article on the receipt of the *Magazine*. If he has not read it, Mr. Melville should read, and try to profit by it. It is not right—it is trespassing too much upon the patience and forbearance of the public, when a writer possessing Herman Melville's talent, publishes such puerilities as the *Confidence Man*. The book will sell, of course, because Melville wrote it; but this exceedingly talented author must beware or he will tire out the patience of his readers.

132. Unsigned notice, Boston *Evening Transcript*

10 April 1857

One of the indigenous characters who has figured long in our journals, courts, and cities, is 'the Confidence Man;' his doings form one of the staples of villany, and an element in the romance of roguery. Countless are the dodges attributed to this ubiquitous personage, and his adventures would equal those of Jonathan Wild. It is not to be wondered at, therefore, that the subject caught the fancy of Herman Melville—an author who deals equally well in the material description and the metaphysical insight of human life. He has added by his 'Confidence Man' to the number of original subjects—an achievement for the modern *raconteur*, who has to glean in a field so often harvested. The plan and treatment are alike Melvillish; and the story more popularly eliminated than is usual with the author. *The Confidence Man—His Masquerade*—is a taking title. Dix, Edwards & Co. have brought it out in their best style.

133. From an unsigned review, *Athenæum*

11 April 1857, 462–3

The Confidence-Man is a morality enacted by masqued players. The credulous and the sceptical appear upon the stage in various quaint costumes, and discourse sententiously on the art of human life, as developed by those who believe and those who suspect. We leave the inference to be traced by Mr. Melville's readers,—some of whom, possibly, may wait for a promised sequel to the book before deciding as to the lucidity or opaqueness of the author's final meaning. There is a stage, with a set of elaborate scenery, but there is strictly no drama, the incidents being those of a masquerade, while the theatre is a steam-palace on the Mississippi. Here 'the Confidence-Man' encounters his antagonists and disciples,—and their dialogues occupy the chief part of the volume. Mr. Melville is lavish in aphorism, epigram, and metaphor. When he is not didactic, he is luxuriously picturesque; and, although his style is one, from its peculiarities, difficult to manage, he has now obtained a mastery over it, and pours his colours over the narration with discretion as well as prodigality. All his interlocutors have studied the lore of old philosophy: they have all their wise sayings, of satire or speculation, to enrich the colloquy; so that, while the mighty river-boat, Fidèle, steams up the Mississippi, between low, vine-tangled banks, flat as tow-paths, a voyage of twelve hundred miles, 'from apple to orange, from clime to clime,' we grow so familiar with the passengers that they seem at last to form a little world of persons mutually interested, generally eccentric, but in no case dull. Mr. Melville has a strange fashion of inaugurating his moral miracle-play,—the synopsis of which, in the Table of Contents, is like a reflection of 'The Ancient Mariner,' interspersed with some touches vaguely derived from the dialecticians of the eighteenth century. One sentence, leading into the first chapter, immediately fixes the attention:—

> At sunrise on a first of April, there appeared, suddenly as Manco Capac at the lake Titicaca, a man in cream colours, at the water-side, in the city of St.-Louis.

This is a mute. The other personages are fantastically attired, or rather, by an adroit use of language, common things are suggested under uncommon aspects. . . .

Full of thought, conceit, and fancy, of affectation and originality, this book is not unexceptionably meritorious, but it is invariably graphic, fresh, and entertaining.

134. Unsigned review, *Leader*

11 April 1857, 356

Under 'Three Works of Fiction,' the reviewer discusses *The Metaphysicians*—on the lives of Franz Carvel and Harold Fremdling—*The Confidence-Man*, and *Madaron* by D'Aubigné White—'*an Historical Romance of the Sixteenth Century*.'

In this book, also, philosophy is brought out of its cloisters into the living world; but the issue raised is more simple:—whether men are to be trusted or suspected? Mr. Melville has a manner wholly different from that of the anonymous writer who has produced *The Metaphysicians*. He is less scholastic, and more sentimental; his style is not so severe; on the contrary, festoons of exuberant fancy decorate the discussion of abstract problems; the controversialists pause ever and anon while a vivid, natural Mississippi landscape is rapidly painted before the mind; the narrative is almost rhythmic, the talk is cordial, bright American touches are scattered over the perspective—the great steamboat deck, the river coasts, the groups belonging to various gradations of New-World life. In his Pacific stories Mr. Melville wrote as with an Indian pencil, steeping the entire relation in colours almost too brilliant for reality; his books were all stars, twinkles, flashes, vistas of green and crimson, diamond and crystal; he has now tempered himself, and studied the effect of neutral tints. He has also added satire to his repertory, and, as he uses it scrupulously, he uses it well. His fault is a disposition to discourse upon too large a scale, and to keep his typical characters too long in one attitude upon the stage. Lest we should seem to imply that the masquerade is dramatic in form, it is as well to describe its construction. It is a strangely diversified narration of events taking place during the voyage of a Mississippi river boat, a cosmopolitan philanthropist, the apostle of a doctrine, being the centre and inspiration of the whole. The charm of the book is owing to its originality and to its constant flow of descriptions, character-sketching, and dialogue, deeply toned and skilfully contrasted.

135. Unsigned review, *Literary Gazette*

11 April 1857, 348–9

We notice this book at length for much the same reason as Dr. Livingston describes his travels in Monomotapa, holding that its perusal has constituted a feat which few will attempt, and fewer still accomplish. Those who, remembering the nature of the author's former performances, take it up in the expectation of encountering a wild and stirring fiction, will be tolerably sure to lay it down ere long with an uncomfortable sensation of dizziness in the head, and yet some such introduction under false pretences seems to afford it its only chance of being taken up at all. For who will meddle with a book professing to inculcate philosophical truths through the medium of nonsensical people talking nonsense—the best definition of its scope and character that a somewhat prolonged consideration has enabled us to suggest. A novel it is not, unless a novel means forty-five conversations held on board a steamer, conducted by personages who might pass for the errata of creation, and so far resembling the Dialogues of Plato as to be undoubted Greek to ordinary men. Looking at the substance of these colloquies, they cannot be pronounced altogether valueless; looking only at the form, they might well be esteemed the compositions of a March hare with a literary turn of mind. It is not till a lengthened perusal—a perusal more lengthened than many readers will be willing to accord—has familiarized us with the quaintness of the style, and until long domestication with the incomprehensible interlocutors has infected us with something of their own eccentricity, that our faculties, like the eyes of prisoners accustomed to the dark, become sufficiently acute to discern the golden grains which the author has made it his business to hide away from us.

It is due to Mr. Melville to say, that he is by no means unconscious of his own absurdities, which, in one of his comparatively lucid intervals, he attempts to justify and defend:—

[quotes from chapter 33, 'But ere be given' to 'capers too fantastic.']

This is ingenious, but it begs the question. We do, as Mr. Melville says, desire to see nature 'unfettered, exhilarated,' in fiction we do *not* want to see her 'transformed.' We are glad to see the novelist create imaginary scenes and persons, nay, even characters whose type is not to be found in nature. But we demand that, in so doing, he should observe certain ill-defined but sufficiently understood rules of probability. His fictitious creatures must be such as Nature might herself have made, supposing their being to have entered into her design. We must have fitness of organs, symmetry of proportions, no impossibilities, no monstrosities. As to harlequin, we think it very possible indeed that his coat may be too parti-coloured, and his capers too fantastic, and conceive, moreover, that Mr. Melville's present production supplies an unanswerable proof of the truth of both positions. We should be sorry, in saying this, to be confounded with the cold unimaginative critics, who could see nothing but extravagance in some of our author's earlier fictions—in the first volume of *Mardi*, that archipelago of lovely descriptions is led in glittering reaches of vivid nautical narrative—the conception of *The Whale*, ghostly and grand as the great grey sweep of the ridged and rolling sea. But these wild beauties were introduced to us with a congruity of outward accompaniment lacking here. The isles of 'Mardi' were in Polynesia, not off the United States. Captain Ahab did not chase Moby Dick in a Mississippi steamboat. If the language was extraordinary, the speakers were extraordinary too. If we had extravaganzas like the following outpouring on the subject of port wine, at least they were not put into the mouths of Yankee cabin passengers:—

[quotes from chapter 29, 'A shade passed' to 'murderous drugs!" ']

The best of it is, that this belauded beverage is all the time what one of the speakers afterwards calls 'elixir of logwood.'

This is not much better than Tilburina in white satin, yet such passages form the staple of the book. It is, of course, very possible that there may be method in all this madness, and that the author may have a plan, which must needs be a very deep one indeed. Certainly we can obtain no inkling of it. It may be that he has chosen to act the part of a mediæval jester, conveying weighty truths under a semblance antic and ludicrous; if so, we can only recommend him for the future not to jingle his bells so loud. There is no catching the accents of wisdom amid all this clattering exuberance of folly. Those who wish to teach should not begin by assuming a mask so grotesque as to keep listeners on the laugh, or frighten them away. Whether Mr. Melville really does mean to teach anything is, we are aware, a matter of considerable uncertainty. To describe his book, one had need to be a Höllen-Breughel; to understand its purport, one should be something of a Sphinx. It may be a *bonâ fide* eulogy on the blessedness of reposing 'confidence'—but we are not at all confident of this. Perhaps it is a hoax on the public—an emulation of Barnum. Perhaps the mild man in mourning, who goes about requesting everybody to put confidence in him, is an emblem of Mr. Melville himself, imploring toleration for three hundred and fifty-three pages of rambling, on the speculation of there being something to the purpose in the three hundred and fifty-fourth; which, by the way, there is not, unless the oracular announcement that 'something further may follow of this masquerade,' is to be regarded in that light. We are not denying that this tangled web of obscurity is shot with many a gleam of shrewd and subtle thought—that this caldron, so thick and slab with nonsense, often bursts into the bright, brief bubbles of fancy and wit. The greater the pity to see these good things so thrown away. The following scene, in the first chapter, for example, seems to us sufficiently graphic to raise expectations very indifferently justified by the sequel:—

[quotes from chapter I, 'Pausing at this spot' to 'but also deaf.']

It will be seen that Mr. Melville can still write powerfully when it pleases him. Even when most wayward, he yet gives evidence of much latent genius, which, however, like latent heat, is of little use either to him or to us. We should wish to meet him again in his legitimate department, as the prose-poet of the ocean; if, however, he will persist in indoctrinating us with his views concerning the *vrai*,[1] we trust he will at least condescend to pay, for the future, some slight attention to

[1] *Vrai:* true.

the *vraisemblable*.[1] He has ruined this book, as he did *Pierre*, by a strained effort after excessive originality. When will he discover that—

Standing on the head makes not
Either for ease or dignity?

136. Unsigned review, *Spectator*

11 April 1857, 398–9

The precise design of Mr. Herman Melville in *The Confidence-Man, his Masquerade*, is not very clear. Satire on many American smartnesses, and on the gullibility of mankind which enables those smartnesses to succeed, is indeed an evident object of the author. He stops short of any continuous pungent effect; because his plan is not distinctly felt, and the framework is very inartistical; also because the execution is upon the whole flat, at least to an English reader, who does not appreciate what appear to be local allusions.

A Mississippi steam-boat is the scene of the piece; and the passengers are the actors, or rather the talkers. There is a misanthropist, looking like a dismissed official soured against the government and humanity, whose pleasure it is to regard the dark side of things and to infuse distrust into the compassionate mind. There is the President and Transfer Agent of the 'Black Rapids Coal Company,' who does a little business on board, by dint of some secret accomplices and his own pleasant plausibility and affected reluctance. A herb-doctor is a prominent person, who gets rid of his medicine by immutable patience and his dexterity in playing upon the fears and hopes of the sick. The 'Confidence-Man' is the character most continually before the reader. He is collecting subscriptions for a 'Widow and Orphan Asylum recently founded among the Seminoles,' and he succeeds greatly in fleecing the passengers by his quiet impudence and his insinuating fluency; the persons who effectually resist being middle-aged or elderly well-to-do

[1] *Vraisemblable:* probable.

gentlemen, who cut short his advances: 'You—pish! why will the captain suffer these begging fellows to come on board?' There are various other persons who bear a part in the discourses: one or two tell stories; and the author himself sometimes directly appears in a chapter of disquisition.

Besides the defective plan and the general flatness of execution, there seems too great a success on the part of the rogues, from the great gullibility of the gulls. If implicit reliance could be placed on the fiction as a genuine sketch of American society, it might be said that poverty there as elsewhere goes to the wall, and that the freedom of the constitution does not extend to social intercourse unless where the arms and physical strength of some border man compel the fears of the genteel to grudgingly overcome their reluctance for the time. This reliance we cannot give. The spirit of the satire seems drawn from the European writers of the seventeenth and eighteenth centuries, with some of Mr. Melville's own Old World observations superadded. It sometimes becomes a question how much belongs to the New World, how much to the Old, and how much to exaggerated representation, impressing a received truth in the form of fiction. The power of wealth, connexion, and respectability, to overbear right, while poor and friendless innocence suffers, may be illustrated in the following story of a begging cripple, told to the herb-doctor; or it may instance the unscrupulous invention of vagrant impostors; but it can scarcely be taken as a true picture of justice towards the poor at New York.

[quotes from chapter 19, ' "Well, I was born' to 'and I hobbled off." ']

137. Unsigned notice, New York *Times* Supplement

11 April 1857

The author of *Typee* has again come upon us in one of his strange vagaries, and calls himself *The Confidence Man*. His publishers are DIX, EDWARDS & Co., who seem to have an affection for our young authors. Mr. MELVILLE's *Confidence Man* is almost as ambiguous an apparition as his *Pierre*, who was altogether an impossible and un-understandable creature. But, in the *Confidence Man* there is no attempt at a novel, or a romance, for MELVILLE has not the slighest qualifications for a novelist, and therefore he appears to much better advantage here than in his attempts at story books. The scene of the *Confidence Man* is on the Mississippi on board a steamboat, and the whole element of the work, though full of book learning, is as essentially Western and Indianesque as one of COOPER's *Leather-Stocking Tales*. It is, in short, a Rabelaisian piece of patch-work without any of the Rabelaisian indecency. And here it may be well to remark that one of the distinguishing traits of the Young American literature is its perfect decency. You can read any of these books aloud to your grandmother or your daughter, which is more than can be done by the majority of British books. Some of the local descriptions in the *Confidence Man* are as striking and picturesque as the best things in *Typee*, and the oddities of thought, felicities of expression, the wit, humor, and rollicking inspirations are as abundant and original as in any of the productions of this most remarkable writer. The volume has an end, but there is no conclusion to the book; the last chapter might have been the first, and the author intimates that there is more of the same sort to come.

138. Unsigned notice, Worcester, Massachusetts, *Palladium*

22 April 1857

There is a great deal of material in the work; material which deserves better setting than the author has given it. Even the most partial of Mr. Melville's friends must allow that the book is not wholly worthy of him. It has a careless and rambling style which would seem to have been easier for the author to write than his readers to peruse. There are bright flashes in it; scintillations of poetic light, and much common sense well expressed, but the book as a whole is somewhat heavy. Still, there are minds with which it will chord; and, as it pictures nineteenth century notions it will command attention. 'The Confidence Man' is a character common enough to be easily recognised in Mr Melville's portraiture. We see him every day, and often in the same light as does our author. Z. Baker & Co.; have the book.

139. From an unsigned review, London *Illustrated Times*

25 April 1857, 266

We can make nothing of this masquerade, which, indeed, savours very much of a mystification. We began the book at the beginning, and, after reading ten or twelve chapters, some of which contained scenes of admirable dramatic power, while others presented pages of the most vivid description, found, in spite of all this, that we had not yet obtained the slightest clue to the meaning (in case there should happen to be any) of the work before us. This novel, comedy, collection of dialogues, repertory of anecdotes, or whatever it is, opens (and opens brilliantly, too) on the deck of a Mississippi steamer. It appeared an excellent idea to lay the opening of a fiction (for the work is a fiction, at all events) on the deck of a Mississippi steamer. The advantage of selecting a steamer, and above all a Mississippi steamer, for such a purpose, is evident: you can have all your characters present in the vessel, and several of your scenes taking place in different parts of the vessel, if necessary, at the same time; by which means you exhibit a certain variety in your otherwise tedious uniformity. For an opening, the Mississippi steamer is excellent; and we had read at least eight chapters of the work, which opens so excellently, before we were at all struck with the desirability of going ashore. But after the tenth chapter, the steamer began to be rather too much for us; and with the twelfth we experienced symptoms of a feeling slightly resembling nausea. Besides this, we were really getting anxious to know whether there was a story to the book; and, if the contrary should be the case, whether the characters were intended—as seemed probable—not for actual living beings, but for philosophical abstractions, such as might be introduced with more propriety, or with less impropriety, floating about in the atmosphere of the planet Sirius, than on the deck and in the cabin of a Mississippi steamer, drinking, smoking, gambling, and talking about 'confidence.' Having turned to the last chapter, after the manner of the professed students of novels from the circulating library, we convinced ourselves that, if there was almost no beginning to the story, there was altogether no end to it. Indeed, if the negative of 'all's well that ends well' be true, the *Confidence-man* is certainly a very bad book.

After reading the work forwards for twelve chapters and backwards for five, we attacked it in the middle, gnawing at it like Rabelais's dog at the bone, in the hope of extracting something from it at last. But the book is without form and void. We cannot continue the chaotic comparison and say that 'darkness is on the face thereof;' for, although a sad jumble, the book is nevertheless the jumble of a very clever man, and of one who proves himself to be such even in the jumble of which we are speaking.

As a last resource, we read the work from beginning to end; and the result was we liked it even less than before—for then we had at all events not *suffered* from it. Such a book might have been called 'Imaginary Conversations,' and the scene should be laid in Tartarus, Hades,

Tophet, Purgatory, or at all events some place of which the manners, customs, and mode of speech are unknown to the living.

Perhaps, as we cannot make the reader acquainted with the whole plot or scheme of the work before us, he may expect us to tell him at least why it is called the *Confidence-Man*. It is called the *Confidence-Man* because the principal character, type, spectre, or *ombre-chinoise*[1] of the book, is always talking about confidence to the lesser characters, types, &c., with whom he is brought into contact. Sometimes the 'Confidence-Man' succeeds in begging or borrowing money from his collocutors; at other times he ignominiously fails. But it is not always very evident why he fails, nor in the other cases is it an atom clear why he succeeds. For the rest, no one can say whence the 'Confidence-Man' comes, nor whither he is going. . . .

In conclusion, the *Confidence-Man* contains a mass of anecdotes, stories, scenes, and sketches undigested, and, in our opinion, indigestible. The more voracious reader may, of course, find them acceptable; but we confess that we have not 'stomach for them all.' We said that the book belonged to no particular class, but we are almost justified in affirming that its *génre* is the *génre ennuyeux*.[2] The author in his last line promises 'something more of this masquerade.' All we can say, in reply to the brilliant author of *Omoo* and *Typee* is, 'the less the merrier.'

140. Unsigned review, London *Saturday Review*

23 May 1857, 484

There are some books which it is almost impossible to review seriously or in a very critical spirit. They occupy among books the same position as Autolycus, or Falstaff, or Flibbertigibbet do among men. Of course they are quite wrong—there are other people in the world besides those

[1] *Ombre-chinoise:* the shadow of the actor in a shadow play.

[2] *Ennuyeux:* boring.

who cheat and those who are cheated—all pleasant folks are not rogues, and all good men are not dull and disagreeable. On the contrary, the truth is for the most part, we are thankful to say, the exact opposite of this, and therefore Mr. Melville's view of life, were it gravely intended, should no doubt be gravely condemned. But that he has no such intention we quote his own words to show. He says:—

> There is another class, and with this class we side, who sit down to a work of amusement tolerably as they sit at a play, and with much the same expectations and feeling. They look that fancy shall evoke scenes different from those of the same old crowd round the custom-house counter, and same old dishes on the boarding-house table, with characters unlike those of the same old acquaintances they meet in the same old way every day in the same old street.
>
> In this way of thinking, the people in a fiction, like the people in a play, must dress as nobody exactly dresses, talk as nobody exactly talks, act as nobody exactly acts. It is with fiction as with religion: it should present another world, and yet one to which we feel the tie.
>
> If, then, something is to be pardoned to well-meant endeavour, surely a little is to be allowed to that writer who, in all his scenes, does but seek to minister to what, as he understands it, is the implied wish of the more indulgent lovers of entertainment, before whom harlequin can never appear in a coat too parti-coloured, or cut capers too fantastic.

Whether this is a very high aim, is another question. All we can say is that it has been fully attained in the volume before us; and we lay our frowns aside, and give ourselves up to watch the eccentric transformations of the Confidence-Man, in much the same spirit as we listen to the first verse of the song of Autolycus.

The scene of this comedy is one of the large American steamers on the Mississippi—the time of its action, one day—and its hero a clever impostor, who, under the successive disguises of a deaf mute, a crippled negro, a disconsolate widower, a charitable collector, a transfer agent, a herb doctor, a servant of the 'Philosophical Intelligence Office,' and a cosmopolitan traveller, contrives to take in almost every one with whom he comes in contact, and to make a good deal of money by these transactions. The characters are all wonderfully well sustained and linked together; and the scene of his exploits gives unlimited scope for the introduction of as many others as Mr. Melville's satirical pencil likes to sketch, from the good simple country merchant to the wretched miser, or the wild Missourian who had been worried into misanthropy by the pranks of thirty-five boys—and no wonder, poor man, if they were all like the one whose portrait we subjoin:—

[quotes from chapter 22, 'I say, this thirtieth' to 'all are rascals." ']

We likewise recommend to those readers who like tales of terror the story of Colonel John Moredock, the Indian hater. It opens up a dark page in American history, and throws some light on the feelings with which the backwoodsmen and red men mutually regard each other, and apparently with very good reason. Let those who are fond of borrowing money study the fate of the unlucky China Aster, and take warning by it. The portrait of the mystic philosopher, who 'seemed a kind of cross between a Yankee pedler and a Tartar priest,' is good in its way; and so is the practical commentary on his philosophy, contained in the following chapters, which attack severely, and with considerable power, the pretended philanthropical, but really hard and selfish optimist school, whose opinions seemed not long ago likely to gain many disciples.

There is one point on which we must speak a serious word to Mr. Melville before parting with him. He is too clever a man to be a profane one; and yet his occasionally irreverent use of Scriptural phrases in such a book as the one before us, gives a disagreeable impression. We hope he will not in future mar his wit and blunt the edge of his satire by such instances of bad taste. He has, doubtless, in the present case fallen into them inadvertently, for they are blemishes belonging generally to a far lower order of mind than his; and we trust that when the sequel of the masquerade of the Confidence-Man appears, as he gives us reason to hope that it soon will, we shall enjoy the pleasure of his society without this drawback.

Of the picture of American society which is here shown us, we cannot say much that is favourable. The money-getting spirit which appears to pervade every class of men in the States, almost like a monomania, is vividly portrayed in this satire; together with the want of trust and honour, and the innumerable 'operations' or 'dodges' which it is certain to engender. We wish that our own country was free from this vice, but some late commercial transactions prove us to be little, if at all, behind our Transatlantic cousins in this respect, and we gladly hail the assistance of so powerful a satirist as Mr. Melville in attacking the most dangerous and the most debasing tendency of the age.

141. Ann Sophia Stephens, unsigned review, *Mrs. Stephens' New Monthly Magazine*

June 1857, ii, 288

Mrs Stephens (1813–86) was an author of historical tales as well as an editor of a number of periodicals besides her own, including *Graham's* and *Peterson's*.

Mr. Herman Melville has also issued a new book, through the publishing house of Dix, Edwards & Co. It is called *The Confidence Man*. It is the most singular of the many singular books of this author. Mr. Melville seems to be bent upon obliterating his early successes. *Typee* and *Omoo* give us a right to expect something better than any of his later books have been. He appears now, to be merely trying how many eccentric things he can do. This is the more to be condemned, because in many important points he has sensibly advanced. His style has become more individualized—more striking, original, sinewy, compact; more reflective and philosophical. And yet, his recent books stand confessedly inferior to his earlier ones. As to *The Confidence Man*, we frankly acknowledge our inability to understand it. The scene is laid upon a Mississippi steamboat, on a voyage from St. Louis to New Orleans. In the course of the voyage The Confidence Man assumes innumerable disguises—with what object it is not clear—unless for the sake of dogmatizing, theorizing, philosophizing, and amplifying upon every known subject; all of which, philosophy, we admit to be sharp, comprehensive, suggestive, and abundantly entertaining. But the object of this masquerade? None appears. The book ends where it begins. You might, without sensible inconvenience, read it backwards. You are simply promised in the last line, that something further shall be heard of the hero; until which consummation, the riddle must continue to puzzle you unsolved.

142. Unsigned review, *Westminster and Foreign Quarterly Review*

July 1857, (n.s.) xii, 310–11

We are not among those who have had faith in Herman Melville's South Pacific travels so much as in his strength of imagination. The *Confidence-Man* shows him in a new character—that of a satirist, and a very keen, somewhat bitter, observer. His hero, like Mr. Melville in his earlier works, asks confidence of everybody under different masks of mendicancy, and is, on the whole, pretty successful. The scene is on board an American steamboat—that epitome of the American world—and a variety of characters are hustled on the stage to bring out the Confidence-Man's peculiarities: it is, in fact, a puppet-show; and, much as Punch is bothered by the Beadle, and calmly gets the better of all his enemies, his wife in the bargain, the Confidence-Man succeeds in baffling the one-legged man, whose suspicions and snappish incredulity constantly waylay him, and in counting a series of victims. Money is of course the great test of confidence, or credit in its place. Money and credit follow the Confidence-Man through all his transformations—misers find it impossible to resist him. It required close knowledge of the world, and of the Yankee world, to write such a book and make the satire acute and telling, and the scenes not too improbable for the faith given to fiction. Perhaps the moral is the gullibility of the great Republic, when taken on its own tack. At all events, it is a wide enough moral to have numerous applications, and sends minor shafts to right and left. Several capital anecdotes are told, and well told; but we are conscious of a certain hardness in the book, from the absence of humour, where so much humanity is shuffled into close neighbourhood. And with the absence of humour, too, there is an absence of kindliness. The view of human nature is severe and sombre—at least, that is the impression left on our mind. It wants relief, and is written too much in the spirit of Timon; who, indeed, saw life as it is, but first wasted his money, and then shut his heart, so that for him there was nothing save naked rock, without moss and flower. A moneyless man and a heartless man are not good exponents of our state. Mr. Melville has delineated with passable correctness, but he has forgotten to infuse the colours that exist in nature. The fault may lie in the uniqueness of the construction. Spread over a larger canvas, and taking in more of the innumerable sides of humanity, the picture might have been as accurate, the satire as sharp, and the author would not have laid himself open to the charge of harshness. Few Americans write so powerfully as Mr. Melville, or in better English, and we shall look forward with pleasure to his promised continuation of the masquerade. The first part is a remarkable work, and will add to his reputation.

143. Henry T. Tuckerman, from 'Authors At Home. Authors in Berkshire,' initialled essay, Philadelphia, Pennsylvania, *American Literary Gazette*

16 November 1863, 38–40

Tuckerman (1813–71), a well-known author, essayist, and critic, discusses in this article the homes of a number of American writers living in the Berkshires, including Nathaniel Hawthorne and Oliver Wendell Holmes, whose 'old residence' he describes immediately before Melville's.

Not far from his old residence lives Herman Melville, author of *Typee*, *Omoo*, *Moby Dick*, and other adventurous narratives, which have more of the genuine Robinson Crusoe spell about them than any American writings. The first and second were entirely new subjects, treated with a mingled simplicity and spirit that at once made the author's name a household and a shipboard word; the last, for curious and eloquent descriptions and details about the whale and whale fishing, rivals

Michelet's brilliant and copious brochures on the sea, woman, and other generic themes; but Melville is more scientific as to his facts, and more inventive as to his fiction. *Moby Dick*, indeed, has the rare fault of redundant power; the story is wild and wonderful enough without being interwoven with such a thorough, scientific, and economical treatise on the whale; it is a fine contribution to natural history and to political economy, united to an original and powerful romance of the sea. Melville has written other and more casual things, indicative of great versatility; witness his *Life of Israel Potten*, and his remarkable sketch of a Wall Street scrivener in *Putnam's Monthly*. Impaired health induced him to retire to this beautiful region, and in the care of his fruits and flowers, and the repose of domestic life, he seems to have forsworn the ambition of authorship, but we trust only for a time.

BATTLE PIECES

1866

144. Unsigned review, New York *Herald*

3 September 1866

A rough time of it the country had during our four years' war, and many of the lines in which Herman Melville, in his new character as a poet, commemorates it are not inappropriately rugged enough. The beginning of one of his 'Battle Pieces' characterizes his poetical style:—

Plain be the phrase, not apt the verse,
More ponderous than nimble.

In a prefatory note he says:—'I seem, in most of these verses, to have but placed a harp in a window and noted the contrasted airs which wayward winds have played upon the strings.' But we wish to direct special attention to the 'supplement' which Mr. Melville has added, in obedience to a claim overriding all literary scruples—a claim urged by patriotism not free from solicitude. So far from spoiling the symmetry of the book, this supplement completes it, and converts it into what is better than a good book—into a good and patriotic action. The writer sees clearly that there is no reason why patriotism and narrowness should go together, or why intellectual impartiality should be confounded with political trimming, or why serviceable truth should keep cloistered because not partisan. And therefore, 'in view of the infinite desirableness of re-establishment, and considering that, so far as feeling is concerned, it depends not mainly on the temper in which the South regards the North, but rather conversely. One who never was a blind adherent feels constrained to submit some thoughts, counting on the indulgence of his countrymen.' We are confident that 'the second sober thought' of his countrymen will endorse his views. We welcome these 'words in season,' not only as the deliberate, impartial testimony of a highly cultivated individual mind, but as hopeful signs of a change in public opinion and sentiment. A few extracts will show the laudable spirit in which Mr. Melville writes:—

[quotes from the Supplement, 'is Reason still waiting' to 'have had with individuals.']

145. 'More Poetry Of The War,' unsigned review, *Nation*

6 September 1866, 187–8

This is a review of *Battle Pieces* and of *The Old Sergeant* by Forceythe Willson.

It is only the great poet who is fitly inspired by great events. It is he alone who can express them worthily. But the same storm that piles up the waves of the sea sets all the duck-ponds in ineffectual commotion. The literary productiveness and facility of America display themselves just now in what is called poetry of the war; but most of what is thus designated is as ephemeral as the newspaper in which it usually appears. Our war has produced, at the outside, not more than half-a-dozen lyrics that deserve a place in literature, and has inspired but one truly great and lasting poem. Lowell's 'Commemoration Ode' takes its place securely, not only among the finest works of our generation, but among the noblest poems of all time. It is happy for us that the spirit of the war found a poet capable alike of receiving and expressing its full inspiration. No one who has felt the power of the master in this poem but must sometimes feel a little impatience and weariness with the common handiwork of the journeymen and apprentices, however much he may approve their industry or sympathize with the emotion which, in their degree, they experienced and attempt to express.

But the grandeur of the war—alike in its principles and its events—

must be the measure of the poetry of the war. It is only the highest art that can illustrate the highest deeds. The severest literary criticism on this poetry is not so hard as the criticism of the facts themselves. Unless the poet is as great as his theme, he must submit to be crushed by it, and the literary critic has little to do but to confront the verse and its subject.

If measured by this standard, Mr. Melville must take his place with the herd of recent versifiers. But his literary reputation gives his volume special claims to notice, and the abilities which he has shown in some of his other works entitle whatever he produces to respectful consideration. It is impossible, in view of what Mr. Melville has done and of his intention in his present book, not to read his *Battle Pieces* with a certain melancholy. Nature did not make him a poet. His pages contain at best little more than the rough ore of poetry. Here and there gleams of imaginative power shine out like the grains of gold in a mass of quartz. But, accustomed as we have been of late, in certain works professing to be poetry, to astonishing crudity and formlessness, we yet cannot refrain from expressing surprise that a man of Mr. Melville's literary experience and cultivation should have mistaken some of these compositions for poetry, or even for verse. There are some of them in which it is difficult to discover rhythm, measure, or consonance of rhyme. The thought is often involved and obscure. The sentiment is weakened by incongruous imagery. We quote the first piece in the volume lest our criticism be thought too severe:

THE PORTENT.

(1859.)

Hanging from the beam,
   Slowly swaying (such the law)
Gaunt the shadow on your green,
   Shenandoah!
The cut is on the crown
   (Lo, John Brown),
And the stabs shall heal no more.

Hidden in the cap
   Is the anguish none can draw;
So your future veils its face,
   Shenandoah!
But the streaming beard is shown
   (Weird John Brown),
The meteor of the war.

It would seem that only a writing medium could mistake such stuff as this for poetry. And, alas! there is more of it, and our regret is the keener when we find such simple and feeling verses as the following:

BALL'S BLUFF.

A REVERIE.

(October, 1861.)

One noonday, at my window in the town,
  I saw a sight—saddest that eyes can see—
  Young soldiers marching lustily
      Unto the wars
With fifes, and flags, and mottoed pageantry;
  While all the porches, walks, and doors
Were rich with ladies cheering royally.

They moved like Juny morning on the wave,
  Their hearts were fresh as clover in its prime
  (It was the breezy summer time),
      Life throbbed so strong;
How should they dream that death in a rosy clime
  Would come to thin their shining throng?
Youth feels immortal, like the gods sublime.

Weeks passed; and at my window, leaving bed,
  By night I mused, of easeful sleep bereft,
  On those brave boys (ah! war, thy theft);
      Some marching feet
Found pause at last by cliffs Potomac cleft;
  Wakeful I mused, while in the street
Far footfalls died away till none were left.

There are very few pieces in the volume so direct in expression and so natural in thought as this; but there are single lines, couplets, or quatrains in which genuine power is shown as well as genuine feeling. Take, for instance, the two following lines at the end of 'Misgivings,' the second piece in the volume:

And storms are formed behind the storm we feel;
The hemlock shakes in the rafter, the oak in the driving keel.

Here is another good couplet from a later poem:

All wars are boyish, and are fought by boys,
The champions and enthusiasts of the state;

and the following line from 'A Utilitarian View of the Monitor's Fight,'

> The clangor of that blacksmith's fray,

is not without a touch of imagination.

But these brief citations only serve to show how much better a very small part of the book is than the whole.

It is a misfortune that the special events which have moved Mr. Melville to write are the same, in several instances, which have already been put into verse by other writers, and that these earlier poems, already more or less familiar to the public, are necessarily brought into comparison with his. Thus his brief verses entitled 'Shiloh: a Requiem' almost inevitably suggest, by contrast, the very striking poem of Mr. Forceythe Willson's, of which a great part of the scene is laid on the battle-field of Shiloh, called 'The Old Sergeant.' The author of this poem has not as yet won the position in literature which may be predicted for him if he be really master of the qualities of which this poem gives evidence. We doubt if the war has inspired a narrative poem more imaginatively conceived, or more vigorously told. It is the work of an imaginative realist, and its power and pathos lie in the straightforward truthfulness of the poet in dealing alike with the spiritual and the material elements of the story. The narrative is conducted with great simplicity; it is entirely free from 'padding' or 'rhetoric,' and it is of so much interest that the defects which exist in it as a work of art may readily be overlooked. It first appeared, in 1863 (?), in the *Louisville Journal*, and has since been widely copied; and we are glad now to read it again in a form better suited to its merits.

146. Unsigned notice, *Godey's Lady's Book and Magazine*

December 1866, lxxiii, 540

This volume of poetry, which will, doubtless, find many admirers, is 'dedicated to those who fell fighting under the stars and stripes.'

147. Richard Henry Stoddard, unsigned review, New York *World*

19 October 1866

Stoddard (1825–1903), a contributor to several New York periodicals, was a customs inspector at the New York Customs House when Melville began his duties there in 1866. Stoddard's interest in Melville may have some relation to the fact that his father, Reuben Stoddard, was a seaman and, later, master of his own ship. He was lost at sea when his son was three years old. From 1860 to 1870 Stoddard wrote reviews for the *World* and from 1880 to 1903, for the New York *Mail and Express*.

Mr. Melville's earliest prose *chef d'œuvre*[1] established his claim to the possession of the poetic nature. It is now understood that *Typee* and *Omoo* were constructed upon a substantial basis of fact; but that concession degenerates nothing from the wonderful power of narrative manifested by the author—the gorgeous picturesqueness, the masterly management of intense dramatic situations, and the ability to infuse into the mind of all readers, high and low, the local coloring of an hitherto unknown barbarism, where the savage and the sumptuous were blended in one inextricable pageant of terror and glamour. Partaking partly of the *Arabian Nights*, and partly of *Robinson Crusoe*, it is not too much to say that Mr. Melville's earlier books have been promoted to a place beside those common favorites of boyhood and manhood, on the shelves of every mind which revelled in them.

The collection of battle-pieces exemplifies the fact that the poetic nature and the technical faculty of poetry writing are not identical. Whole pages of Mr. Melville's prose are, in the highest sense, poetic, and nearly all the battle-pieces would be much more poetic if they were thrown into the external prose form. The habit of his mind is not lyric, but historical, and the *genre* of historic poetry in which he most congenially expatiates finds rythm not a help but a hindrance. The exi-

[1] *Chef d'œuvre:* masterpiece.

gencies of rhyme hamper him still more, and against both of these trammels his vigorous thought habitually recalcitrates, refusing from time to time the harness which by adopting the verse-form it had voluntarily assumed. That it is not the nature of his thought which is at fault, may be plainly perceived from multitudes of strong and beautiful images, many thoughts picturesquely put, which, belonging legitimately to the poetic domain, still refuse to obey the rigid regimental order of the stanza, but outly its lines, deployed as irregular, though brilliant skirmishers. From the book, which treats in something like chronological order, a selection from the more prominent passages of our late war, we may extract, turning at random, a few passages to illustrate our meaning.

'The March into Virginia—ending in the first Manassas,' contains this beautiful descriptive fragment:

> The banners play, the bugles call,
> The air is blue and prodigal.
>   No berrying party, pleasure-woed,
> No pic-nic party in the May
> Ever went less loth than they
>   Into that leafy neighborhood.
> In Bacchic glee they file toward Fate
> Molock's uninitiate.

The last stanza of the same poem, making a forcible antithesis to that just quoted, has its artistic value, and simultaneously much of its vigor, marred by the change in the last line from an heroic to an entirely different lyric metre:

> But some who this blithe mood present,
>   As on in lightsome files they fare,
> Shall die experienced ere three days are spent—
>   Perish, enlightened by the vollied glare;
> Or shame survive, and, like to adamant,
>   *The throe of Second Manassas share.*

In the poem, 'Lyon-Battle of Springfield,' twice occurs the inadmissible rhyme of 'iron' and 'Lyon,' as well as this fine expression:

> By candlelight he wrote the will
>   And left his all
> *To her for whom 'twas not enough to fall.*

The last stanza says that he

—Foresaw his soldier doom,
Yet willed the fight.
He never turned; his only flight
Was up to Zion,
Where prophets now and armies greet brave Lyon.

It is easy to see that the allusion here is to the 'goodly fellowship of the prophets,' and 'the noble army of martyrs' of the *Te Deum*; but the adjective 'brave' greatly weakens the last line, and makes it a disproportionate *finale* to the fine thought of the two preceding ones.

We might go on to instance such technical blemishes as the rhyming of 'law' and 'Shenandoah,' 'more' and 'Kenesaw,' but we forbear, lest we should seem carping at a book which, without having one poem of entire artistic *ensemble* in it, possesses numerous passages of beauty and power. For these it is well worth going through, and belongs, at any rate, to a place on the shelves of those who are collecting the literature of the war, as well as of that much larger class who would not be without a book of *Typee*'s gifted author.

148. Unsigned notice, *Harper's New Monthly Magazine*

January 1867, xxxiv, 265

Mr Melville has broken a long silence in a manner hardly to have been expected of the author of *Typee* and *Mardi*. Among these poems are some—among them 'The March to the Sea' and that upon 'Stonewall Jackson, ascribed to a Virginian'—which will stand as among the most stirring lyrics of the war.

149. Unsigned review, *Atlantic Monthly*

February 1867, xix, 252–3

Mr. Melville's work possesses the negative virtues of originality in such degree that it not only reminds you of no poetry you have read, but of no life you have known. Is it possible—you ask yourself, after running over all these celebrative, inscriptive, and memorial verses—that there has really been a great war, with battles fought by men and bewailed by women? Or is it only that Mr. Melville's inner consciousness has been perturbed, and filled with the phantasms of enlistments, marches, fights in the air, parenthetic bulletin-boards, and tortured humanity shedding, not words and blood, but words alone?

Mr. Melville chooses you a simple and touching theme, like that of the young officer going from his bride to hunt Mosby in the forest, and being brought back to her with a guerrilla's bullet in his heart,—a theme warm with human interests of love, war, and grief, and picturesque with green-wood lights and shadows,—and straight enchants it into a mystery of thirty-eight stanzas, each of which diligently repeats the name of Mosby, and deepens the spell, until you are lost to every sense of time or place, and become as callous at the end as the poet must have been at the beginning to all feeling involved, doubting that

> The living and the dead are but as pictures.

Here lies the fault. Mr. Melville's skill is so great that we fear he has not often felt the things of which he writes, since with all his skill he fails to move us. In some respects we find his poems admirable. He treats events as realistically as one can to whom they seem to have presented themselves as dreams; but at last they remain vagaries, and are none the more substantial because they have a modern speech and motion. We believe ghosts are not a whit more tangible now that they submit to be photographed in the sack-coats and hoop-skirts of this life, than before they left off winding-sheets, and disappeared if you spoke to them.

With certain moods or abstractions of the common mind during the war, Mr. Melville's faculty is well fitted to deal: the unrest, the strangeness and solitude, to which the first sense of the great danger reduced all souls, are reflected in his verse, and whatever purely mystic aspect occurrences had seems to have been felt by this poet, so little capable of giving their positive likeness.

The sentiment and character of the book are perhaps as well shown in its first poem as in any other part of it. Mr. Melville calls the verses 'The Portent (1859)'; but we imagine he sees the portent, as most portents are seen, after the event portended.

Hanging from the beam,
    Slowly swaying (such the law),
Gaunt the shadow on your green,
    Shenandoah!
The cut is on the crown
(Lo, John Brown),
And the stabs shall heal no more.

Hidden in the cap
    Is the anguish none can draw;
So your future veils its face,
    Shenandoah!
But the streaming beard is shown
(Weird John Brown),
The meteor of the war.

There is not much of John Brown in this, but, as we intimated, a good deal of Mr. Melville's method, and some fine touches of picturesque poetry. Indeed, the book is full of pictures of many kinds,—often good,—though all with an heroic quality of remoteness, separating our weak human feelings from them by trackless distances. Take this of the death of General Lyon's horse a few moments before he was himself struck at Springfield,—a bit as far off from us as any of Ossian's, but undeniably noble:—

There came a sound like the slitting of air
    By a swift sharp sword—
A rush of the sound; and the sleek chest broad
    Of black Orion
Heaved, and was fixed; the dead mane waved toward Lyon.

We have never seen anywhere so true and beautiful a picture as the following of that sublime and thrilling sight,—a great body of soldiers marching:—

The bladed guns are gleaming—
    Drift in lengthened trim,
Files on files for hazy miles
    Nebulously dim.

A tender and subtile music is felt in many of the verses, and the eccentric metres are gracefully managed. We received from the following lines a pleasure which may perhaps fail to reach the reader, taking them from their context in the description of a hunt for guerillas, in the ballad already mentioned:—

The morning-bugles lonely play,
  Lonely the evening-bugle calls—
Unanswered voices in the wild;
  The settled hush of birds in nest
  Becharms, and all the wood enthralls:
    Memory's self is so beguiled
    That Mosby seems a satyr's child.

He does so; and the other persons in Mr. Melville's poetry seem as widely removed as he from our actual life. If all the Rebels were as pleasingly impalpable as those the poet portrays, we could forgive them without a pang, and admit them to Congress without a test-oath of any kind.

CLAREL

1876

150. Edmund Clarence Stedman, unsigned review, New York *Tribune*

16 June 1876

Stedman (1833–1908), an editor, poet, and critic, showed great interest in Melville's writings and knew Melville personally during the last three years of his life. Stedman joined the staff of the New York *World* in 1860, serving as a correspondent during the American Civil War. His son, Arthur, directed the re-issuing of *Typee*, *Omoo*, *White-Jacket*, and *Moby-Dick* soon after Melville's death.

After a long silence, Mr. Herman Melville speaks again to the world. No more a narrator of marvelous stories of tropical life and adventure, no more a weird and half-fascinating, half-provoking writer of romances, but now as a poet with a single work, in four parts, and about 17,000 lines in length. We knew already that Mr. Melville's genius has a distinctly poetical side; we remember still his stirring lines on Sheridan's Ride, commencing:

> Shoe the steed with silver,
> That bore him to the fray!

But the present venture is no less hazardous than ambitious. A narrative poem of such a length demands all the charms of verse, the strength and interest of plot, the picturesqueness of episode, and the beauty of sentimental or reflective digression which the author's art is capable of creating; and even then it may lack the subtle spell which chains the reader to its perusal. *Clarel*, we must frankly confess, is something of a puzzle, both in design and execution. A short excursion in Palestine—the four parts of the poem being entitled Jerusalem, the Wilderness, Mar

Saba, and Bethlehem—gives a framework of landscape and incident to the characters, who are Clarel, a student, a doubter and dreamer; Nehemiah, an old Rhode Island religious enthusiast; Vine, a problematic character; Rolfe, 'a messmate of the elements;' Derwent, an English clergyman; Glaucon, a Smyrniote Greek; and Mortmain, an eccentric Swede. After a love-passage between Clarel and Ruth, a young Jewish girl, in Jerusalem, the above characters make up a party for Jericho, the Jordan and the Dead Sea, returning by way of the Greek monastery of Mar Saba and Bethlehem. The excursion lasts but a few days: they return to Jerusalem by night, and find Ruth dead and about to be buried by torch-light. Passion Week follows, and with it the poem closes. Clarel with his grief, and the other characters with their several eccentricities, disappear suddenly from our view.

There is thus no plot in the work; but neither do the theological doubts, questions, and disputations indulged in by the characters, and those whom they meet, have any logical course or lead to any distinct conclusions. The reader soon becomes hopelessly bewildered, and fatigues himself vainly in the effort to give personality to speakers who constantly evade it, and connection to scenes which perversely hold themselves separate from each other. The verse, frequently flowing for a few lines with a smooth, agreeable current, seems to foam and chafe against unmanageable words like a brook in a stony glen: there are fragments of fresh, musical lyrics, suggestive both of Hafiz and of William Blake; there are passages so rough, distorted, and commonplace withal, that the reader impatiently shuts the book. It is, in this respect, a medley such as we have rarely perused,—a mixture of skill and awkwardness, thought and aimless fancy, plan shattered by whim and melody broken by discords. It is difficult to see how any one capable of writing such excellent brief passages should also write such astonishingly poor ones—or the reverse.

The descriptive portions of the poem are often bold, clear, and suggestive of the actual scenes. We might make a collection of admirable lines and couplets, which have the ring and sparkle of true poetry. On the other hand it would be equally easy to multiply passages like the following, the sense of which is only reached with difficulty, and then proves to be hardly worth the trouble of seeking:

> But one there was (and Clarel he)
> Who, in his aspect free from cloud,
> Here caught a gleam from source unspied,
> As cliff may take on mountain-side,

When there one small brown cirque ye see,
Lit up in mole, how mellowly,
Day going down in somber shroud—
October pall.
But tell the vein
Of new emotion, inly held
That so the long contention quelled—
Languor and indecision, pain.
Was it abrupt resolve? a strain
Wiser than wisdom's self might teach?
Yea, now his hand would boldly reach
And pluck the nodding fruit to him,
Fruit of the tree of life.

As a contrast, we take at random a few of the lyrical passages scattered through the work:

Noble gods at the board,
Where lord unto lord
Light pushes the care-killing wine:
Urbane in their pleasure,
Superb in their leisure—
Lax ease—
Lax ease after labor divine!

With a rose in thy mouth
Through the world lightly veer;
Rose in the mouth
Makes a rose of the year!

But through such strange illusions have they passed
Who in life's pilgrimage have baffled striven—
Even death may prove unreal at the last,
And stoics be astounded into heaven.

The ordinary reader will find himself in the position of one who climbs over a loose mound of sliding stones and gravel, in the search for the crystals which here and there sparkle from the mass. Some may suspect a graver enigma hidden in the characters of the story, and study them with that patience which the author evidently presupposes; but all will agree that a little attention to the first principles of poetic art would have made their task much more agreeable. An author has the right, simply as an individual, to disregard those principles, and must therefore be equally ready to accept the consequences. There is a vein of earnestness in Mr. Melville's poem, singularly at variance with the carelessness of the execution; but this only increases the impression of confusion which it makes.

151. Richard Henry Stoddard, unsigned review, New York *World*

26 June 1876

The reader who undertakes to read a poem of 600 pages in length, thirty-five lines to the page, is more than apt to receive the reward given by Jupiter to the man whom he caused to seek a grain of wheat in a bushel of chaff—to wit, the chaff. Good lines there must be, but they and their effect will alike be lost in the overwhelming tide of mediocrity. There are very few themes capable of such expansion, and the theme being found, very, very few authors capable of conducting it successfully to the close. In the present instance Mr. Melville has for subject the story of a short pilgrimage in the Holy Land, and as characters an old religious enthusiast of Yankee birth; a Swede; an English clergyman; a Greek; a Jewish girl, Ruth; a very nondescript genius, Vine; and another, Rolfe, who

> Was no scholastic partisan
> Or euphopist of Academe,
> But supplemented Plato's theme
> With dædal life in boats and tents,
> A messmate of the elements.

Last comes the hero who gives the name to the poem, Clarel, a doubting, dreaming student. There is no particular reason why these characters should be assembled, but they are. Clarel falls in love with Ruth at Jerusalem, leaves her for a brief tour through the Holy Land, and returns to, as the French would say, assist at her funeral by torch-light, the book concluding with a description of Passion Week, and the characters vanish with about as much reason as they had for appearing at the first. There is thus no plot to sustain the interest of the reader, but there is a constant opportunity, fatal to such a facile writer as Mr. Melville, for digression, discussion, and, above all, description. Given these characters and that scene, there is no earthly reason why the author should have turned the faucet and cut off his story at 21,000 lines instead of continuing to 221,000. Not being in his confidence we cannot of course say why he wrote the book, and what he intended it to mean, whether it has any cause or object. In the absence of this information, the reader is harassed by constant doubt whether the fact that he hasn't apprehended its motive and moral is due to his own obtuseness, or—distracting thought!—to the entire absence of either. The style is just as provoking. After a lot of jog-trot versifying—Mr. Melville rhymes 'hand' and 'sustained,' and 'day' and 'Epiphany' in the first ten lines—and just as he is prepared to abandon the book as a hopeless case, he stumbles on a passage of striking original thought, or possessing the true lyrical ring and straightway is lured over another thousand lines or so, the process being repeated till the book ends just where it began. There has been much action but nothing has been accomplished. There is some very break-neck reading, as for instance:

> 'The chiffonier!' cried Rolfe: 'e'en grim
> Milcom and Chemosh scowl at him,
> Here nosing underneath their lee
> Of pagod heights.'

The philosophizing of the book is its least agreeable part, nor can the analyzations of character—or what appear to be intended therefor—receive much higher praise. Its best passages, as a rule, are the descriptive ones, which, notwithstanding frequent turgidness and affectation, are frequently bold, clear, and judicious. On the whole, however, it is hardly a book to be commended, for a work of art it is not in any sense or measure, and if it is an attempt to grapple with any particular problem of the universe, the indecision as to its object and processes is sufficient to appal or worry the average reader.

152. From an unsigned review, New York *Times*

10 July 1876

The appearance of a poem in two volumes of three hundred pages each from a writer of Mr. Herman Melville's undoubted talent cannot fail to be a matter of interest to a wide circle of readers. The poem is upon the Holy Land, and is descriptive, narrative, and religious. It is in four parts, 'Jerusalem,' 'The Wilderness,' 'Near Sabe,' and 'Bethlehem,' and among these regions the scene of the work is laid. *Clarel* is not without signs of power such as we should have expected from Mr. Melville. Here and there we have delicate and vigorous pieces of description. But of the poem as a whole we do not think we can be far wrong when we say that it should have been written in prose. The author's genius is evidently not of the kind which must express itself in numbers. Nor has he that minor gift of facile verse which constitutes him one of the 'mob of gentlemen who write with ease.' The metre selected is the octo-syllable, which Scott used in his narrative poems. But from the 'fatal facility' which Byron said inhered in this verse Mr. Melville does not appear to have suffered. It is often very difficult work with the author. In describing the familiar fact that a horseman going down hill leans backward in order to preserve his centre of gravity, Mr. Melville writes:

> How fair
> And light he leaned with easeful air
> Backward in saddle, so to frame
> A counterpoise, as down he came.

The next three lines are better:

> Against the dolorous mountain side
> His Phrygian cap in scarlet pride,
> Burned like a cardinal flower in glen.

Indeed, there are many good pieces of description in the book, showing how sensible the author's mind is to the noble scenery of the East, to the poetic interest which attaches to man's handiwork in those ancient and remote regions, and to the misery of the contemporaneous society, so trifling and transitory do the living in that land of shadow and antiquity seem by the side of the dead. The following, addressed to Clarel as he enters this Gate of Zion by the lepers, is forcible:

> Behold, proud worm, (if such can be,)
> What yet may come, yea, even to thee.
> Who knoweth? Canst forecast the fate
> In infinite ages? Probe thy state:
> Sinless art thou? Then these sinned not,
> These, these are men; and thou art—what?

The following gives poetical expression to a well-known fact:

> Jerusalem, the mountain town
> Is based how far above the sea;
> But down, a lead-line's long reach down,
> A deep-sea lead, beneath the zone
> Of ocean's level, Heaven's decree
> Has sunk the pool whose deep submerged
> The doomed Pentapolis fire-scourged.
>   Long then the slope, though varied oft,
> From Zion to the seats abject;
> For rods and roods ye wind aloft
> By verges where the pulse is checked;
> And chief both height and steepness show
> Ere Achor's gorge the barrier rends
> And like a thunder-cloud impends
> Ominous over Jerico.

The thread of the story which *Clarel* contains the reader will find some difficulty in deciphering. If Mr. Melville had condescended to follow the example of Milton, he might have eased the reader's task by placing before his poem an 'argument.' . . .

. . . If Mr. Melville has any special tenets of religion to advance he has chosen a vehicle somewhat at variance with intelligibility, and the reader will have some trouble in making them out. In the 'epilogue' the poet thus speaks of faith and science:

> Yes, ape and angel, strife and old debate—
> The harps of heaven and dreary gongs of hell;
> Science the feud can only aggravate—
> No umpire she betwixt the chimes and knell:
> The running battle of the star and clod
> Shall run forever—if there be no God.

Such merit as Mr. Melville's poem has is in its descriptions and in the Oriental atmosphere which he has given his work. There is no nonsense about the book; it is written in an honest and sincere style, but verse is certainly not the author's forte.

153. Unsigned notice, *Galaxy*

August 1876, xxii, 282

We confess that we are puzzled by the title of Mr. Herman Melville's last volume—*Clarel: a Poem and Pilgrimage in the Holy Land*. How a book can be a poem in the Holy Land, or a pilgrimage in the Holy Land, or a pilgrimage at all, or how it can be both a poem and a pilgrimage, we really cannot discover. The fact of the matter, set forth in simple English, is, that *Clarel* is a poem which narrates and comments upon a pilgrimage in the Holy Land. We are by no means in a captious, or a dissenting, or even a fastidious mood, but we cannot praise Mr. Melville's poem or pilgrimage, or poem-pilgrimage. It is sadly uninteresting. It is not given even to the gods to be dull; and Mr. Melville is not one of the gods.

154. Unsigned review, London *Academy*

19 August 1876, 185

These volumes are thoroughly described in their title. An American traveller in the Holy Land, full of Western thought, formed by modern civilisation, wanders among Eastern shrines where dawned a faith which seems now dying, now possessed of a strange vitality: at one time changeless, at another capable of adapting itself to every age and time. The traveller falls in with companions in his journey and makes new friends, nor is a more tender element wholly wanting. The scenes of the pilgrimage, the varying thoughts and emotions called up by them, are carefully described, and the result is a book of very great interest, and poetry of no mean order. The form is subordinate to the matter, and a rugged inattention to niceties of rhyme and metre here and there seems rather deliberate than careless. In this, in the musical verse where the writer chooses to be musical, in the subtle blending of old and new thought, in the unexpected turns of argument, and in the hidden connexion between things outwardly separate, Mr. Melville reminds us of A. H. Clough. He probably represents one phase of American thought as truly as Clough did one side of the Oxford of his day. The following lines on the Holy Sepulchre are striking:—

In Crete they claimed the tomb of Jove,
In glen o'er which his eagles soar;
But through a peopled town ye rove
To Christ's low tomb, where, nigh the door,
Settles the dove. So much the more
The contrast stamps the human God
Who dwelt among us, made abode
With us, and was of woman born;
Partook our bread and thought no scorn
To share the humblest, homeliest hearth,
Shared all of man except the sin and mirth.
—Vol. i., p. 16.

We must make room for one more quotation, which is typical of the tone and spirit as well as the poetry of the whole:—

He espied
Upon the mountain humbly kneeling
Those shepherds twain, while morning tide
Rolled o'er the hills with golden healing.
It was a rock they kneeled upon,
Convenient for their rite avowed—
Kneeled and their turbaned foreheads bowed—
Bowed over till they kissed the stone:
Each shaggy sur-coat heedful spread
For rug such as in mosque is laid.
About the ledge's favoured hem
Mild fed their sheep enringing them,
While facing as by second sight
Toward Mecca they direct the rite.
'Look; and their backs on Bethlehem turned,'
Cried Rolfe. The priest then, who discerned
The drift, replied 'Yes, for they pray
To Allah.' Well, and what of that?
Christ listens standing in heaven's gate,
Benignant listens, nor doth stay
Upon a syllable in creed,
Vowels and consonants indeed.

—Vol. ii., p. 477.

We advise our readers to study this interesting poem, which deserves more attention than we fear it is likely to gain in an age which craves for smooth, short, lyric song, and is impatient for the most part of what is philosophic or didactic.

GENERAL ESTIMATE

1884

155. W. Clark Russell, from 'Sea Stories,' article, *Contemporary Review*

September 1884, xlvi, 343–63

Russell (1844–1911) was a well-known English sea-novelist and became a great proponent of Melville's writings of the sea. His years in the merchant service resulted in his writing many articles on sea topics, especially regarding the grievances of merchant seamen—one of the major themes in 'Sea Stories.' Russell and Melville exchanged letters, and Melville dedicated *John Marr* to the Englishman.

Cooper pleases and has pleased, and is to this day read and admired by thousands; but speaking from a sailor's point of view, I really have no words to express the delight with which I quit his novels for the narratives of his countrymen, Dana and Herman Melville.

Whoever has read the writings of Melville must I think feel disposed to consider *Moby Dick* as his finest work. It is indeed all about the sea, whilst *Typee* and *Omoo*, are chiefly famous for their lovely descriptions of the South Sea Islands, and of the wild and curious inhabitants of those coral strands; but though the action of the story is altogether on shipboard, the narrative is not in the least degree nautical in the sense that Cooper's and Marryat's novels are. . . .

. . . *Moby Dick* is not a sea-story—one could not read it as such—it is a medley of noble impassioned thoughts born of the deep, pervaded by a grotesque human interest, owing to the contrast it suggests between the rough realities of the cabin and the forecastle, and the phantasms of men conversing in rich poetry, and strangely moving and acting in that dim weather-worn Nantucket whaler. There is a chapter where the sailors are represented as gathered together on the forecastle; and what is made to pass among them, and the sayings which are put into their mouths, might truly be thought to have come down to us from some giant mind of the Shakspearean era. As we read, we do not need to be told that seamen don't talk as those men do; probabilities are not thought of in this story. It is like a drawing by William Blake, if you please; or, better yet, it is of the 'Ancient Mariner' pattern, madly fantastic in places, full of extraordinary thoughts, yet gloriously coherent—the work of a hand which, if the desire for such a thing had ever been, would have given a sailor's distinctness to the portrait of the solemn and strange Miltonic fancy of a ship built in the eclipse and rigged with curses dark. In *Typee*, and *Omoo*, and *Redburn*, he takes other ground, and writes—always with the finest fancy—in a straight-headed way. I am concerned with him only as a seafarer. In *Redburn* he tells a sailor's yarn, and the dream-like figures of the crew of the *Pequod* make place for Liverpool and Yankee seamen, who chew tobacco and use bad language. His account of the sufferings of the emigrants in this book leaves a deep impression upon the mind. His accuracy is unimpeachable here, for the horrors he relates were as well known thirty and forty years ago as those of the middle passages were in times earlier still. In *Omoo*, again, he gives us a good deal of the sea, and presumably relates his own experiences on board a whaler. . . .

He . . . charms the nautical reader with the faithfulness of his portraiture, and the humour and the poetry he puts into it. There is some remarkable character-drawing in this book: notably John Jermin, the mate of the *Little Jule*, and Doctor Long Ghost, the nickname given by the sailors to a man who shipped as a physician, and was rated as a gentleman and lived in the cabin, until both the captain and he falling drunk, he drove home his views on politics by knocking the skipper down, after which he went to live forward. He is as quaint, striking, and original a personage as may be found in English fiction, and we find him in the dingy and leaky forecastle of the *Little Jule*, where he is surrounded by coarse and worn whalemen in Scotch caps and ragged clothes quoting Virgil, talking of Hobbes, 'besides repeating poetry by the canto, especially "Hudibras."' Yet his portrait does not match that of John Jermin, the mate, whom, in spite of his love of rum and homely method of reasoning with a man by means of a handspike, one gets to heartily like and to follow about with laughter as, intoxicated, he chases the sun all over the deck at noon with an old quadrant at his eye, or tumbles into the forecastle after a seaman who has enraged him by contemptuous remarks. Both Melville and Dana, who deal with the Merchant Service, show us in their books how trifling has been the change in the inner life of the sea during the forty or fifty years since they wrote about it. The merchant sailor of 1884 has still the same complaint to make that was made by his predecessor in 1840 and during many a long year before. . . . It is well indeed when men who have suffered the experiences and preserved the knowledge of sailors write books about the sea, that they should include all harsh facts which may help to teach the world what the mariner's life is. Dana and Melville have written thus, and whatever they say is stamped with genius and truth. The ocean is the theatre of more interests than boys would care to follow. We laugh with Marryat; we read Cooper for his 'plots;' we find much that is dashing and flattering to our patriotism in the 'Tom Bowlings,' and 'Will Watches,' and 'Tough Yarns,' and 'Topsail Sheet-blocks;' in the sprawling and fighting and drinking school of sea yarns; but when we turn to Dana and Melville, we find that the real life of the sea is not to be found between yellow covers adorned with catching cuts; that all the romance does not lie in cocked-hats and epaulets, but that by far the largest proportion of the sentiment, the pathos of the deep, the bitterness and suffering of the sailor's life, must be sought in the gloomy forecastle of the humble coaster, in the deckhouses of the deep-laden cargo-steamer, in the crew's dwelling-place on board the big ship trading to Australia and India and China. It is because only two or three writers have kept their eye steadfastly on this walk of the marine calling, and it is because all the rest who have written about the sea have represented the sailor as a jolly, drinking, dancing, skylarking fellow, that the shore-going public have come to get the wildest, absurdest notion of Jack's real character and professional life. For one who reads Dana and Melville, thousands read Marryat and Michael Scott, and Chamier, and Cupples, and Neale. . . .

JOHN MARR

1888

156. Richard Henry Stoddard, unsigned review, New York *Mail and Express*

20 November 1888

The reputation of no American writer stood higher forty years ago than that of Herman Melville. Like his predecessor, Richard Henry Dana, Jr., he went to sea before the mast, starting, if we have not forgotten, from Nantucket or New Bedford on a whaler. Familiar from boyhood with such eminent writers of sea stories as Smollett and Marryat, he adventured into strange seas in *Omoo* and *Typee*, which were speedily followed by *Mardi*, a not very skillful allegory, and *Moby Dick*, which is probably his greatest work. He was the peer of Hawthorne in popular estimation, and was by many considered his superior. His later writings were not up to the same high level. With all his defects, however, Mr. Melville is a man of unquestionable talent, and of considerable genius. He is a poet also, but his verse is marked by the same untrained imagination which distinguishes his prose. He is the author of the second best cavalry poem in the English language, the first being Browning's 'How They Brought the Good News from Ghent to Aix.' His prose is characterized by a vein of true poetical feeling, as elemental as the objects to which it is directed. Nothing finer than his unrhymed poems exists outside of the sea lyrics of Campbell. The present text of these observations is to be found in the little volume, *John Marr, and Other Sailors*, of which only a limited edition is published, and which contains about twenty poems of varying degrees of merit, but all with the briny flavor that should belong to songs of the sea.

GENERAL ESTIMATES

1889–92

157. H. S. Salt, 'Herman Melville,' article, *Scottish Art Review*

November 1889, ii, 186–90

Henry S. Salt (1851–1939), another English admirer of Melville, wrote biographies of James Thompson ('B.V.') and Thoreau and critical studies of Shelley and Tennyson. He and Melville corresponded in Melville's last years, concerning in particular Salt's plan to reprint *Typee* in the Camelot Series, which included writings of Hazlitt and Landor.

'Instead of a landsman's grey-goose quill, he seems to have plucked a quill from a skimming curlew, or to have snatched it, a fearful joy, from a hovering albatross, if not from the wings of the wind itself.'

This extract, from the pages of a bygone review, is a sample of the outburst of interest and admiration which greeted the appearance of Herman Melville's earlier volumes more than forty years ago. Such books as *Typee*, *Omoo*, and *Mardi* challenged attention by the originality of their style, their suggestive piquancy of tone, the strangeness of the experiences of which they purported to be the record, and not least by the very grotesqueness of the titles themselves. Who and what was the narrator of these mysterious adventures among the islands of the Pacific? Was he, as his stories implied, a common seaman serving before the mast—now on a whaler, now on an American frigate, and devoting the interim of his voyages to the publication of his diary; or was he rather, as might be surmised from the cultured tone of his writings and the fictitious aspect of some of his 'narratives,' a man of liberal education and imaginative temperament, who promulgated these romantic accounts of perils in the South Seas from some comfortable quarters in London or New York? The critics, intent on such questions as these, were fairly puzzled as to Herman Melville's identity; even his name was declared by some to be a *nom de plume*. 'Separately,' said one wiseacre, 'the names are not uncommon; we can urge no valid reason against their juncture; yet, in this instance, they fall suspiciously on our ear.' . . .

His books may be roughly divided into two classes, according to the predominance of the practical or the fantastic element. *Typee*, the 'narrative of a four months' residence in the Marquesas Islands,' appeared in 1846, and takes precedence of all his other writings, in merit no less than in date. Few indeed are the books of adventure that can vie with this charming little volume in freshness, humour, and literary grace, above all in the extraordinary interest which the story, simple as it is, inspires in the mind of the reader, from the first page to the last. . . . —all this is depicted with the firmness of outline indicative of a true narrative, yet invested (such is the literary skill of the narrator) with the filmy mystery of a fairy tale. The characters of those particular islanders among whom 'Tommo's' lot was cast are drawn with wonderful clearness; the warrior-chief Mehevi, the aged Marheyo, the housewife Tinor, the faithful but officious Kory-Kory, and above all the gentle and beautiful Fayaway—surely one of the most charming maidens ever sketched by poet or novelist—stand before us to the life. There is much valuable information in the book about various native customs, such as the mysterious edict of the 'taboo,' the process of tatooing, the manufacture of the white 'tappa' cloth, the polyandrous marriage system, and certain superstitious creeds and ceremonials. The remarks also on the comparative happiness of civilised and uncivilised nations are extremely interesting and suggestive. . . .

Omoo (*i.e.*, in Polynesian dialect, 'a rover') was published a year later than *Typee*, to which it supplies the sequel. It is altogether a more desultory and discursive book than its predecessor; but there is much vigour in the narrator's description of his voyage from Typee to Tahiti on board the 'Little Jule,' and his subsequent adventures in the Society Islands. Some remarks in which he commented severely on the errors committed by Christian missionaries in their treatment of the native Polynesians gave great offence to the critics, who attempted to discount the effect by impeaching the character of the sailor-novelist, especially on the subject of his relations with the charming Fayaway. . . .

Redburn (1849) and *White Jacket* (1850) complete the category of

Melville's distinctly autobiographical writings. . . . *White Jacket* is a careful study of all the doings on board a man-of-war, its sum and substance being a strong protest, on humane grounds, against the over-bearing tyranny of the naval officers and the depravity of the crew. 'So long as a man-of-war exists,' he says, 'it must ever remain a picture of much that is tyrannical and repelling in human nature.' The serious tone of the book is, however, relieved and diversified by some brilliant touches of humorous description . . . .

Melville's later works must be considered as phantasies rather than a relation of sober facts. He was affected, like so many of his countrymen, by the transcendental tendency of the age, and the result in his case was a strange blending of the practical and the metaphysical, his stories of what purported to be plain matter-of-fact life being gradually absorbed and swallowed up in the wildest mystical speculations. This process was already discernible in *Mardi*, published as early as 1849, the first volume of which is worthy to rank with the very finest achievements of its author, while the rest had far better have remained altogether un-written. . . .

Moby Dick; or, The White Whale (1851) is perhaps more successful as a whole than *Mardi*, since its very extravagances, great as they are, work in more harmoniously with the outline of the plot. . . . The book is a curious compound of real information about whales in general and fantastic references to this sperm-whale in particular, that 'portentous and mysterious monster,' which is studied (as the bird is studied by Michelet) in a metaphysical and ideal aspect—'a mass of tremendous life, all obedient to one volition, as the smallest insect.' Wild as the story is, there is a certain dramatic vigour in the 'quenchless feud' between Ahab and Moby Dick which at once arrests the reader's attention, and this interest is well maintained to the close, the final hunting-scene being a perfect nightmare of protracted sensational description.

Moby Dick was published when Melville was still a young man of thirty-three. Before he was forty he produced several other volumes, none of which were calculated to add in any degree to his fame, one of them, entitled *Pierre; or, The Ambiguities*, being perhaps the *ne plus ultra*[1] in the way of metaphysical absurdity.

> Physic of metaphysic begs defence,
> And metaphysic calls for aid on sense.

It may seem strange that so vigorous a genius, from which stronger

[1] *Ne plus ultra:* furthest point.

and stronger work might reasonably have been expected, should have reached its limit at so early a date; but it must be remembered that the six really notable books of which I have made mention were produced within a period of less than six years. Whether the transcendental obscurities in which he latterly ran riot were the cause or the consequence of the failure of his artistic powers is a point which it would be difficult to determine with precision. His contemporary critics were inclined, not unnaturally, to regard his mysticism as a kind of *malice prepense*,[1] and inveighed mournfully against the perversity of 'a man born to create, who resolves to anatomise, a man born to see, who insists upon speculating,' and warned him, after the publication of *Pierre*, that his fame was on the edge of a precipice, and that if he were wise he would thenceforth cease to affect the style of Sir Thomas Browne, and study that of Addison. . . .

The chief characteristic of Herman Melville's writings is this attempted union of the practical with the ideal. Commencing with a basis of solid fact, he loves to build up a fantastic structure, which is finally lost in the cloudland of metaphysical speculation. He is at his best, as in *Typee*, when the mystic element is kept in check, and made subservient to the clear development of the story; or when, as in certain passages of *Mardi* and *Moby Dick*, the two qualities are for the time harmoniously blended. His strong attraction to the sea and to ships, which has already been alluded to as dating from his earliest boyhood, was closely connected with this ideality of temperament; for the sea, he tells us, was to him 'the image of the ungraspable phantom of life,' while a ship was 'no piece of mechanism merely, but a creature of thoughts and fancies, instinct with life, standing at whose vibrating helm you feel her beating pulse.' 'I have loved ships,' he adds, 'as I have loved men.'

The tone of Melville's books is altogether frank and healthy, though of direct ethical teaching there is little or no trace, except on the subject of humanity, on which he expresses himself with strong and genuine feeling. He speaks with detestation of modern warfare, and devotes more than one chapter of *White Jacket* to an exposure of the inhuman system of flogging, then prevalent in the navy, asking at the close if he be not justified 'in immeasurably denouncing this thing.' In *Typee* and *Omoo* he again and again protests against the shameful ill-usage of the harmless Pacific islanders by their 'civilised' invaders. . . .

That Melville, in spite of his early transcendental tendencies and final lapse into the 'illimitable inane,' possessed strong powers of obser-

[1] *Malice prepense:* malice aforethought.

vation, a solid grasp of facts, and a keen sense of humour, will not be denied by any one who is acquainted with his writings. . . . His literary power, as evidenced in *Typee* and his other early volumes, is also unmistakable, his descriptions being at one time rapid, concentrated, and vigorous, according to the nature of his subject, at another time dreamy, suggestive, and picturesque. The fall from the mast-head in *White Jacket* is a swift and subtle piece of writing of which George Meredith might be proud; the death of the white whale in *Moby Dick* rises to a sort of epic grandeur and intensity. . . .

. . . In an age which has witnessed a marked revival of books of travel and adventure, and which, in its greed for narrative or fiction of this kind is often fain to content itself with works of a very inferior quality, it is a cause for regret that the author of *Typee* and *Mardi* should have fallen to a great extent out of notice, and should be familiar only to a small circle of admirers, instead of enjoying the wide reputation to which his undoubted genius entitles him.

158. Edward William Bok, from New York *Publishers' Weekly*

15 November 1890, 705

Bok (1863–1930), who came to the United States from the Netherlands in 1870, founded with his brother the Bok Syndicated Press that distributed columns to subscribing periodicals. One such column was Edward Bok's weekly letter of literary gossip, 'Bok's Literary Leaves,' a syndicated column carried in a number of papers and in this instance reprinted in the *Publishers' Weekly*.

There are more people to-day, writes Edward Bok, who believe Herman Melville dead than there are those who know he is living. And yet if one choose to walk along East Eighteenth Street, New York City, any morning about 9 o'clock, he would see the famous writer of sea stories—stories which have never been equalled perhaps in their special line. Mr. Melville is now an old man, but still vigorous. He is an employé of the Customs Revenue Service, and thus still lingers around the atmosphere which permeated his books. Forty-four years ago, when his most famous tale, *Typee*, appeared, there was not a better known author than he, and he commanded his own prices. Publishers sought him, and editors considered themselves fortunate to secure his name as a literary star. And to-day? Busy New York has no idea he is even alive, and one of the best-informed literary men in this country laughed recently at my statement that Herman Melville was his neighbor by only two city blocks. 'Nonsense,' said he. 'Why, Melville is dead these many years!' Talk about literary fame? There's a sample of it!

159. 'Herman Melville,' unsigned article, New York *Times*

2 October 1891

On 29 September the *Times* carried the following under 'Obituary Notes': 'Herman Melville died yesterday at his residence, 104 East Twenty-sixth Street, this city, of heart failure, aged seventy-two. He was the author of *Typee*, *Omoo*, *Mobie Dick*, and other sea-faring tales, written in earlier years. He leaves a wife and two daughters, Mrs. M. B. Thomas and Miss Melville.'

There has died and been buried in this city, during the current week, at an advanced age, a man who is so little known, even by name, to the generation now in the vigor of life that only one newspaper contained an obituary account of him, and this was but of three or four lines. Yet forty years ago the appearance of a new book by HERMAN MELVILLE was esteemed a literary event, not only throughout his own country, but so far as the English-speaking race extended. To the ponderous and quarterly British reviews of that time, the author of *Typee* was about the most interesting of literary Americans, and men who made few exceptions to the British rule of not reading an American book not only made MELVILLE one of them, but paid him the further compliment of discussing him as an unquestionable literary force. Yet when a visiting British writer a few years ago inquired at a gathering in New-York of distinctly literary Americans what had become of HERMAN MELVILLE, not only was there not one among them who was able to tell him, but there was scarcely one among them who had ever heard of the man concerning whom he inquired, albeit that man was then living within a half mile of the place of the conversation. Years ago the books by which MELVILLE's reputation had been made had long been out of print and out of demand. The latest book, now about a quarter of a century old, *Battle Pieces and Aspects of the War*, fell flat, and he has died an absolutely forgotten man.

In its kind this speedy oblivion by which a once famous man so long survived his fame is almost unique, and it is not easily explicable. Of course, there are writings that attain a great vogue and then fall entirely out of regard or notice. But this is almost always because either the interest of the subject matter is temporary, and the writings are in the nature of journalism, or else the workmanship to which they owe their temporary success is itself the produce or the product of a passing fashion. This was not the case with HERMAN MELVILLE. Whoever, arrested for a moment by the tidings of the author's death, turns back now to the books that were so much read and so much talked about forty years ago has no difficulty in determining why they were then read and talked about. His difficulty will be rather to discover why they are read and talked about no longer. The total eclipse now of what was then a literary luminary seems like a wanton caprice of fame. At all events, it conveys a moral that is both bitter and wholesome to the popular novelists of our own day.

MELVILLE was a born romancer. One cannot account for the success of his early romances by saying that in the Great South Sea he had found and worked a new field for romance, since evidently it was not his experience in the South Sea that had led him to romance, but the irresistible attraction that romance had over him that led him to the South Sea. He was able not only to feel but to interpret that charm, as it never had been interpreted before, as it never has been interpreted since. It was the romance and the mystery of the great ocean and its groups of islands that made so alluring to his own generation the series of fantastic tales in which these things were celebrated. *Typee* and *Omov* and *Mardi* remain for readers of English the poetic interpretation of the

Polynesian Islands and their surrounding seas. MELVILLE's pictorial power was very great, and it came, as such power always comes, from his feeling more intensely than others the charm that he is able to present more vividly than others. It is this power which gave these romances the hold upon readers which it is surprising that they have so completely lost. It is almost as visible in those of his books that are not professed romances, but purport to be accounts of authentic experiences—in *White Jacket*, the story of life before the mast in an American man-of-war; in *Moby Dick*, the story of a whaling voyage. The imagination that kindles at a touch is as plainly shown in these as in the novels, and few readers who have read it are likely to forget MELVILLE's poetizing of the prosaic process of trying out blubber in his description of the old whaler wallowing through the dark and 'burning a corpse.' Nevertheless, the South Pacific is the field that he mainly made his own, and that he made his own, as those who remember his books will acknowledge, beyond rivalry. That this was a very considerable literary achievement there can be no question. For some months a contemporaneous writer, of whom nobody will dispute that he is a romancer and a literary artist, has been working in the same field, but it cannot seriously be pretended that Mr. STEVENSON has taken from HERMAN MELVILLE the laureateship of the Great South Sea. In fact, the readers of STEVENSON abandon as quite unreadable what he has written from that quarter.

160. From 'The Literary Wayside,' unsigned article, Springfield, Massachusetts, *Republican*

4 October 1891

Herman Melville, one of the most original and virile of American literary men, died at his home on Twenty-sixth street, New York, a few days ago, at the age of 72. He had long been forgotten, and was no doubt unknown to the most of those who are reading the magazine literature and the novels of the day. Nevertheless, it is probable that no work of imagination more powerful and often poetic has been written by an American than Melville's romance of *Moby Dick; or the Whale*, published just 40 years ago; and it was Melville who was the first of all writers to describe with imaginative grace based upon personal knowledge, those attractive, gentle, cruel and war-like peoples, the inhabitants of the South Sea islands. His *Typee*, *Omoo* and *Mardi* made a sensation in the late forties, when they were published, such as we can hardly understand now; and from that time until Pierre Loti began to write there has been nothing to rival these brilliant books of adventure, sufficiently tinged with romance to enchain the attention of the passing reader as well as the critic. Melville wrote many books, but ceased to write so long ago as 1857, having since that date published only two volumes of verse which had no obvious relation to his previous work, and gave no addition to his literary reputation. . . .

Herman Melville later was appointed to a clerkship in the New York custom-house, and since then his home has been in New York city, where in the society of a few friends he has been content to see the world go by. He published a volume of war poems in 1866, and 10 years later his versified record of travel, *Clarel, a Pilgrimage in the Holy Land.* Mr Melville has not gained a place as poet, yet no one can read his book of *Battle Pieces* without much admiration for the vigor of the verse, and the frequent flashes of prophetic fire which they show. It is startling to read these lines, called 'The Portent':—

Hanging from the beam
  Slowly swaying (such the law),
Gaunt the shadow on your green,
  Shenandoah!
The cut is on the crown,
(Lo! John Brown),
And the stabs shall heal no more.

Hidden in the cap
  Is the anguish none can draw;
So your future veils its face,
  Shenandoah!
But the streaming beard is shown
(Weird John Brown),
The meteor of the war!

The book is exceptional in that its verse was not suggested and put forth at the time of the events it wraps in rhythmic guise, but after the fall of

Richmond Melville wrote nearly all of the poems; they show, nevertheless, such differences of proportion as might have occurred from the spontaneity of immediate impulse. The verses on Worden, 'In the Turret,' on Cushing, 'At the Cannon's Mouth,' are not ordinary writing nor is the poem 'Chattanooga' on the battle fought in November, 1863 . . . .

Yet the better evidence of the divine afflatus that was in him appeared in his South Sea romances and in *Moby Dick;* his *Clarel* cannot be read except as a task, and contains probably nothing worth quoting, although some very patient reader might discover here and there lines of some consequence. Melville was very interesting in his personality,—a man above the ordinary stature, with a great growth of hair and beard, and a keen blue eye; and full of vigor and quickness of thought in his age,—which he felt and yielded to earlier than would have been expected of one of so stalwart a frame.

Although as aforesaid Melville's early novels are not now read, they are as well worth reading as the more sensuous stories of Pierre Loti, or the vivacious ventures of Robert Louis Stevenson, whose scenes are laid in the same region of 'lotus eating,' to describe in a fit phrase the common life of the Pacific islands. *Typee*, particularly, would be found to retain its charm for even the sophisticated readers of to-day. But the crown of Melville's sea experience was the marvelous romance of *Moby Dick*, the White whale, whose mysterious and magical existence is still a superstition of whalers,—at least such whalers as have not lost touch with the old days of Nantucket and New Bedford glory and grief. This book was dedicated to Nathaniel Hawthorne, and Hawthorne must have enjoyed it, and have regarded himself as honored in the inscription. This story is unique; and in the divisions late critics have made of novels, as it is not a love-story (the only love being that of the serious mate Starbuck for his wife in Nantucket, whom he will never see again), it is the other thing, a hate-story. And nothing stranger was ever motive for a tale than Capt Ahab's insane passion for revenge on the mysterious and invincible White whale, Moby Dick, who robbed him of a leg, and to a perpetual and fatal chase of him the captain binds his crew. The scene of this vow is marvelously done, and so are many other scenes, some of them truthful depictions of whaling as Melville knew it; some of the wildest fabrications of imagination. An immense amount of knowledge of the whale is given in this amazing book, which swells, too, with a humor often as grotesque as Jean Paul's, but not so genial as it is sardonic. Character is drawn with great power too, from Queequeg the ex-cannibal, and Tashtego the Gay Header, to the crazy and awful Ahab, the grave Yankee Starbuck, and the terrible White whale, with his charmed life, that one feels can never end. Certainly it is hard to find a more wonderful book than this *Moby Dick*, and it ought to be read by this generation, amid whose feeble mental food, furnished by the small realists and fantasts of the day, it would appear as Hercules among the pygmies, or as Moby Dick himself among a school of minnows.

161. Richard Henry Stoddard, from 'Herman Melville,' New York *Mail and Express*

8 October 1891

A remarkable man of letters recently passed away in the person of Mr. Herman Melville, at the age of 72. If he had died forty years ago his death would have attracted as much attention as the death of Mr. Lowell at that time, for his books were of a kind that was more widely read than those of Mr. Lowell, whose reputation, such as it was, rested upon his serious and satiric verse, and not upon his prose, which in critical directions, was masterly and authoritative. The early career of Mr. Melville was adventurous enough to make him famous among his countrymen, who, less literary in their tastes and demands than at present, were easily captivated by stories of maritime life like *Omoo* and *Typee*, and *Moby Dick*.

They read Marryatt then, and Cooper, and Dana, and it was natural that they should read Melville, whose gifts in writing were rather those of a sailor of genius than a landsman of talent. He knew the sea as only sailors know it; for, beginning before the mast at the age of 18, he went to Liverpool and London and elsewhere in England, and then returned to New York, where he was born and lived, and where he was not content to remain long. A descendant of a member of the Boston 'tea party,' there was that in his blood which chafed at the limitations of modern city life, its artificial conventionalities and proprieties, and a spirit in his feet, which, spurning the ground, impelled him to seek again the life and freedom, the delights and dangers, that are so dear to those who go down to the sea in ships. . . .

Popular among his own countrymen, who read him without quite knowing why, except that he entertained them, for they were not critical, though they had persuaded themselves that they were, Mr. Melville was a revelation to the English, who as a people have never grown weary of reading the stories of adventurous navigators, whether they were written in the days of Drake and Cavendish, or are written in our more prosaic days of ocean steamers that beat the record, and who could not but be charmed, critics and all, with the wild, and spirited, and picturesque prose poetry of Mr. Melville. It was as new in their literature as it was in ours, and they admired it accordingly, not more ardently, perhaps, than we, but more lastingly, for the fame of Melville, as we were assured a few years ago by Mr. Clark Russell, is still perennial in the mother country.

It cannot be said to be so here, for after *Mardi* (1849), a clumsy attempt at an allegory, which was a great disappointment to Mr. Melville's readers, and still more after *Pierre, or the Ambiguities* (1852), his reputation declined. Not that he was other than he had been from the beginning, but that a new king had arisen who knew not Joseph; not that he was written out, for a man of genius is never written out so long as he understands what is best in himself, but that writing like his was no longer cared for or read. It is easy to decry changes of popular taste in letters, in art, in music, but whether they are wise or unwise, it is impossible to prevent them, and they must be submitted to, like changes in government, the seasons, and most other mundane matters.

Mr. Melville was a man of great genius, but he cannot be said to have understood the limitation of his genius, or the things which it could, or could not, accomplish, and he cannot be said to have understood, or to have cultivated, literature as an art. He wrote as he felt, following out his moods and whims, confessing himself to his readers, of whose condemnation, or absolution, he took no thought, satisfied to be what he was, and to do what he did. *Typee* and *Omoo* are full of light and color, of sensations that seem to be reflections, and of the restlessness of thought that seems to imply activity of mind. We drift with him through his Pacific splendors and dangers as if we had partaken of the lotus plant; everything about us is wonderful, is marvelous, is miraculous, but nothing is tangible, real, 'of the earth, earthy.'

There was a wealth of imagination in the mind of Mr. Melville, but it was an untrained imagination, and a world of the stuff out of which poetry is made, but no poetry, which is creation and not chaos. He saw like a poet, felt like a poet, thought like a poet, but he never attained any proficiency in verse, which was not among his natural gifts. His vocabulary was large, fluent, eloquent, but it was excessive, inaccurate and unliterary. He wrote too easily, and at too great length, his pen sometimes running away with him, and from his readers. There were strange, dark, mysterious elements in his nature, as there were in Hawthorne's, but he never learned to control them, as Hawthorne did from the beginning, and never turned their possibilities into actualities. The suggestive comparison with Hawthorne reminds us that Mr. Melville and that great writer, who were personal friends, were at one time neighbors or nearly such, the one living at Pittsfield and other at Lenox, on the brink of the Stockbridge Bowl, and that in Mr. Julian Hawthorne's memoir of his parents—*Nathaniel Hawthorne and His Wife*—there are references to this friendship, besides several letters that passed between them at this time.

As none of these letters have as yet (so far as we know) been quoted in any literary notice of Mr. Melville, we copy one of them, which was written at Pittsfield in the summer of 1851, after the finishing of *The House with the Seven Gables* on the one hand, and during the composition of *Moby Dick* on the other, and which represents the peculiarities of the writer with a force and a faithfulness which leaves nothing to be desired:

[quotes almost all of Melville's letter to Hawthorne, 1(?) June 1851. See No. 75]

This is a very curious letter, and a very interesting one, from a personal point of view; but it is a strange and sad one, for a man of 32, who had written four or five remarkable books, and whose promise of fame was voluble in mouths of wisest censure. But, whatever it was, it was unfortunately prophetic, for, whether its writer knew it or not, his development had 'come to the inmost leaf of the bulb' when he wrote *Moby Dick*. He wrote other books afterward—four in prose, stories and what not, and three in verse—but they added nothing to his reputation; why, it is not easy to determine, since they were conceived in the same spirit, and informed with the same qualities, as *Omoo* and *Typee*, which are landmarks in American literature, in which the name of Herman Melville must ever hold an honorable place.

162. Julian Hawthorne and Leonard Lemmon, 'Herman Melville, An early sea-novelist,' *American Literature*

Boston, 1892, 208–9

Julian Hawthorne (1846–1934), Nathaniel's only son, was his parents' biographer in *Nathaniel Hawthorne and His Wife* (1884). He also wrote novels, sketches, and reviews and a book, *The Subterranean Brotherhood*, based on his observations of life in the Atlanta penitentiary where he was confined several months in 1913 for mail fraud.

Leonard William Lemmon (1860–?) was an educator and editor of text books.

American Literature was a text book designed 'for the use of Schools and Colleges.'

Herman Melville (1819–91). Forty years ago, few American authors had so wide a reputation as Melville, whose books of sea-adventure, part fact and part fancy, were read and praised in England quite as much and as warmly as in this country. Not to have read *Typee* and *Omoo* was not to have made the acquaintance of the most entertaining and novel current literature: and those who take them up to-day find their charm and interest almost unimpaired. The leading sea-novelist of the present day has acknowledged Melville as his master; and there is no doubt that he possessed not only exhaustive technical knowledge of his chosen field, but that his talent for exploiting it amounted to genius. The main substance of his books is plainly founded on fact: but the facts are so judiciously selected as to produce the effect of art, while the flavoring of fiction is so artfully introduced as to seem like fact. All the stories are told in the first person, and there is a fascination and mystery in the narrator's personality that much enhances the interest of the tale. But Melville's imagination has a tendency to wildness and metaphysical extravagance; and when he trusted to it alone, he becomes difficult and sometimes repulsive. There seems, also, to be a background of gloom in his nature, making itself felt even in the midst of his sunshine: and now and then his speculations and rhapsodies have a tinge almost of insanity. *Typee* and *Omoo* are stories of adventure in the Pacific archipelago, as is also *Mardi*, but the latter merges into a quasi-symbolic analysis of human life, perplexing to the general reader, though the splendor and poetic beauty of the descriptions win his admiration. *Redburn* is the narrative of a voyage to Liverpool before the mast, in an American clipper, and is a model of simplicity and impressiveness: *White Jacket* describes life on an American man-of-war, and overflows with humor, character, adventure and absorbing pictures of a kind of existence which has now ceased forever to exist. *Moby Dick, or the Whale* takes up the whole subject of whaling, as practised in the '30's and '40's, and is, if anything, more interesting and valuable than *White Jacket*; the scenes are grouped about a wildly romantic and original plot, concerned with the chase round the world of an enormous white whale—Moby Dick—by a sea-captain who has previously lost a limb in a conflict with the monster, and has sworn revenge. This is the most powerful of Melville's books; it was also the last of any literary importance. *Pierre, or The Ambiguities* is a repulsive, insane and impossible romance, in which the sea has no part, and one or two later books need not be mentioned. But Melville's position in literature is secure and solitary: he surpasses Cooper, when Cooper writes of the sea; and no subsequent writer has even challenged a comparison with him on that element.

163. W. Clark Russell, from 'A Claim for American Literature,' *North American Review*

February 1892, cliv, 138–49

Until Richard H. Dana and Herman Melville wrote, the commercial sailor of Great Britain and the United States was without representation in literature. Dana and Melville were Americans. They were the first to lift the hatch and show the world what passes in a ship's forecastle; how men live down in that gloomy cave, how and what they eat, and where they sleep; what pleasures they take, what their sorrows and wrongs are; how they are used when they quit their black sea-parlors in response to the boatswain's silver summons to work on deck by day or by night. These secrets of the deep Dana and Melville disclosed. By doing so, they—the one by a single volume, the other by four or five remarkable narratives—expanded American literature immeasurably beyond the degree to which English literature had been expanded by, say, the works of two-thirds of the poets named in Johnson's *Lives*, or by the whole series of the Waverley novels, or by half the fiction, together with much of the philosophy, theology, poetry, and history, that has been published since the death of Charles Dickens.

For compare what the vast proportion of poets and novelists and philosophers and the rest have done with what these two men did. Dana and Melville created a world, not by the discovery, but by the interpretation of it. They gave us a full view of the life led by tens of thousands of men whose very existence, until these wizards arose, had been as vague to the general land intelligence as the shadows of clouds moving under the brightness of stars. . . .

Herman Melville, as I gather from an admirable account of this fine author by Mr. Arthur Stedman, a son of the well-known poet, went to sea in 1841. He shipped before the mast on board a whaler and cruised continuously for eighteen months in the Pacific. He saw much ocean life, and his experiences were wild and many. I will not compare him with Dana: his imagination was soaring and splendid, yet there are such passages of pathos and beauty in Dana's book as persuade me that he might have matched Melville's most startling and astonishing inventions, had taste prompted him or leisure invited. There is nothing in Melville to equal in simple, unaffected beauty Dana's description of an old sailor lying over a jibboom on a fine night and looking up at the stirless canvas white as sifted snow with moonlight. Full of rich poetry, too, is Dana's description of the still night broken by the breathing of shadowy shapes of whales. Melville is essentially American: Dana writes as a straight-headed Englishman would; he is clear, convincing utterly unaffected. A subtle odor of the sea freshens and sweetens his sentences. An educated sailor would swear to Dana's vocation by virtue of his style only—a style as plain and sturdy as Defoe's. In truth, I know of no American writer whose style is so good. Yet are Melville's pictures of the forecastle life, his representation of what goes on under the deck of that part of the ship which is thumped by the handspike of the boatswain when he echoes in thunder the order of 'All hands!' marvellously and delightfully true. I will not speak of his faithful and often beautiful and often exquisite sketches of the life and scenery of the South Sea Islands, nor of his magnificent picture of Liverpool, and the descriptions of London and of English scenery in *Redburn*, and the wonderful opening chapters of *Moby Dick*. I link him with Dana; I place the two side by side as men of genius, but sailors first of all, and I claim, in their name, that to American literature the world owes the first, the best, and the enduring revelation of the secrets of one great side of the ocean life. . . .

Melville wrote out of his heart and out of wide and perhaps bitter experience; he enlarged our knowledge of the life of the deep by adding many descriptions to those which Dana had already given. His 'South Seaman' is typical. Dana sighted her, but Melville lived in her. His books are now but little read. When he died the other day,—to my sorrow! for our correspondence had bred in me a deeper feeling than kindness and esteem,—men who could give you the names of fifty living American poets and perhaps a hundred living American novelists owned that they had never heard of Herman Melville; which simply means that to all intents and purposes the American sailor is a dead man, and the American merchant service to all intents and purposes a dead industry. Yet a famous man he was in those far days when every sea was bright with the American flag, when the cotton-white canvas shone starlike on the horizon, when the nasal laugh of the jolly Yankee tar in China found its echo in Peru. Famous he was; now he is neglected; yet his name and works will not die. He is a great figure in shadow; but the shadow is not that of oblivion. . . .

Two American sailors, men of letters and of genius, seizing the pen for a handspike, prized open the sealed lid under which the merchant-seaman lay caverned. The light of heaven fell down the open hatch, and the story of what had been happening for centuries in the British service, for years in the American, was read. Did any good come of it? I should have to ask your patience for a much longer paper than this to answer *that* question. But as a literary feat! in an age, too, when men thought most things known. Americans! honor your Dana and your Melville. Greater geniuses your literature has produced, but none who have done work so memorable in the history of their native letters.

164. Henry S. Salt, from 'Marquesan Melville,' *Gentleman's Magazine*

March 1892, cclxxii, 248–57

Has America a literature? I am inclined to think it a grave mistake to argue seriously with those afflicted persons who periodically exercise themselves over this idlest of academic questions. It is wiser to meet them with a practical counter-thrust, and pointedly inquire, for example, whether they are familiar with the writings of Herman Melville. Whereupon, confusion will in most cases ensue, and you will go on to suggest that to criticise *Hamlet*, with the prince's part omitted, would be no whit more fatuous than to demonstrate the non-existence of an American literature, while taking no account of its true intellectual giants. When it was announced, a few months ago, that 'Mr. Herman Melville, the author,' had just died in New York at the age of seventy-two, the news excited but little interest on this side of the Atlantic; yet, forty years ago, his name was familiar to English, as to American readers, and there is little or no exaggeration in Robert Buchanan's remark, that he is 'the one great imaginative writer fit to stand shoulder to shoulder with Whitman on that continent.'

It was in 1846 that Melville fairly took the world by storm with his *Typee: the Narrative of a four months' residence in the Marquesas Islands*, the first of a brilliant series of volumes of adventure, in which reality was so deftly encircled with a halo of romance that readers were at once captivated by the force and freshness of the style and puzzled as to the personality of the author. Who and what was this mysterious sojourner in the far islands of the Pacific—this 'Marquesan Melville,' as a writer in *Blackwood* denominated him? Speculation was rife, and not unaccompanied by suspicion; for there were some critics who not only questioned the veracity of Herman Melville's 'Narratives,' but declared his very name to be fictitious. 'Separately,' remarked one sagacious reviewer, 'the names are not uncommon; we can urge no valid reason against their juncture; yet in this instance they fall suspiciously on our ear.'

Herman Melville, however, was far from being a mythical personage, though in his early life, as in his later, he seems to have instinctively shrunk from any other publicity than that which was brought him by his books. He was a genuine child of nature, a sort of nautical George Borrow, on whom the irresistible sea-passion had descended in his boyhood, and won him away from the ordinary routine of respectable civilised life, until, to quote his own words, to travel had become a necessity of his existence, 'a way of driving off the spleen and regulating the circulation.' . . .

There is no doubt that Melville's characteristic reticence on personal matters, together with his increasing love of retirement, was in large measure the cause of his otherwise unaccountable loss of literary fame; for even the well-merited failure of such books as *Pierre* and *The Confidence Man*, would be in itself insufficient to explain the neglect of his genuine masterpieces. It is true that for a few years he was induced to lecture, in various parts of the States, on the subject of his voyages to the South Seas; but, as a rule, he could not, or would not, cultivate the indispensable art of keeping his name before the public. The man who could win the affections of a cannibal community in the Pacific was less at home in the intricacies of self-advertisement and 'business.' 'Dollars damn me,' he remarks in one of his letters. 'When I feel most moved to write, that is banned—it will not pay. Yet, altogether, write the *other* way I cannot. So the product is a final hash, and all my books are botches.' That he felt keenly mortified at the ill success of *Pierre*, is beyond question. When, on the occasion of a tour in Europe, in 1856, he visited Hawthorne at the Liverpool consulate, he told his friend that 'the spirit of adventure had gone out of him.' He is described by Hawthorne as looking 'a little paler, perhaps, and a little sadder, and with his characteristic gravity and reserve of manner. . . . He has suffered from too constant literary occupations, pursued without much success latterly; and his writings, for a long while past, have indicated a morbid state of mind.'

In 1863, Melville found it necessary, for the better education of his children, to leave his home at Pittsfield, and to take up his quarters at New York, where for many years he held an inspectorship in the custom-house. His life became now altogether one of quietude and retirement; content to let the noisy world go by, he made no attempt to recover the fame which had once been his, and to which he still possessed an inalienable title. During these years, however, he published two volumes of poetry; *Battle Pieces*, which deals mainly with incidents of the civil war, and *Clarel, a Pilgrimage in the Holy Land*, described by Melville himself, in a letter to an English correspondent, as 'a metrical affair, a pilgrimage or what not, of several thousand lines, eminently adapted for unpopularity.' More interesting than these is a little story, *John Marr and other Sailors*, issued in 1888, and limited to twenty-five copies—a limitation which affords a pathetic and significant comment on the acumen of a 'reading public' which had allowed itself to become almost entirely oblivious of the author of *Typee* and *The Whale*! We need not doubt, however, that Melville found ample compensation for this neglect in that assurance of ultimate and lasting recognition which is seldom denied to men of genius. . . .

His love of literature was fully sustained to the end. I have before me a most interesting batch of letters, dated between 1884 and 1888, addressed by him to Mr. James Billson, of Leicester, and mostly dealing with the poems of James Thomson ('B.V.'), of which he was a great admirer. Some of these comments and appreciations are in Melville's best style. ' "Sunday up the River," ' he writes, 'contrasting with the "City of Dreadful Night," is like a Cuban humming-bird, beautiful in faery tints, flying against the tropic thundercloud. Your friend was a sterling poet, if ever one sang. As to pessimism, although neither pessimist nor optimist myself, nevertheless I relish it in the verse, if for nothing else than as a counterpoise to the exorbitant hopefulness, juvenile and shallow, that makes such a muster in these days—at least in some quarters.'

'Exorbitant hopefulness' could indeed have been hardly otherwise than distasteful to one who, like his own 'John Marr' (a retired sailor whose fate it was to live on a 'frontier-prairie,' among an unresponsive inland people who cared nothing for the sea), had so long experienced the solitude of disappointed genius. But it is impossible to believe that this undeserved neglect can be permanent. The opinion of those competent judges who are students of Melville's works is so clear and emphatic in his favour, that it is not too much to say that to read his books is generally to appreciate them; nor is it only those who have what is called an 'educated taste' who are thus impressed, for I have been told of instances in which English working-men became his hearty admirers. It is satisfactory to know that a new edition of his best books is forthcoming, both in America and England, and that the public will thus have an opportunity, I will not say of repairing a wrong done to a distinguished writer, for, as I have already shown, the decay of his fame was partly due to circumstances of his own making, but at least of rehabilitating and confirming its earlier and truer judgment. Herman Melville will then resume his honourable place in American literature (for, to end as I began, I hold that the existence of an American literature is a fact and not a supposition), as the prose-poet of the Pacific—

> the sea-compelling man,
> Before whose wand Leviathan
> Rose hoary-white upon the deep,
> With awful sounds that stirred its sleep;
> Melville, whose magic drew Typee,
> Radiant as Venus, from the sea.[1]

[1] Robert Buchanan's *Socrates in Camden*. [Salt's note.]

165. 'Herman Melville's Romances,' unsigned review, New York *Critic*

3 December 1892, 308–9

This is a review of the reissued *Typee* (New York: United States Book Company, 1892) with a 'Biographical and Critical Introduction' by Arthur Stedman.

Since Captain Cook was killed and, perhaps, eaten by cannibals, the Pacific, especially the South, seas have afforded a basilisk-like fascination to the romance-writer. Coleridge and Wordsworth wrote a weird poem about the slaying of the albatross, a creature under the *taboo* of Polynesian superstition; Poe wrote a romance still more weird on a kindred line; Darwin's voyage covered the region with delightful mystery; and poet, naturalist and romance-writer have vied with each other since in reproducing the beauty and strangeness of that wild and virginal waste of waters, dotted only here and there by the Sandwich, the Tahiti, the Marquesan, the Samoan, and the Fiji groups of islands. Many of these islands, doubtless, represent the gigantic cup-like summits of volcanoes that have risen from the sea and filled themselves with life and vegetation, holding them aloft to the cloudless skies in their volcano-vases that give forth perpetual fragrance. What *mise-en-scène* could be imagined more striking or more dramatic for the display of rare or peculiar knowledge, of singular experience, of marvellous adventure, of imaginative and artistic manipulation? Victor Hugo, in his sublime ode, 'Oceano Nox,' speculates on the fate of vanished mariners.

Sont-ils devenus rois dans quelque île?[1]

Homer long before had sent the most fascinating of his heroes a-voyaging in the trail of the western sun on a train of adventure which for 2500 years has filled the world with delight. Fifty years ago the same magic caress of the siren Adventure sent Herman Melville, a New Yorker of Dutch ancestry, and therefore entitled to navigator-blood in

[1] *Sont-ils devenus rois dans quelque île?*: Have they become kings on some island?

his veins, afloat in a sperm-whaler on a search not so much for oil as for the precious gold which the author of *Two Years Before the Mast* had brought back, a gold wrought to dazzling brightness in the twin crucibles of experience and fancy. The result was a string of romances of real life which have never been excelled for vividness, verisimilitude, recondite information and miniature-like finish of detail. The first of these—*Typee*—was published in England by John Murray in 1846 (five years after Dana's *Two Years*), to be followed in tolerably quick succession by its sequel, *Omoo*, by *Moby Dick*, and by *White Jacket*. These romances are all autobiographic, bits of real adventure or detail lived out on sperm-whalers or men-of-war cruising in these distant seas. A famous 'old tar' informs us that *his* favorite is *White Jacket*, probably because he himself was a man-of-war's-man. Of *Typee*, the story of the castaway in the 'Happy Valley' of a Marquesan cannibal isle, the reader must judge for himself. Its *Robinson-Crusoe*-like minuteness and realism carry with them the stamp of truth, and it will remain a classic in spite of its well-directed attacks on the pseudo-missionaries. Mr. Arthur Stedman furnishes a welcome biographical and critical introduction to this new edition, and gives us interesting personal glimpses of the recluse-author who latterly abandoned himself to Schopenhauer and philosophy.

Select bibliography

The following books contain either examinations of the critical reception of Melville's works in the nineteenth century or transcriptions of reviews and essays by his contemporaries. While many of the twentieth-century editions of Melville's books do include editorial commentary that mentions the early reviews, the ones listed below either have particularly useful studies of the reviews or reprint original documents.

Battle-Pieces and Aspects of The War, ed. Sidney Kaplan. Amherst: University of Massachusetts Press, 1972.

The Complete Stories of Herman Melville, ed. Jay Leyda. New York: Random House, 1949.

Complete Works of Herman Melville, Hendricks House edition, general ed.: Howard P. Vincent. Chicago and New York: Hendricks House. Published to date: *Omoo* (1969), *Moby-Dick* (1952), *Pierre* (1949), *Piazza Tales* (1948), *The Confidence-Man* (1954), *Clarel* (1960), *Collected Poems* (1947).

The Confidence-Man, ed. Hershel Parker. New York: Norton, 1971.

Moby-Dick, eds Harrison Hayford and Hershel Parker. New York: Norton, 1967.

The Writings of Herman Melville, Northwestern-Newberry edition, eds Harrison Hayford, Hershel Parker, G. Thomas Tanselle. Evanston and Chicago: Northwestern University Press. Published to date: *Typee* (1968), *Omoo* (1969), *Mardi* (1970), *Redburn* (1969), *White-Jacket* (1970), *Pierre* (1971).

ANDERSON, CHARLES ROBERTS, *Melville in the South Seas*. New York: Columbia University Press, 1939. Reprinted, New York: Dover, 1966.

HETHERINGTON, HUGH W., *Melville's Reviewers, British and American, 1846–1891*. Chapel Hill: University of North Carolina Press, 1961.

HOWARD, LEON, *Herman Melville: A Biography*. Berkeley: University of California Press, 1951.

LEYDA, JAY, *The Melville Log: A Documentary Life of Herman Melville, 1819–1891*, 2 vols. New York: Harcourt, Brace, 1951. Reprinted, 'With a New Supplementary Chapter,' 2 vols. New York: Gordian Press, 1969.

MILLER, PERRY, *The Raven and the Whale: The War of Words and Wits in the Era of Poe and Melville*. New York: Harcourt, Brace, 1956.

MINNIGERODE, MEADE, *Some Personal Letters of Herman Melville and a Bibliography*. New York: Brick Row Book Shop, 1922.

PARKER, HERSHEL AND HAYFORD, HARRISON, eds, *Moby-Dick as Doubloon: Essays and Extracts (1851–1970)*. New York: Norton, 1970.

PARKER, HERSHEL, ed., *The Recognition of Herman Melville*. Ann Arbor: University of Michigan Press, 1967.

ROUNTREE, THOMAS J., ed., *Critics on Melville*. Coral Gables: University of Miami Press, 1972.

THORP, WILLARD, ed., *Herman Melville: Representative Selections, with Introduction, Bibliography, and Notes*. American Writers Series. New York: American Book Company, 1938.

Select Index

A figure in italic indicates the initial page of a review or article reprinted in this volume.

THE CRITICAL HERITAGE SERIES

GENERAL EDITOR: B. C. SOUTHAM

Volumes published and forthcoming

MATTHEW ARNOLD: THE POETRY	Carl Dawson
JANE AUSTEN	B. C. Southam
THE BRONTËS	Miriam Allott
BROWNING	Boyd Litzinger and Donald Smalley
ROBERT BURNS	Donald A. Low
BYRON	Andrew Rutherford
THOMAS CARLYLE	Jules Paul Seigel
CLARE	Mark Storey
CLOUGH	Michael Thorpe
COLERIDGE	J. R. de J. Jackson
CONRAD	Norman Sherry
FENIMORE COOPER	George Dekker and John P. McWilliams
CRABBE	Arthur Pollard
STEPHEN CRANE	Richard M. Weatherford
DEFOE	Pat Rogers
DICKENS	Philip Collins
DRYDEN	James and Helen Kinsley
GEORGE ELIOT	David Carroll
HENRY FIELDING	Ronald Paulson and Thomas Lockwood
FORD MADOX FORD	Frank MacShane
E. M. FORSTER	Philip Gardner
GISSING	Pierre Coustillas and Colin Partridge
GOLDSMITH	G. S. Rousseau
THOMAS HARDY	R. G. Cox
HAWTHORNE	J. Donald Crowley
IBSEN	Michael Egan
HENRY JAMES	Roger Gard

Continued